The Guitar Grimoire®

A Compendium of Formulas for Guitar Scales and Modes

BY ADAM KADMON

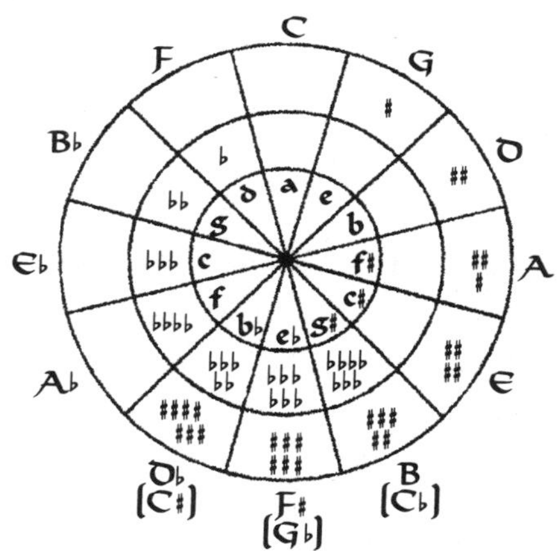

Produced by

for

CARL FISCHER®

65 Bleecker Street, New York, NY 10012

GT1

ISBN 0-8258-2171-1

Neophyte and Adept alike, Welcome to

THE GUITAR GRIMOIRE

In the pages that ensue, the mystical veil that enshrouds music theory will be removed. Theory will be explained for the guitarist as easily as possible, with clear concise graphic diagrams. For the advanced players who already understand music theory, this book will have scales for you to readily explore new realms of music. For the intermediate players who know how to play chords, etc. but never really knew how they were built, this book will help put the pieces of the puzzle into place. Although this book is essentially designed for the intermediate and advanced player, this book will lay an excellent foundation for the beginner.

This book is a "where to" book, showing you exactly where to find any scale in any key on your fretboard. It is a professional reference tool to enhance your music library and playing that you will use for many years to come.

This book is dedicated to all the pioneering guitarists who will take music to depths and levels never before explored.

gri·moire \grėm'wär\ *n* (*rhymes with guitar*)
[F., book of magical formulas]:
magician's manual

For more information on **The Guitar Grimoire®** Series and other music instructional products by Adam Kadmon check out the following Web sites:
http://www.guitargrimoire.com
http://www.adamkadmon.com

CONTENTS

HOW TO USE THIS BOOK

This book is divided into sections according to scale groups. The groups are 7 tone, 5 tone, 6 tone, and 8 tone scales. Each scale group is then subdivided into different scales. For instance, the 7 note group has 14 scales, etc.. Each individual scale in every scale group consists of a title page, and pattern breakdown pages depicting that particular scale's usage in all 12 keys. Each title page contains various charts. The charts are your tools in analyzing how the modes are derived, compatible chords, keyboard fingerings (for those of you with sequencers and midi equipment), modal generation charts, and guitar fingering patterns for conventional and sweeping. The guitar sweeping patterns are then broken down for complete fretboard in all 12 keys.

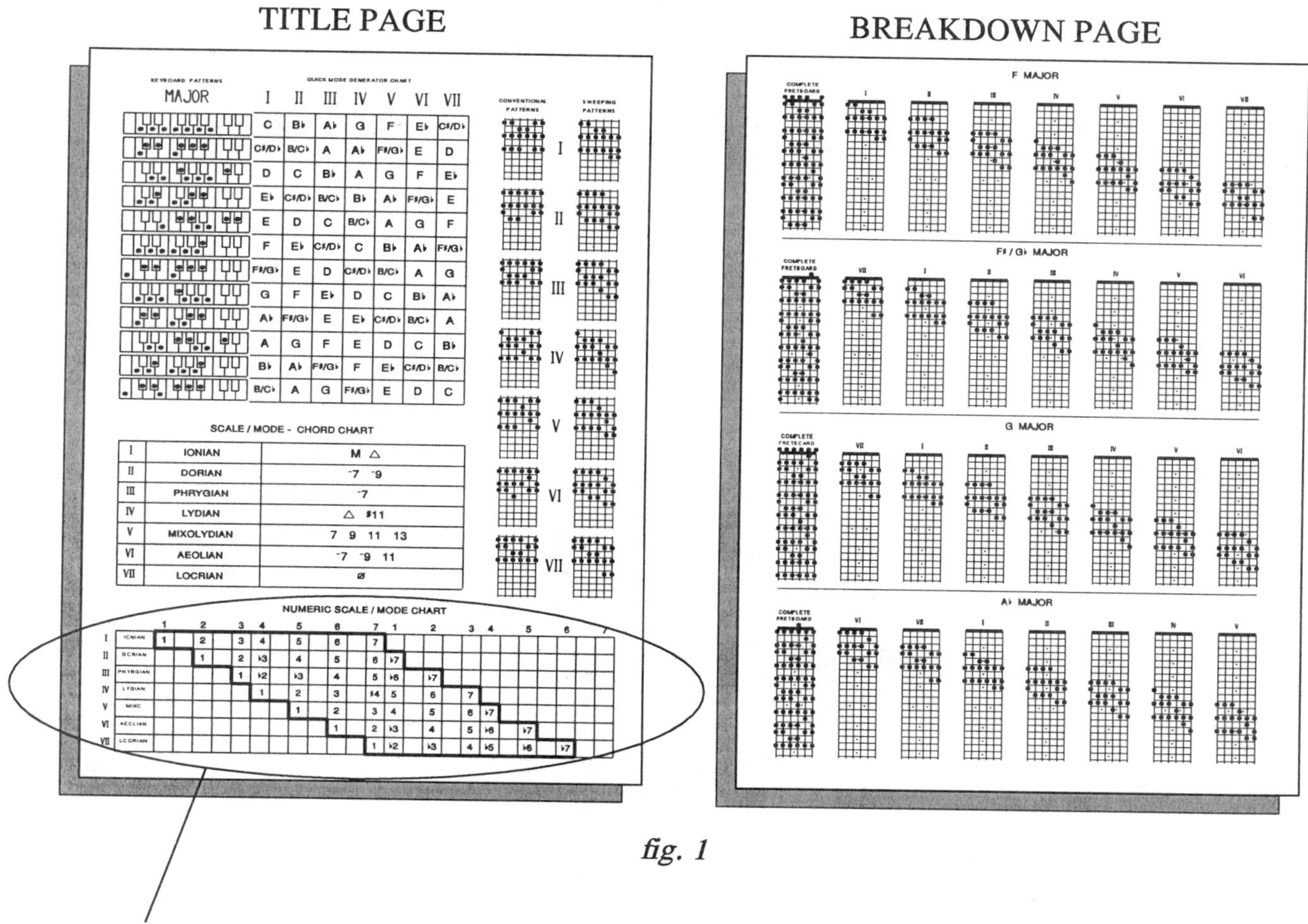

fig. 1

NUMERIC SCALE / MODE CHART

Before we start with the scales, we will show you how each section of the title page works. The first section we will explain is the **Numeric Scale / Mode** chart at the bottom of the page (fig. 1).

THE BUILDING BLOCKS OF MUSIC

Music is sound. But for now imagine that it is a set of 12 equal blocks (fig. 2). The distance from one block to the next block is a half-step. From block 1 to block 2 is a half-step, from 8 to block 9 is a half-step, etc..

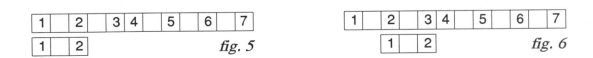

fig. 2 *fig. 3*

7 of these 12 tones or blocks have been given positions of "major" importance (fig. 3). Looking at the diagram we only see 7 numbers, but there are still 12 tones or blocks. The empty blocks are reserved for flats ♭ and sharps ♯ . The distance from block 1 to the 1st empty block is still a half-step. The blocks that are numbered are the tones that make up the Major scale.

The various combinations of half-steps are called intervals. Basically, an interval is the distance between 2 tones. The names of the intervals are then divided into 2 sets: the majors and the perfects. The majors are 2, 3, 6, and 7 ; the perfects are 1,4, 5, and 8. 1 would be a unison, such as 2 instruments playing the same note. An 8 would be the octave. Altering the intervals with flats or sharps changes them from major and perfect into minor, diminished, and augmented (fig. 4).

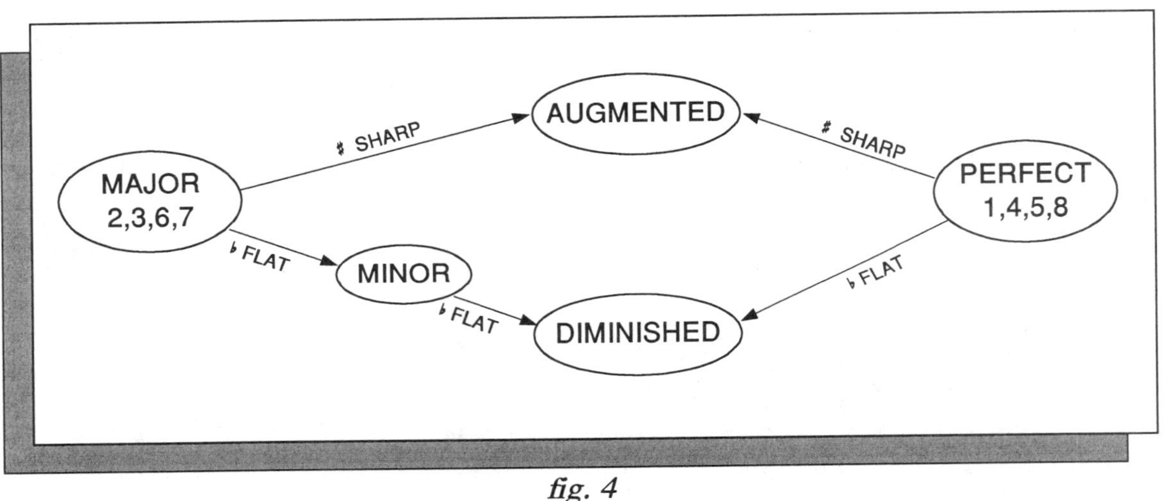

fig. 4

In essence, flat a major get a minor, flat a minor get a diminished, sharp a major get an augmented, sharp a perfect get an augmented, flat a perfect get a diminished. The entire set of major and perfect intervals are called diatonic intervals.

Let's look at an easy way for memorizing interval distances by counting the amount of blocks. There are 12 building blocks within the major scale. Therefore, an interval has to consist of so many building blocks. We'll demonstrate first with a major 2nd. There are 3 blocks in a major 2nd (fig. 5), but the distance from the 2 to the 3 is also a major 2nd (fig. 6).

1		2		3	4		5		6		7
1		2									

fig. 5

1		2		3	4		5		6		7
		1		2							

fig. 6

Fig. 7 is a complete chart of intervals showing you a breakdown in building block format. Also observe, the chart tells you how many half- and whole steps make up each interval.

1	1 BLOCK = UNISON	(0 STEPS)
1 ♭2	2 BLOCKS = MINOR 2ND	(½ STEP)
1 2	3 BLOCKS = MAJOR 2ND	(1 WHOLE STEP)
1 ♭3	4 BLOCKS = MINOR 3RD	(1½ STEPS)
1 3	5 BLOCKS = MAJOR 3RD	(2 WHOLE STEPS)
1 4	6 BLOCKS = PERFECT 4TH	(2½ STEPS)
1 ♭5	7 BLOCKS = DIMINISHED 5TH	(3 WHOLE STEPS)
1 5	8 BLOCKS = PERFECT 5TH	(3½ STEPS)
1 ♭6	9 BLOCKS = MINOR 6TH	(4 WHOLE STEPS)
1 6	10 BLOCKS = MAJOR 6TH	(4½ STEPS)
1 ♭7	11 BLOCKS = MINOR 7TH	(5 WHOLE STEPS)
1 7	12 BLOCKS = MAJOR 7TH	(5½ STEPS)

fig. 7

Now let's look at all the individual components of the major scale in building block breakdown (fig. 8).

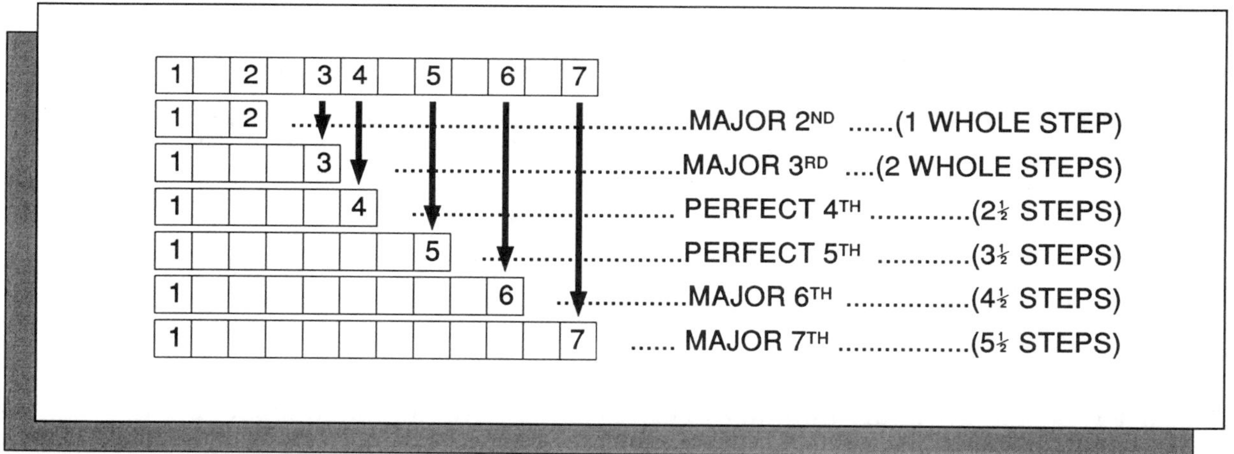

fig. 8

We can clearly see here the individual intervals. We have a 2nd, 3rd, 4th, 5th, 6th, and 7th. With the block diagram we can also see exactly how many steps make up each interval.

Using the same building block breakdown method, we can also analyze the intervallic relationship between the intervals themselves.

Fig. 9 clearly shows us the distance of the intervals from the intervals. For instance, from the major 2nd to the major 3rd is a major 2nd or a whole step. From the 3rd to the 4th is a minor 2nd or a half-step, etc.

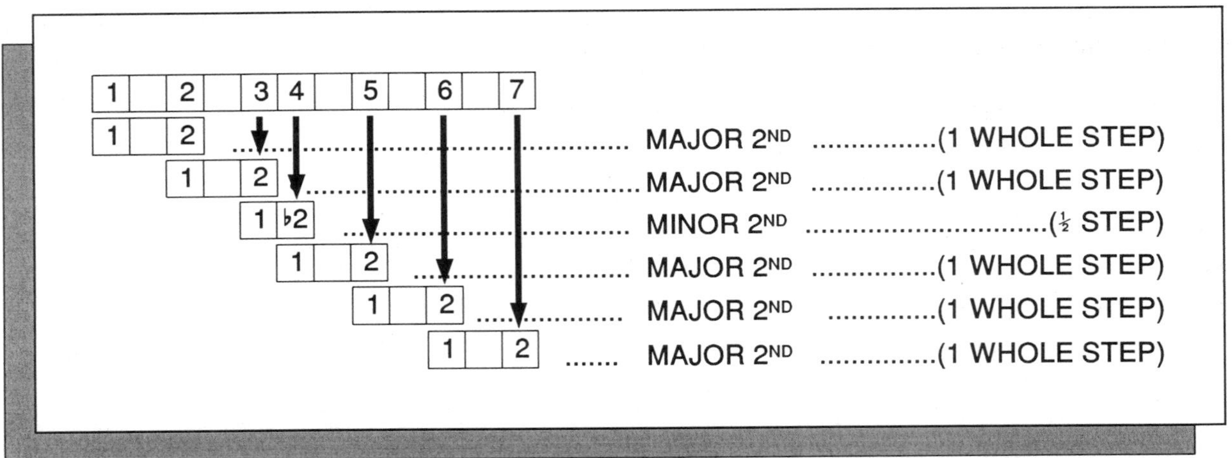

fig. 9

In studying the altered intervals, many of them will look differently on paper and in theory, but sonically, they are the same (fig. 10).

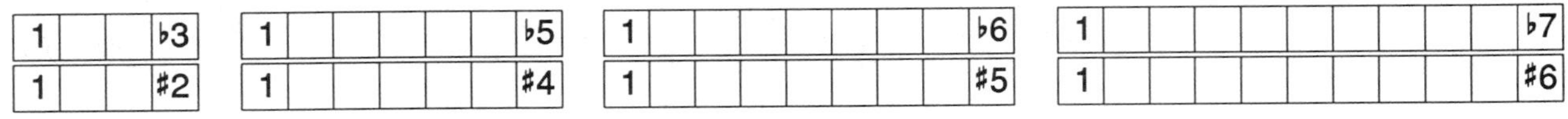

fig. 10

Notice, that the numbers to the right of each set above are different between the upper and the lower, yet each has the same number of blocks. The minor 3rd is the same as the augmented 2nd,the diminished 5th is the same as the augmented 4th, the minor 6th is the same as the augmented 5th, and the minor 7th is the same as the augmeted 6th.

In the next example, we see that the diminished 7th (a double-flat 7th) is the same as the major 6th in sound; although in theory, again, they are two very different intervals (fig. 11).

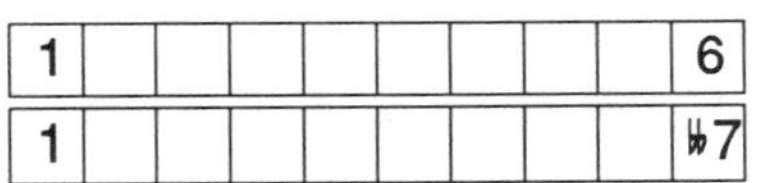

fig. 11

The complete group of intervals which make up the scale, in this case the major scale, can be theoretically repeated infinitely in both directions; although, in practice there are only so many octaves the human ear can hear (fig. 12).

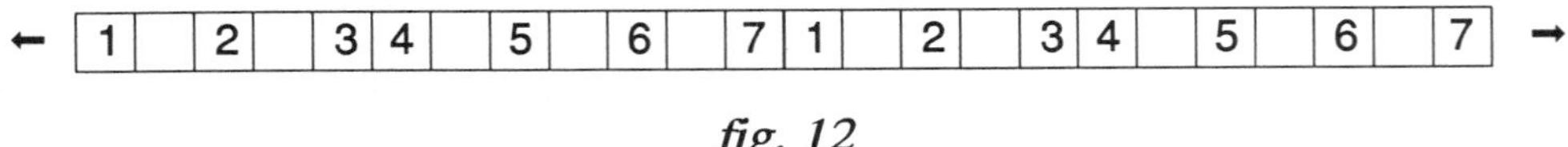

fig. 12

This is the mathematics of music theory. It is important that you memorize the numerics behind the building blocks, in order to form a solid foundation for your musical creations.

SCALES AND MODES

A scale is a sequence of tones comprised of varying intervals. Modes can be described as scales based upon the tones of the main scale. The Major scale has 7 modes, because it has 7 tones. The 1st mode of any modal system is the scale itself. For many scales, the individual modes have been given names because they are used as scales themselves.

The modes of the Major scale are the Ionian, Dorian, Phrygian, Lydian, Mixolydian, Aeolian, and Locrian. The mode called Ionian is the Major scale. Of all the scales, the Major is the only one that has a different name for the 1st mode.

The II mode of any scale is based upon the 2nd tone of the main scale, in this case the Major scale. A mode uses the exact tones of the main scale; however, what was a 2 becomes a 1, what was a 3 becomes a 2, etc. (fig. 13).

1		2		3	4		5		6		7	1		2		3	4		5		6		7
		1		2	♭3		4		5		6	♭7											

fig. 13

The process then continues for the other modes. For the III mode, the 3 becomes the 1, the 4 becomes the 2, etc. (fig. 14).

1		2		3	4		5		6		7	1		2		3	4		5		6		7
				1	♭2		♭3		4		5	♭6		♭7									

fig. 14

For the IV mode, the 4 becomes the 1, the 5 becomes the 2, etc. (fig. 15).

1		2		3	4		5		6		7	1		2		3	4		5		6		7
					1		2		3		♯4	5		6		7							

fig. 15

For the V mode, the 5 becomes the 1, the 6 becomes the 2, etc. (fig. 16)

1		2		3	4		5		6		7	1		2		3	4		5		6		7
							1		2		3	4		5		6	♭7						

fig. 16

For the VI mode the 6 becomes the 1, the 7 becomes the 2, etc. (fig. 17).

1		2		3	4		5		6		7	1		2		3	4		5		6		7
									1		2	♭3		4		5	♭6		♭7				

fig. 17

For the VII, mode, the 7 becomes the 1, the 1 becomes the 2, the 2 becomes the 3, etc. (fig. 18).

1		2		3	4		5		6		7	1		2		3	4		5		6		7
											1	♭2		♭3		4	♭5		♭6		♭7		

fig. 18

As you can see in all of the examples above, every mode has 7 tones; however, it has some kind of a 2, some kind of a 3, some kind of a 4, etc.. In other words, though you are using the same tones, the numeric value changes when you shift the tone center — that is the tone which you now designated as 1.

At the bottom of the title page of each scale, the relative relationship of each mode to the main scale is graphed out for you along with the numeric formula for each mode (fig. 17).

NUMERIC SCALE / MODE CHART

		1		2		3	4		5		6		7	1		2		3	4		5		6		7
I	IONIAN	1		2		3	4		5		6		7	1		2		3	4		5		6		7
II	DORIAN			1		2	♭3		4		5		6	♭7											
III	PHRYGIAN					1	♭2		♭3		4		5	♭6		♭7									
IV	LYDIAN						1		2		3		#4	5		6		7							
V	MIXOLYD•								1		2		3	4		5		6	♭7						
VI	AEOLIAN										1		2	♭3		4		5	♭6		♭7				
VII	LOCRIAN												1	♭2		♭3		4	♭5		♭6		♭7		
		1		2		3	4		5		6		7												

fig. 17

In the case of some of the exotic scales in this book, you will get some pretty weird combinations for the numeric anaysis of the modes such as *double flats* 𝄫 and *double sharps* 𝄪 . Also note some of the modes don't have names, they are merely called mode II, mode III, etc. (fig. 18).

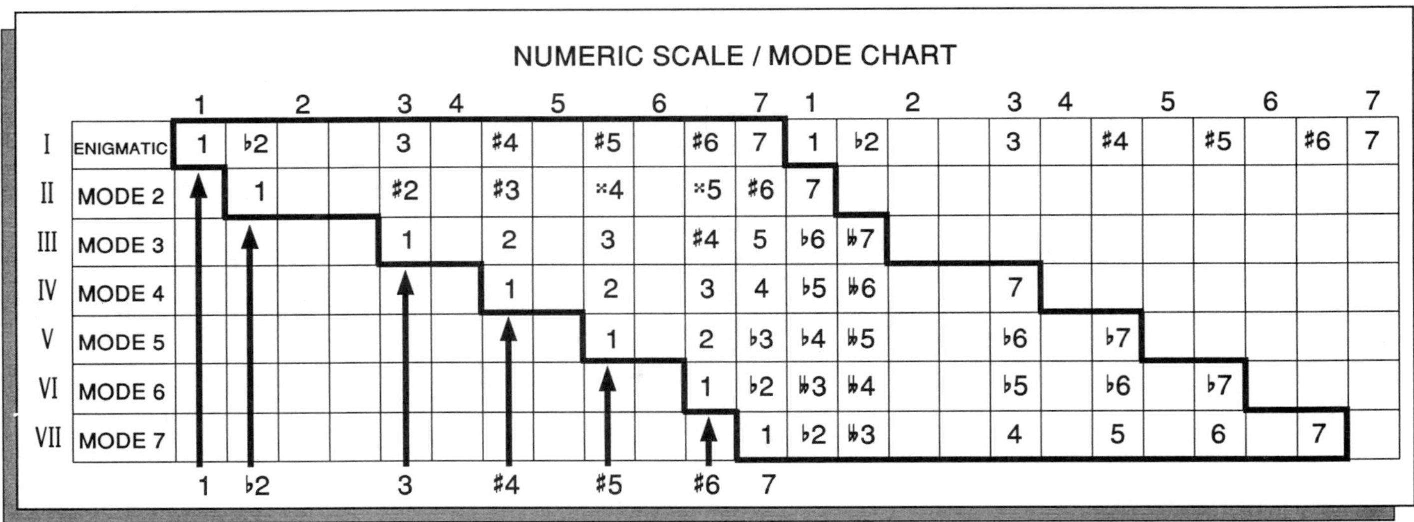

NUMERIC SCALE / MODE CHART

		1		2		3	4		5		6		7	1		2		3	4		5		6		7
I	ENIGMATIC	1	♭2			3		#4		#5		#6	7	1	♭2			3		#4		#5		#6	7
II	MODE 2		1			#2		#3		𝄪4		𝄪5	#6	7											
III	MODE 3					1		2		3		#4	5	♭6	𝄫7										
IV	MODE 4							1		2		3	4	♭5	𝄫6			7							
V	MODE 5									1		2	♭3	♭4	𝄫5			♭6		♭7					
VI	MODE 6											1	♭2	𝄫3	𝄫4			♭5		♭6		♭7			
VII	MODE 7												1	♭2	𝄫3			4		5		6		7	
		1	♭2			3		#4		#5		#6	7												

fig. 18

The numbers above the graph will always be the major scale numbers, so you can see how the new scale and its modes relate to the major scale.

There is actually only 1 scale, the Major scale and its modes. All other scales can be thought of as derived modes which also have modes. This may be a bit confusing at first, but an interesting thought to ponder. For the sake of simplicity, they will be called "scales" in this text.

As you study the numeric formulas for each scale or mode, there is a simple 4-step system which will help you in understanding how the tones become flats or sharps. The 3 examples in fig. 19 demonstrate the application of this 4-step rule. When you compare your tones to the Major, the number of boxes to the left or right of the original tone decides whether standard flats and sharps or double flats and sharps are used. 1 box over is a standard, 2 boxes is a double (fig. 19).

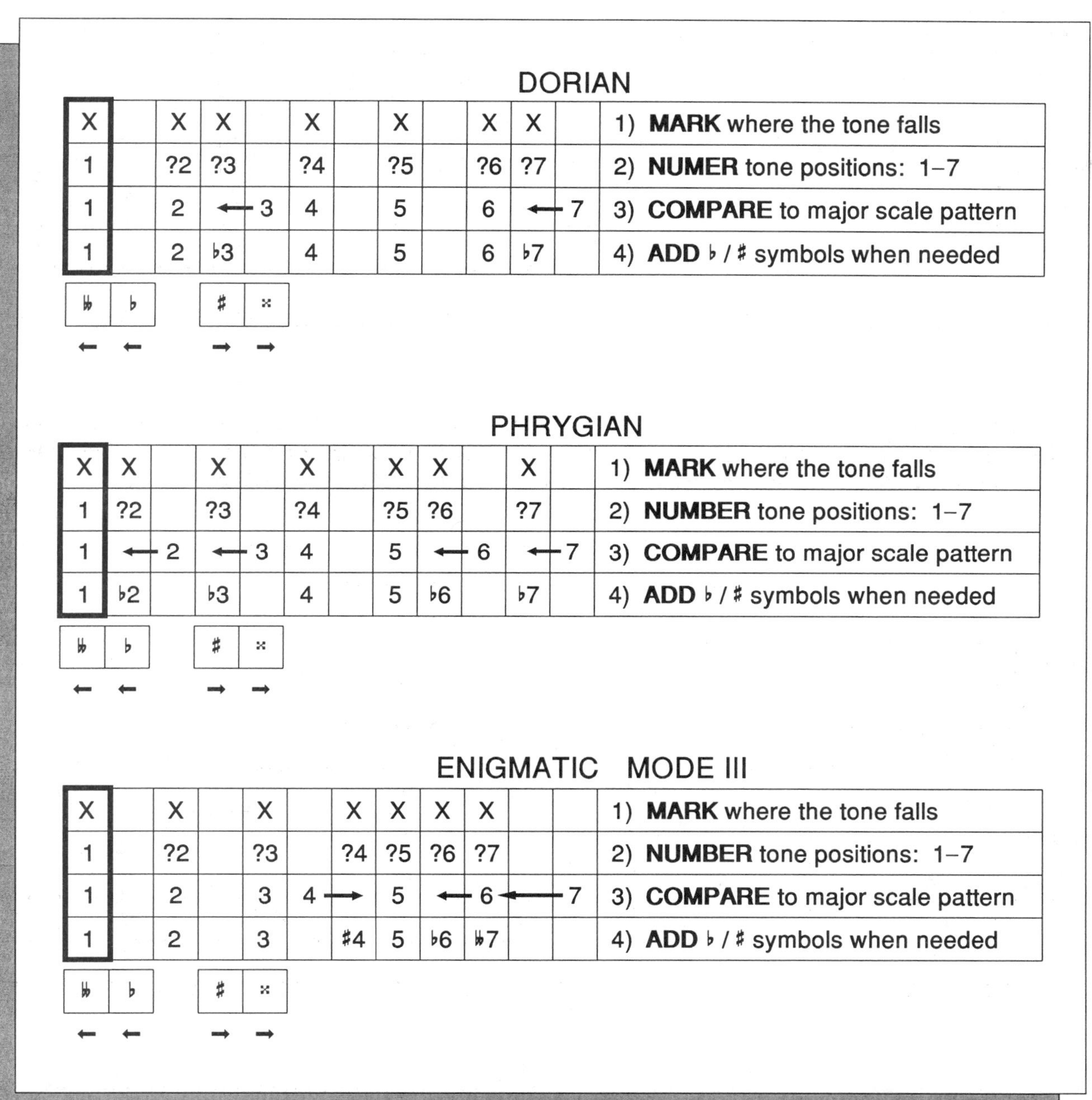

DORIAN

X		X	X		X		X		X	X		1) **MARK** where the tone falls
1		?2	?3		?4		?5		?6	?7		2) **NUMER** tone positions: 1–7
1		2	←	3	4		5		6	←	7	3) **COMPARE** to major scale pattern
1		2	♭3		4		5		6	♭7		4) **ADD** ♭ / ♯ symbols when needed

PHRYGIAN

X	X		X		X		X	X		X		1) **MARK** where the tone falls
1	?2		?3		?4		?5	?6		?7		2) **NUMBER** tone positions: 1–7
1	←	2	←	3	4		5	←	6	←	7	3) **COMPARE** to major scale pattern
1	♭2		♭3		4		5	♭6		♭7		4) **ADD** ♭ / ♯ symbols when needed

ENIGMATIC MODE III

X		X		X		X	X	X	X			1) **MARK** where the tone falls
1		?2		?3		?4	?5	?6	?7			2) **NUMBER** tone positions: 1–7
1		2		3	4 →	→	5	←	6 ←	←	7	3) **COMPARE** to major scale pattern
1		2		3		♯4	5	♭6	𝄫7			4) **ADD** ♭ / ♯ symbols when needed

fig. 19

MODES AND RELATIVE SCALES

Scales and modes are the foundation of your composition and improvisation. Modes are treated as scales. Just as we can change the pitch of the main scale, in order to play in one of the 12 keys, the same concept or principle can be used when using a mode. The mode generator chart of each title page will show you the main scale equivalent for each mode (fig. 20).

The **Quick Mode Generator Chart** is placed next to the keyboard chart for those of you who are guitarists with limited keyboard ability, but have sequencers and keyboard controllers. However, the concept and principles behind the mode generator chart are the same regardless of what instrument you play.

The letters in column I indicate the pitch of the starting point. In other words it tells you what key you are in. The other columns tell you what key the relative scale is in.

Let's demonstrate this below with a G Mixolydian (fig. 21). The Mixolydian is the V mode of the Major scale.

Beneath column I we go down to the G, because that will be our starting pitch or key. Over to where it meets column V we come to a C, therefore, if we are playing a G Mixolydian we are actually playing a C Major with the root note shifted to the G.

Step 1 Place left finger on desired key in column I.

Step 2 Place right finger on column of desired mode (in roman numerals at the top).

Step 3 Run fingers across and down until they meet.

The point where they meet is the relative scale.

It's as simple as 1 - 2 - 3 !

MODE GENERATOR CHART

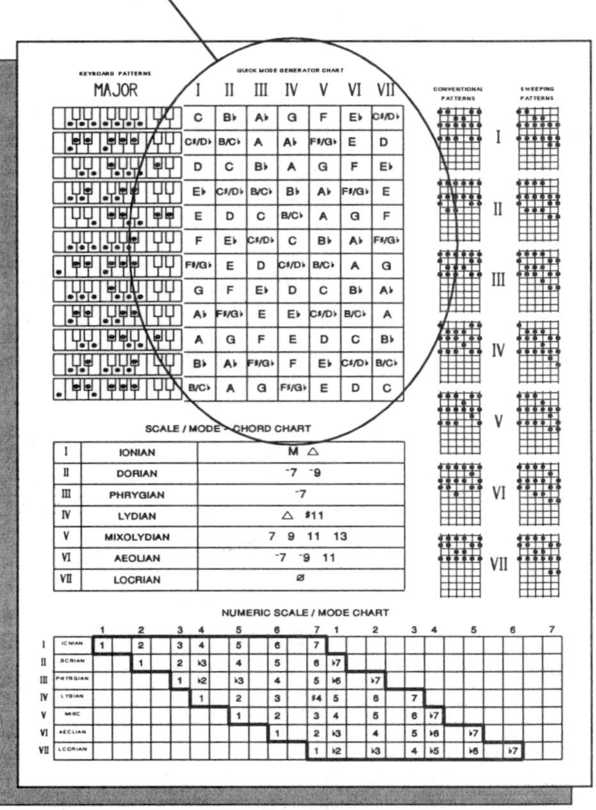

fig. 20

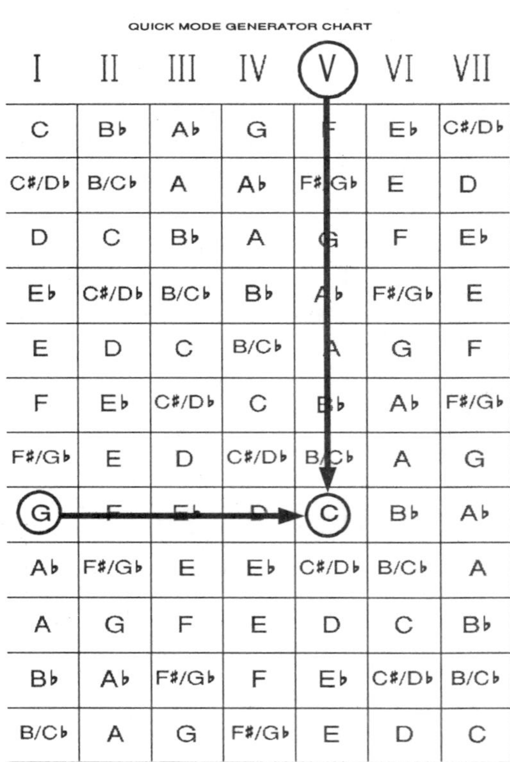

QUICK MODE GENERATOR CHART

I	II	III	IV	V	VI	VII
C	B♭	A♭	G	F	E♭	C♯/D♭
C♯/D♭	B/C♭	A	A♭	F♯/G♭	E	D
D	C	B♭	A	G	F	E♭
E♭	C♯/D♭	B/C♭	B♭	A♭	F♯/G♭	E
E	D	C	B/C♭	A	G	F
F	E♭	C♯/D♭	C	B♭	A♭	F♯/G♭
F♯/G♭	E	D	C♯/D♭	B/C♭	A	G
G	F	E♭	D	C	B♭	A♭
A♭	F♯/G♭	E	E♭	C♯/D♭	B/C♭	A
A	G	F	E	D	C	B♭
B♭	A♭	F♯/G♭	F	E♭	C♯/D♭	B/C♭
B/C♭	A	G	F♯/G♭	E	D	C

fig. 21

CHORDS

One of the most frequently asked questions by inexperienced musicians is, "What chords can I play with such and such scale?" The **Scale / Mode - Chord Chart** for *chord and scale compatibility* on each title page takes the guess work out of that question. Clearly depicted are the compatible chords for every mode (fig. 22).

CHORD / SCALE CHART

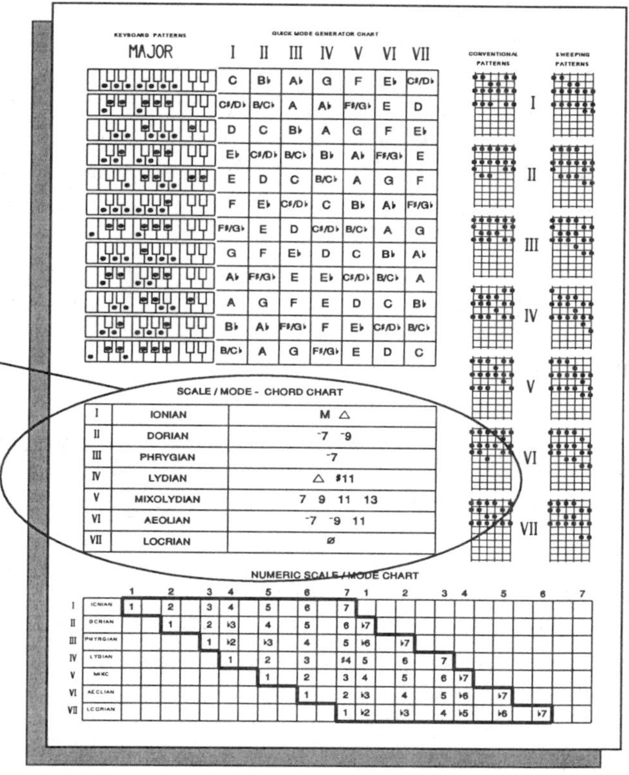

fig. 22

In order to use this chart, you must have an understanding how chords are built. For the sake of those who might be total beginners, we will review the basics behind chord theory and harmony.

We have already studied intervals. An interval is the distance between 2 tones. Therefore, let's define a chord. A chord is 2 or more intervals played simultaneously.

A basic chord "formula" for building chords is to use every other tone of the scale you are in. For example, a Major chord would consist of 1 - 3 - 5. A Major 7th chord would be 1 - 3 - 5 - 7.

Using the building blocks format compare the Major scale, the Major chord, and the Major 7th chord (fig. 23).

Major Scale	1		2		3	4		5		6		7
Major Chord	1				3			5				
Major 7th	1				3			5				7

fig. 23

What about those big fancy chords like 9ths, 11ths, and 13ths? Using 2 octaves of our Major scale, we can clearly see that a 9th is a 2nd, an 11th is a 4th, and the 13th is a 6th (fig. 24). This should help remove the mystery behind big chords.

Major Scale	1		2		3	4		5		6		7	1		2		3	4		5		6		7
Major 9th	1				3			5				7			9									
Major 11th	1				3			5				7			9			11						
Major 13th	1				3			5				7			9			11				13		

fig. 24

CHORD NAMING SYSTEM

In order to fully understand the numeric formulas, you first have to understand the chord naming system in this text. There are certain rules or guidelines which help the musician when he is communicating to other musicians. Once you fully understand music theory, you'll understand all naming systems. We feel that the system in this book is the most effecient ***if used properly.***

In the chart (fig. 25) there are 7 symbols. The 7 symbols are used to denote the status of specific tones within the chord. The flat and sharp symbols are used when altering any other tones. Some systems will use - and + as flats and sharps. Although this is not incorrect, we have found it more systematic to use them as represented in the chart below. Memorize these symbols and the tones they represent, as they will be your best friends when dealing with chords.

CHORDS	SYMBOL	DENOTES STATUS OF	CHANGE	RESULT	NAME	EXAMPLE AND FORMULA
3 TONE	−	3	♭	♭3	MINOR	C$^-$ = 1 - ♭3 - 5
	+	5	♯	♯5	AUGMENTED	C$^+$ = 1 - 3 - ♯5
	°	3,5	♭	♭3,♭5	DIMINISHED	C° = 1 - ♭3 - ♭5
4 TONE	△	7	same	7	DELTA	C△ = 1 - 3 - 5 - 7
	7	7	♭	♭7	DOMINANT	C7 = 1 - 3 - 5 -♭7
	ø	3,5,7	♭	♭3,♭5,♭7	HALF-DIMINISHED	Cø = 1 - ♭3 - ♭5 - ♭7
	°7	7 of ø	extra ♭	𝄫7	DIMINISHED 7TH	C°7= 1- ♭3 - ♭5 - 𝄫7

fig. 25

Let's list a few chords and analyze their components within the name. What we have in fig. 26 is some kind of 13th chord. The letter tells us what pitch the " 1" (root note) of our formula is on. The △ (delta) tells us that it's a Major 7th chord. The + tells us to raise the 5th a half-step, as in 1 sharp. And the 13th is flat. The chord is an E flat delta augmented, flat 13.

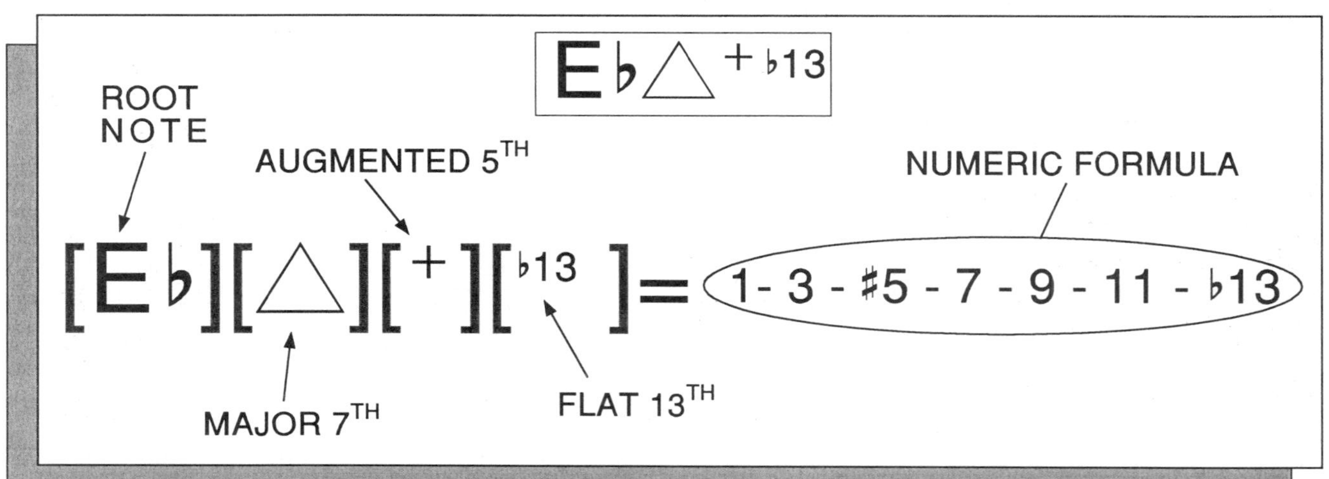

fig. 26

Study the names of the chords in relationship to the formulas in the numeric chord charts.

POLYCHORDS

As you study the numeric chord charts, you will see some of the larger chords have 6 or 7 tones. Many times this can be cumbersome, even for a keyboard player, let alone a guitarist. How do you play 7 notes when you only have 6 strings? The way to do this is to simulate the large chords with what we call polychords. In other words, use several smaller chords to make 1 big chord. Let's look at a $13^{\sharp 11}$ chord with building blocks (fig.27).

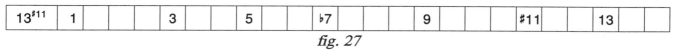

$13^{\sharp 11}$	1				3			5			♭7				9				#11			13		

fig. 27

Now let's look at 1 possible polychord formula (there could be several) and analyze the equation. To the left of the equal sign is the chord name. On the right side of the equal sign it tells us to play a delta augmented over the root at the flated 7th.

$$13^{\sharp 11} = \frac{\triangle^{+}}{\flat 7}$$ *fig. 28*

Let's see what this chord represents (fig. 29):

$13^{\sharp 11}$	1				3			5			♭7				9				#11			13		
	ROOT ↑										↕				↕				↕			↕		
										$\triangle^{+}$	1				3				#5			7		

fig. 29

Placing the 1 of our $\triangle^{+}$ (delta augmented) at the dominant 7th from the root, we see that the tones are the tones of our desired chord. Therefore, we have simulated our $13^{\sharp 11}$. Now let's look at the same chord except with a different polychord formula. The capital M is a Major triad over the root at the 9th. It looks like this: fig. 30 and fig. 31. You could also place the Major triad on the 2nd, since the 2nd is also a 9th (fig. 32 and fig. 33). The result would also be the same.

$$13^{\sharp 11} = \frac{M}{9}$$ *fig. 30*

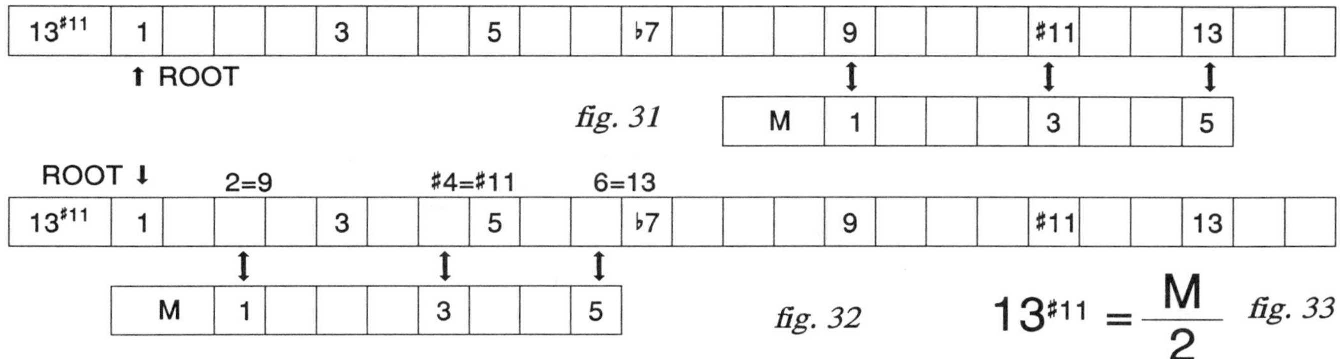

$$13^{\sharp 11} = \frac{M}{2}$$ *fig. 33*

The bass player will usually play the root note, while the guitar or keyboard will play the 3 or 4 tone chord at the appropriate interval.

The formula for polychords is depicted in the chart, fig. 34.

$$X = \frac{Y}{Z}$$

X (DESIRED CHORD) = (3 OR 4 TONE CHORD) Y / OVER THE ROOT AT (INTERVAL) Z

fig. 34

NUMERIC ANALYSIS OF CHORDS

	1		2		3	4		5		6		7	1		2		3	4		5		6		7
M	1				3			5																
−	1			♭3				5																
sus2	1		2					5																
sus	1					4		5																
♭5	1				3		♭5																	
○	1			♭3			♭5																	
$\genfrac{}{}{0pt}{}{5}{8}$	1							5					8											
+	1				3				♯5															
♭6	1				3			5	♭6															
−♭6	1			♭3				5	♭6															
6	1				3			5		6														
−6	1			♭3				5		6														
°7	1			♭3			♭5			𝄫7														
Q(3)	1					4					♭7			QUARTAL or DOUBLE FOURTH										
7	1				3			5			♭7													
−7	1			♭3				5			♭7													
7^{sus2}	1		2					5			♭7													
7^{sus}	1					4		5			♭7													
$7^{\flat 5}$	1				3		♭5				♭7													
ø	1			♭3			♭5				♭7													
7^{+}	1				3				♯5		♭7													
△	1				3			5				7												
−△	1			♭3				5				7												
△^{sus2}	1		2					5				7												
△^{sus}	1					4		5				7												
△$^{\flat 5}$	1				3		♭5					7												
△$^{\circ}$	1			♭3			♭5					7												
△$^{+}$	1				3				♯5			7												
−△$^{+}$	1			♭3					♯5			7												
$\genfrac{}{}{0pt}{}{7}{6}$	1				3			5		6	♭7													
$\genfrac{}{}{0pt}{}{9}{6}$	1				3			5		6					9									
− $\genfrac{}{}{0pt}{}{9}{6}$	1			♭3				5		6					9									

NUMERIC ANALYSIS OF CHORDS continued

	1		2		3	4		5		6		7	1		2		3	4		5		6		7
9	1				3			5			♭7				9									
-9	1			♭3				5			♭7				9									
♭9	1				3			5			♭7			♭9										
-♭9	1			♭3				5			♭7			♭9										
#9	1				3			5			♭7					#9								
△9	1				3			5				7			9									
-△9	1			♭3				5				7			9									
△♭9	1				3			5				7		♭9										
-△♭9	1			♭3				5				7		♭9										
△#9	1				3			5				7				#9								
ALT	1				3		♭5				♭7					#9								
ALT	1				3		♭5				♭7			♭9										
ALT	1				3				#5		♭7			♭9										
ALT	1				3				#5		♭7					#9								
11	1				3			5			♭7				9			11						
-11	1			♭3				5			♭7				9			11						
#11	1				3			5			♭7				9				#11					
-#11	1			♭3				5			♭7				9				#11					
△11	1				3			5				7			9			11						
-△11	1			♭3				5				7			9			11						
△#11	1				3			5				7			9				#11					
-△#11	1			♭3				5				7			9				#11					
13	1				3			5			♭7				9			11				13		
-13	1			♭3				5			♭7				9			11				13		
13#11	1				3			5			♭7				9				#11			13		
-13#11	1			♭3				5			♭7				9				#11			13		
△13	1				3			5				7			9			11				13		
-△13	1			♭3				5				7			9			11				13		
△13#11	1				3			5				7			9				#11			13		
-△13#11	1			♭3				5				7			9				#11			13		

COMPATIBILITY

Now that we have covered chords and polychords, let's return to the Scale/ Mode-Chord Compatibility Chart, which is found on the title page of each new scale (fig. 35)

The roman numerals on the left side of the chart will tell you the mode you are in. Next will be the name of the mode, where applicable. On the right half are the chords that fit or match that mode. In other words, compatible chords you can use.

Taking the Dorian, let's see how this works (fig. 36).

SCALE / MODE - CHORD CHART

I	IONIAN	M △
II	DORIAN	-7 -9
III	PHRYGIAN	-7
IV	LYDIAN	△ ♯11
V	MIXOLYDIAN	7 9 11 13
VI	AEOLIAN	-7 -9 -11
VII	LOCRIAN	ø

fig. 35

DORIAN	1		2	♭3		4		5		6	♭7		1		2	♭3		4		5		6	♭7	
-7	1			♭3				5			♭7													
-9	1			♭3				5			♭7				9									

Comparing it in this way we see that all the tones in the -7 and -9 chords are in the scale, or in this case, mode.

fig. 36

The same 2 chords will also fit with the Aeolian, fig. 37.

AEOLIAN	1		2	♭3		4		5	♭6		♭7		1		2	♭3		4		5	♭6		♭7	
-7	1			♭3				5			♭7													
-9	1			♭3				5			♭7				9									

fig. 37

The Minor 7th and the Minor 9th (-7, -9) will not, however, work with the Locrian. But the half-diminished will (fig. 38).

LOCRIAN	1	♭2		♭3		4	♭5		♭6		♭7		1	♭2		♭3		4	♭5		♭6		♭7	
ø	1			♭3			♭5				♭7													

fig. 38

As you become more familiar with the mathematics or numerics behind scales, modes, and chords, compatibility will become an automatic response. Till then, you have the scale-chord compatibility charts to help you. Volume II of the Guitar Grimoire™ will deal entirely with chords.

THE PATTERNS

On the title page of each scale, you will find a set of keyboard fingerings and 2 sets of guitar fingerings (fig. 39). The scale key for the keyboard fingerings are designated by the letter symbol next to the keyboard fingering in the I column of the Quick Mode Generator Chart (fig. 40).

The conventional guitar fingerings are given merely for the sake of comparison and analysis. If you study carefully you will notice that in most cases each sweeping pattern is comprised of parts from 2 of the conventional patterns. For instance, sweeping pattern I, has the 6th through 4th strings of conventional I and the 1st and 2nd strings of conventional II. This is because the sweeping pattern compensates for the idiosyncrasies of the guitar's design in tuning the 2nd string to the 4th fret of the 3rd string rather than tuning all strings in 4ths. The format of these patterns then, allow you to sweep 3 notes per string systematically and symmetrically.

The 1st 4 scales (Major, Melodic, Harmonic Minor, and Harmonic Major) have all the patterns set up for you per mode to help you along until you get used to the Quick Mode Generator Chart. One thing you must remember, when you are in the II mode, the II pattern from the title page now becomes the I and the rest follow in sequence. Just as when you are in the III mode, the III pattern becomes the I. This will become more apparent when you study the fingering patterns on the breakdown pages.

In the section titled "Intervals and Instrument" we have included interval maps. An interval map will show you the numerics (1,2,3,4,5,6,7) for all 12 keys. This will help you when you are composing using the polychord technique as well as when studying complete fret and pattern breakdowns and how they compare to the major scale. It will benefit you greatly to memorize the numerics for all 12 keys, but until then we have laid it out for you in each key so that you may use it as a reference tool.

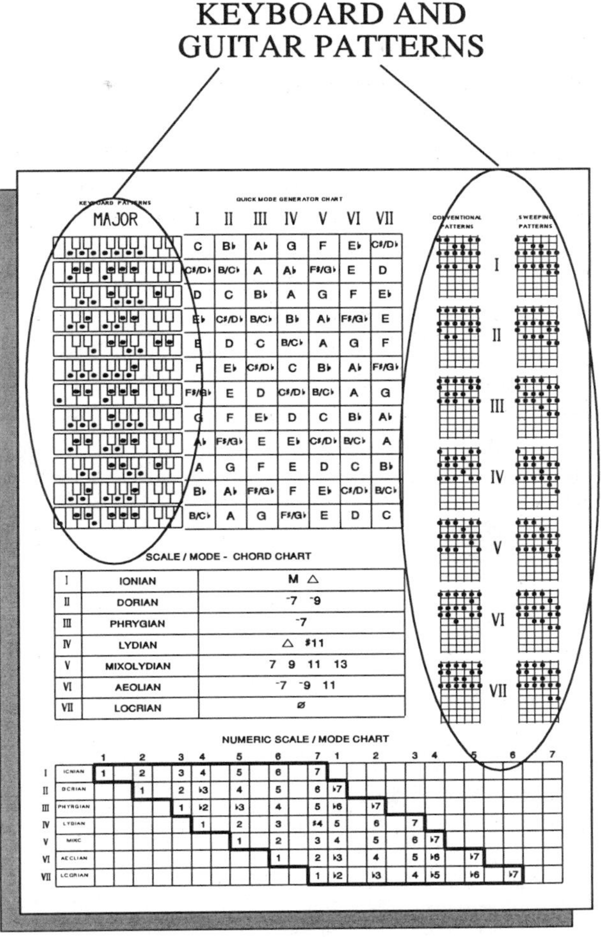

fig. 39

PATTERN

KEY

KEYBOARD PATTERNS

QUICK MODE GENERATOR CHART

MAJOR

I	II	III	IV	V	VI	VII
C	B♭	A♭	G	F	E♭	C♯/D♭
C♯/D♭	B/C♭	A	A♭	F♯/G♭	E	D
D	C	B♭	A	G	F	E♭
E♭	C♯/D♭	B/C♭	B♭	A♭	F♯/G♭	E
E	D	C	B/C♭	A	G	F
F	E♭	C♯/D♭	C	B♭	A♭	F♯/G♭
F♯/G♭	E	D	C♯/D♭	B/C♭	A	G
G	F	E♭	D	C	B♭	A♭
A♭	F♯/G♭	E	E♭	C♯/D♭	B/C♭	A
A	G	F	E	D	C	B♭
B♭	A♭	F♯/G♭	F	E♭	C♯/D♭	B/C♭
B/C♭	A	G	F♯/G♭	E	D	C

fig. 40

INTERVALS AND INSTRUMENT

Now that we've learned about intervals, the building blocks of music, let's see how they tie into our instrument. We are going to take 2 octaves of the intervals which make up the Major scale and see how they match up to the guitar in the key of F.

Looking at the diagram, (fig. 41) we can see that each block corresponds to a fret. Putting your 1st finger on the 1st string, the 1st fret will give you a 1, in this case an F. On the 3rd fret you'll have your major 2nd, on the 5th fret your major 3rd, etc..

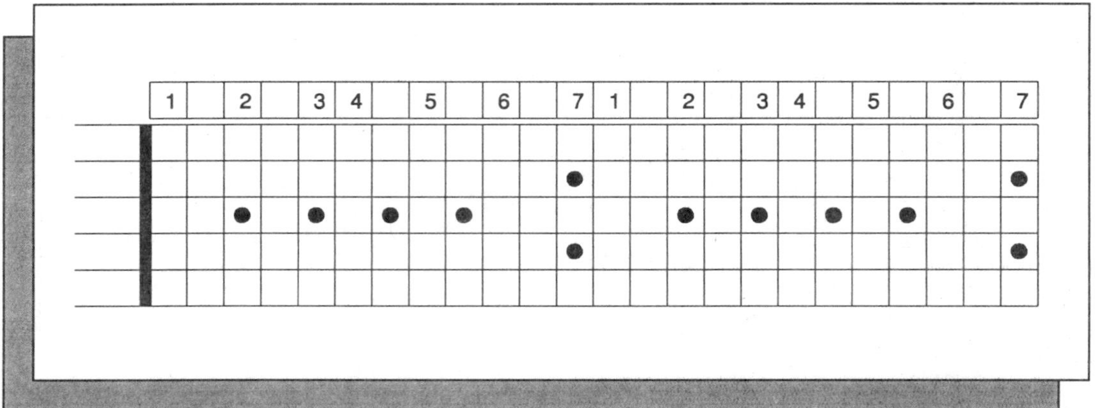

fig. 41

An example for the keyboard, in the key of C, shows that the blocks which make up the Major scale align with the "white" keys (fig. 42).

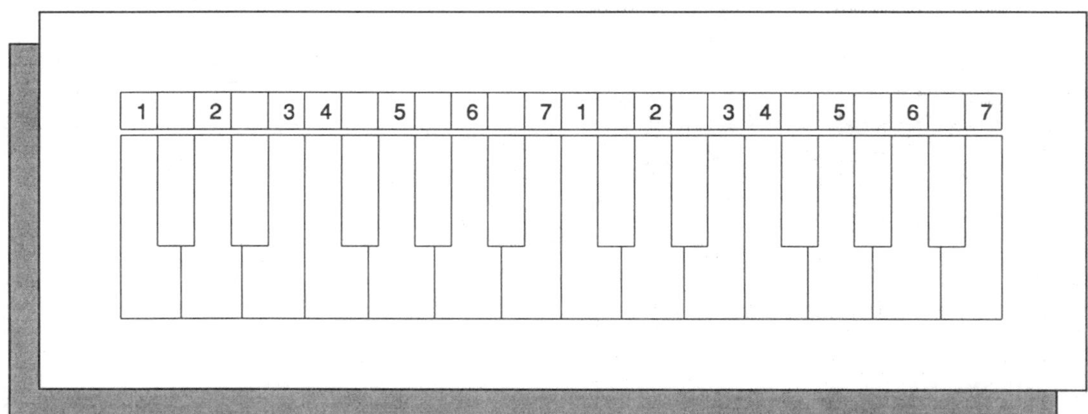

fig. 42

To change keys, you change the pitch of the starting note, in other words, you have to shift your mathematical formula, in this case the Major scale, to the appropriate pitch or key. Until you have memorized this process for yourself, we have done it for you.

The following pages are interval maps for the guitar and the keyboard. The key is designated above each fretboard or next to each keyboard digaram, and as you will notice, they are laid out for you in all 12 keys. Open notes are represented by the circles above the fretboard. Study these well, for they will help you as you analyze the pattern breakdowns later on in the book.

GUITAR INTERVAL MAPS

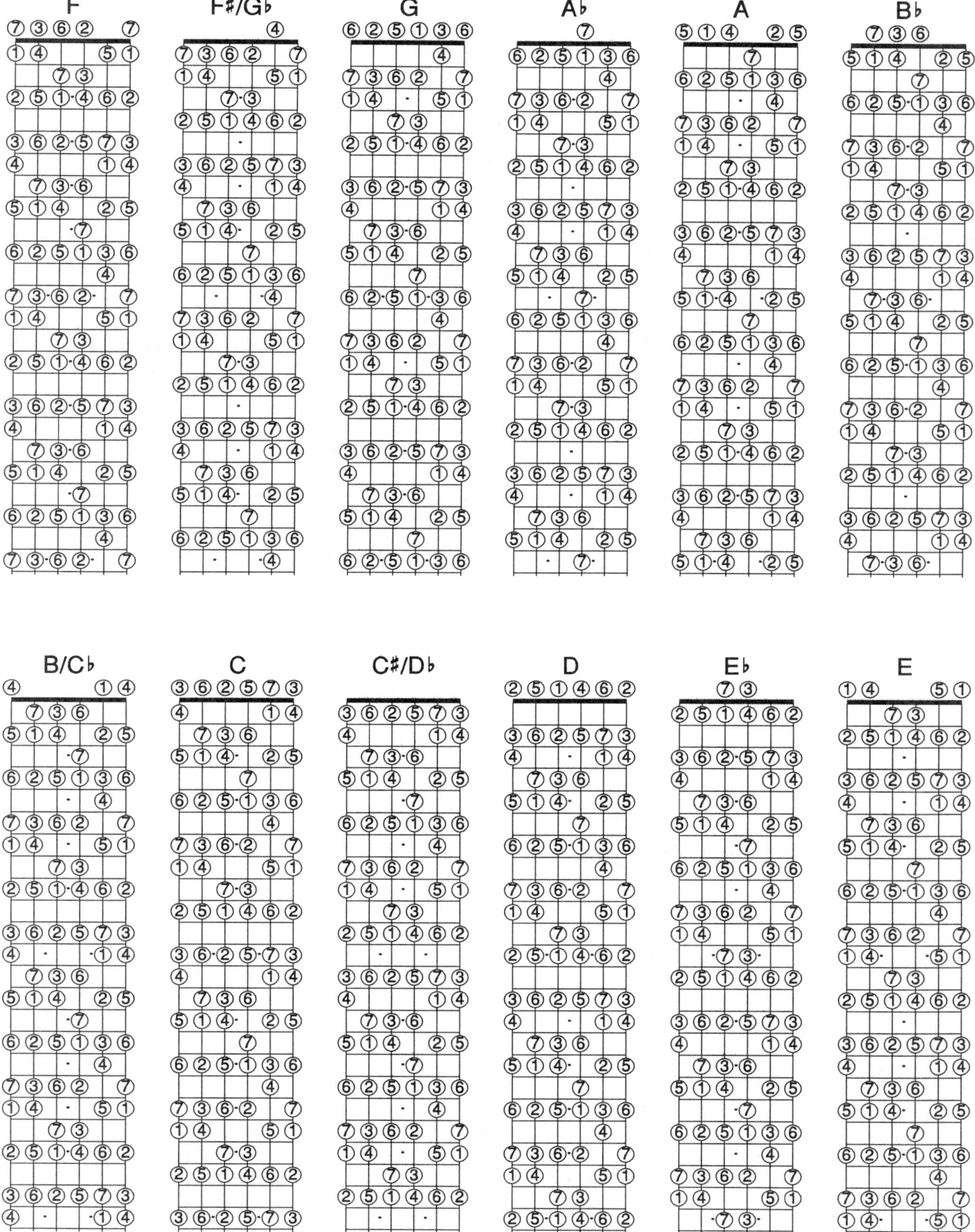

KEYBOARD INTERVAL MAPS

Key	Interval numbers (left to right)
C	1 2 3 4 5 6 7 1 2 3 4 5 6 7 1 2 3 4 5 6 7
C♯/D♭	7 1 2 3 4 5 6 7 1 2 3 4 5 6 7 1 2 3 4 5 6
D	7 1 2 3 4 5 6 7 1 2 3 4 5 6 7 1 2 3 4 5 6
E♭	6 7 1 2 3 4 5 6 7 1 2 3 4 5 6 7 1 2 3 4 5
E	6 7 1 2 3 4 5 6 7 1 2 3 4 5 6 7 1 2 3 4 5
F	5 6 7 1 2 3 4 5 6 7 1 2 3 4 5 6 7 1 2 3 4
F♯/G♭	5 6 7 1 2 3 4 5 6 7 1 2 3 4 5 6 7 1 2 3
G	4 5 6 7 1 2 3 4 5 6 7 1 2 3 4 5 6 7 1 2 3
A♭	3 4 5 6 7 1 2 3 4 5 6 7 1 2 3 4 5 6 7 1 2
A	3 4 5 6 7 1 2 3 4 5 6 7 1 2 3 4 5 6 7 1 2
B♭	2 3 4 5 6 7 1 2 3 4 5 6 7 1 2 3 4 5 6 7 1
B/C♭	2 3 4 5 6 7 1 2 3 4 5 6 7 1 2 3 4 5 6 7 1

7 TONE SCALES

All other scales come from the 7 tone scales, therefore the 7 tone scales are listed first.

Every possible pattern in the sweeping is composed of 8 mini-patterns as follows (fig. 43):

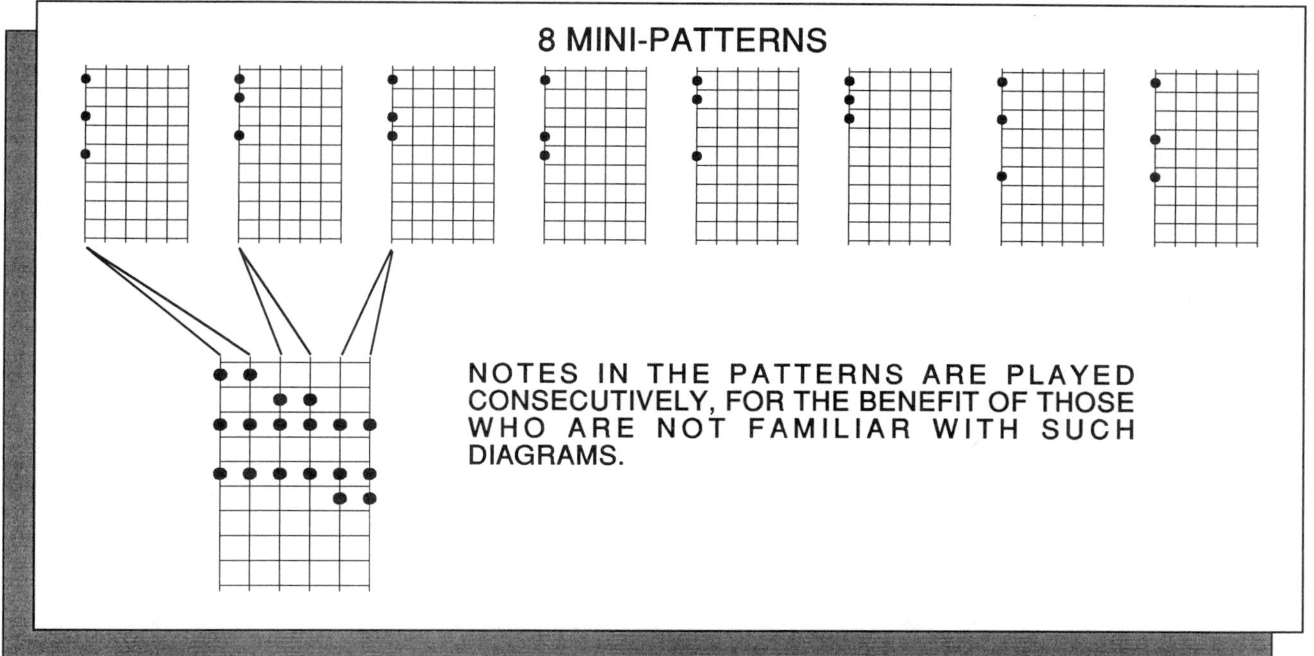

fig. 43

The many combinations of mini-patterns make up the Patterns I through VII for each different scale. By the time you have gotten to the Hungarian Major, you have used all 8 mini-patterns. There are 4 other mini-patterns, but they are used in abstract pentatonics and will be covered in that section.

The breakdowns are shown only as high as the 19th fret, since everything from the 13th fret on is a repeat of the 1st through the 12th. The complete fretboard, of the breakdown pages, depicts every note on every string for that key, that then is broken down into patterns. The first tone of each pattern corresponds to a tone number as you ascend the scale.

QUICK MODE GENERATOR CHART

MAJOR

I	II	III	IV	V	VI	VII
C	B♭	A♭	G	F	E♭	C#/D♭
C#/D♭	B/C♭	A	A♭	F#/G♭	E	D
D	C	B♭	A	G	F	E♭
E♭	C#/D♭	B/C♭	B♭	A♭	F#/G♭	E
E	D	C	B/C♭	A	G	F
F	E♭	C#/D♭	C	B♭	A♭	F#/G♭
F#/G♭	E	D	C#/D♭	B/C♭	A	G
G	F	E♭	D	C	B♭	A♭
A♭	F#/G♭	E	E♭	C#/D♭	B/C♭	A
A	G	F	E	D	C	B♭
B♭	A♭	F#/G♭	F	E♭	C#/D♭	B/C♭
B/C♭	A	G	F#/G♭	E	D	C

CONVENTIONAL PATTERNS / SWEEPING PATTERNS

I, II, III, IV, V, VI, VII

SCALE / MODE - CHORD CHART

I	IONIAN	M, $\triangle$, $\triangle^{9}$
II	DORIAN	$^{-}7$, $^{-}9$
III	PHRYGIAN	$^{-}7$
IV	LYDIAN	$\triangle$, $\triangle^{9}$, $\triangle^{\#11}$
V	MIXOLYDIAN	7, 9, 11, 13
VI	AEOLIAN	$^{-}7$, $^{-}9$, $^{-}11$
VII	LOCRIAN	ø

NUMERIC SCALE / MODE CHART

		1		2		3	4		5		6		7	1		2		3	4		5		6		7
I	IONIAN	1		2		3	4		5		6		7	1		2		3	4		5		6		7
II	DORIAN			1		2	♭3		4		5		6	♭7											
III	PHRYGIAN					1	♭2		♭3		4		5	♭6		♭7									
IV	LYDIAN						1		2		3		#4	5		6		7							
V	MIXOLYD								1		2		3	4		5		6	♭7						
VI	AEOLIAN										1		2	♭3		4		5	♭6		♭7				
VII	LOCRIAN												1	♭2		♭3		4	♭5		♭6		♭7		

F MAJOR

F♯ / G♭ MAJOR

G MAJOR

A♭ MAJOR

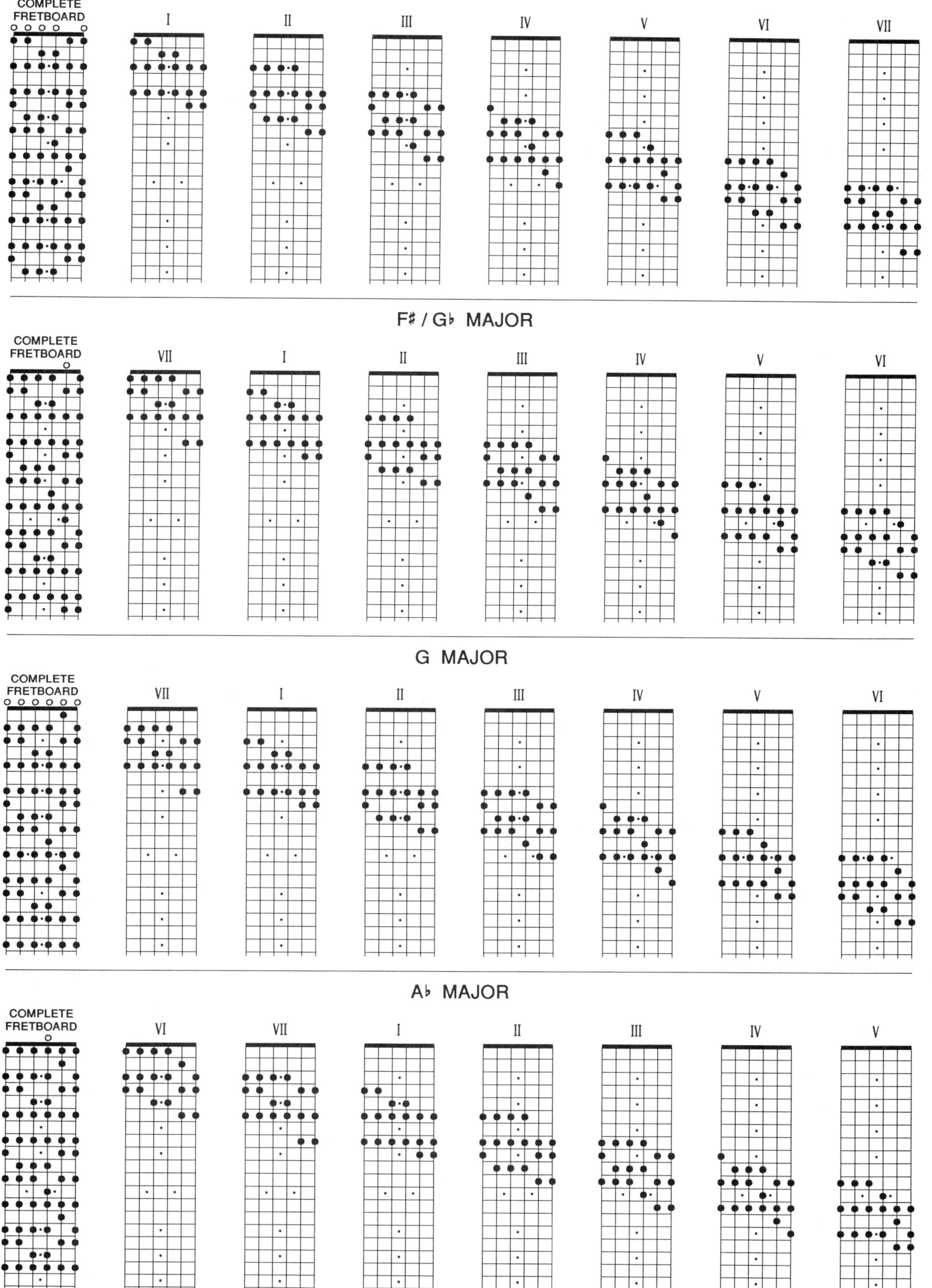

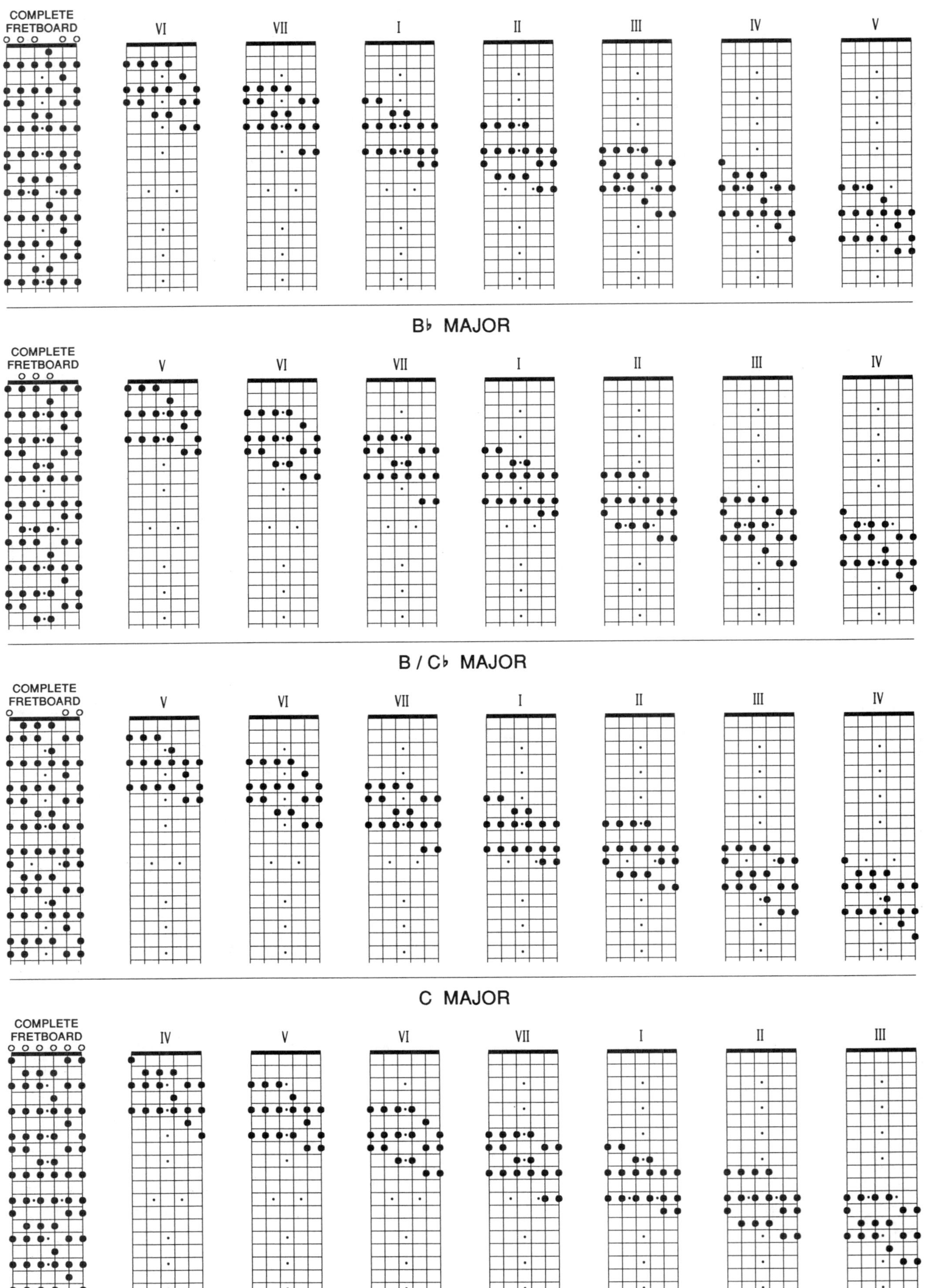
A MAJOR
COMPLETE FRETBOARD
VI
VII
I
II
III
IV
V
B♭ MAJOR
COMPLETE FRETBOARD
V
VI
VII
I
II
III
IV
B / C♭ MAJOR
COMPLETE FRETBOARD
V
VI
VII
I
II
III
IV
C MAJOR
COMPLETE FRETBOARD
IV
V
VI
VII
I
II
III

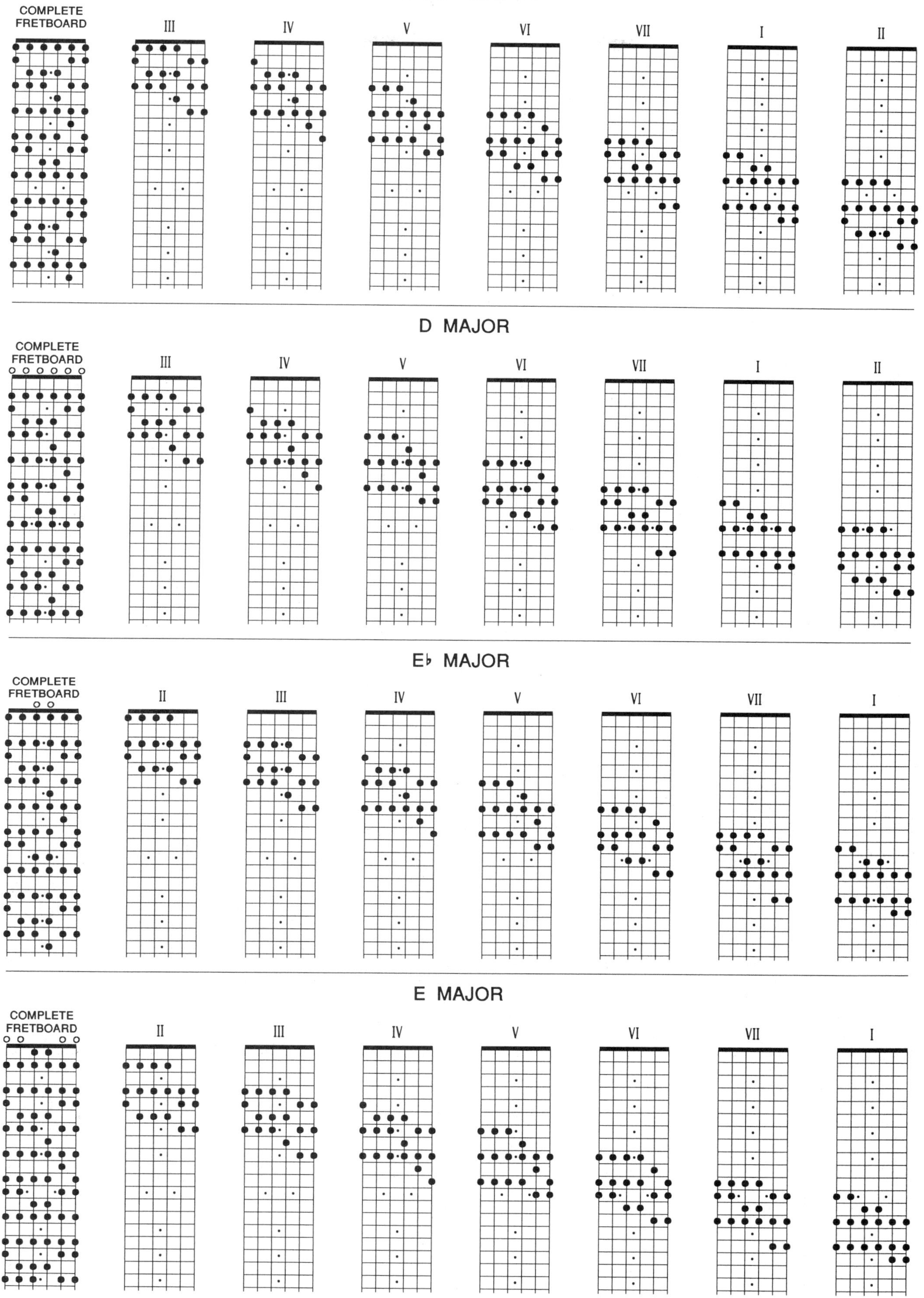
C♯ / D♭ MAJOR
COMPLETE FRETBOARD
III
IV
V
VI
VII
I
II
D MAJOR
COMPLETE FRETBOARD
III
IV
V
VI
VII
I
II
E♭ MAJOR
COMPLETE FRETBOARD
II
III
IV
V
VI
VII
I
E MAJOR
COMPLETE FRETBOARD
II
III
IV
V
VI
VII
I

F DORIAN

F♯ / G♭ DORIAN

G DORIAN

A♭ DORIAN

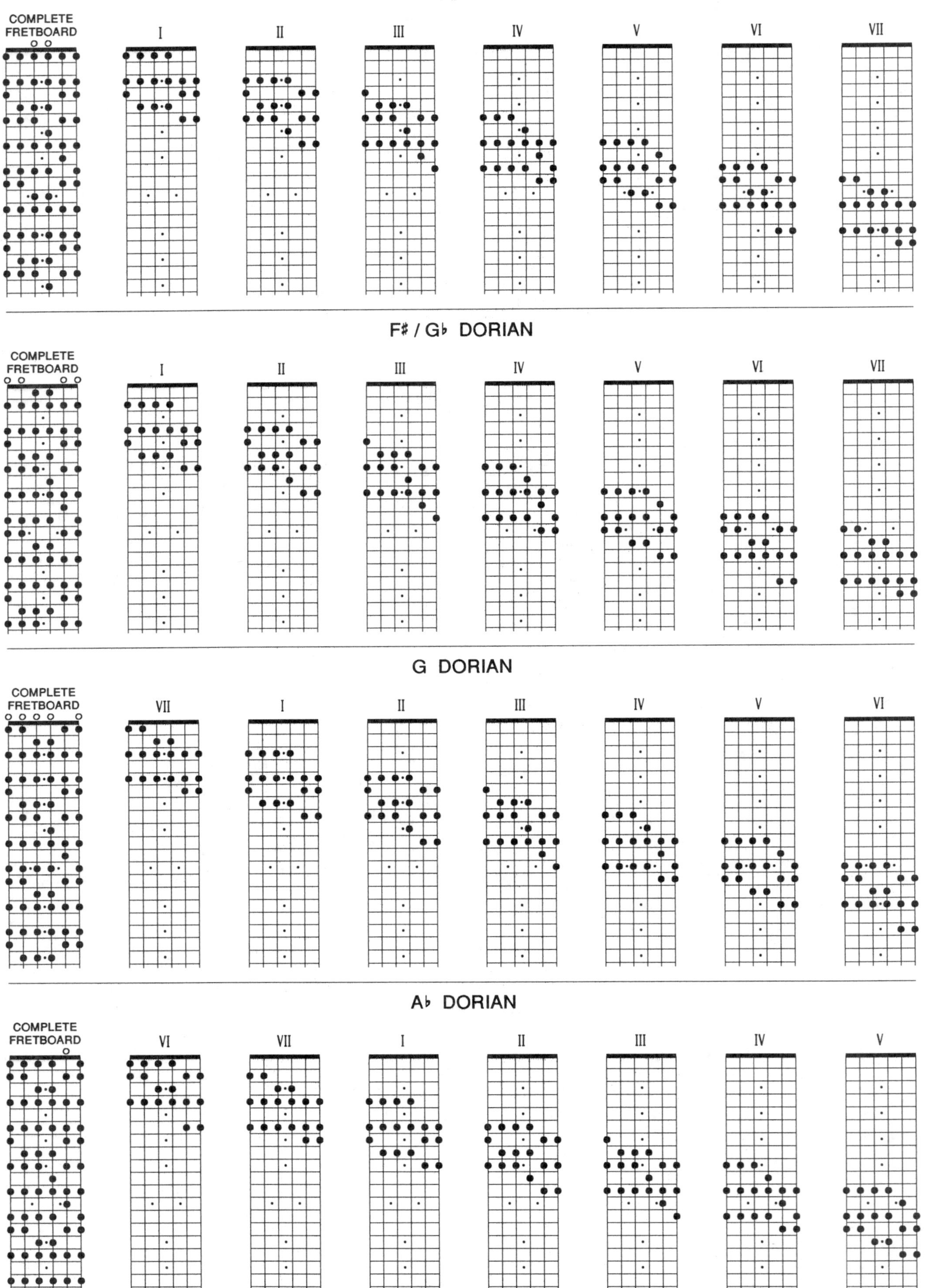

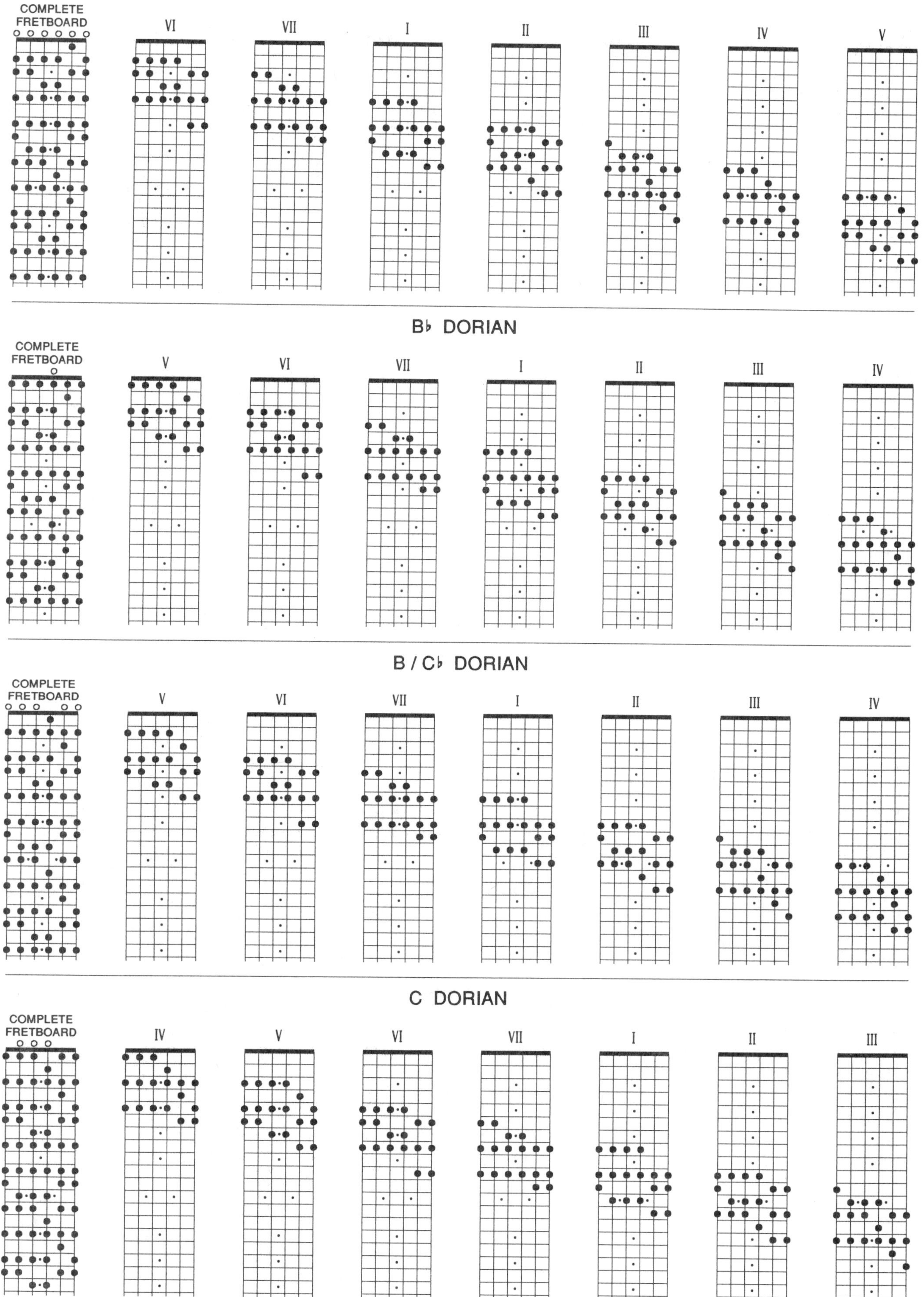
A DORIAN
COMPLETE FRETBOARD
VI
VII
I
II
III
IV
V
B♭ DORIAN
COMPLETE FRETBOARD
V
VI
VII
I
II
III
IV
B / C♭ DORIAN
COMPLETE FRETBOARD
V
VI
VII
I
II
III
IV
C DORIAN
COMPLETE FRETBOARD
IV
V
VI
VII
I
II
III

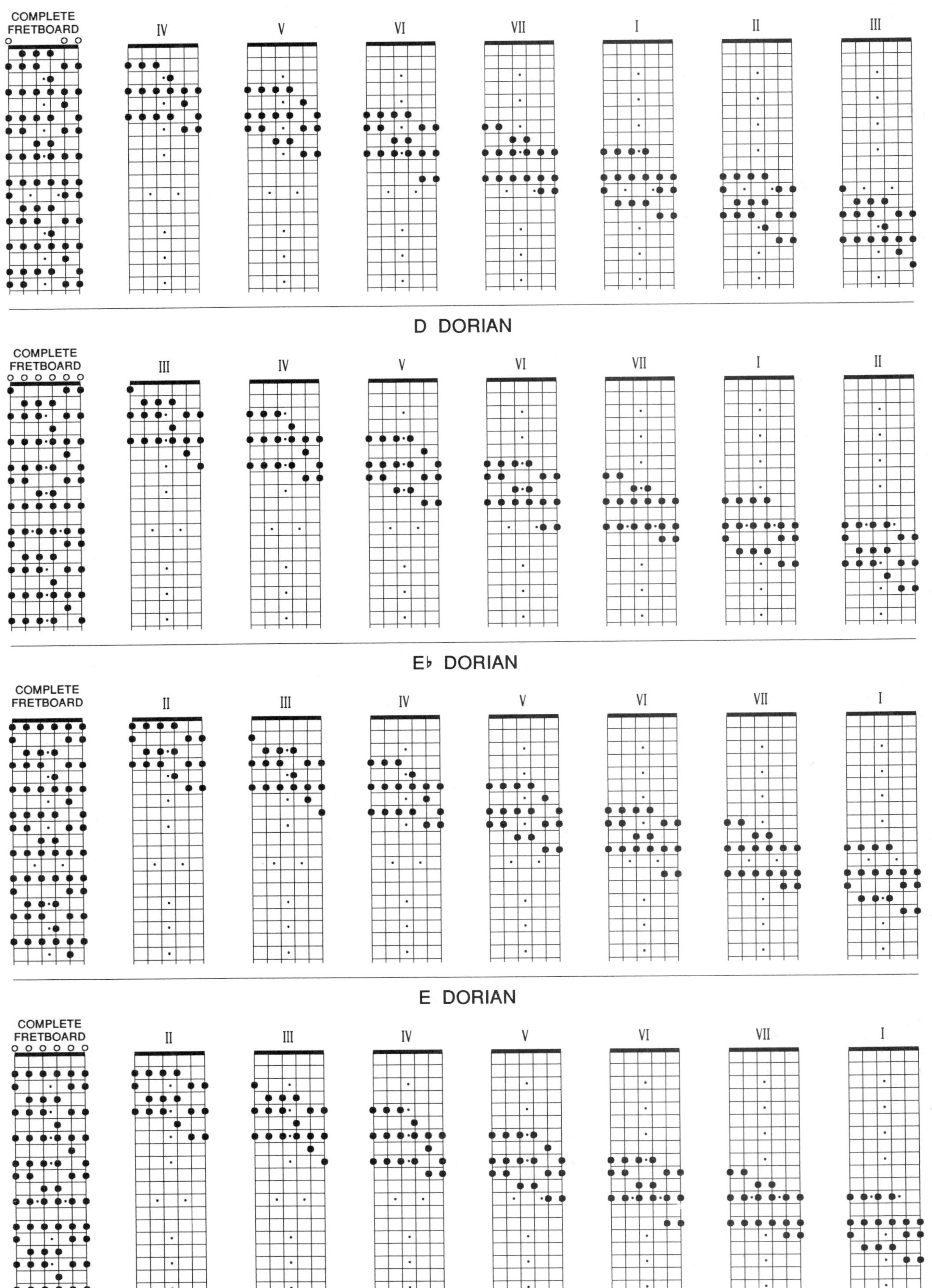
C♯ / D♭ DORIAN
COMPLETE FRETBOARD
IV
V
VI
VII
I
II
III
D DORIAN
COMPLETE FRETBOARD
III
IV
V
VI
VII
I
II
E♭ DORIAN
COMPLETE FRETBOARD
II
III
IV
V
VI
VII
I
E DORIAN
COMPLETE FRETBOARD
II
III
IV
V
VI
VII
I

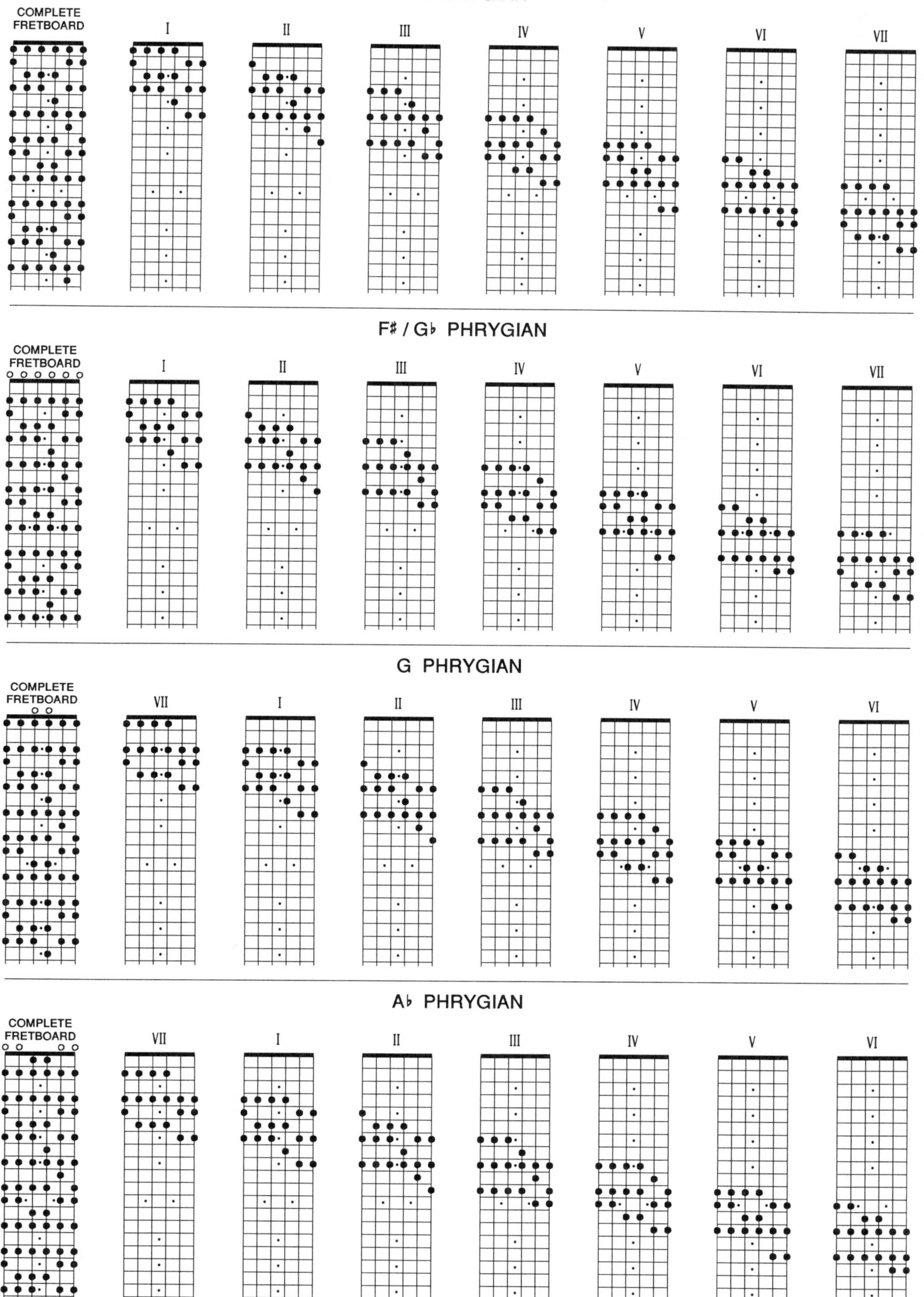
F PHRYGIAN
COMPLETE FRETBOARD
I
II
III
IV
V
VI
VII
F♯ / G♭ PHRYGIAN
COMPLETE FRETBOARD
I
II
III
IV
V
VI
VII
G PHRYGIAN
COMPLETE FRETBOARD
VII
I
II
III
IV
V
VI
A♭ PHRYGIAN
COMPLETE FRETBOARD
VII
I
II
III
IV
V
VI

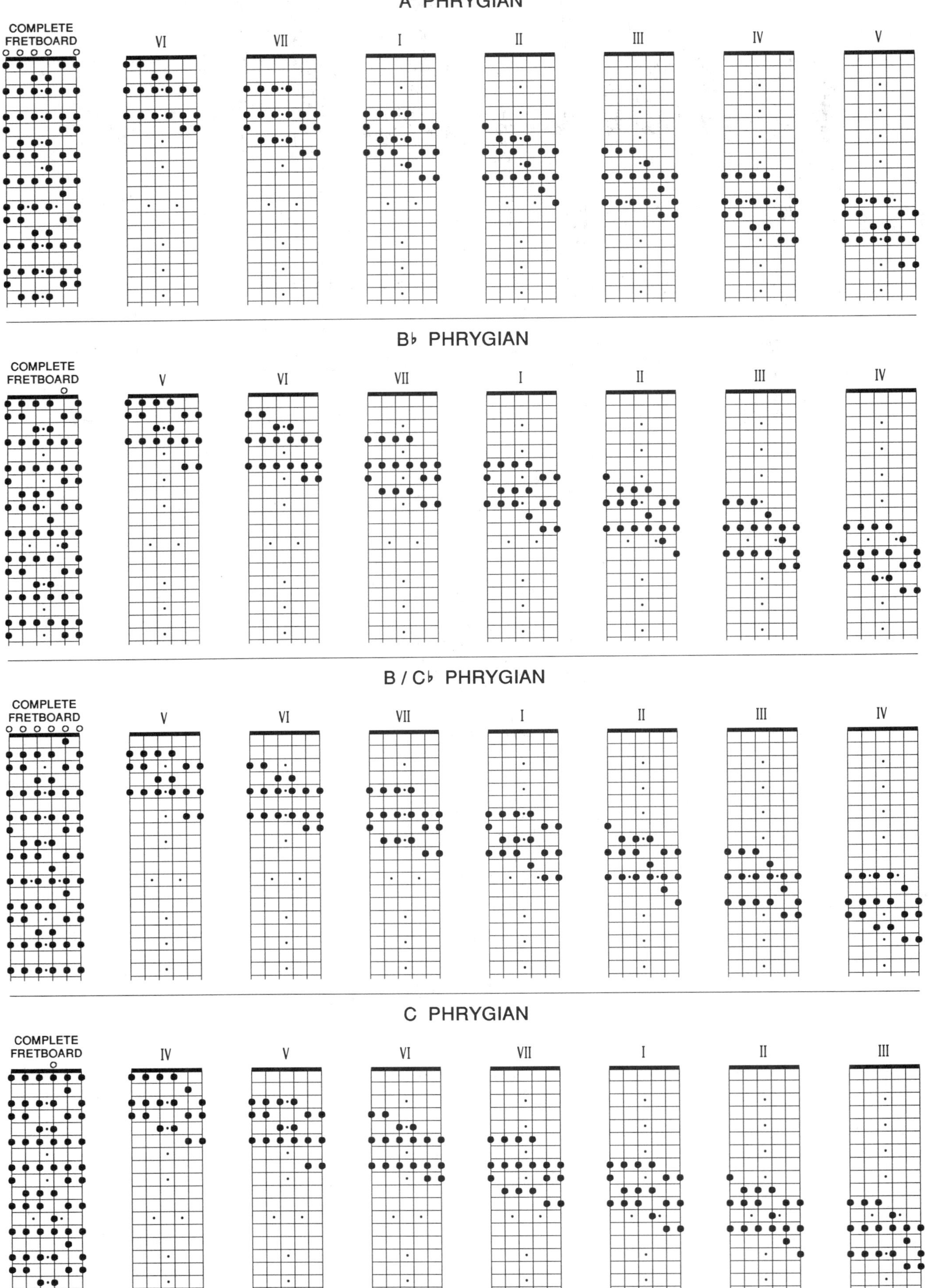
A PHRYGIAN
COMPLETE FRETBOARD
VI
VII
I
II
III
IV
V
B♭ PHRYGIAN
COMPLETE FRETBOARD
V
VI
VII
I
II
III
IV
B / C♭ PHRYGIAN
COMPLETE FRETBOARD
V
VI
VII
I
II
III
IV
C PHRYGIAN
COMPLETE FRETBOARD
IV
V
VI
VII
I
II
III

C♯ / D♭ PHRYGIAN

D PHRYGIAN

E♭ PHRYGIAN

E PHRYGIAN

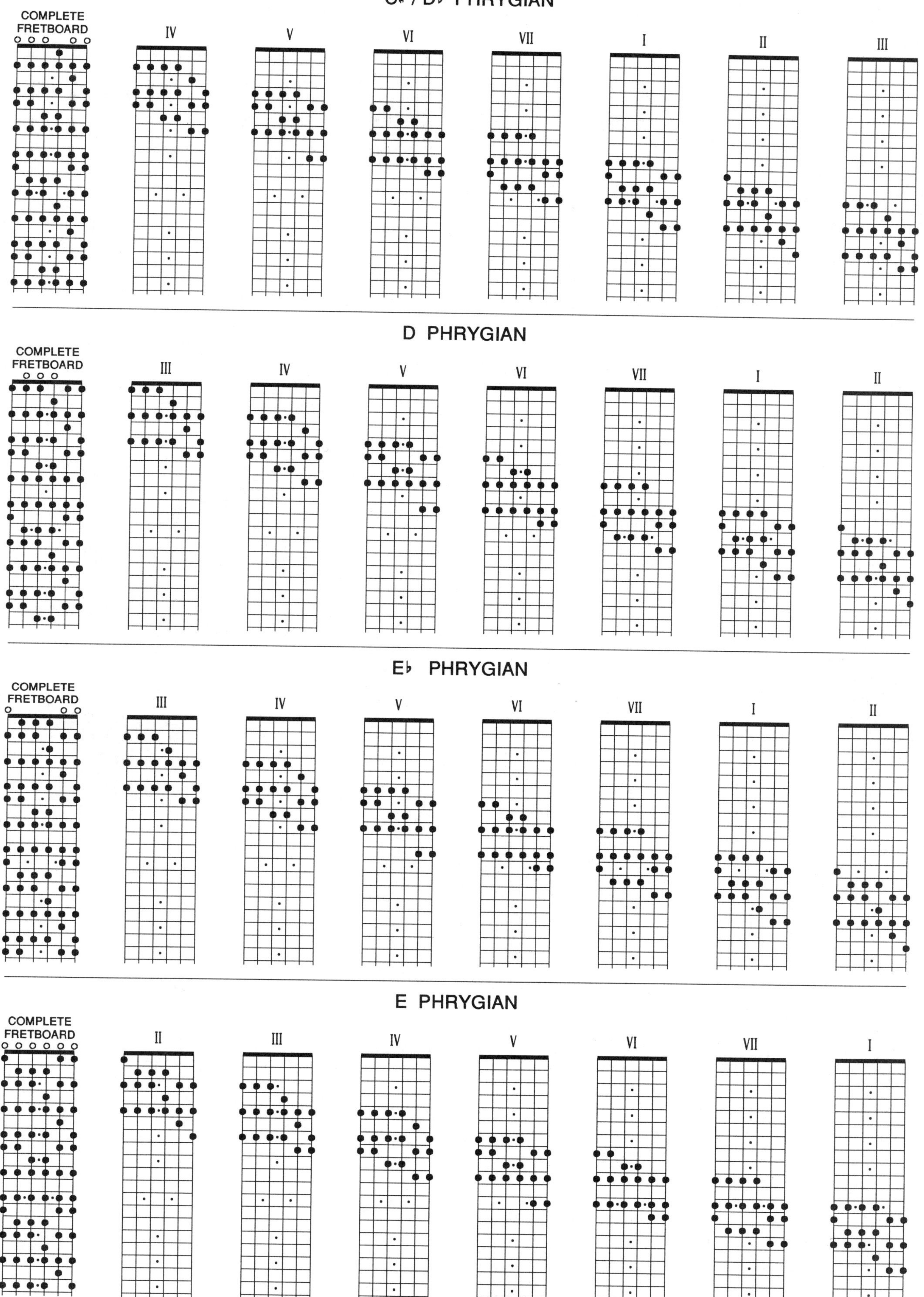

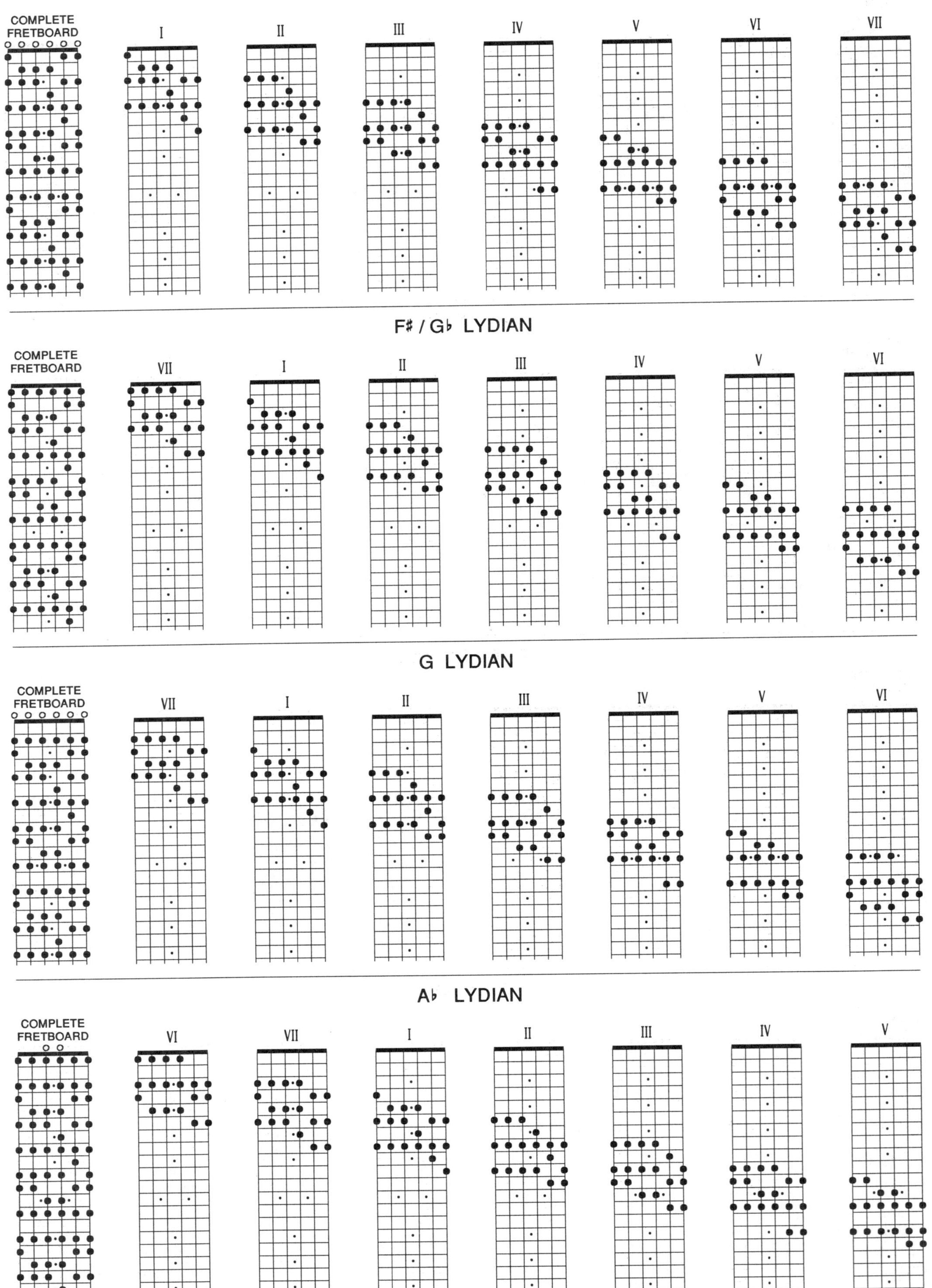
F LYDIAN
COMPLETE FRETBOARD
I
II
III
IV
V
VI
VII
F♯ / G♭ LYDIAN
COMPLETE FRETBOARD
VII
I
II
III
IV
V
VI
G LYDIAN
COMPLETE FRETBOARD
VII
I
II
III
IV
V
VI
A♭ LYDIAN
COMPLETE FRETBOARD
VI
VII
I
II
III
IV
V

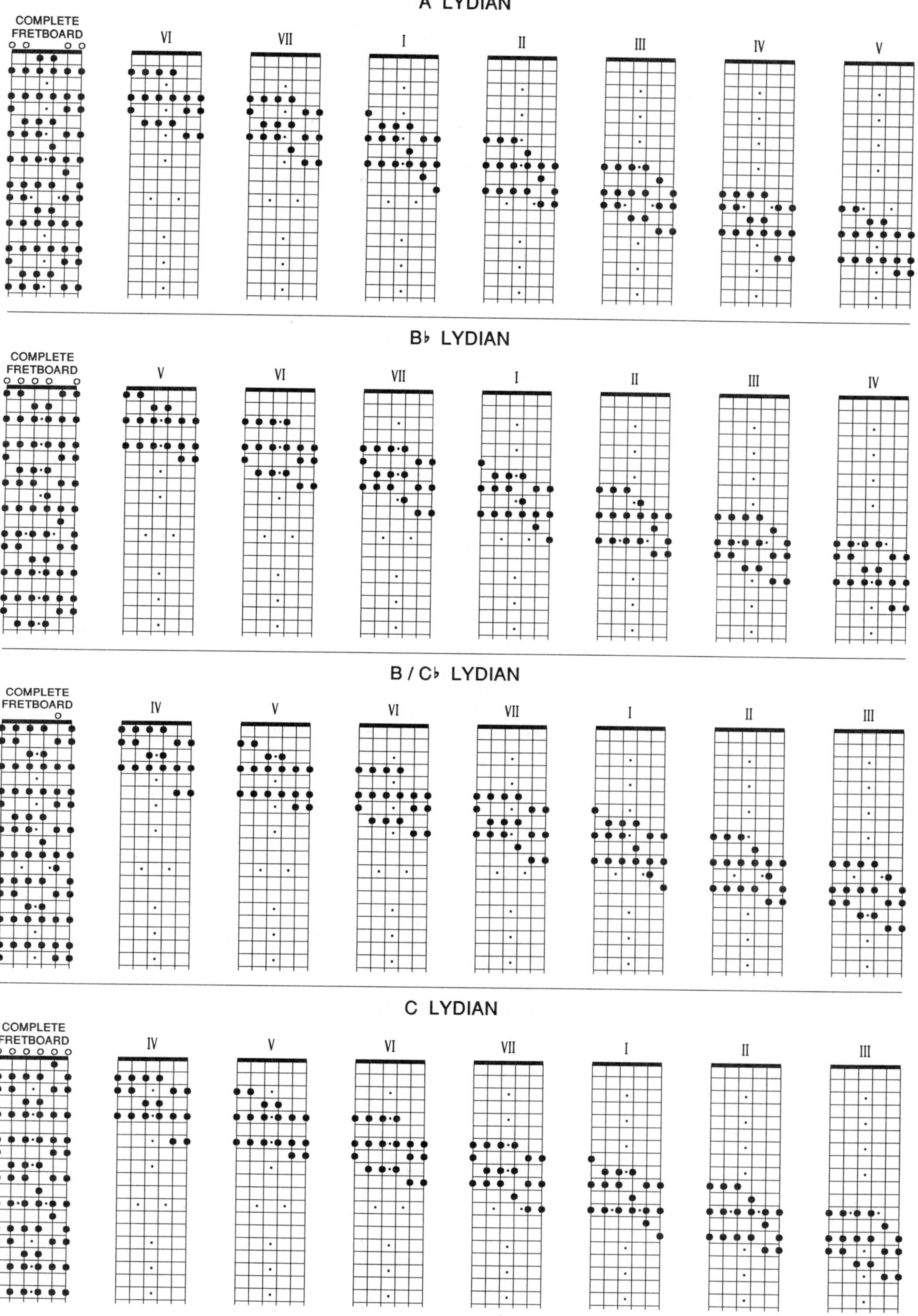
A LYDIAN
COMPLETE FRETBOARD
VI
VII
I
II
III
IV
V
B♭ LYDIAN
COMPLETE FRETBOARD
V
VI
VII
I
II
III
IV
B / C♭ LYDIAN
COMPLETE FRETBOARD
IV
V
VI
VII
I
II
III
C LYDIAN
COMPLETE FRETBOARD
IV
V
VI
VII
I
II
III

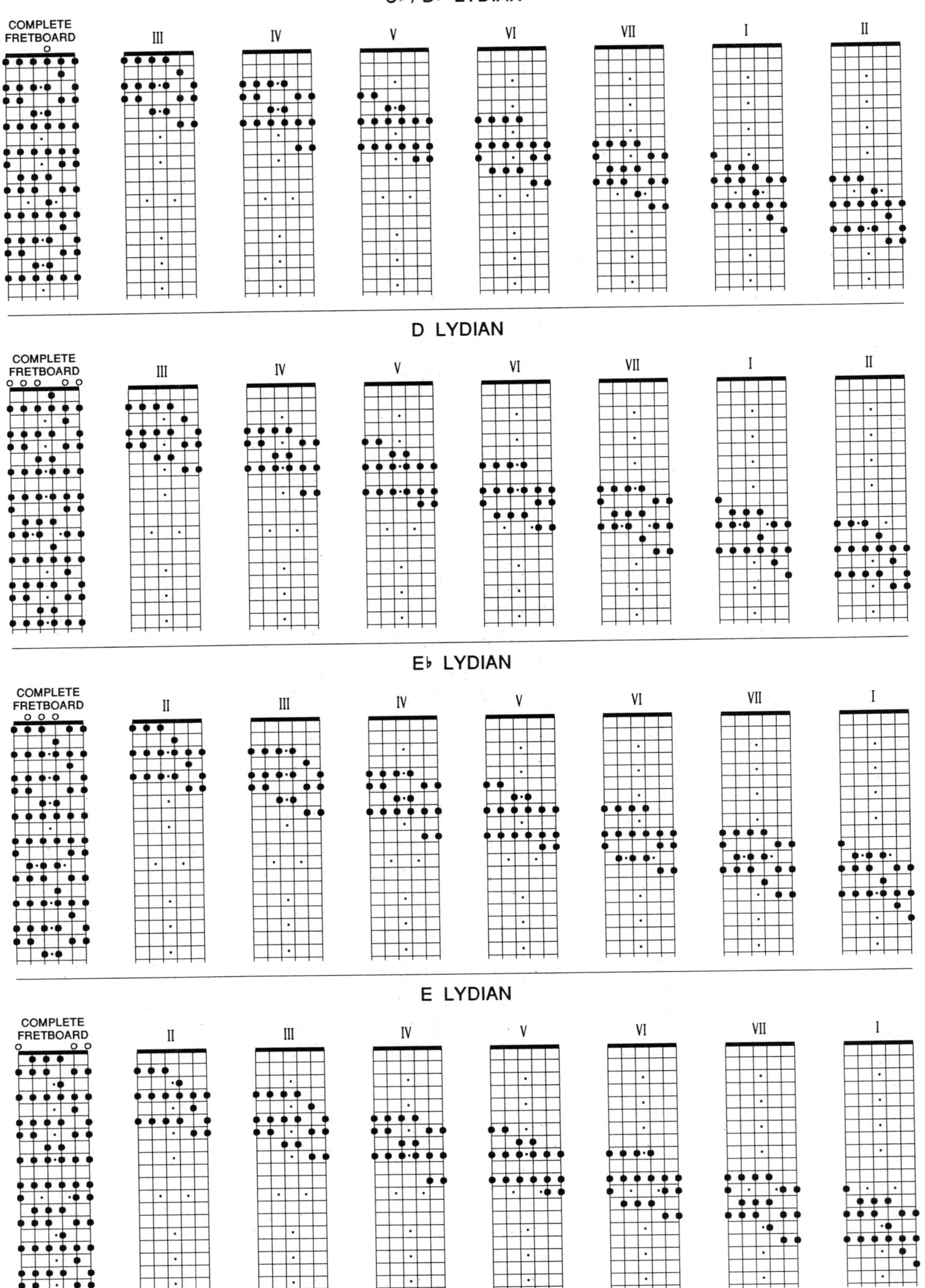
C♯ / D♭ LYDIAN
COMPLETE FRETBOARD
III
IV
V
VI
VII
I
II
D LYDIAN
COMPLETE FRETBOARD
III
IV
V
VI
VII
I
II
E♭ LYDIAN
COMPLETE FRETBOARD
II
III
IV
V
VI
VII
I
E LYDIAN
COMPLETE FRETBOARD
II
III
IV
V
VI
VII
I

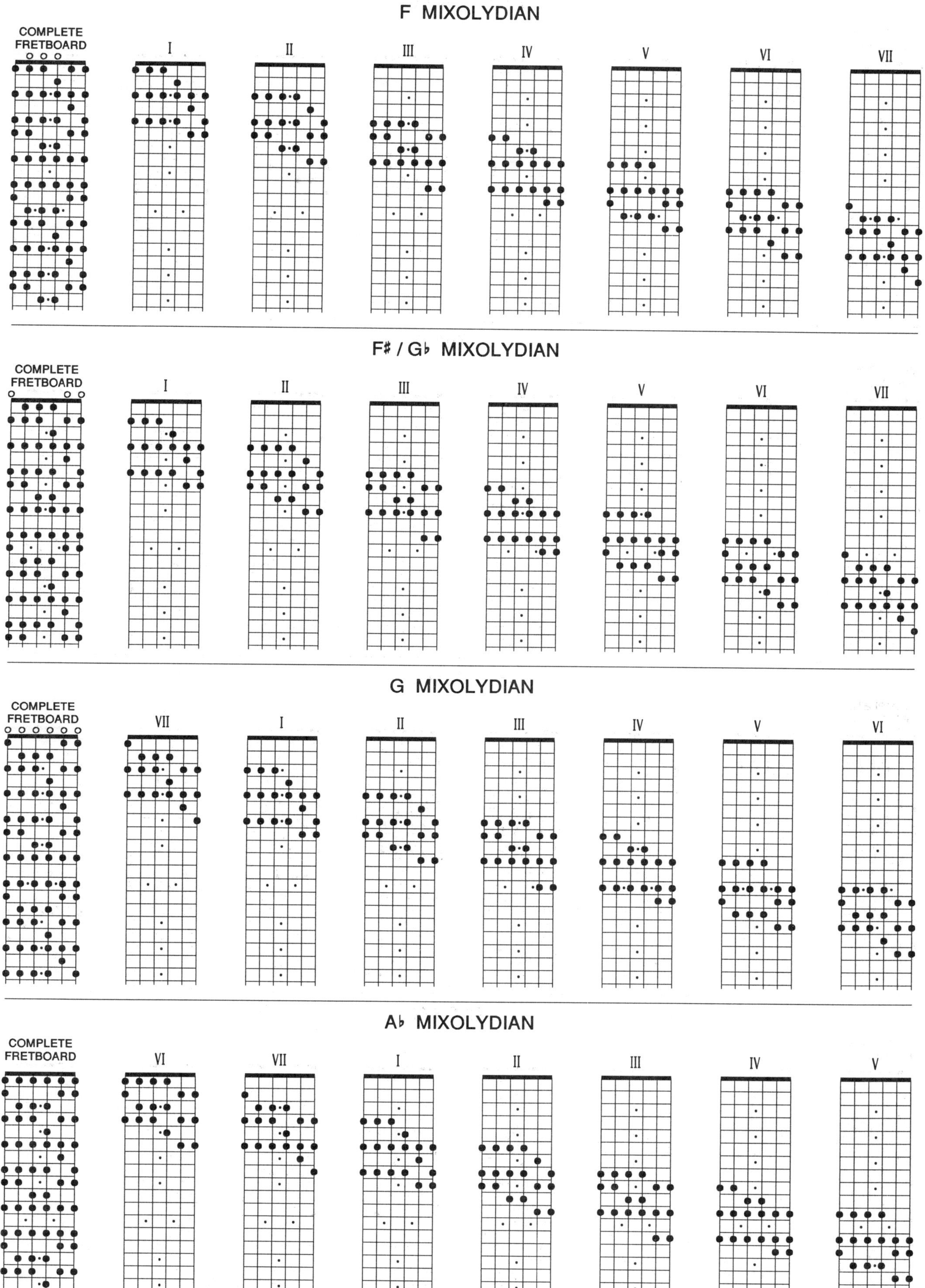
F MIXOLYDIAN
COMPLETE FRETBOARD
I
II
III
IV
V
VI
VII
F♯ / G♭ MIXOLYDIAN
COMPLETE FRETBOARD
I
II
III
IV
V
VI
VII
G MIXOLYDIAN
COMPLETE FRETBOARD
VII
I
II
III
IV
V
VI
A♭ MIXOLYDIAN
COMPLETE FRETBOARD
VI
VII
I
II
III
IV
V

A MIXOLYDIAN

B♭ MIXOLYDIAN

B / C♭ MIXOLYDIAN

C MIXOLYDIAN

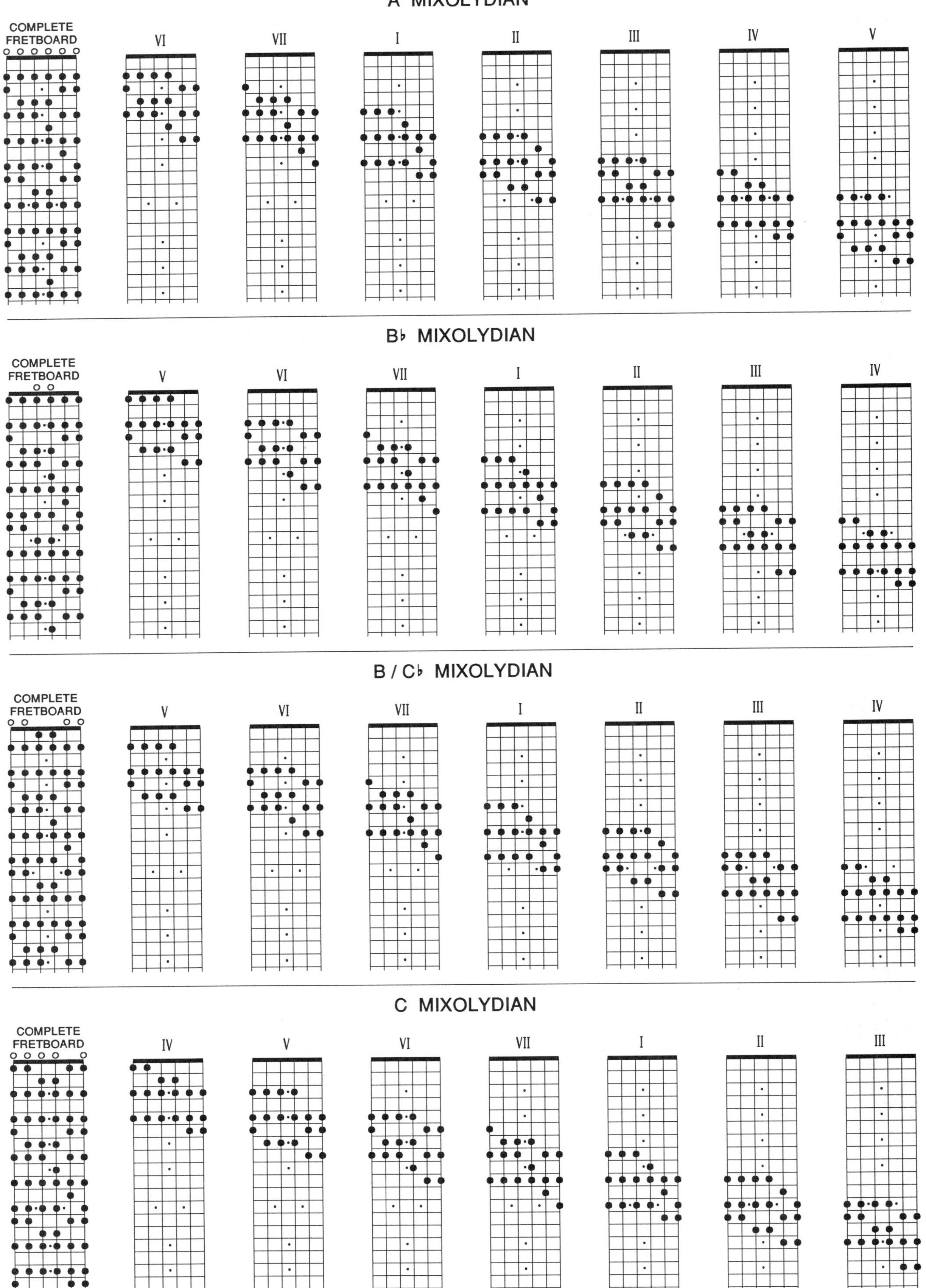

C♯ / D♭ MIXOLYDIAN

D MIXOLYDIAN

E♭ MIXOLYDIAN

E MIXOLYDIAN

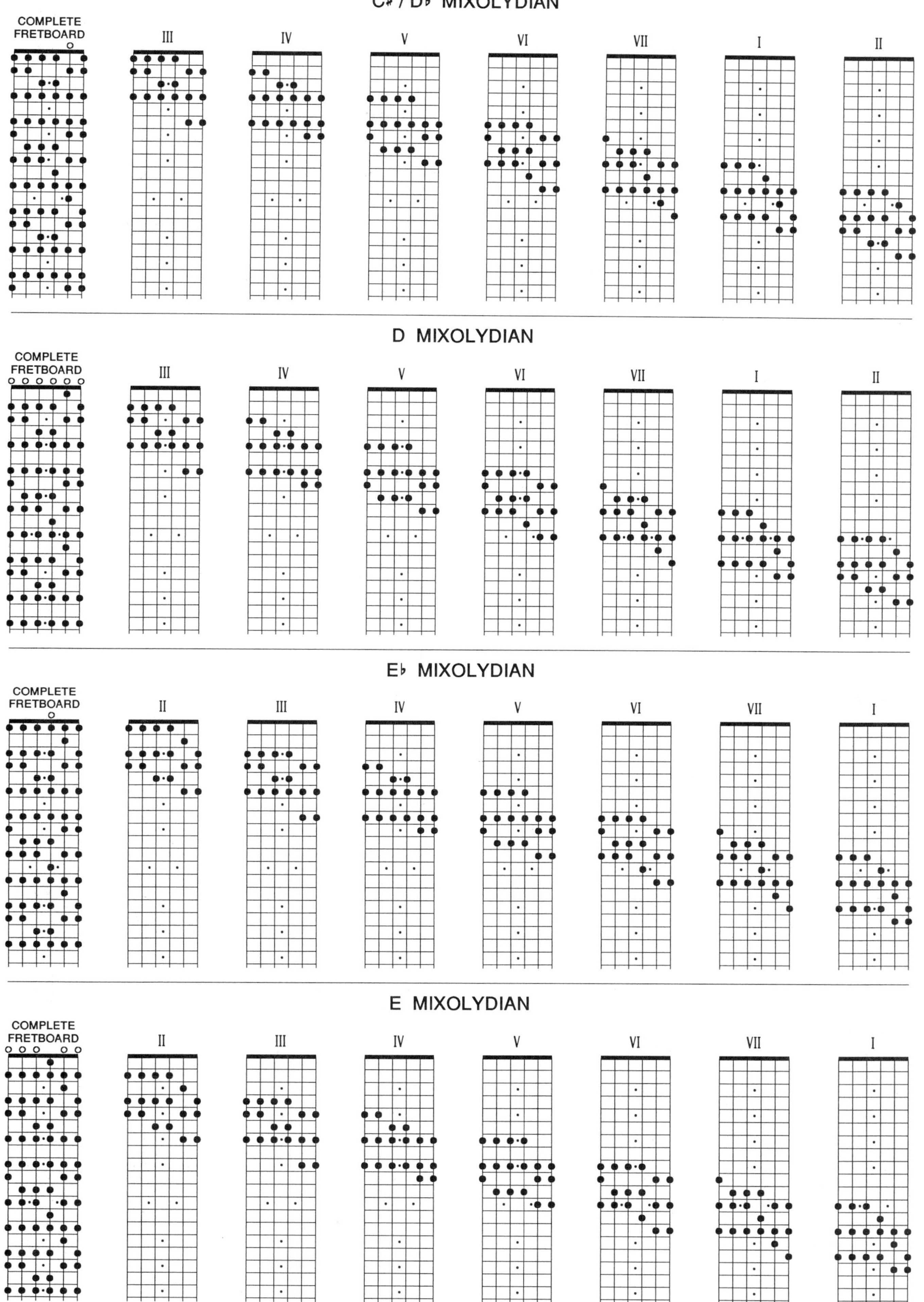

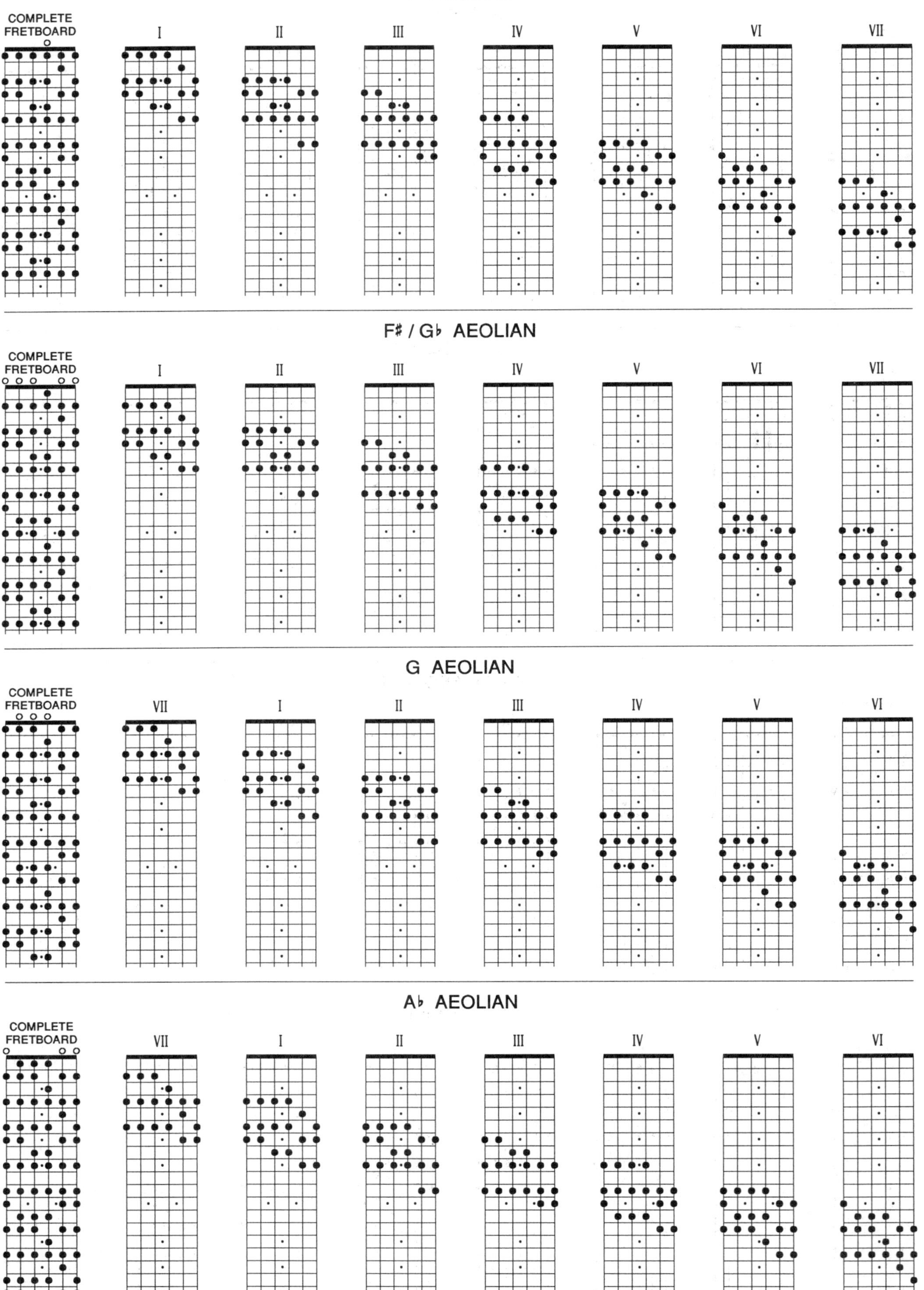

F AEOLIAN
COMPLETE FRETBOARD
I
II
III
IV
V
VI
VII
F♯ / G♭ AEOLIAN
COMPLETE FRETBOARD
I
II
III
IV
V
VI
VII
G AEOLIAN
COMPLETE FRETBOARD
VII
I
II
III
IV
V
VI
A♭ AEOLIAN
COMPLETE FRETBOARD
VII
I
II
III
IV
V
VI

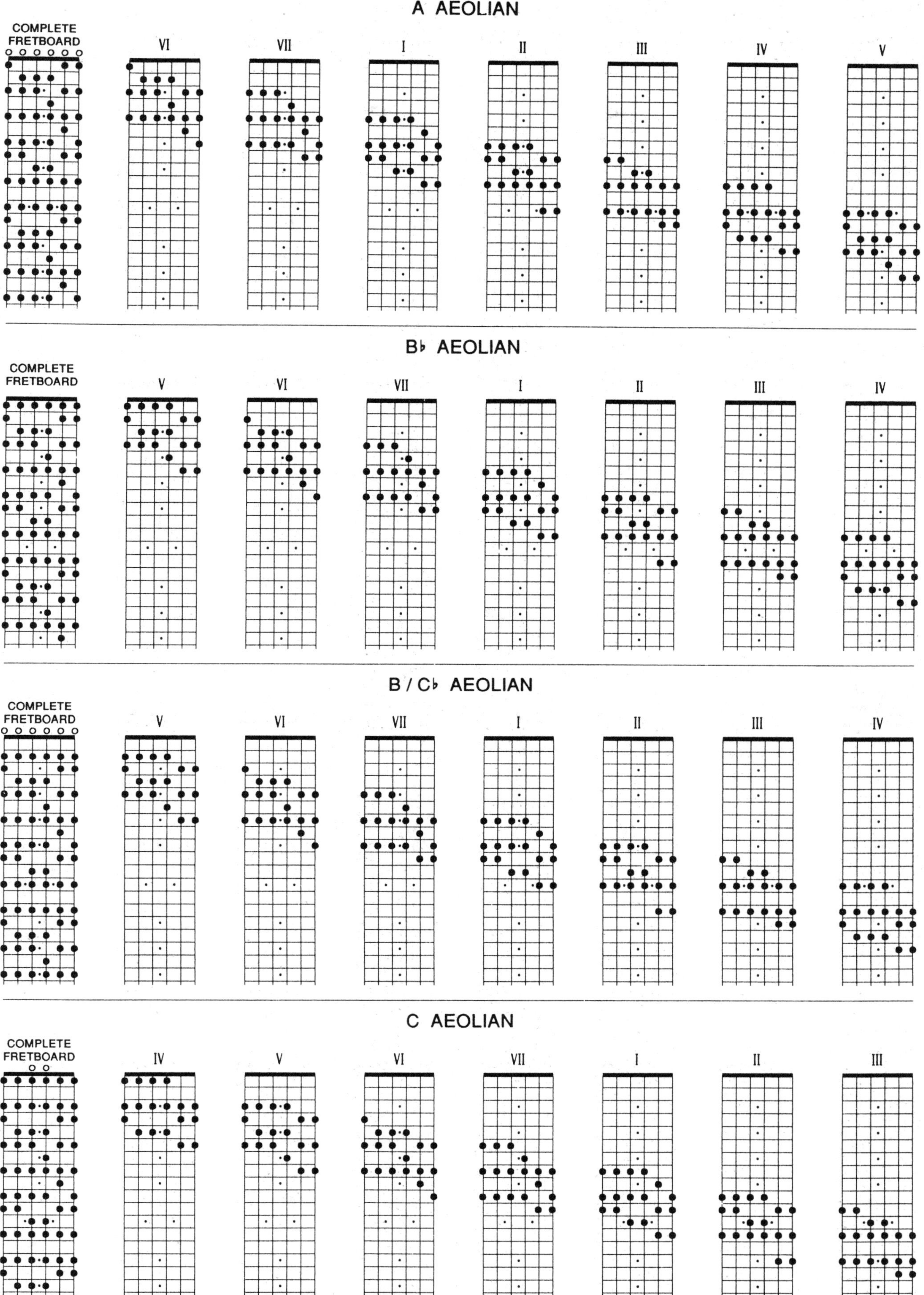
A AEOLIAN
COMPLETE FRETBOARD
VI
VII
I
II
III
IV
V
B♭ AEOLIAN
COMPLETE FRETBOARD
V
VI
VII
I
II
III
IV
B / C♭ AEOLIAN
COMPLETE FRETBOARD
V
VI
VII
I
II
III
IV
C AEOLIAN
COMPLETE FRETBOARD
IV
V
VI
VII
I
II
III

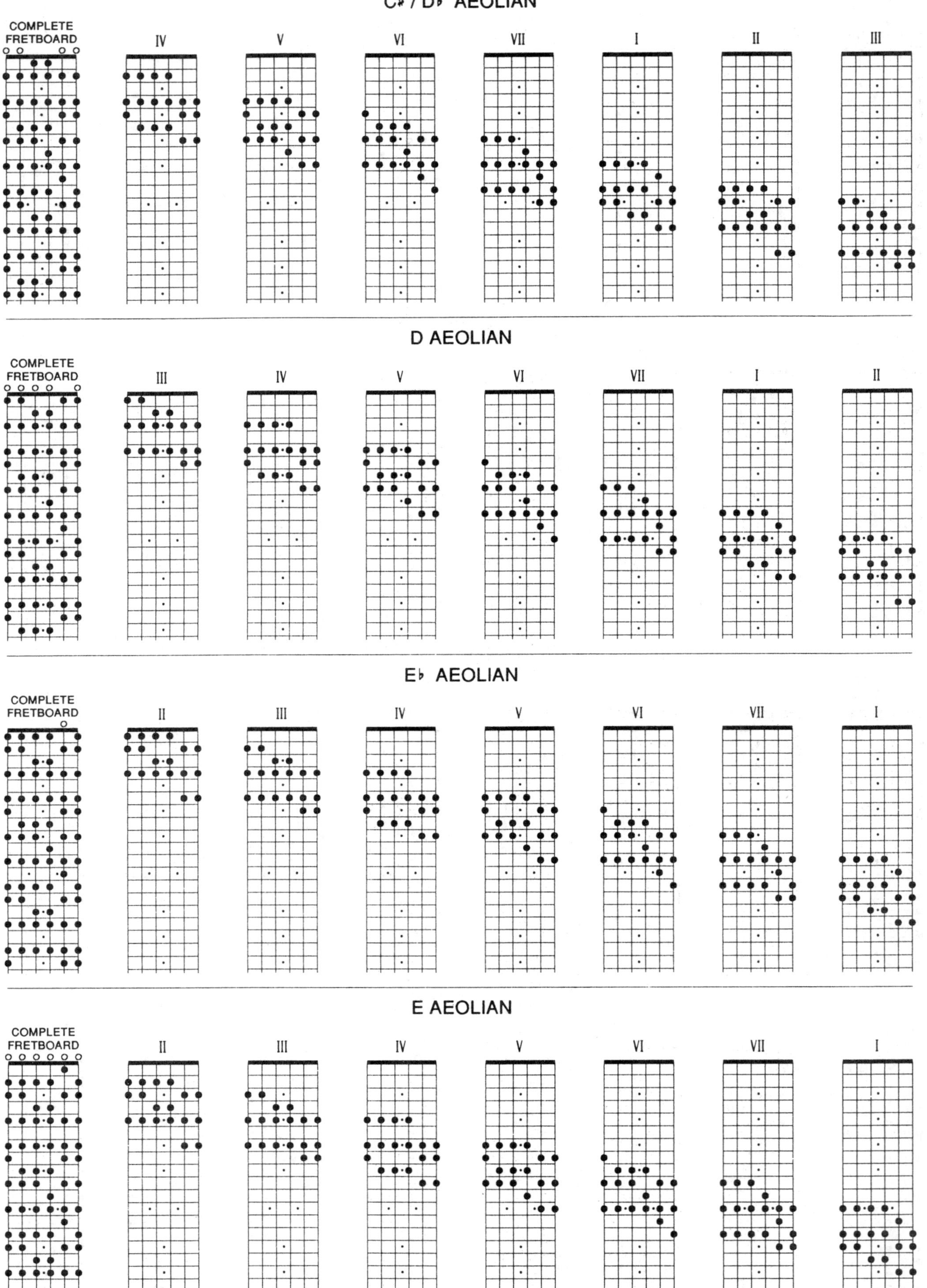
C♯ / D♭ AEOLIAN
COMPLETE FRETBOARD
IV
V
VI
VII
I
II
III
D AEOLIAN
COMPLETE FRETBOARD
III
IV
V
VI
VII
I
II
E♭ AEOLIAN
COMPLETE FRETBOARD
II
III
IV
V
VI
VII
I
E AEOLIAN
COMPLETE FRETBOARD
II
III
IV
V
VI
VII
I

F LOCRIAN

F♯ / G♭ LOCRIAN

G LOCRIAN

A♭ LOCRIAN

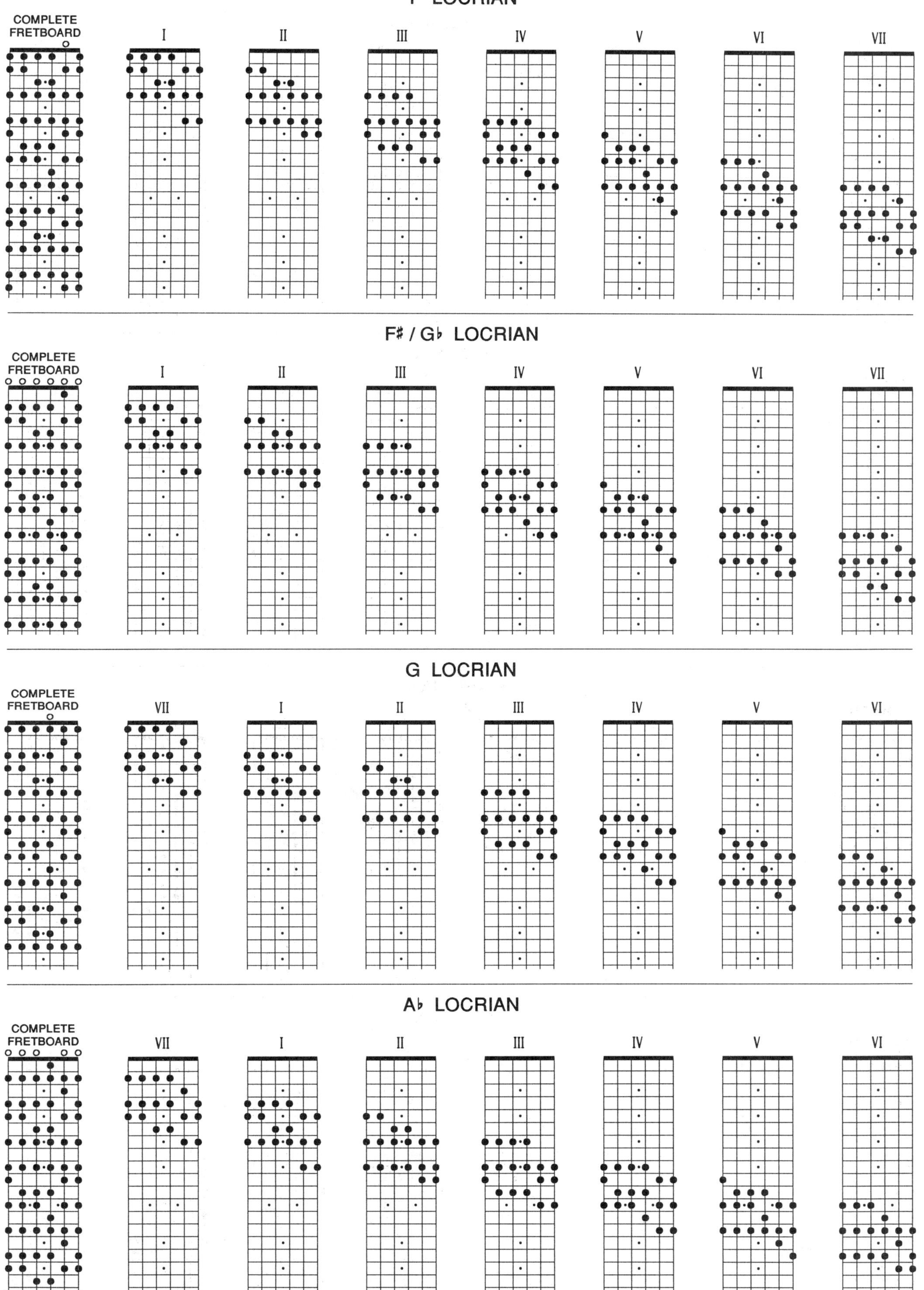

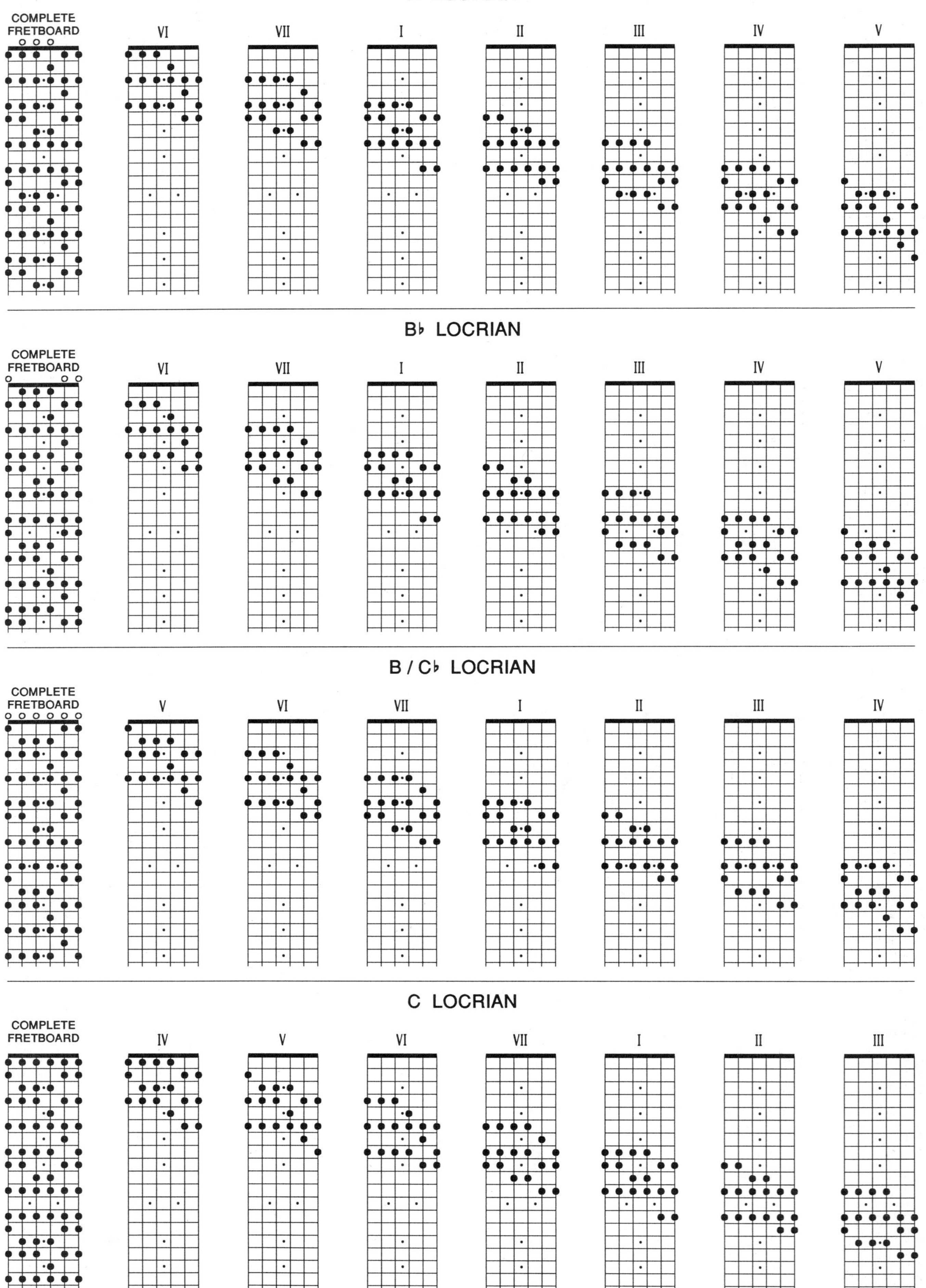
A LOCRIAN
COMPLETE FRETBOARD
VI
VII
I
II
III
IV
V
B♭ LOCRIAN
COMPLETE FRETBOARD
VI
VII
I
II
III
IV
V
B / C♭ LOCRIAN
COMPLETE FRETBOARD
V
VI
VII
I
II
III
IV
C LOCRIAN
COMPLETE FRETBOARD
IV
V
VI
VII
I
II
III

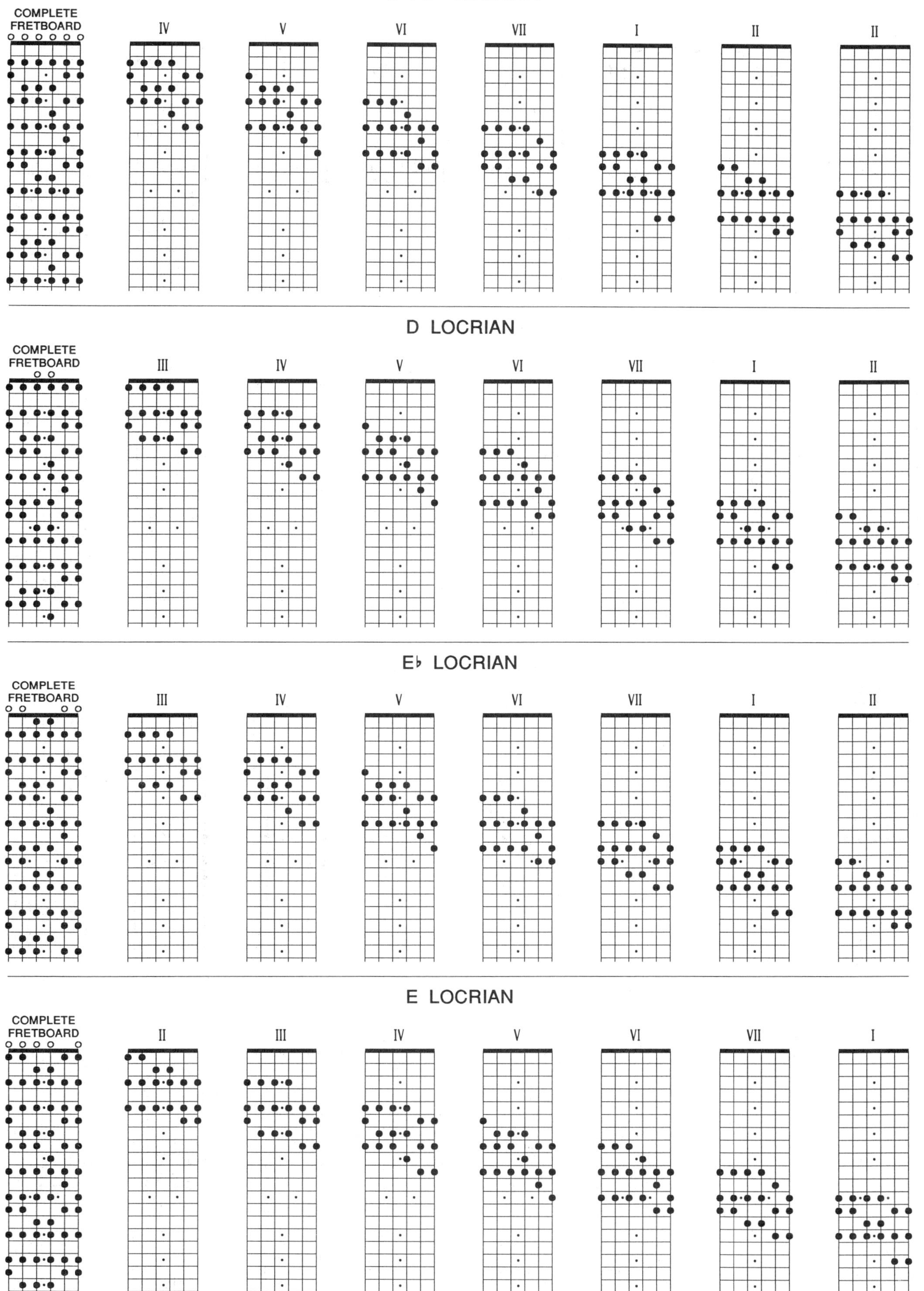
C♯ / D♭ LOCRIAN
COMPLETE FRETBOARD
IV V VI VII I II II
D LOCRIAN
COMPLETE FRETBOARD
III IV V VI VII I II
E♭ LOCRIAN
COMPLETE FRETBOARD
III IV V VI VII I II
E LOCRIAN
COMPLETE FRETBOARD
II III IV V VI VII I

KEYBOARD PATTERNS

QUICK MODE GENERATOR CHART

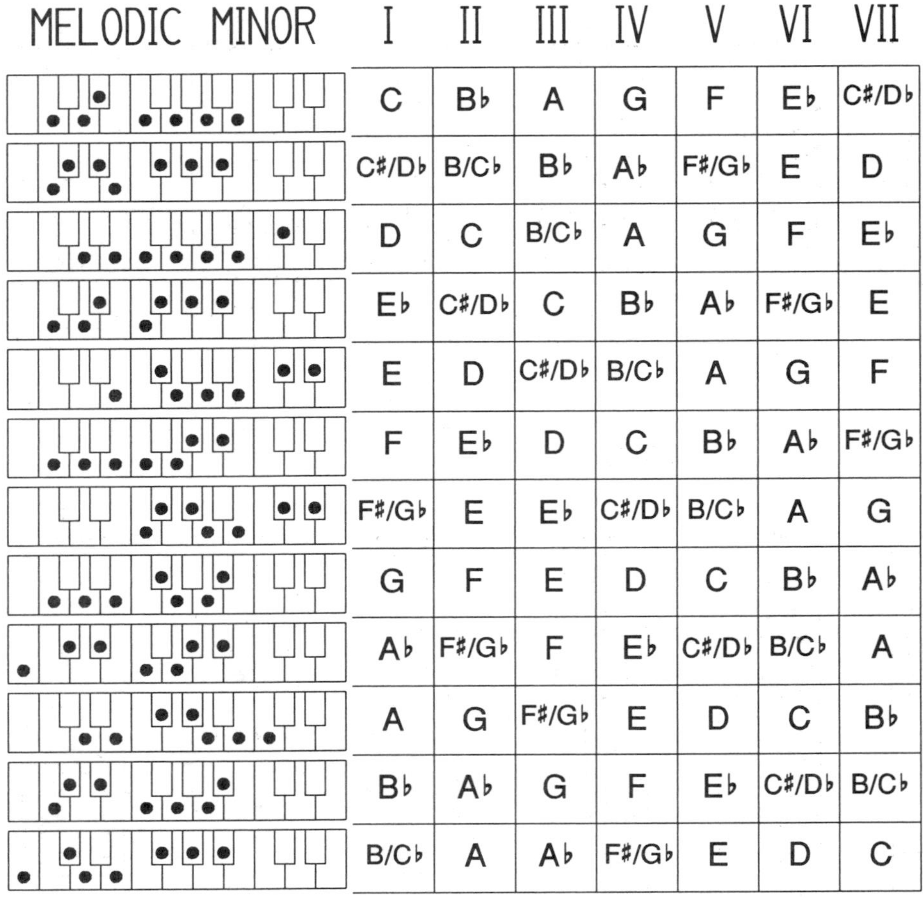

MELODIC MINOR

I	II	III	IV	V	VI	VII
C	B♭	A	G	F	E♭	C#/D♭
C#/D♭	B/C♭	B♭	A♭	F#/G♭	E	D
D	C	B/C♭	A	G	F	E♭
E♭	C#/D♭	C	B♭	A♭	F#/G♭	E
E	D	C#/D♭	B/C♭	A	G	F
F	E♭	D	C	B♭	A♭	F#/G♭
F#/G♭	E	E♭	C#/D♭	B/C♭	A	G
G	F	E	D	C	B♭	A♭
A♭	F#/G♭	F	E♭	C#/D♭	B/C♭	A
A	G	F#/G♭	E	D	C	B♭
B♭	A♭	G	F	E♭	C#/D♭	B/C♭
B/C♭	A	A♭	F#/G♭	E	D	C

CONVENTIONAL PATTERNS

SWEEPING PATTERNS

I

II

III

IV

V

VI

VII

SCALE / MODE - CHORD CHART

I	MELODIC MINOR	$^{-}\triangle$, $^{-}6$
II	DORIAN ♭2	$^{-}7$
III	LYDIAN AUGMENTED	$\triangle^{+}$, $\triangle^{\flat 5}$
IV	LYDIAN DOMINANT	$7^{\flat 5}$
V	HINDU	$7^{\flat 13}$, 7^{+}
VI	LOCRIAN ♮2	$^{ø}9$
VII	SUPER LOCRIAN	ALT

NUMERIC SCALE / MODE CHART

		1		2		3	4		5		6		7	1		2		3	4		5		6		7
I	MELODIC	1		2	♭3		4		5		6		7	1		2	♭3		4		5		6		7
II	DORIAN ♭2			1	♭2		♭3		4		5		6	♭7											
III	LYD AUG				1		2		3		#4		#5	6		7									
IV	LYD DOM						1		2		3		#4	5		6	♭7								
V	HINDU								1		2		3	4		5	♭6		♭7						
VI	LOCRIAN ♮2										1		2	♭3		4	♭5		♭6		♭7				
VII	SUPER LOC												1	♭2		♭3	♭4		♭5		♭6		♭7		

F MELODIC

F♯ / G♭ MELODIC

G MELODIC

A♭ MELODIC

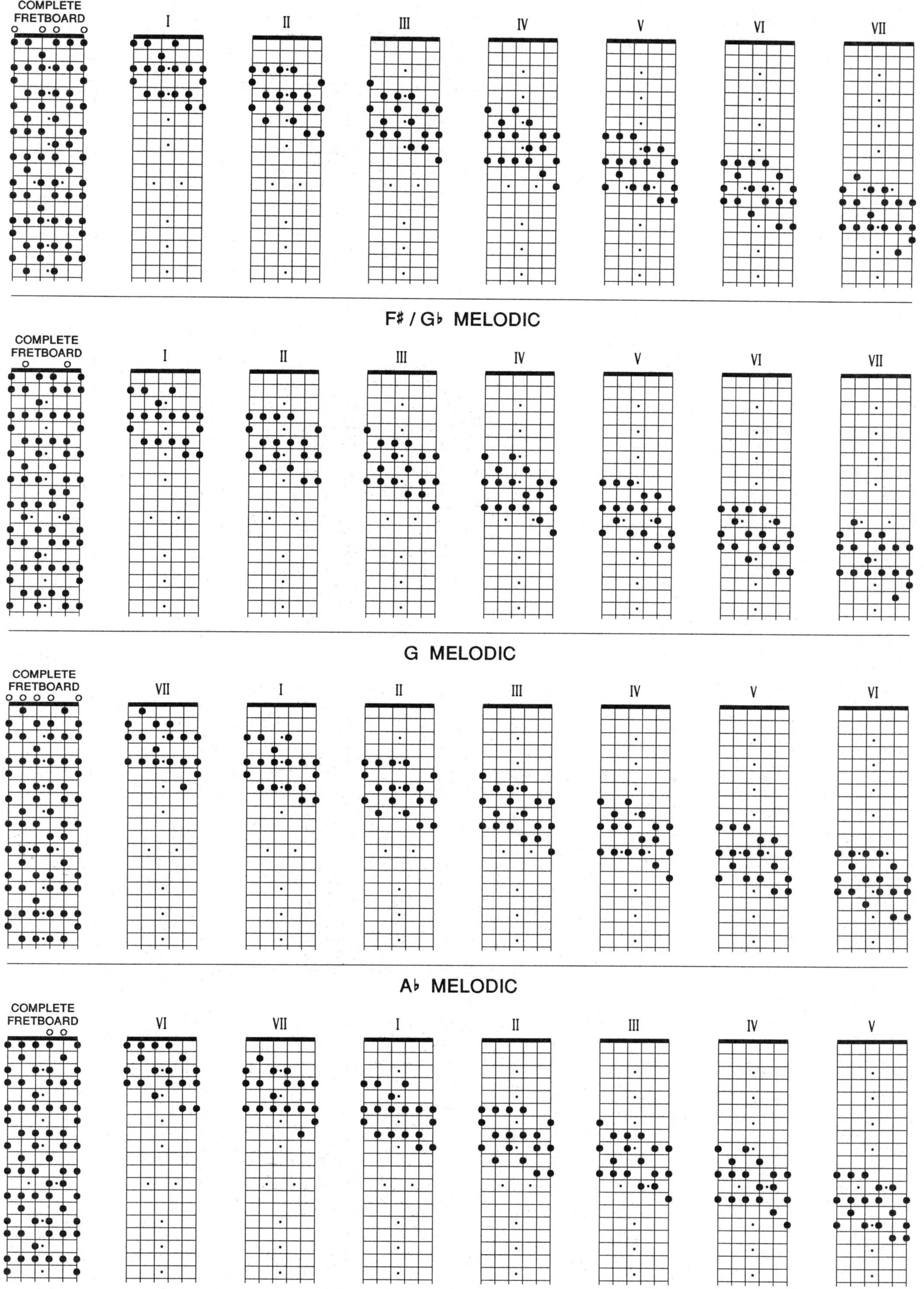

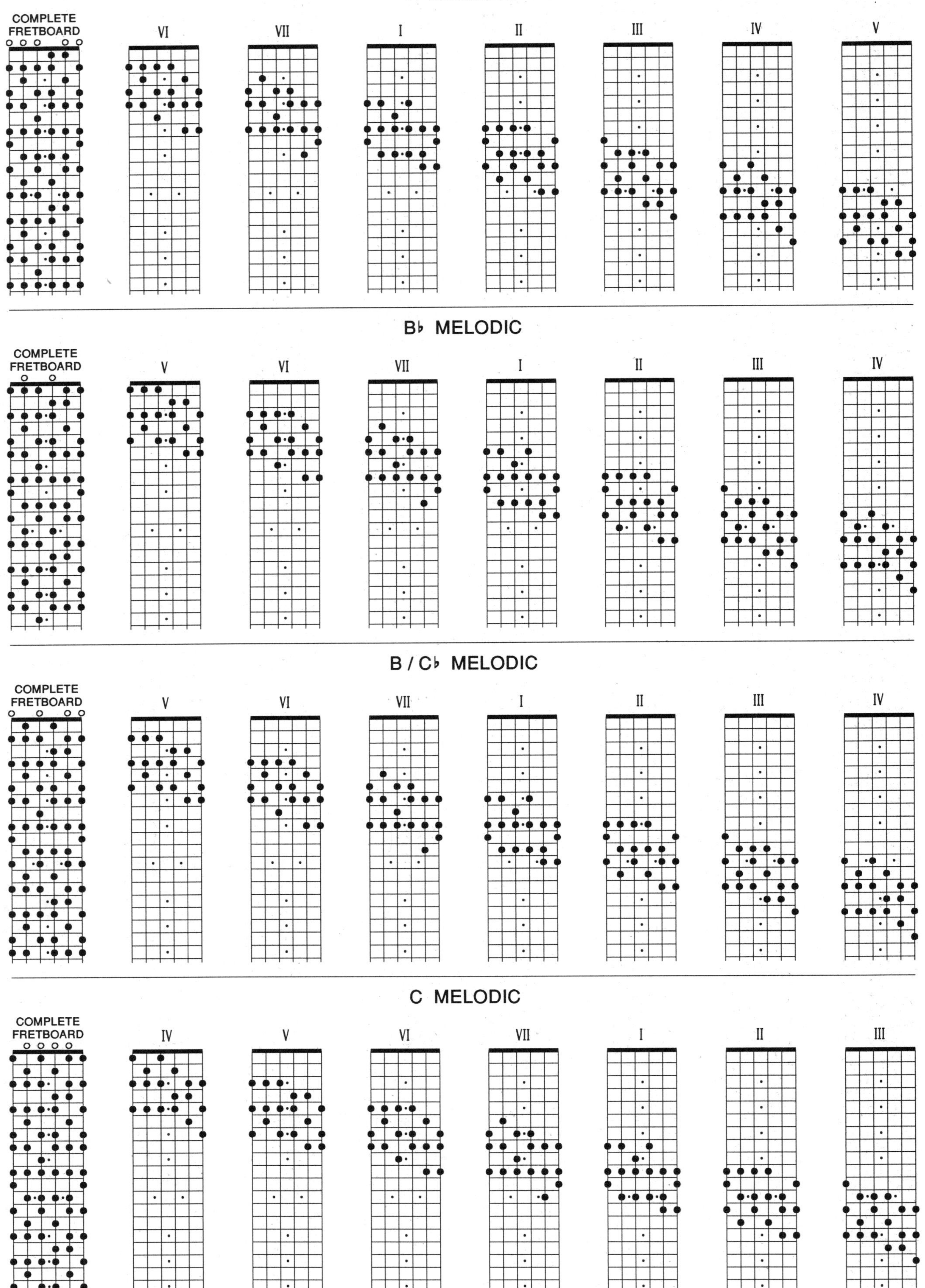
A MELODIC
COMPLETE FRETBOARD
VI
VII
I
II
III
IV
V
B♭ MELODIC
COMPLETE FRETBOARD
V
VI
VII
I
II
III
IV
B / C♭ MELODIC
COMPLETE FRETBOARD
V
VI
VII
I
II
III
IV
C MELODIC
COMPLETE FRETBOARD
IV
V
VI
VII
I
II
III

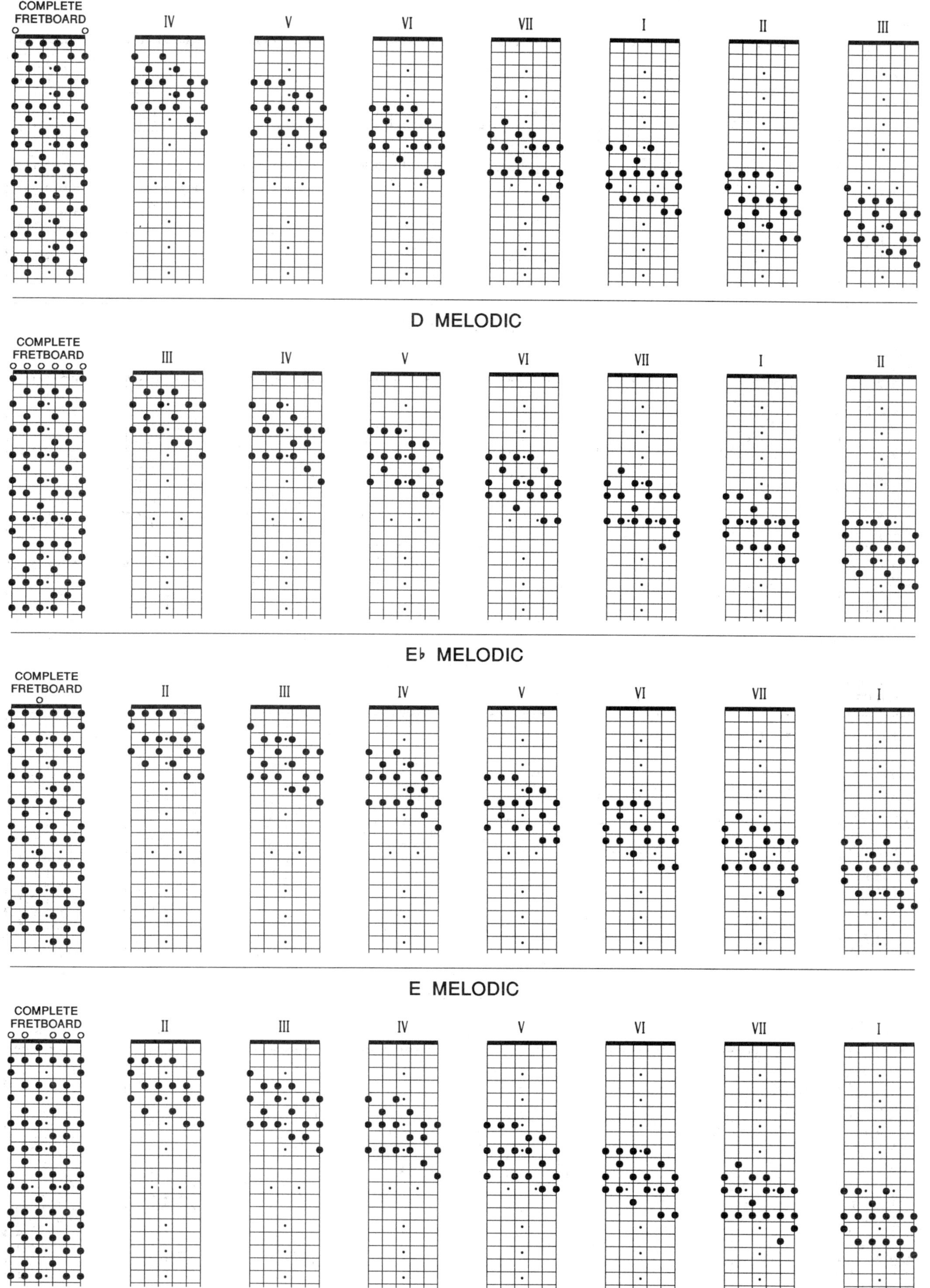
C♯ / D♭ MELODIC
COMPLETE FRETBOARD
IV
V
VI
VII
I
II
III
D MELODIC
COMPLETE FRETBOARD
III
IV
V
VI
VII
I
II
E♭ MELODIC
COMPLETE FRETBOARD
II
III
IV
V
VI
VII
I
E MELODIC
COMPLETE FRETBOARD
II
III
IV
V
VI
VII
I

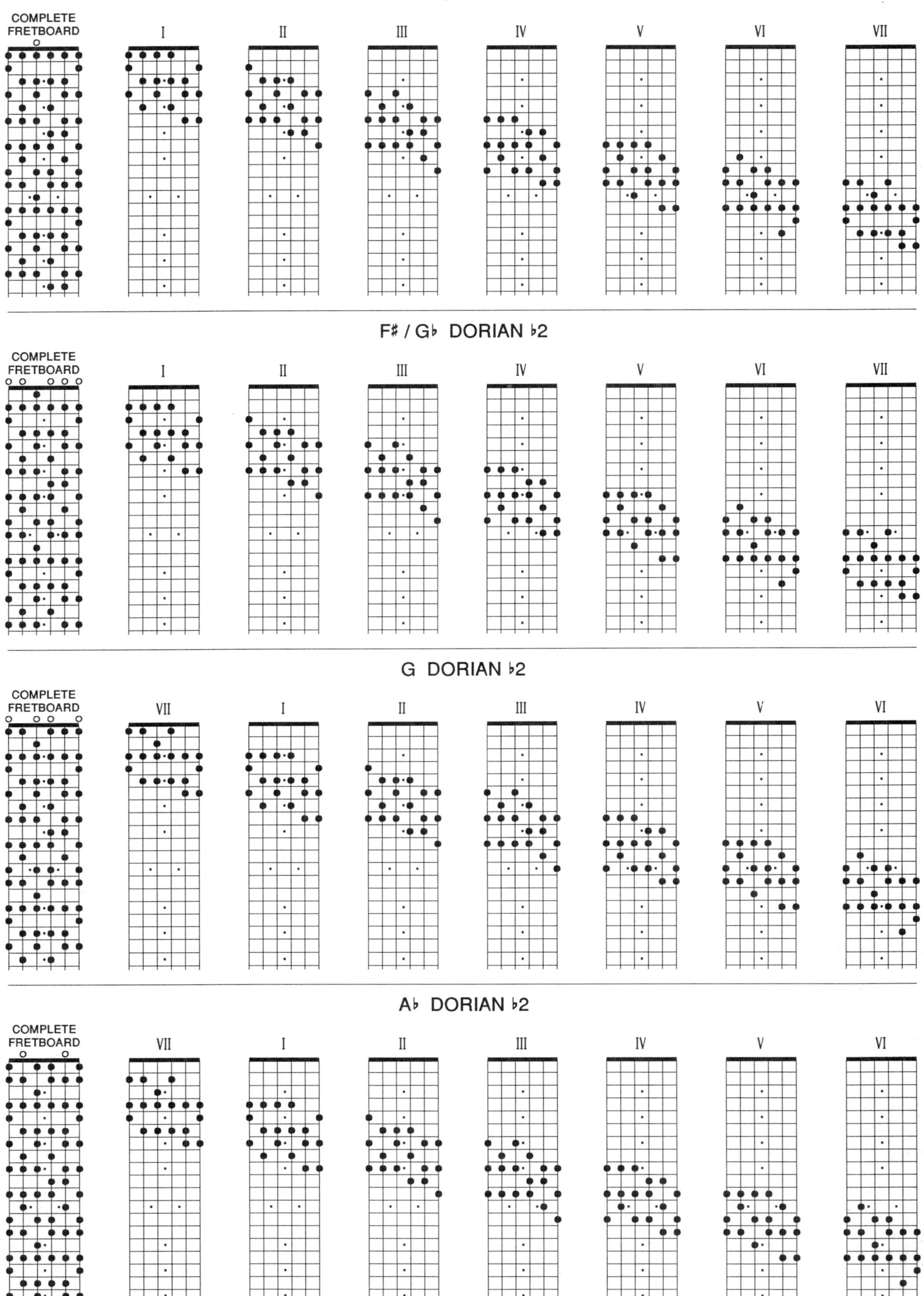
F DORIAN ♭2
COMPLETE FRETBOARD
I
II
III
IV
V
VI
VII
F♯ / G♭ DORIAN ♭2
COMPLETE FRETBOARD
I
II
III
IV
V
VI
VII
G DORIAN ♭2
COMPLETE FRETBOARD
VII
I
II
III
IV
V
VI
A♭ DORIAN ♭2
COMPLETE FRETBOARD
VII
I
II
III
IV
V
VI

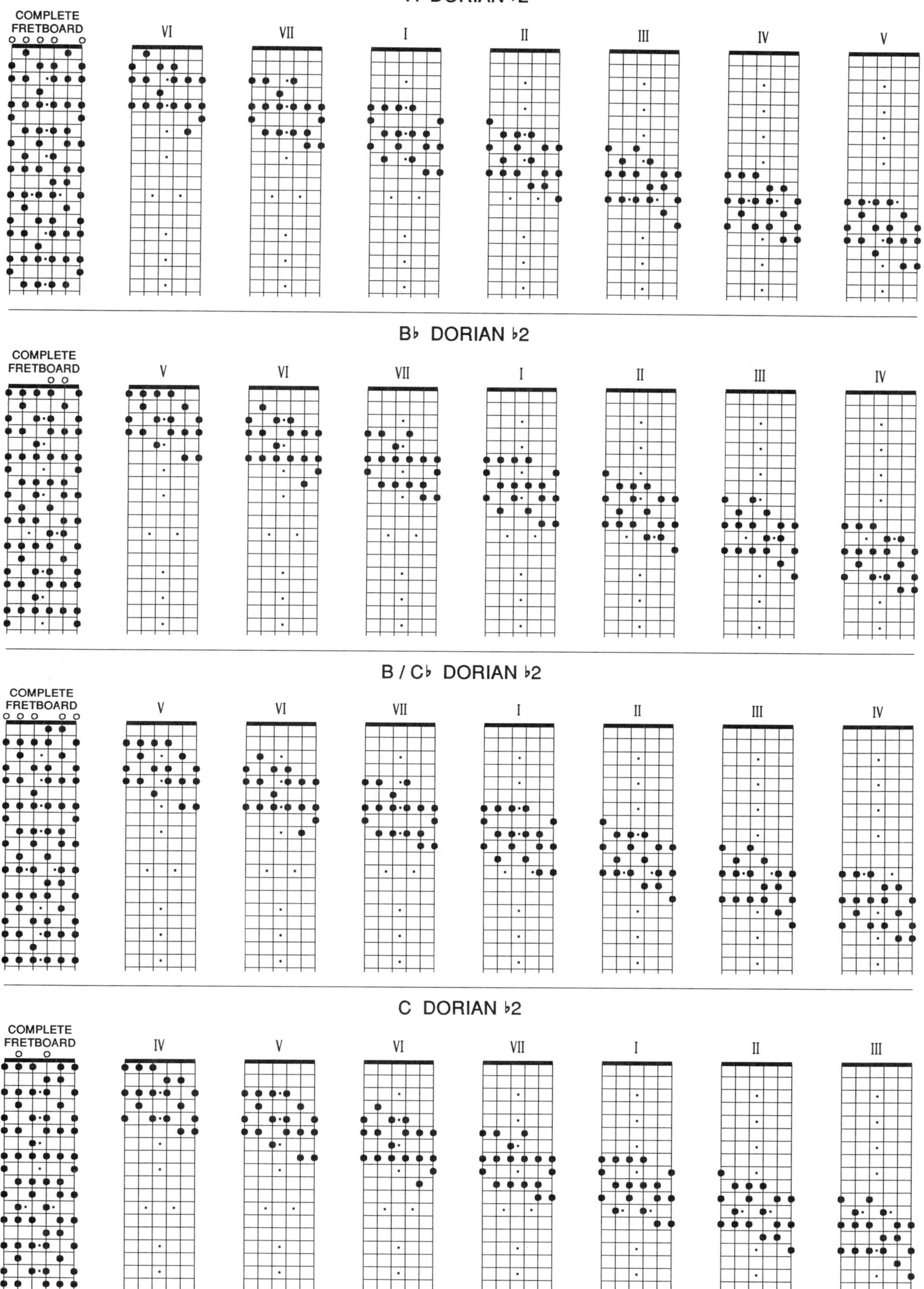
A DORIAN ♭2
COMPLETE FRETBOARD
VI
VII
I
II
III
IV
V
B♭ DORIAN ♭2
COMPLETE FRETBOARD
V
VI
VII
I
II
III
IV
B / C♭ DORIAN ♭2
COMPLETE FRETBOARD
V
VI
VII
I
II
III
IV
C DORIAN ♭2
COMPLETE FRETBOARD
IV
V
VI
VII
I
II
III

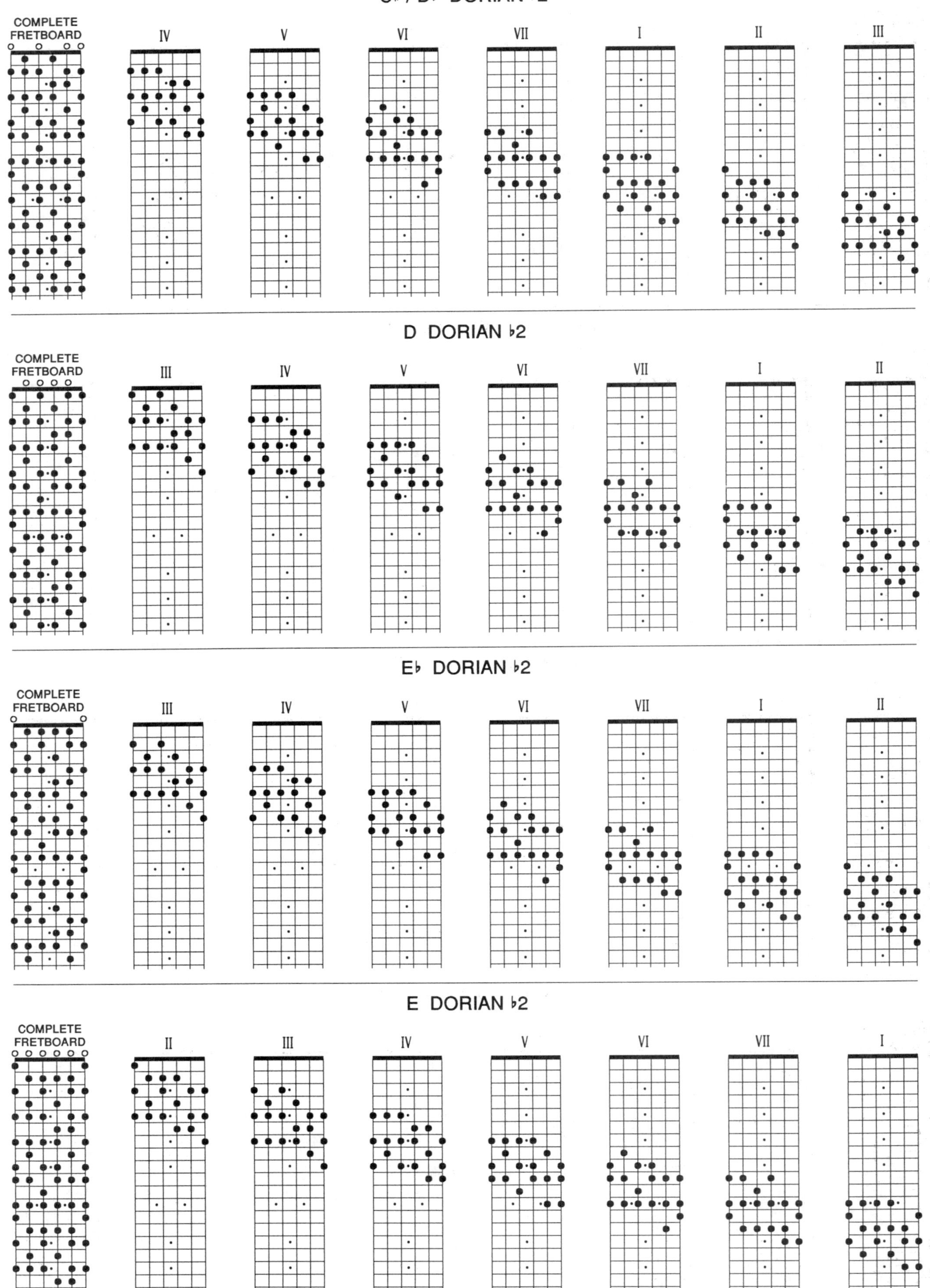
C♯ / D♭ DORIAN ♭2
COMPLETE FRETBOARD
IV
V
VI
VII
I
II
III
D DORIAN ♭2
COMPLETE FRETBOARD
III
IV
V
VI
VII
I
II
E♭ DORIAN ♭2
COMPLETE FRETBOARD
III
IV
V
VI
VII
I
II
E DORIAN ♭2
COMPLETE FRETBOARD
II
III
IV
V
VI
VII
I

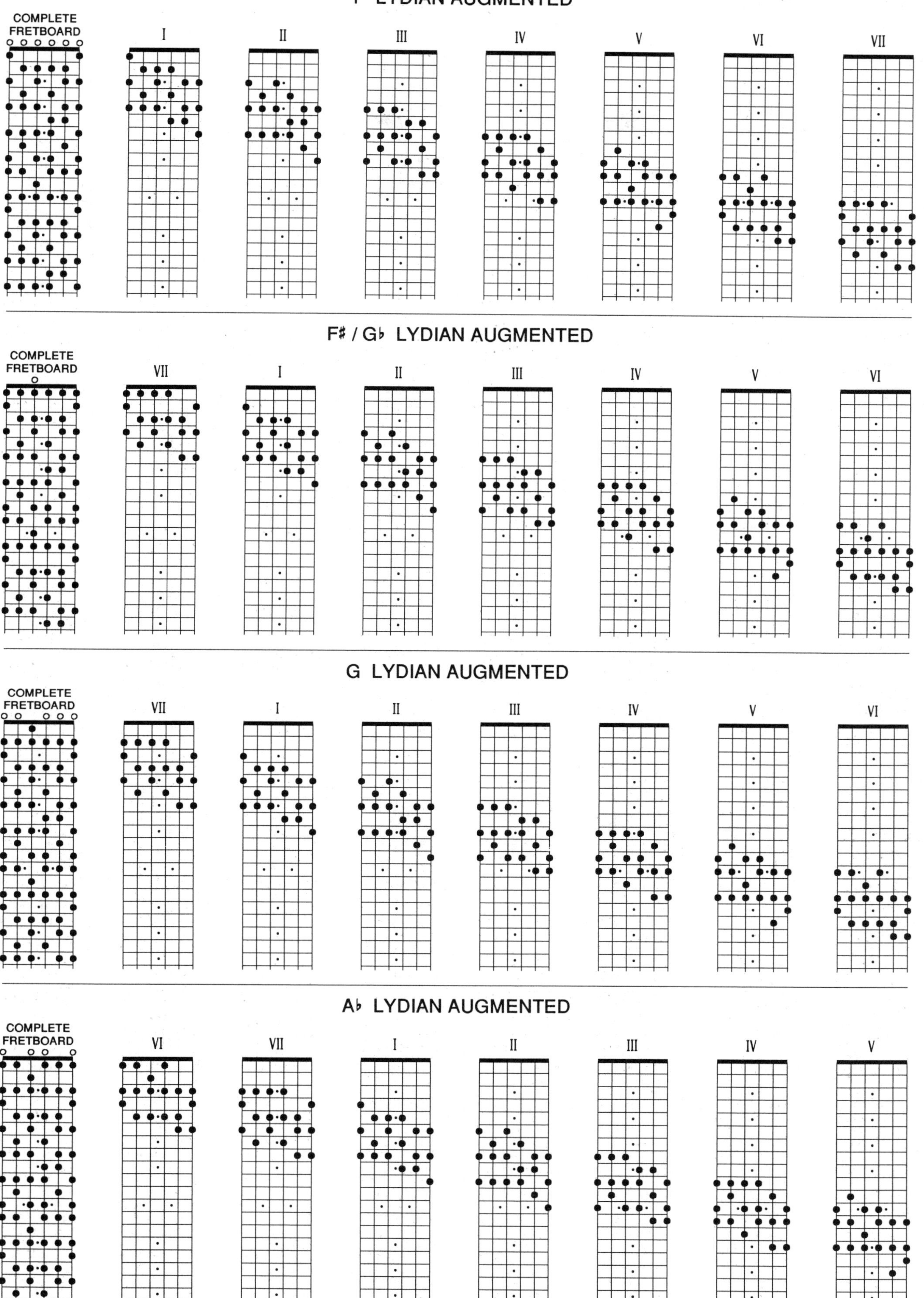
F LYDIAN AUGMENTED
COMPLETE FRETBOARD
I
II
III
IV
V
VI
VII
F♯ / G♭ LYDIAN AUGMENTED
COMPLETE FRETBOARD
VII
I
II
III
IV
V
VI
G LYDIAN AUGMENTED
COMPLETE FRETBOARD
VII
I
II
III
IV
V
VI
A♭ LYDIAN AUGMENTED
COMPLETE FRETBOARD
VI
VII
I
II
III
IV
V

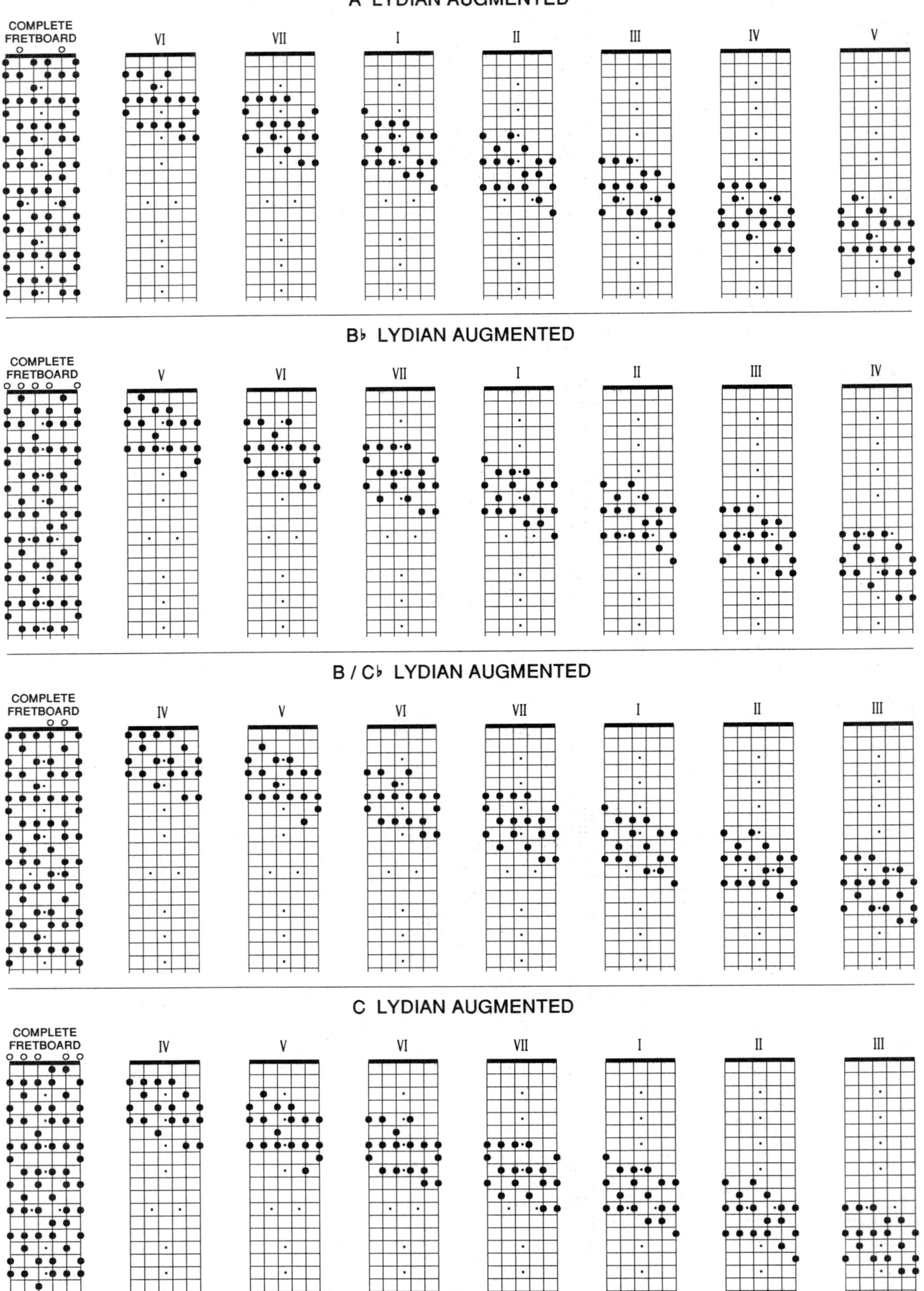
A LYDIAN AUGMENTED
COMPLETE FRETBOARD
VI
VII
I
II
III
IV
V
B♭ LYDIAN AUGMENTED
COMPLETE FRETBOARD
V
VI
VII
I
II
III
IV
B / C♭ LYDIAN AUGMENTED
COMPLETE FRETBOARD
IV
V
VI
VII
I
II
III
C LYDIAN AUGMENTED
COMPLETE FRETBOARD
IV
V
VI
VII
I
II
III

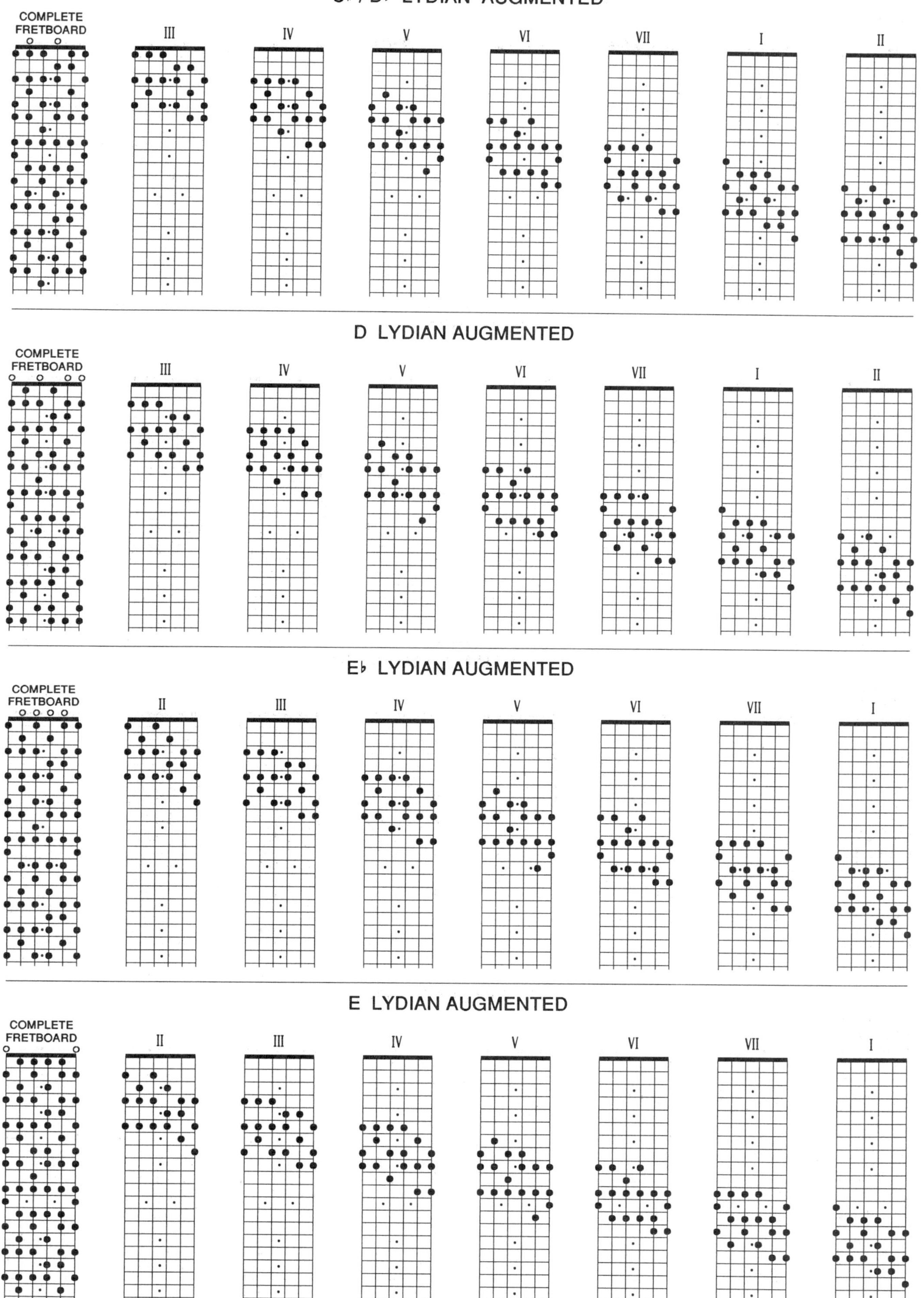
C♯ / D♭ LYDIAN AUGMENTED
COMPLETE FRETBOARD
III
IV
V
VI
VII
I
II
D LYDIAN AUGMENTED
COMPLETE FRETBOARD
III
IV
V
VI
VII
I
II
E♭ LYDIAN AUGMENTED
COMPLETE FRETBOARD
II
III
IV
V
VI
VII
I
E LYDIAN AUGMENTED
COMPLETE FRETBOARD
II
III
IV
V
VI
VII
I

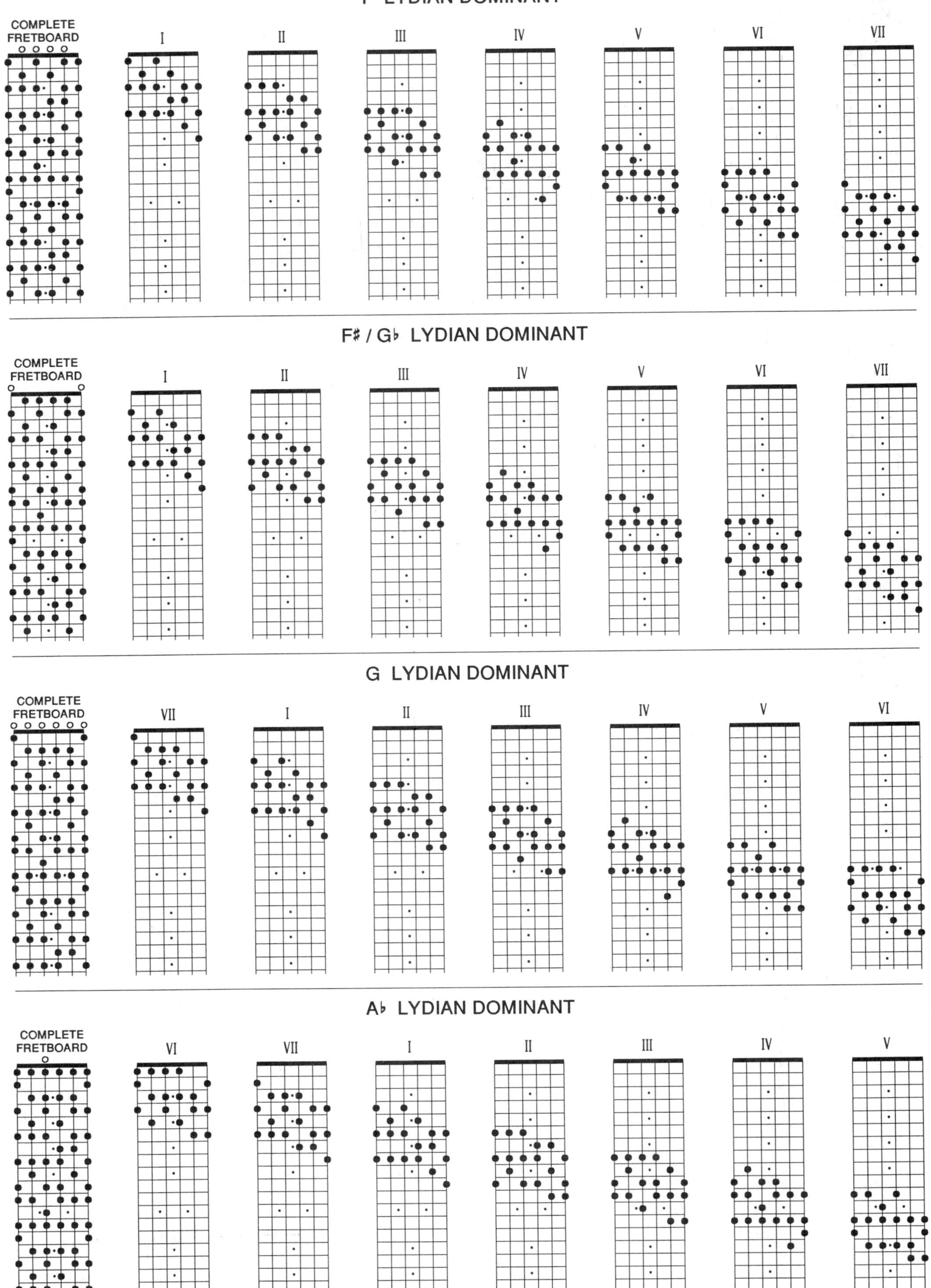
F LYDIAN DOMINANT
COMPLETE FRETBOARD
I
II
III
IV
V
VI
VII
F♯ / G♭ LYDIAN DOMINANT
COMPLETE FRETBOARD
I
II
III
IV
V
VI
VII
G LYDIAN DOMINANT
COMPLETE FRETBOARD
VII
I
II
III
IV
V
VI
A♭ LYDIAN DOMINANT
COMPLETE FRETBOARD
VI
VII
I
II
III
IV
V

A LYDIAN DOMINANT

B♭ LYDIAN DOMINANT

B / C♭ LYDIAN DOMINANT

C LYDIAN DOMINANT

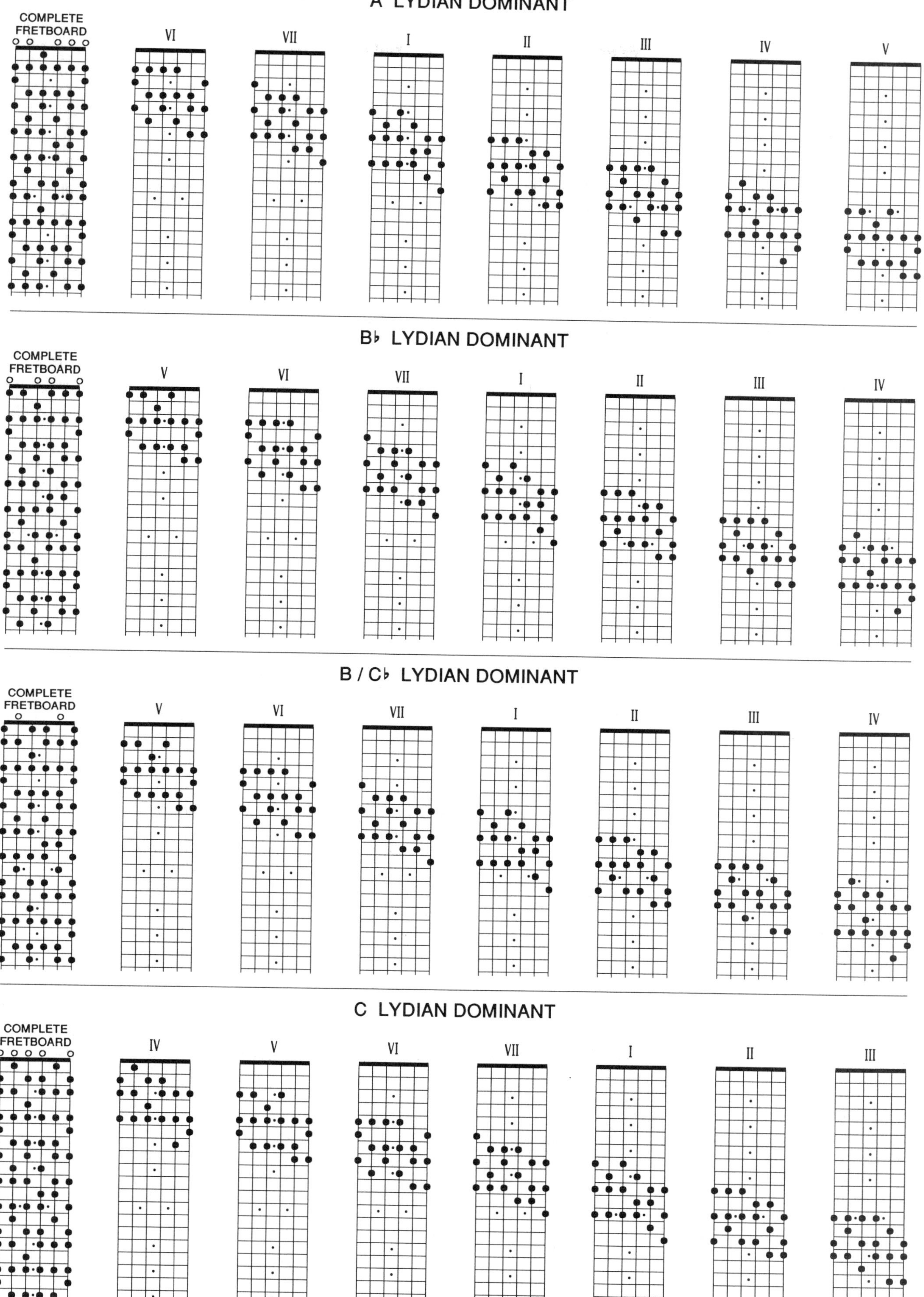

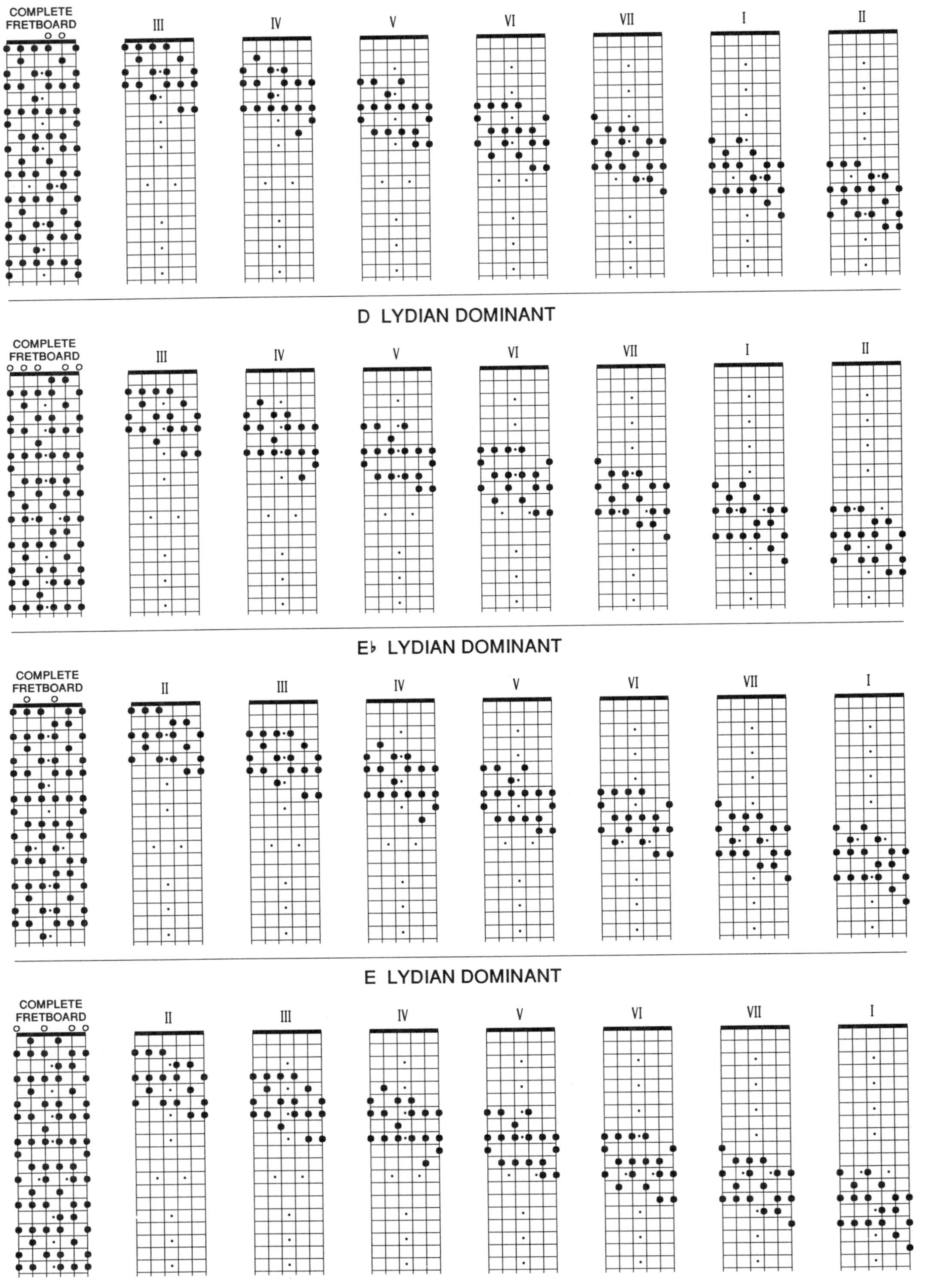
C♯ / D♭ LYDIAN DOMINANT
COMPLETE FRETBOARD
III
IV
V
VI
VII
I
II
D LYDIAN DOMINANT
COMPLETE FRETBOARD
III
IV
V
VI
VII
I
II
E♭ LYDIAN DOMINANT
COMPLETE FRETBOARD
II
III
IV
V
VI
VII
I
E LYDIAN DOMINANT
COMPLETE FRETBOARD
II
III
IV
V
VI
VII
I

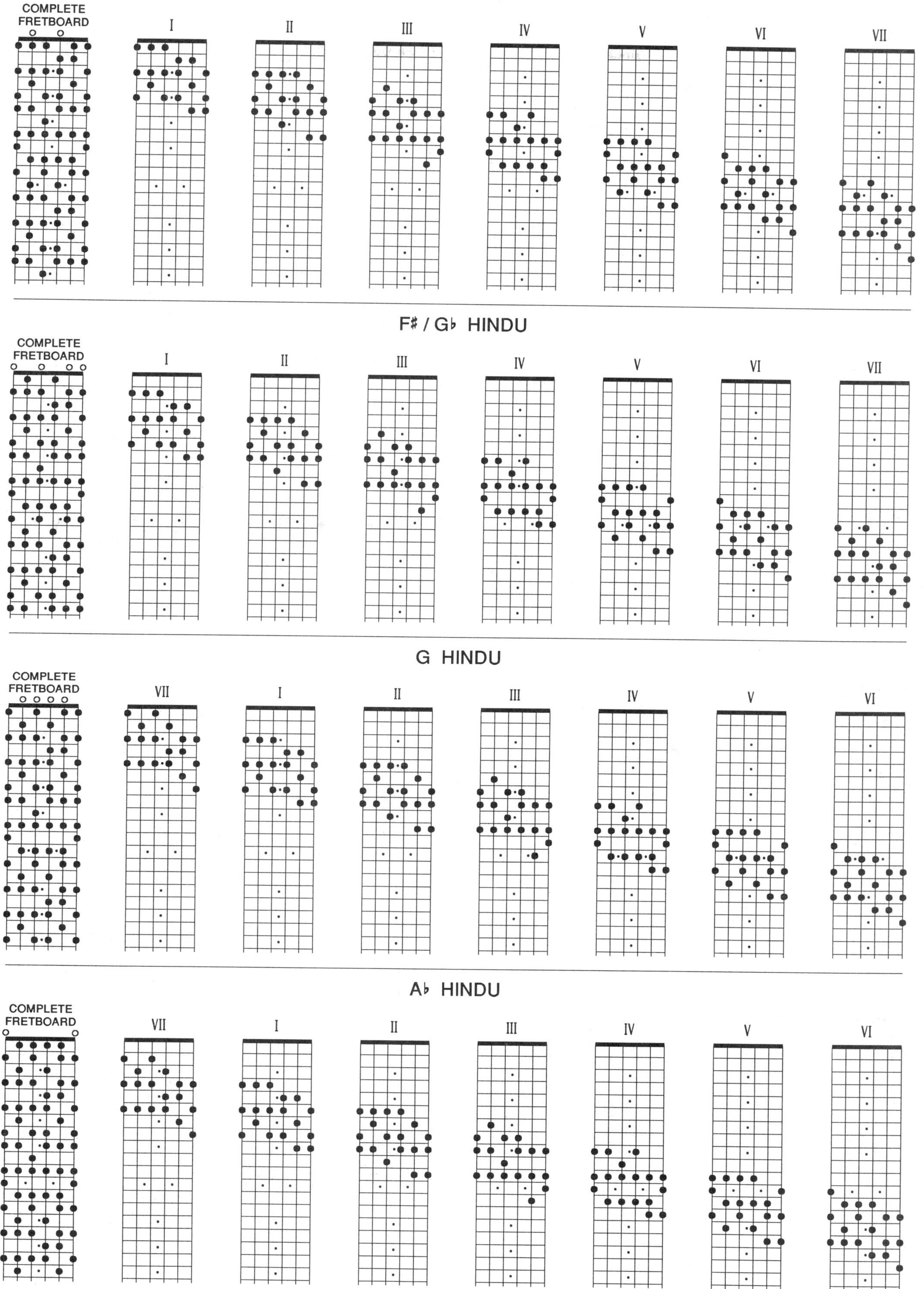

F HINDU
COMPLETE FRETBOARD
I
II
III
IV
V
VI
VII
F♯ / G♭ HINDU
COMPLETE FRETBOARD
I
II
III
IV
V
VI
VII
G HINDU
COMPLETE FRETBOARD
VII
I
II
III
IV
V
VI
A♭ HINDU
COMPLETE FRETBOARD
VII
I
II
III
IV
V
VI

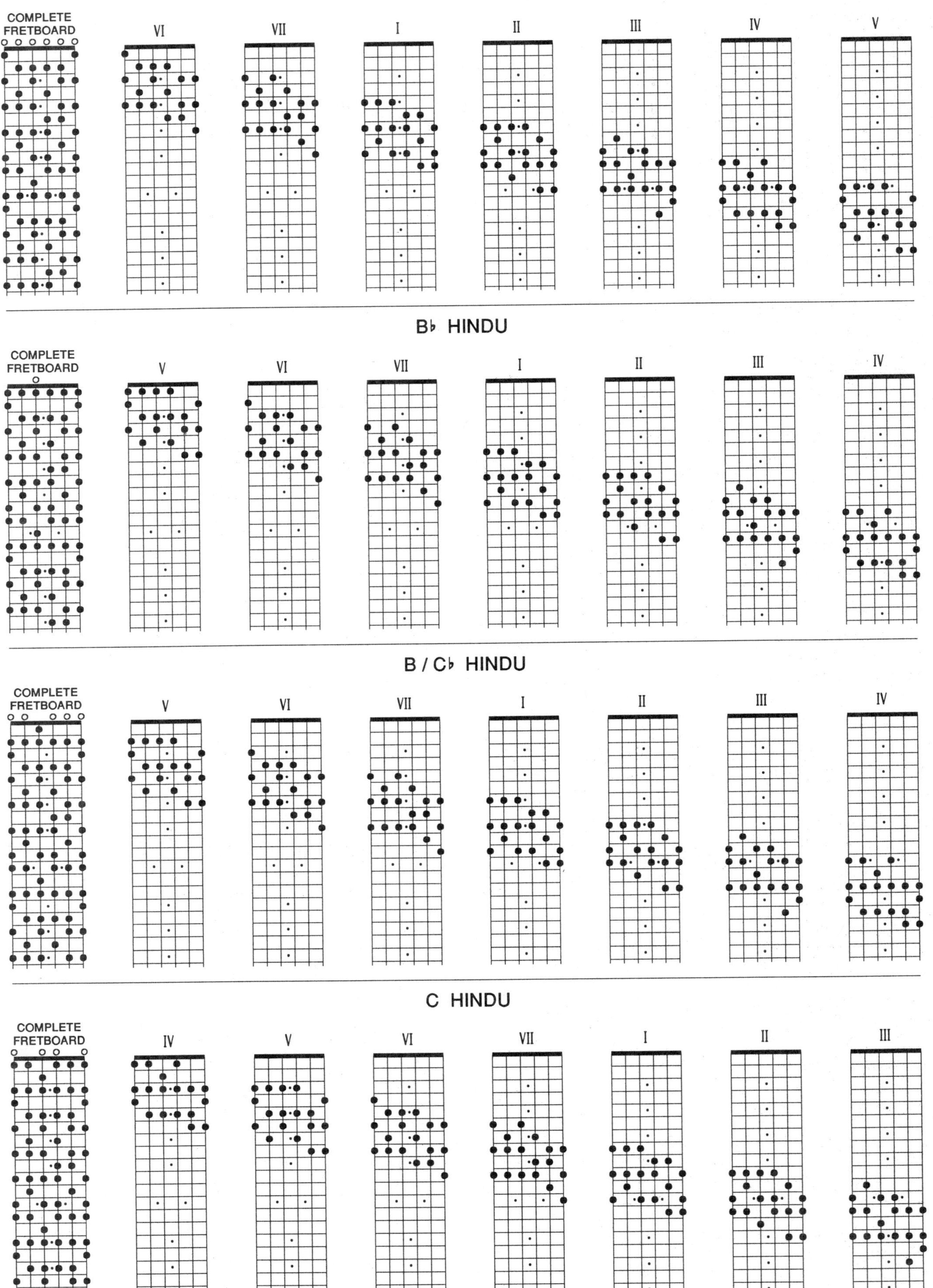
A HINDU
COMPLETE FRETBOARD
VI
VII
I
II
III
IV
V
B♭ HINDU
COMPLETE FRETBOARD
V
VI
VII
I
II
III
IV
B / C♭ HINDU
COMPLETE FRETBOARD
V
VI
VII
I
II
III
IV
C HINDU
COMPLETE FRETBOARD
IV
V
VI
VII
I
II
III

C♯ / D♭ HINDU

D HINDU

E♭ HINDU

E HINDU

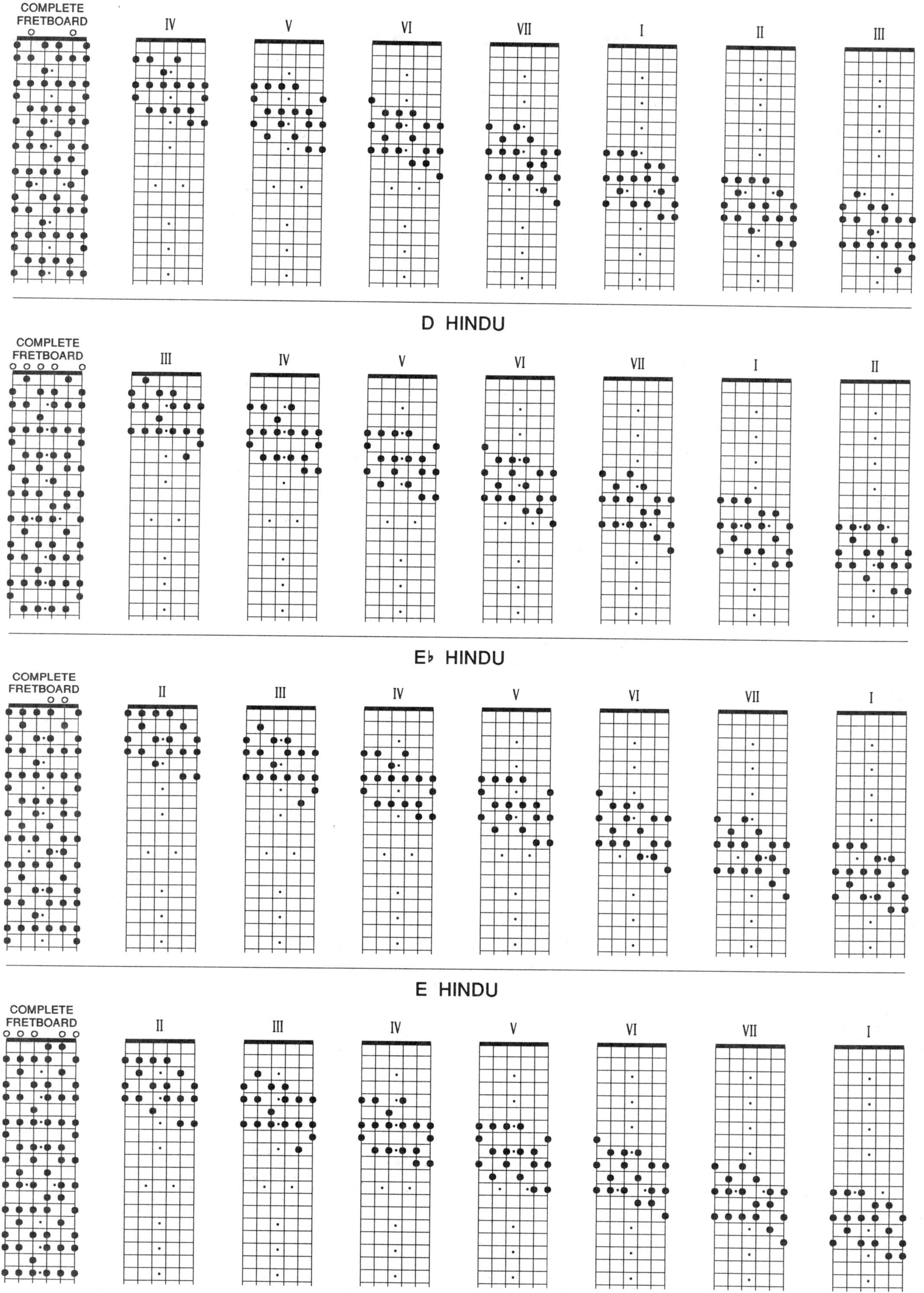

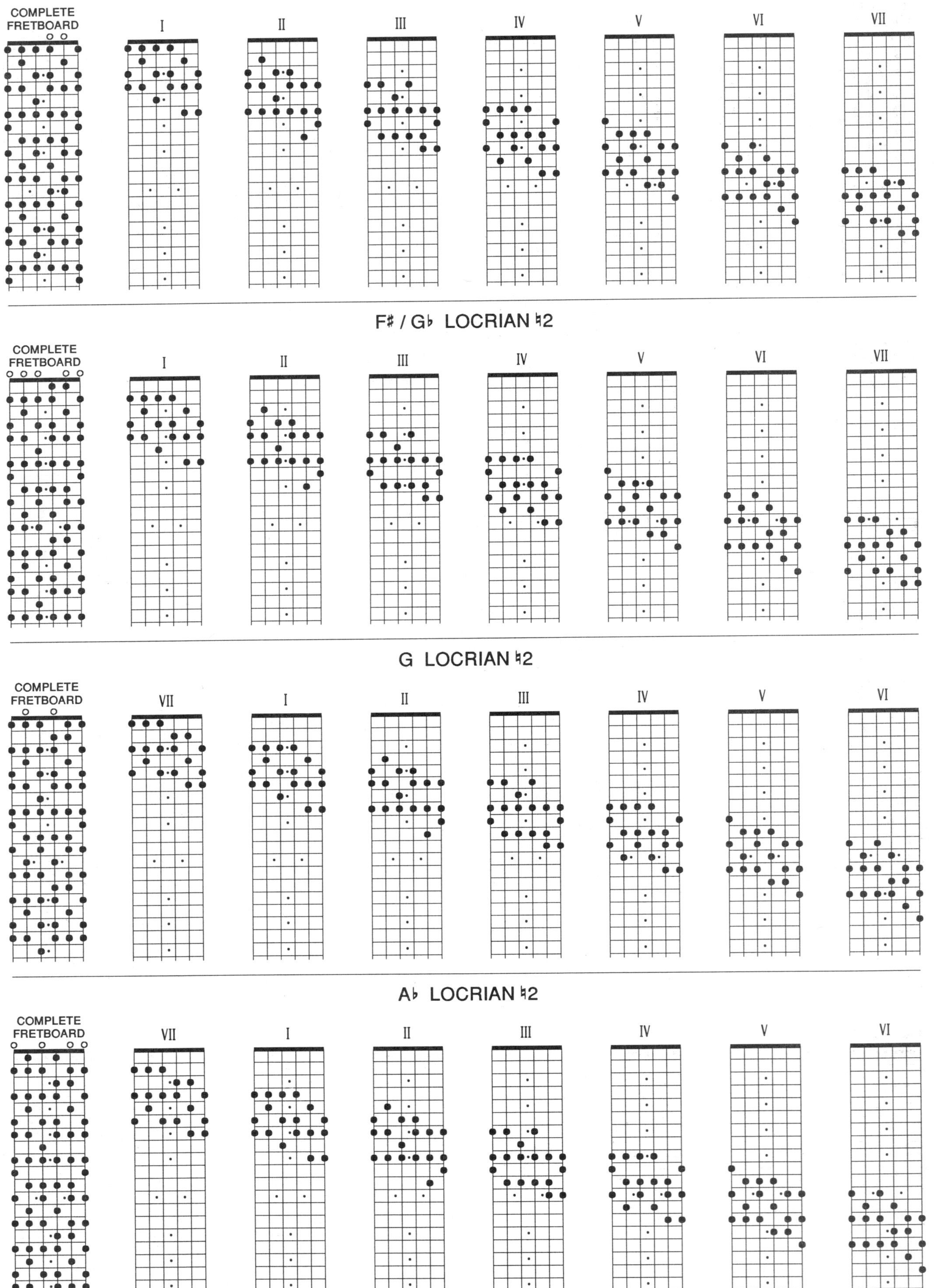
F LOCRIAN ♮2
COMPLETE FRETBOARD
I
II
III
IV
V
VI
VII
F♯ / G♭ LOCRIAN ♮2
COMPLETE FRETBOARD
I
II
III
IV
V
VI
VII
G LOCRIAN ♮2
COMPLETE FRETBOARD
VII
I
II
III
IV
V
VI
A♭ LOCRIAN ♮2
COMPLETE FRETBOARD
VII
I
II
III
IV
V
VI

A LOCRIAN ♮2

COMPLETE FRETBOARD

VI VII I II III IV V

B♭ LOCRIAN ♮2

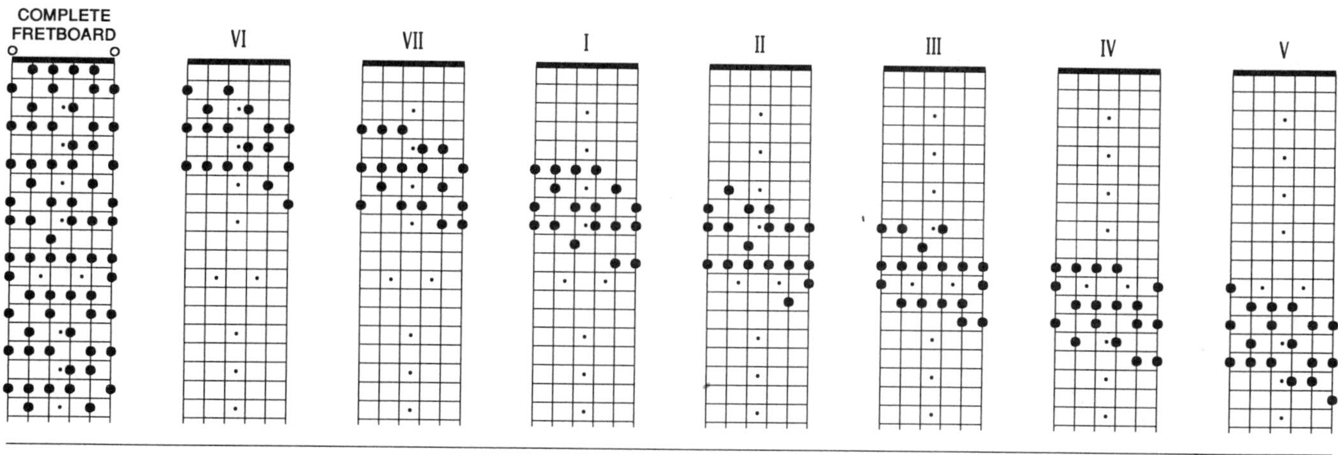

B / C♭ LOCRIAN ♮2

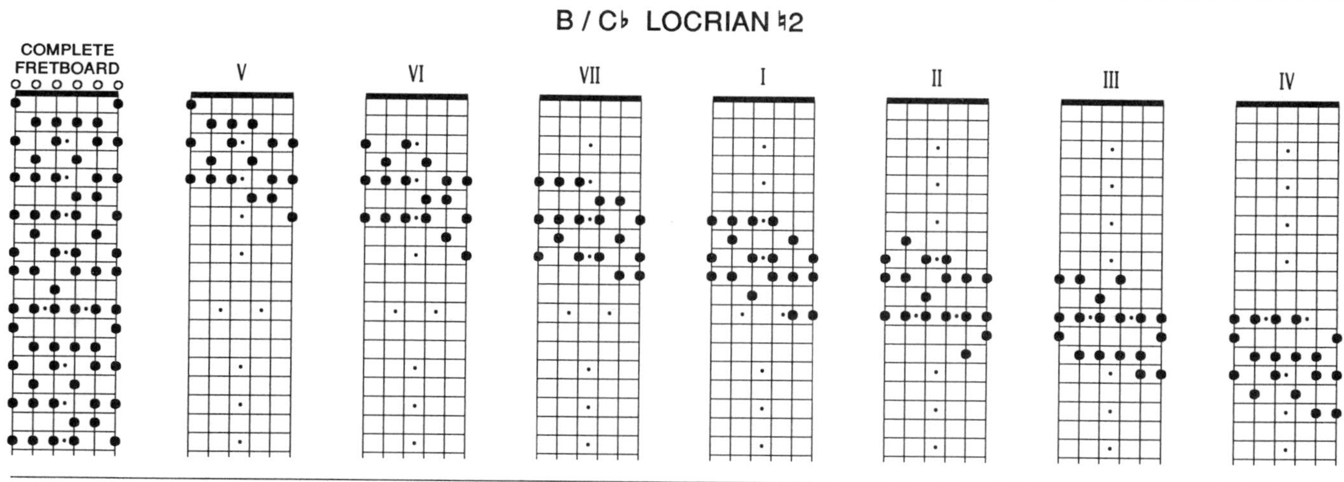

C LOCRIAN ♮2

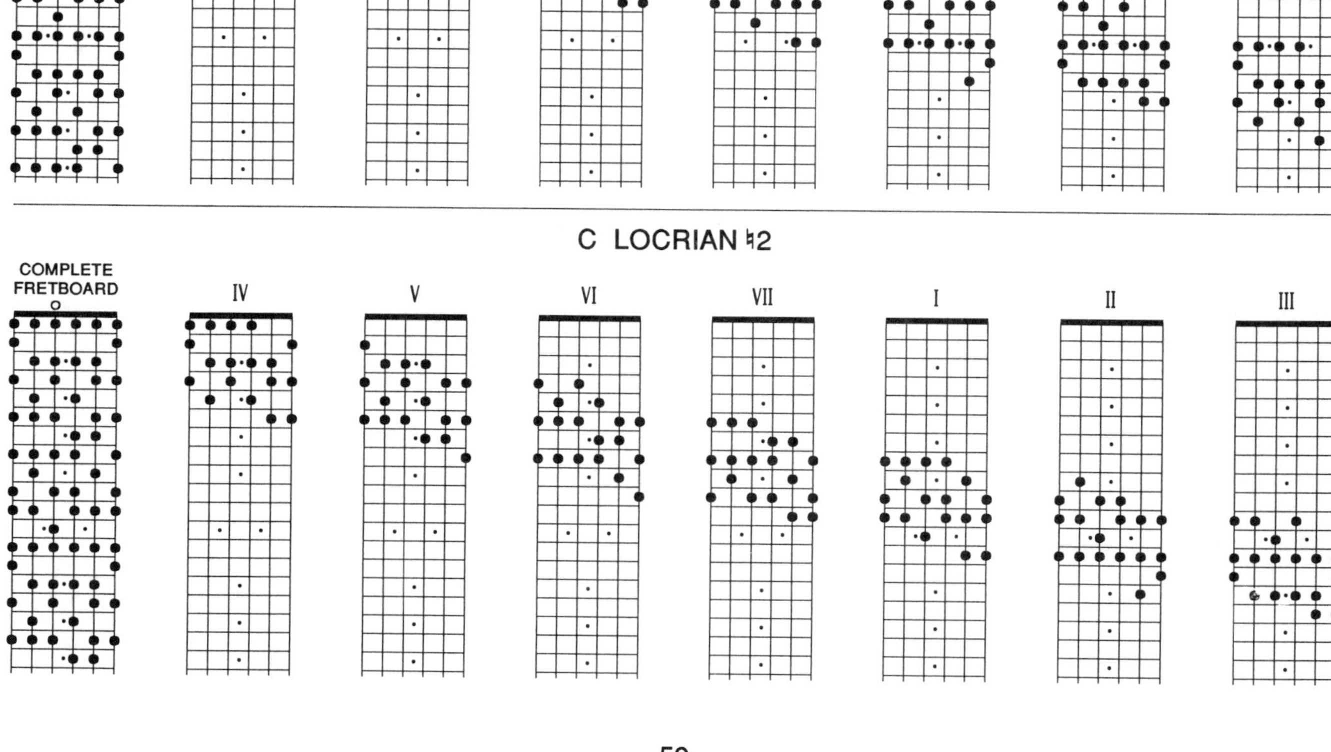

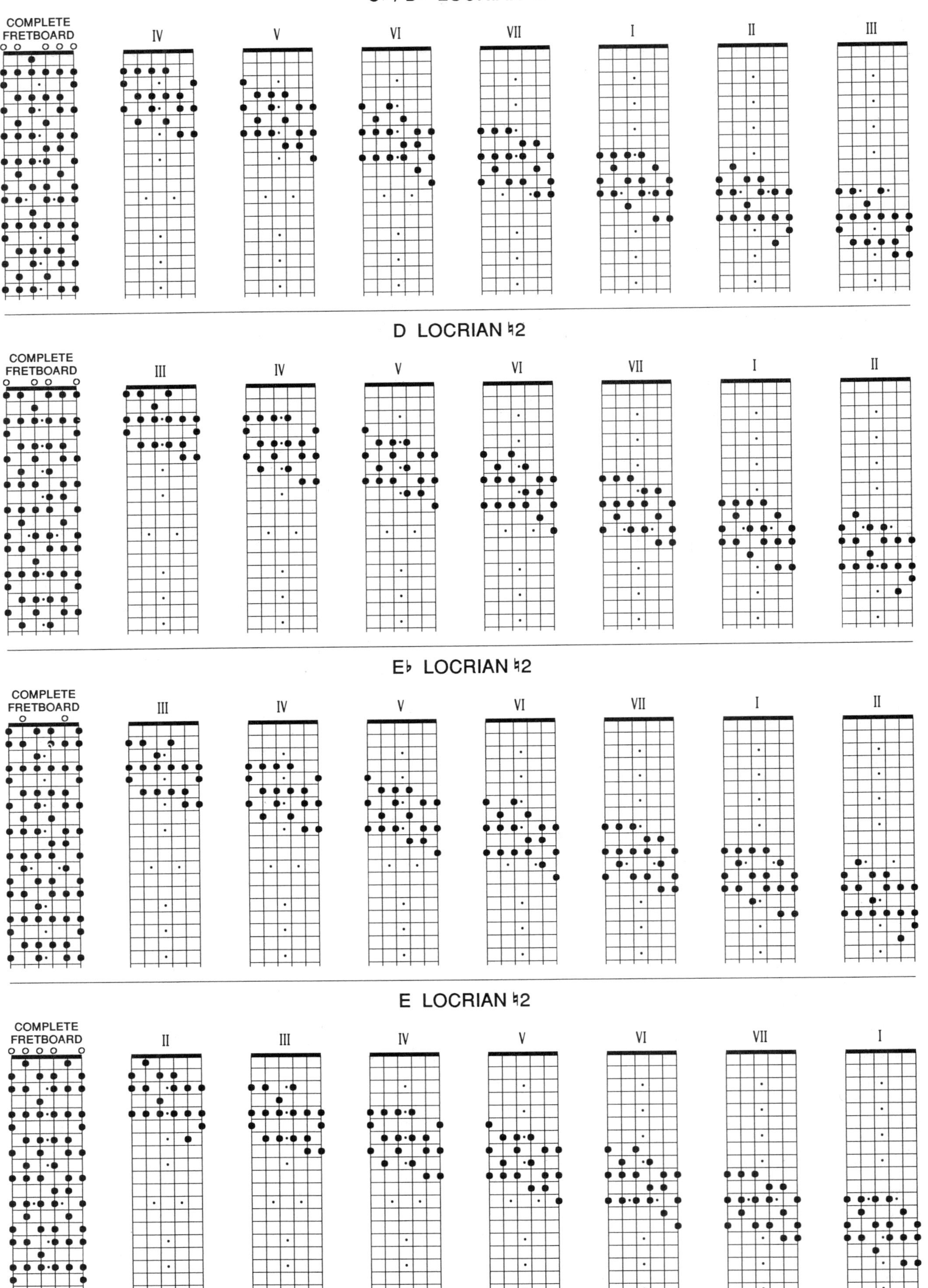
C♯ / D♭ LOCRIAN ♮2
COMPLETE FRETBOARD
IV
V
VI
VII
I
II
III
D LOCRIAN ♮2
COMPLETE FRETBOARD
III
IV
V
VI
VII
I
II
E♭ LOCRIAN ♮2
COMPLETE FRETBOARD
III
IV
V
VI
VII
I
II
E LOCRIAN ♮2
COMPLETE FRETBOARD
II
III
IV
V
VI
VII
I

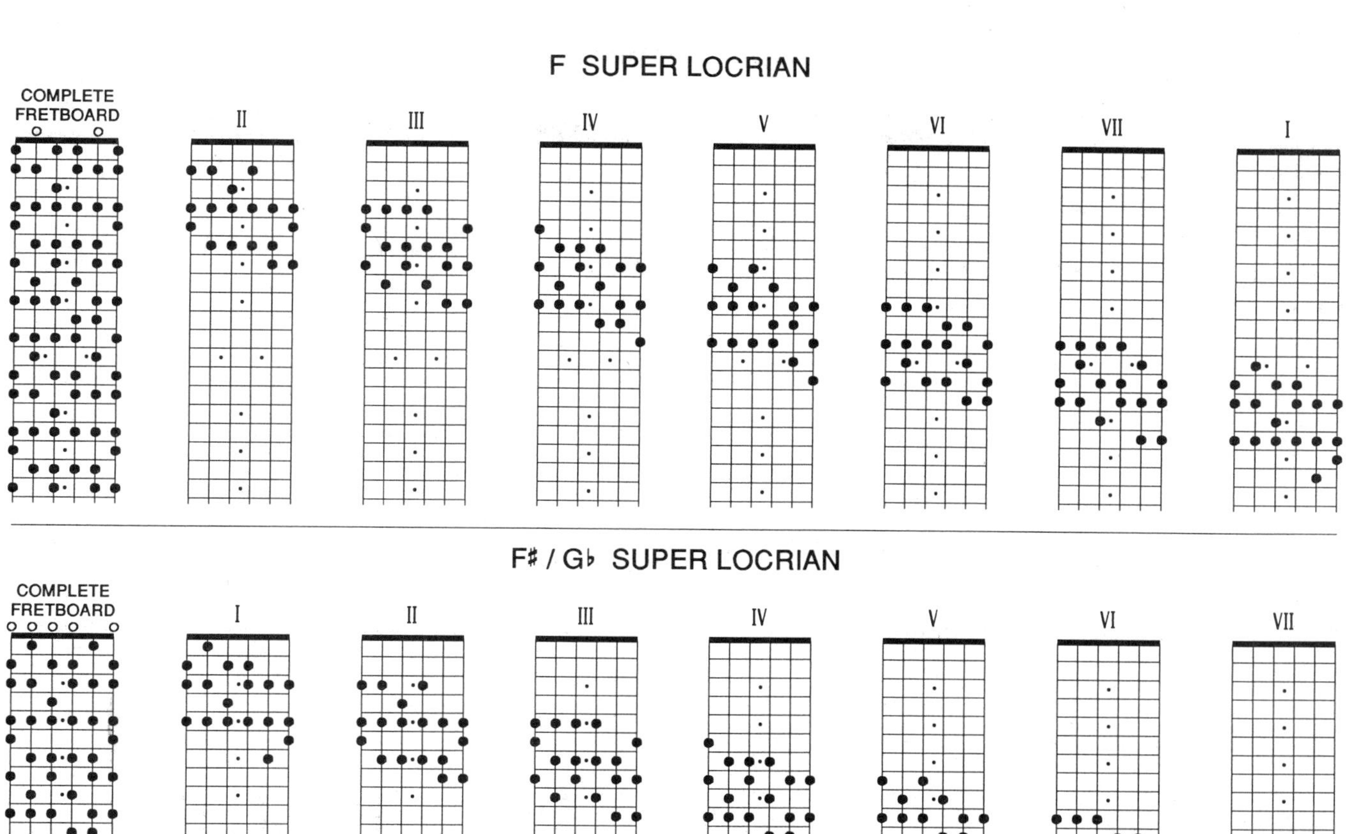
F SUPER LOCRIAN
COMPLETE FRETBOARD
II
III
IV
V
VI
VII
I
F♯ / G♭ SUPER LOCRIAN
COMPLETE FRETBOARD
I
II
III
IV
V
VI
VII

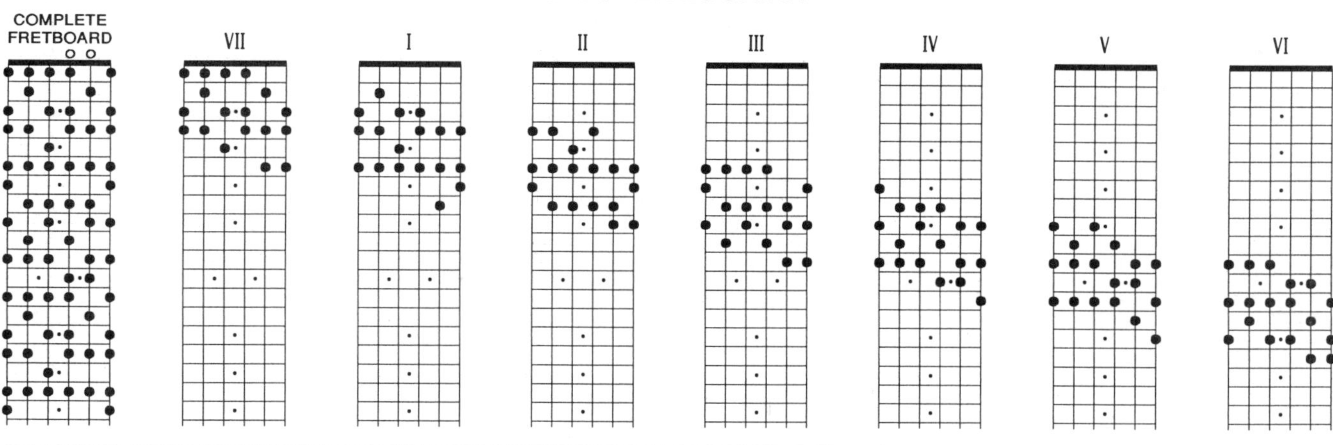
G SUPER LOCRIAN
COMPLETE FRETBOARD
VII
I
II
III
IV
V
VI

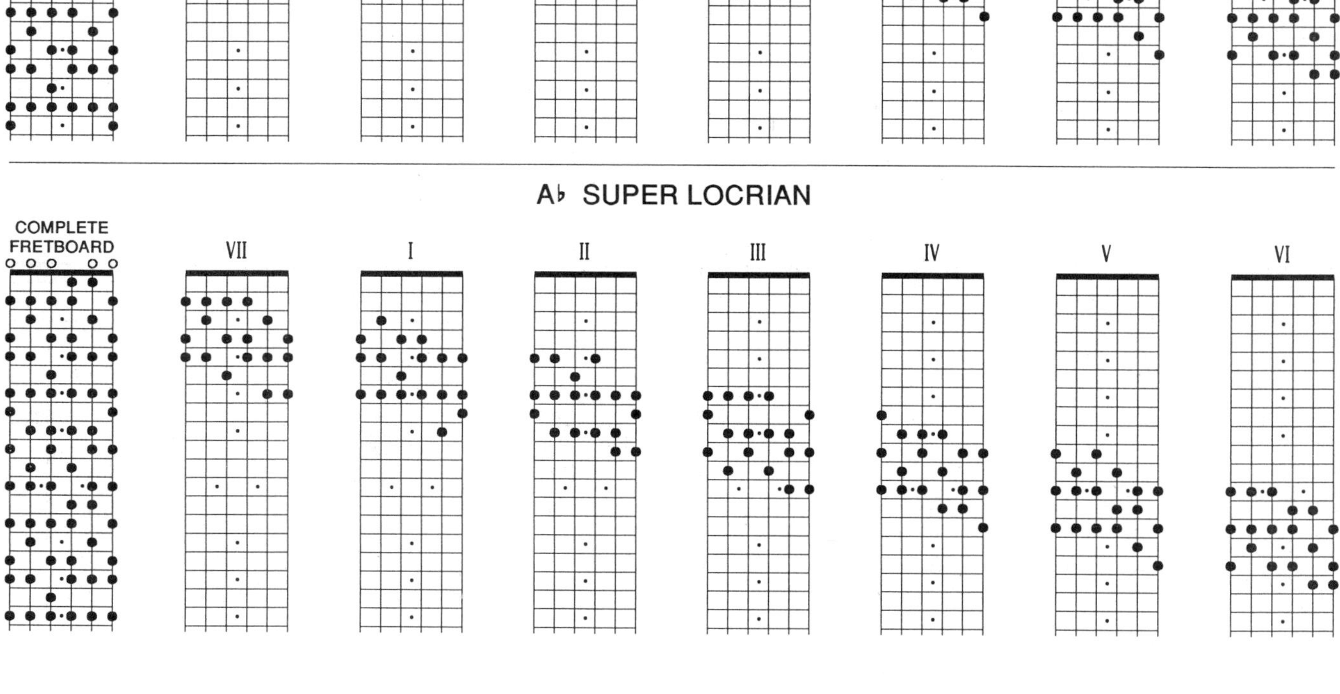
A♭ SUPER LOCRIAN
COMPLETE FRETBOARD
VII
I
II
III
IV
V
VI

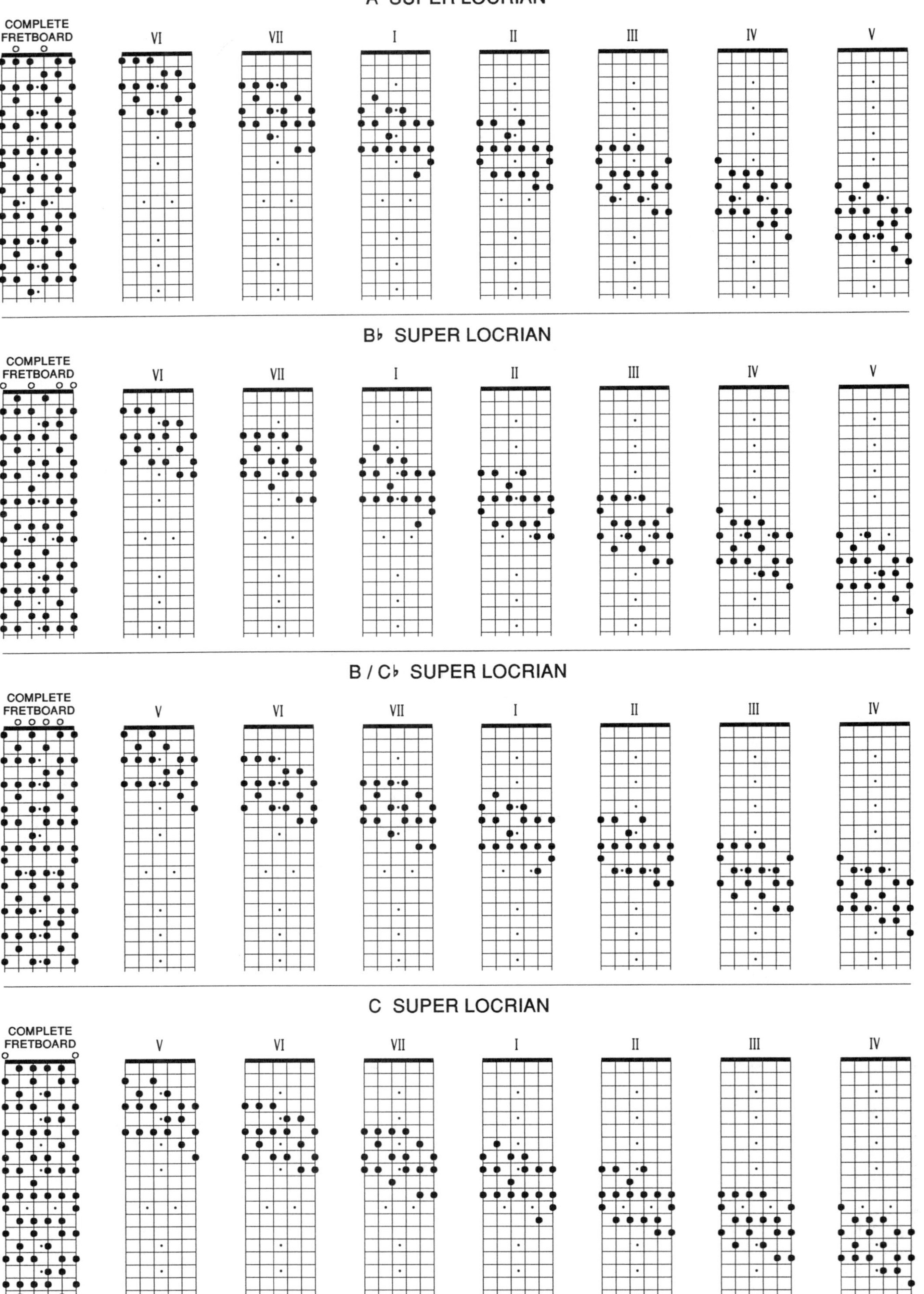
A SUPER LOCRIAN
COMPLETE FRETBOARD
VI
VII
I
II
III
IV
V
B♭ SUPER LOCRIAN
COMPLETE FRETBOARD
VI
VII
I
II
III
IV
V
B / C♭ SUPER LOCRIAN
COMPLETE FRETBOARD
V
VI
VII
I
II
III
IV
C SUPER LOCRIAN
COMPLETE FRETBOARD
V
VI
VII
I
II
III
IV

C♯ / D♭ SUPER LOCRIAN

D SUPER LOCRIAN

E♭ SUPER LOCRIAN

E SUPER LOCRIAN

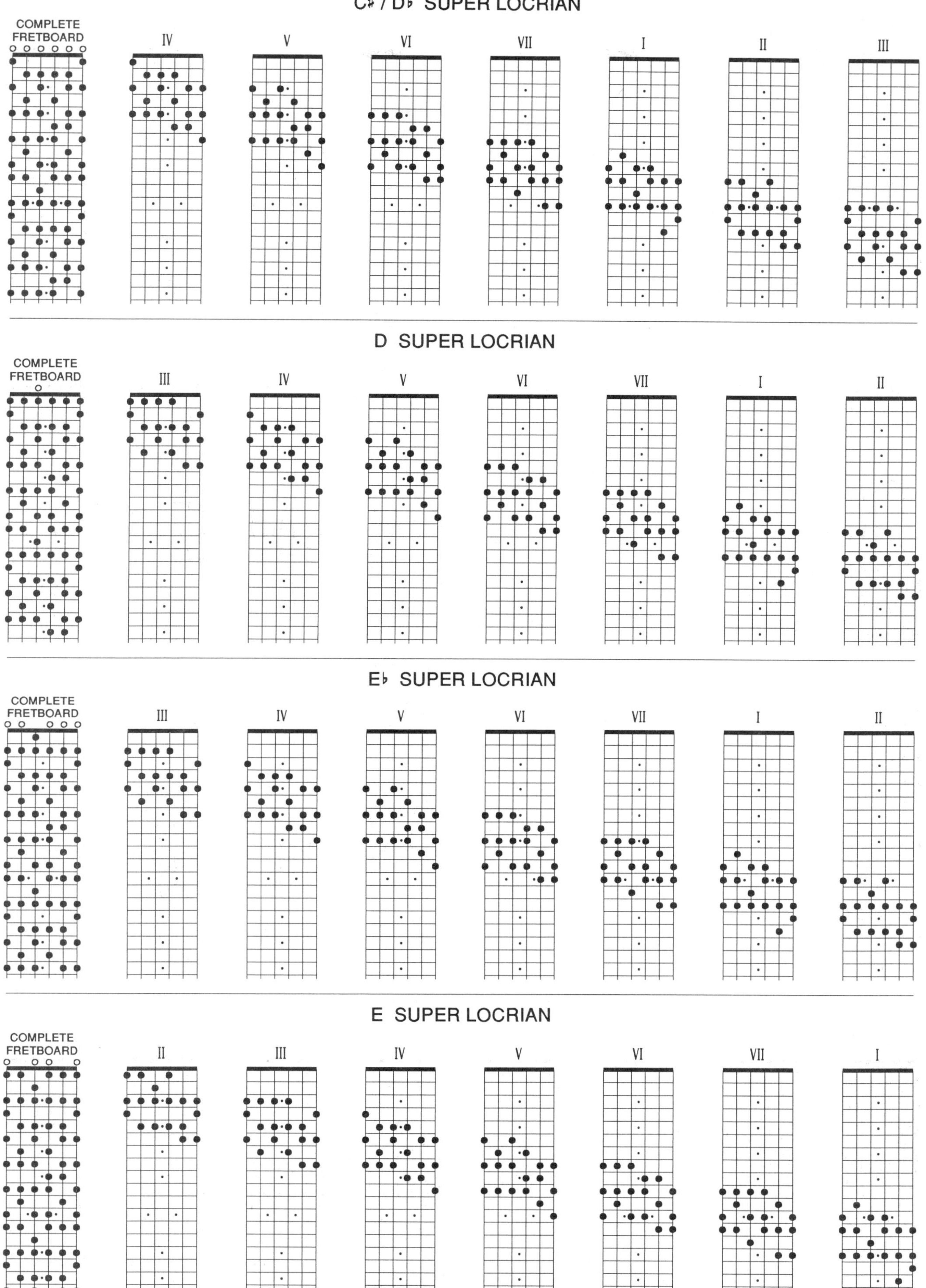

KEYBOARD PATTERNS

QUICK MODE GENERATOR CHART

HARMONIC MINOR

I	II	III	IV	V	VI	VII
C	B♭	A	G	F	E	C♯/D♭
C♯/D♭	B/C♭	B♭	A♭	F♯/G♭	F	D
D	C	B/C♭	A	G	F♯/G♭	E♭
E♭	C♯/D♭	C	B♭	A♭	G	E
E	D	C♯/D♭	B/C♭	A	A♭	F
F	E♭	D	C	B♭	A	F♯/G♭
F♯/G♭	E	E♭	C♯/D♭	B/C♭	B♭	G
G	F	E	D	C	B/C♭	A♭
A♭	F♯/G♭	F	E♭	C♯/D♭	C	A
A	G	F♯/G♭	E	D	C♯/D♭	B♭
B♭	A♭	G	F	E♭	D	B/C♭
B/C♭	A	A♭	F♯/G♭	E	E♭	C

CONVENTIONAL PATTERNS

SWEEPING PATTERNS

I

II

III

IV

V

VI

VII

SCALE / MODE - CHORD CHART

I	HARMONIC MINOR	$-\triangle$, $-\flat 6$
II	LOCRIAN ♮6	ø, °7
III	IONIAN ♯5	$\triangle^{+}$
IV	DORIAN ♯4	ø, ○, -7, -6, $^{ø}9$, °9, -9
V	PHRYGIAN ♮3	+, 7, 7^{+}, $7^{\flat 9}$
VI	LYDIAN ♯2	M, m, 6, $\triangle$, $-\triangle$
VII	ALT 𝄫7	♭5, ○, °7

NUMERIC SCALE / MODE CHART

		1		2		3	4		5		6		7	1		2		3	4		5		6		7
I	HARMONIC MINOR	1		2	♭3		4		5	♭6			7	1		2	♭3		4		5	♭6			7
II	LOCRIAN ♮6			1	♭2		♭3		4	♭5			6	♭7											
III	IONIAN ♯5				1		2		3	4			♯5	6		7									
IV	DORIAN ♯4						1		2	♭3			♯4	5		6	♭7								
V	PHRYGIAN ♮3								1	♭2			3	4		5	♭6		♭7						
VI	LYDIAN ♯2									1			♯2	3		♯4	5		6		7				
VII	ALT 𝄫7												1	♭2		♭3	♭4		♭5		♭6	𝄫7			

F HARMONIC MINOR

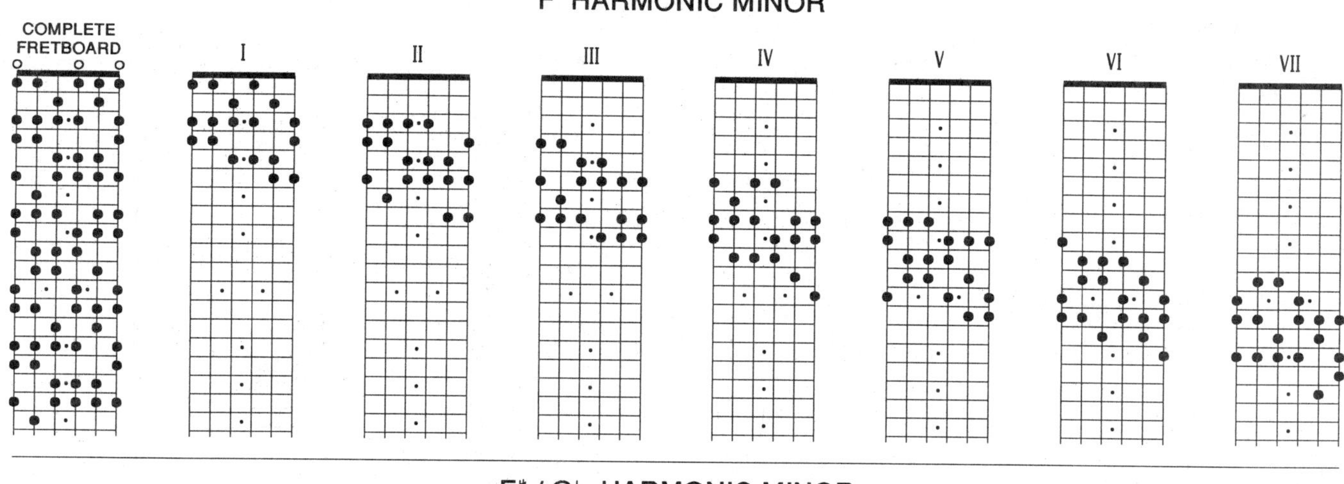

F♯ / G♭ HARMONIC MINOR

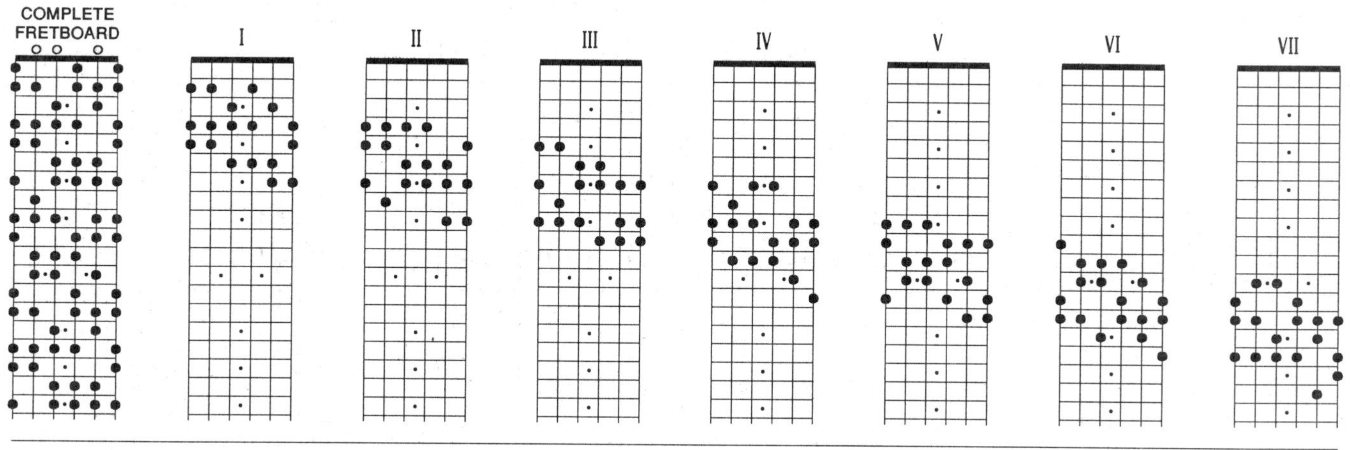

G HARMONIC MINOR

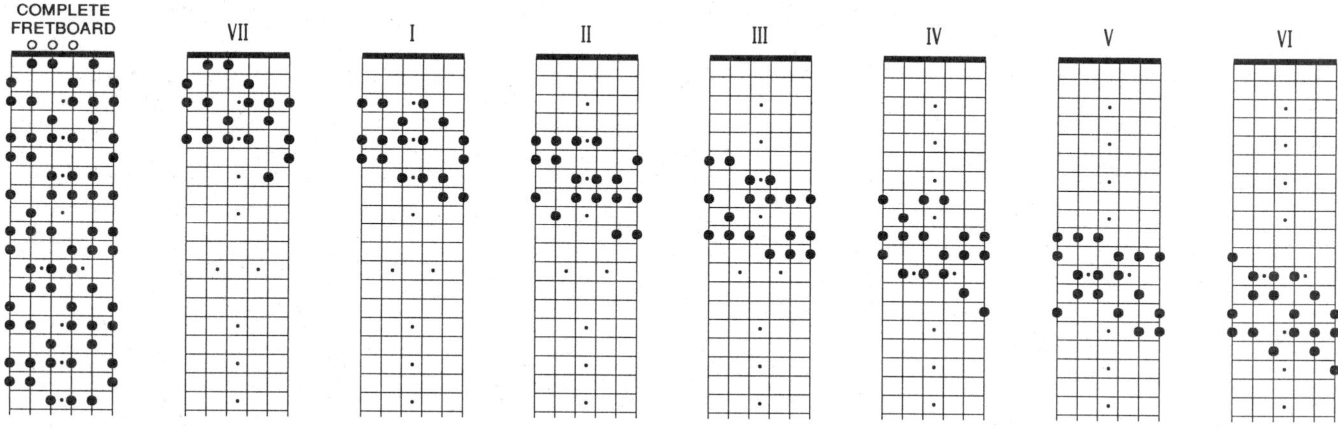

A♭ HARMONIC MINOR

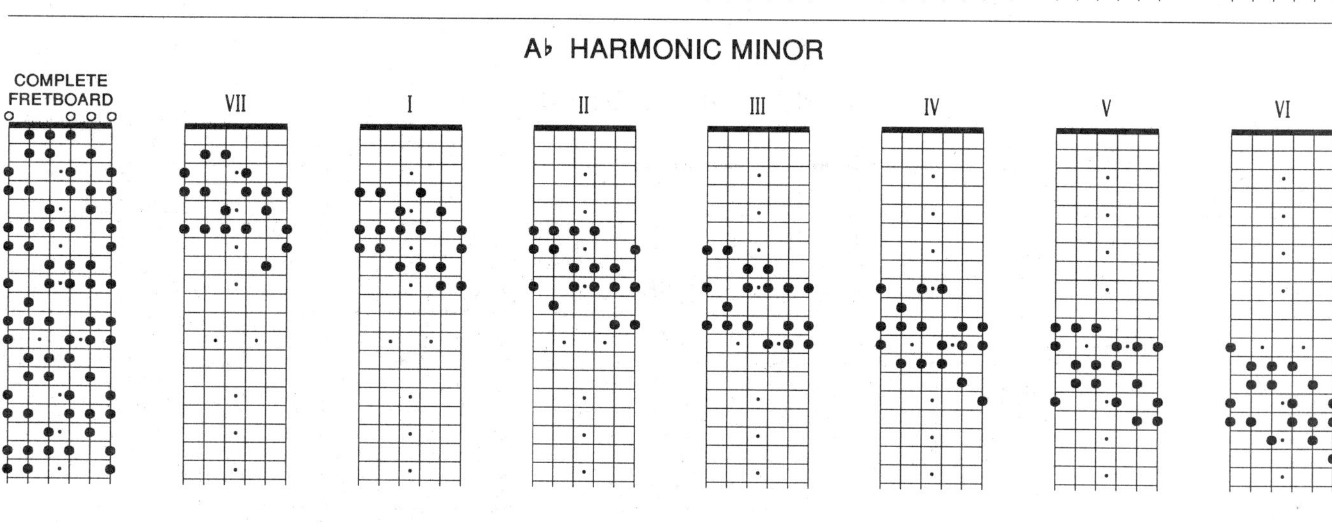

A HARMONIC MINOR

COMPLETE FRETBOARD

VI VII I II III IV V

B♭ HARMONIC MINOR

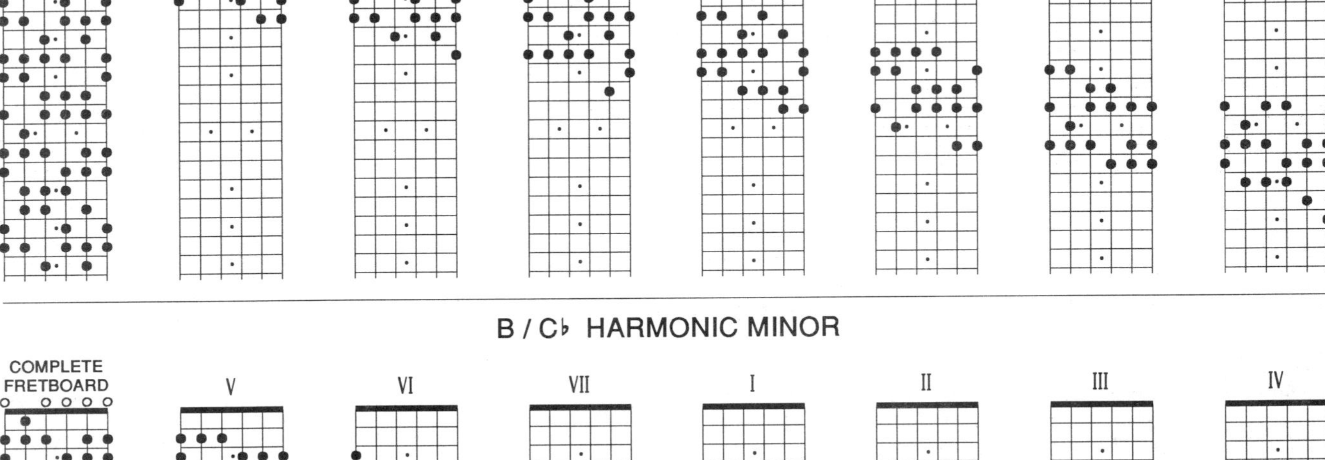

B / C♭ HARMONIC MINOR

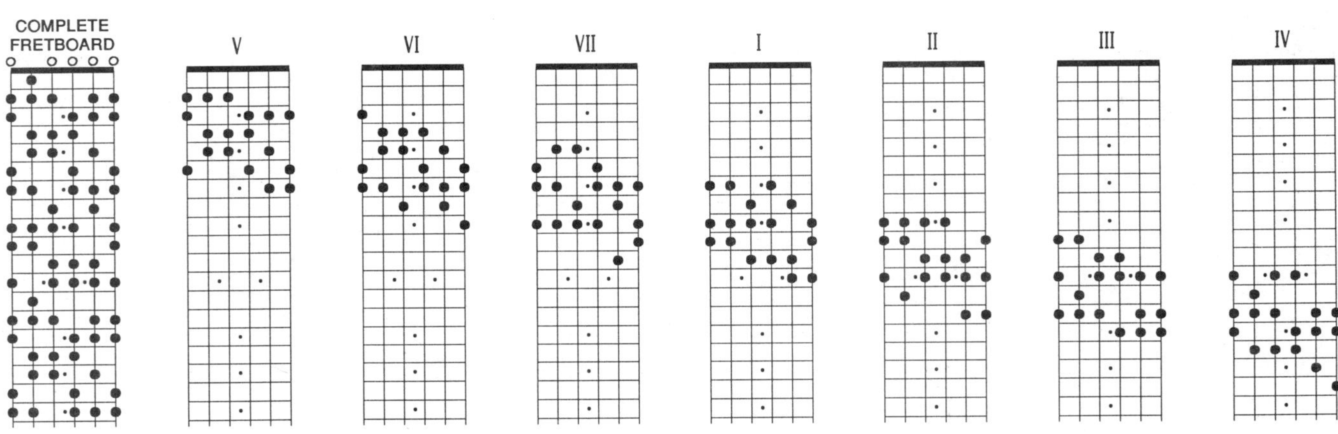

C HARMONIC MINOR

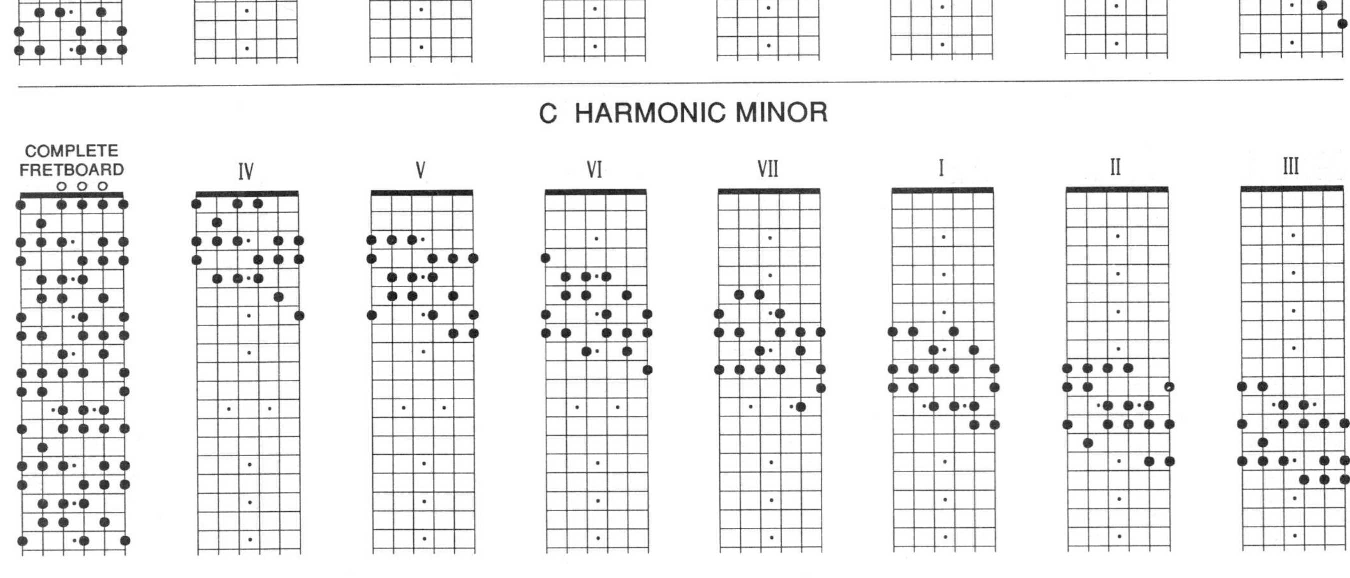

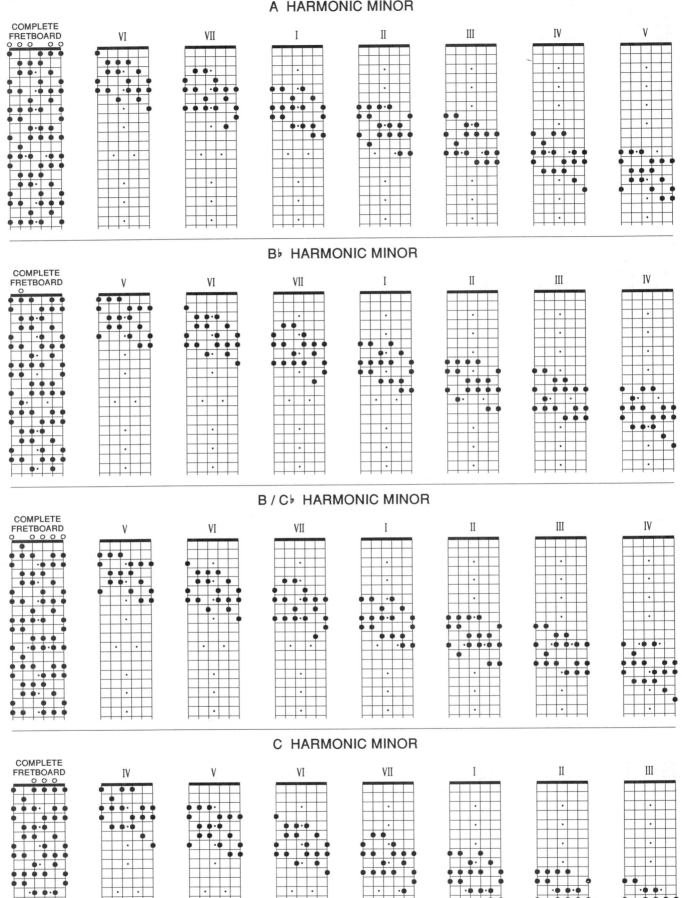

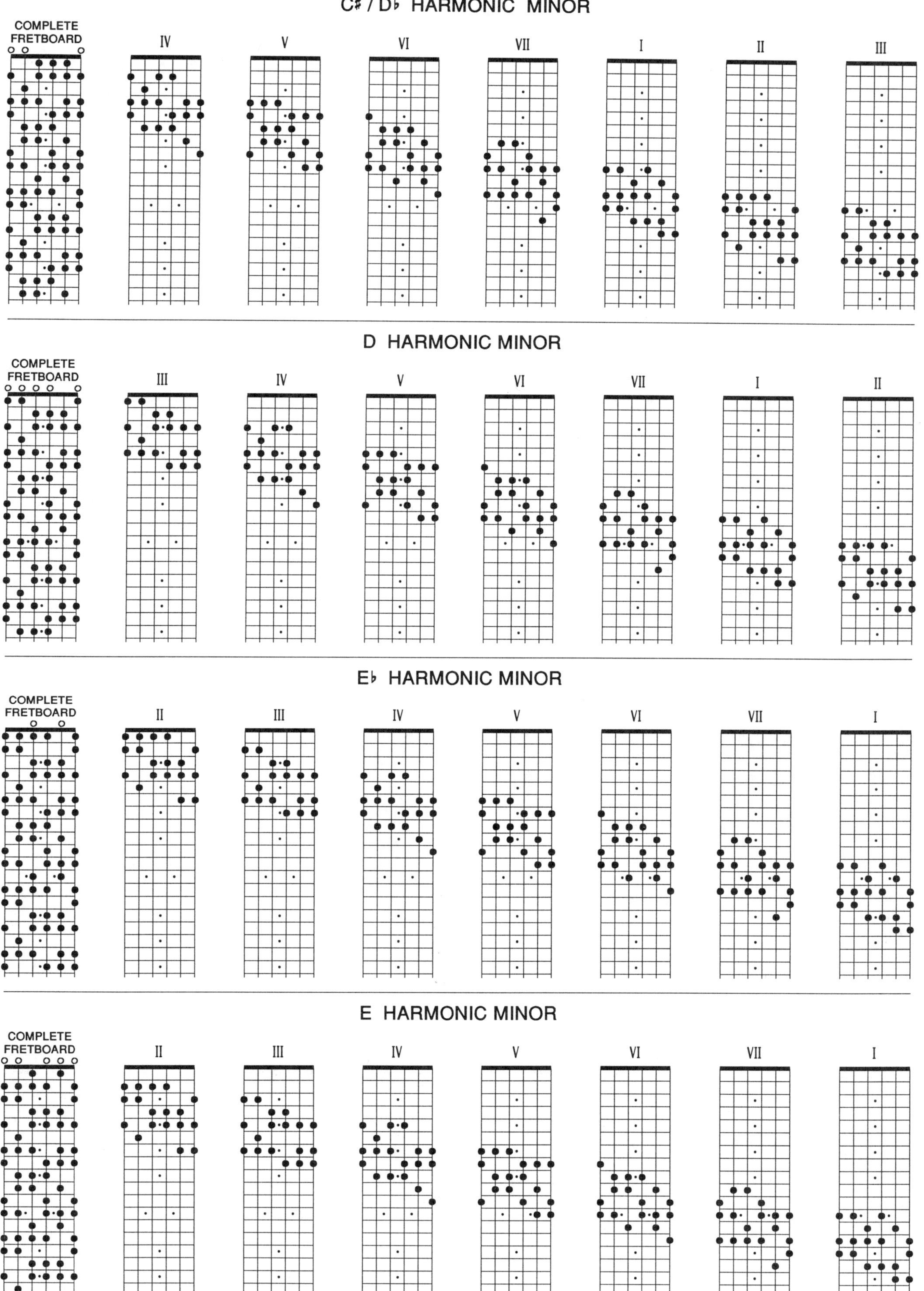
C♯ / D♭ HARMONIC MINOR
COMPLETE FRETBOARD
IV
V
VI
VII
I
II
III
D HARMONIC MINOR
COMPLETE FRETBOARD
III
IV
V
VI
VII
I
II
E♭ HARMONIC MINOR
COMPLETE FRETBOARD
II
III
IV
V
VI
VII
I
E HARMONIC MINOR
COMPLETE FRETBOARD
II
III
IV
V
VI
VII
I

F LOCRIAN ♮6

F♯ / G♭ LOCRIAN ♮6

G LOCRIAN ♮6

A♭ LOCRIAN ♮6

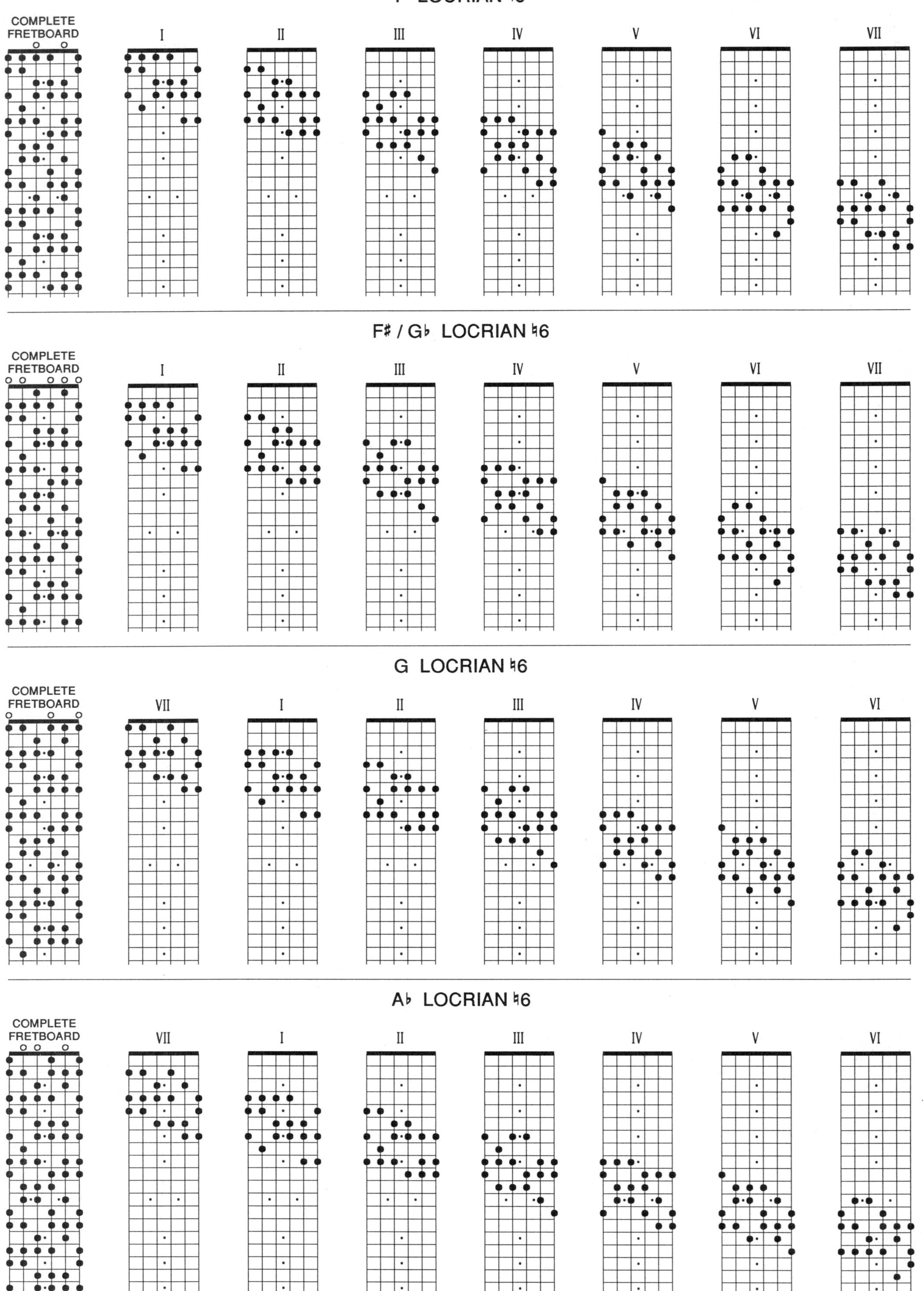

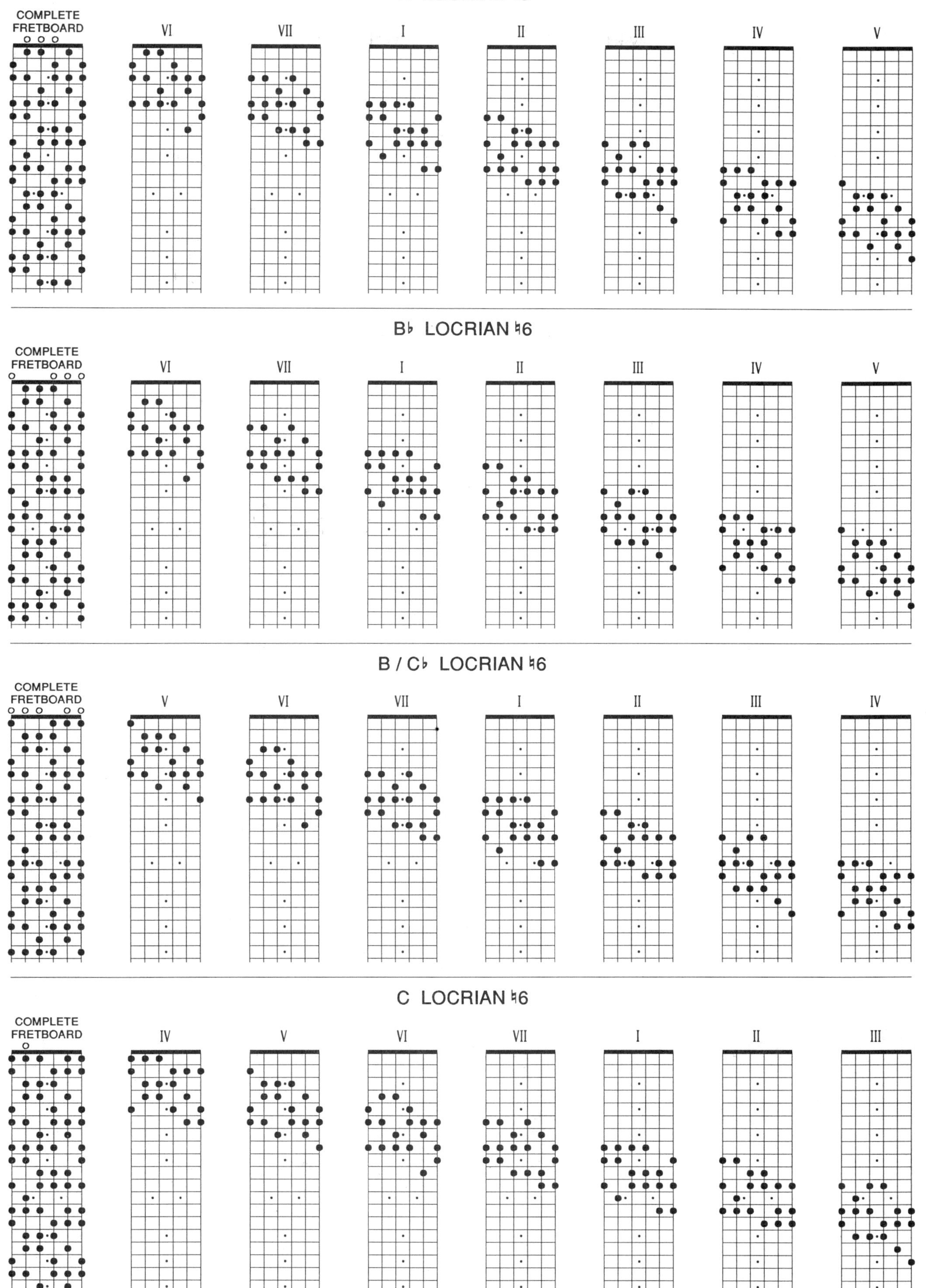
A LOCRIAN ♮6
COMPLETE FRETBOARD
VI
VII
I
II
III
IV
V
B♭ LOCRIAN ♮6
COMPLETE FRETBOARD
VI
VII
I
II
III
IV
V
B / C♭ LOCRIAN ♮6
COMPLETE FRETBOARD
V
VI
VII
I
II
III
IV
C LOCRIAN ♮6
COMPLETE FRETBOARD
IV
V
VI
VII
I
II
III

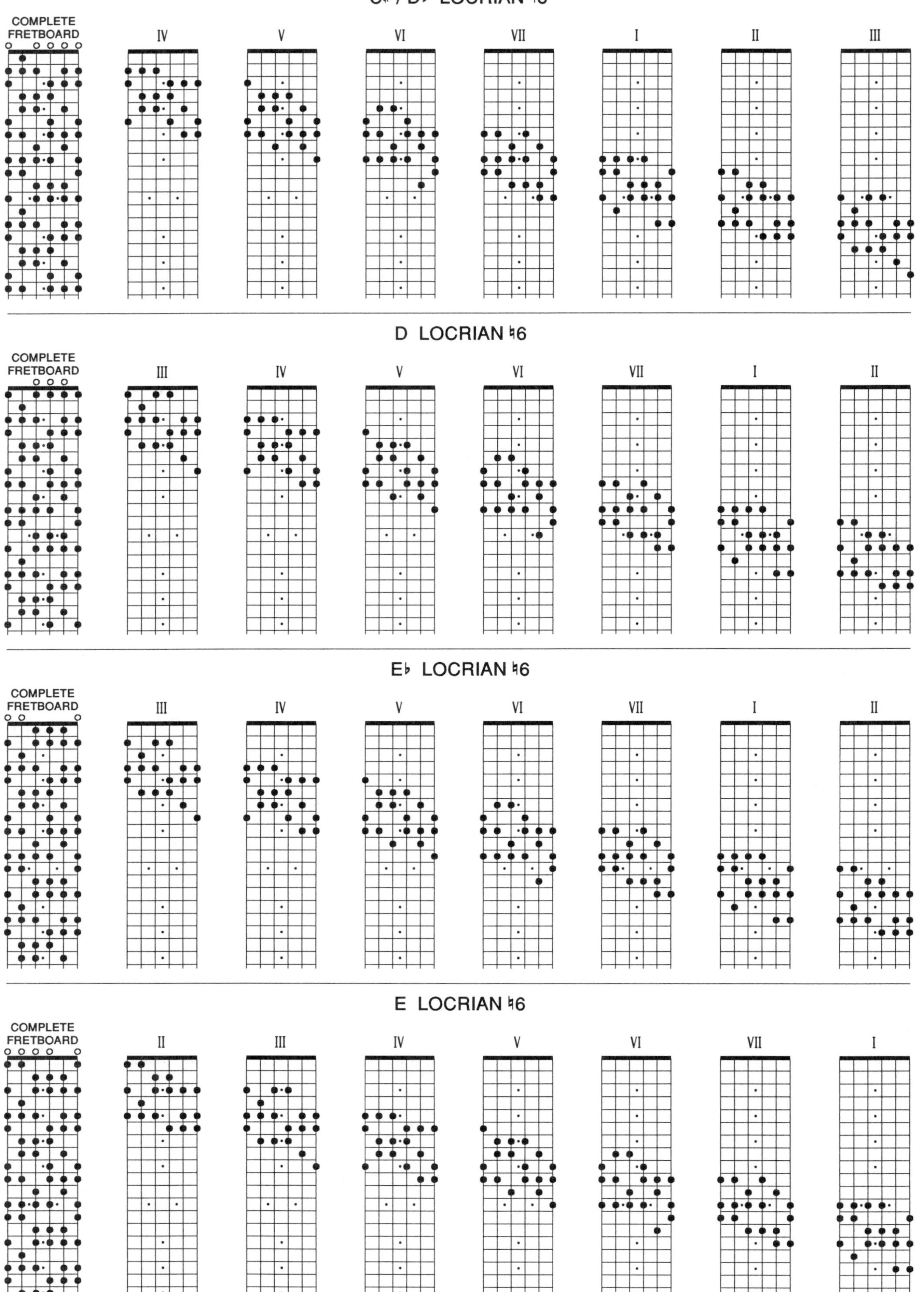
C♯ / D♭ LOCRIAN ♮6
COMPLETE FRETBOARD
IV
V
VI
VII
I
II
III
D LOCRIAN ♮6
COMPLETE FRETBOARD
III
IV
V
VI
VII
I
II
E♭ LOCRIAN ♮6
COMPLETE FRETBOARD
III
IV
V
VI
VII
I
II
E LOCRIAN ♮6
COMPLETE FRETBOARD
II
III
IV
V
VI
VII
I

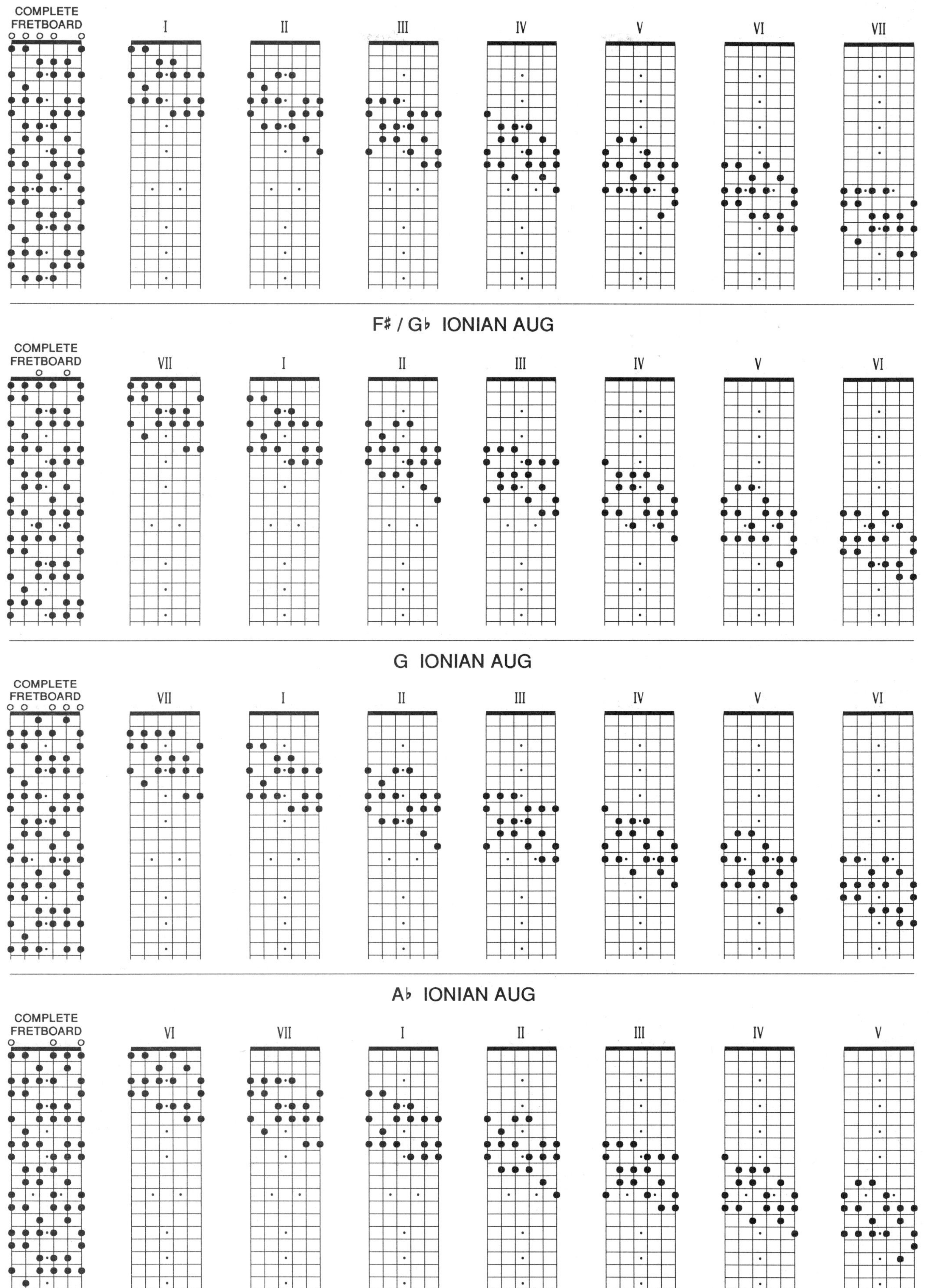
F IONIAN AUG
COMPLETE FRETBOARD
I
II
III
IV
V
VI
VII
F♯ / G♭ IONIAN AUG
COMPLETE FRETBOARD
VII
I
II
III
IV
V
VI
G IONIAN AUG
COMPLETE FRETBOARD
VII
I
II
III
IV
V
VI
A♭ IONIAN AUG
COMPLETE FRETBOARD
VI
VII
I
II
III
IV
V

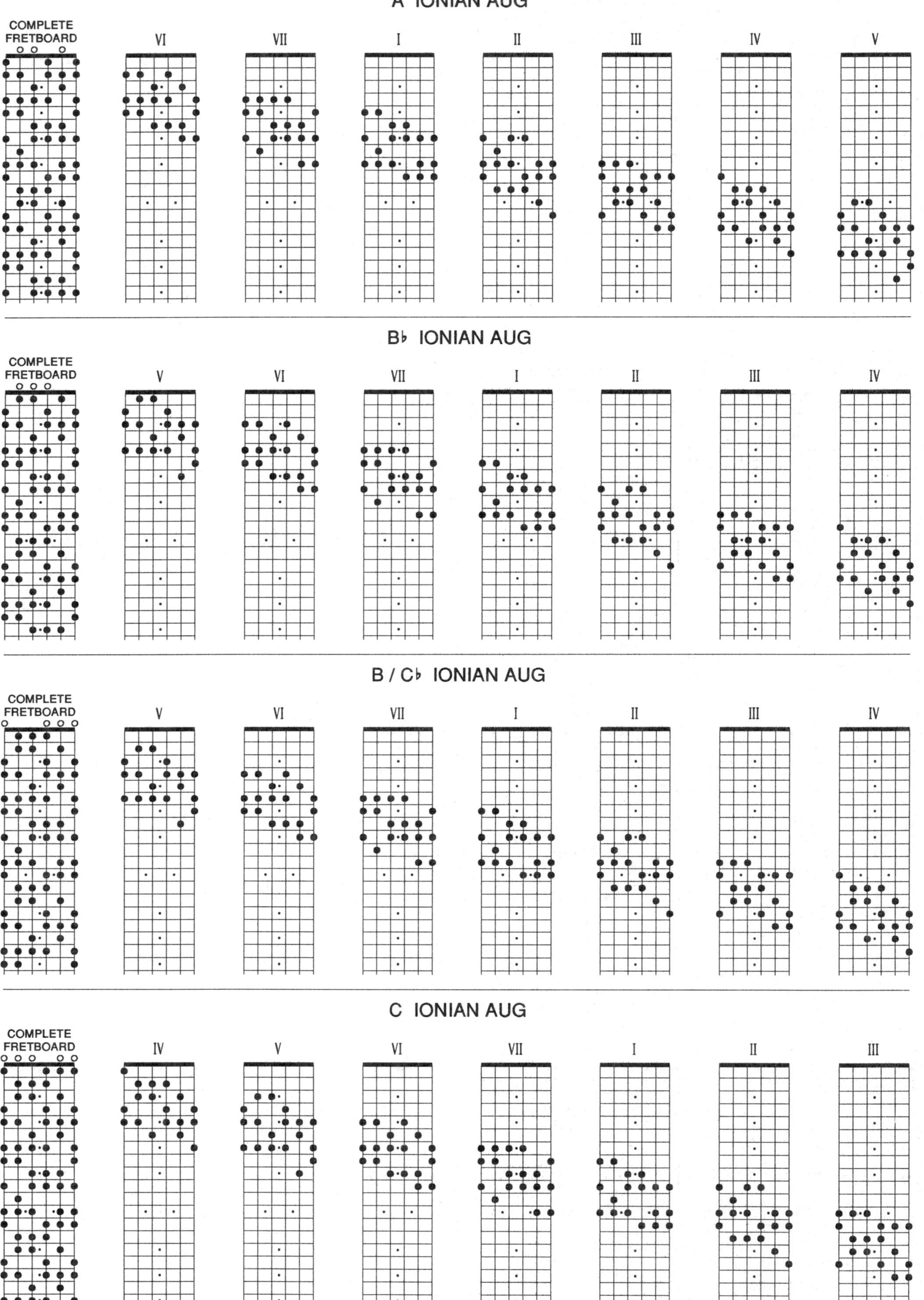
A IONIAN AUG
COMPLETE FRETBOARD
VI
VII
I
II
III
IV
V
B♭ IONIAN AUG
COMPLETE FRETBOARD
V
VI
VII
I
II
III
IV
B / C♭ IONIAN AUG
COMPLETE FRETBOARD
V
VI
VII
I
II
III
IV
C IONIAN AUG
COMPLETE FRETBOARD
IV
V
VI
VII
I
II
III

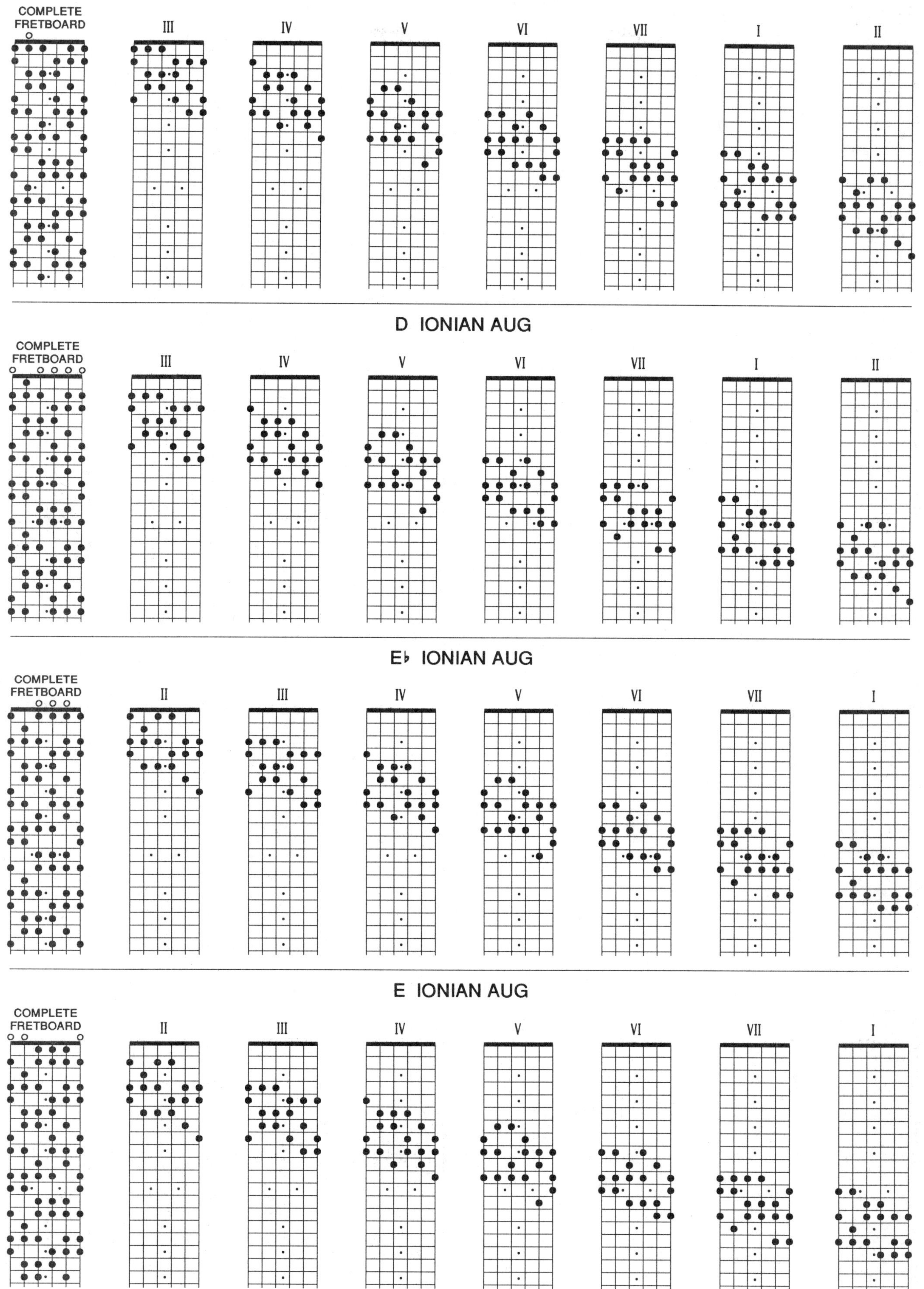
C♯ / D♭ IONIAN AUG
COMPLETE FRETBOARD
III
IV
V
VI
VII
I
II
D IONIAN AUG
COMPLETE FRETBOARD
III
IV
V
VI
VII
I
II
E♭ IONIAN AUG
COMPLETE FRETBOARD
II
III
IV
V
VI
VII
I
E IONIAN AUG
COMPLETE FRETBOARD
II
III
IV
V
VI
VII
I

F DORIAN #4

F# / G♭ DORIAN #4

G DORIAN #4

A♭ DORIAN #4

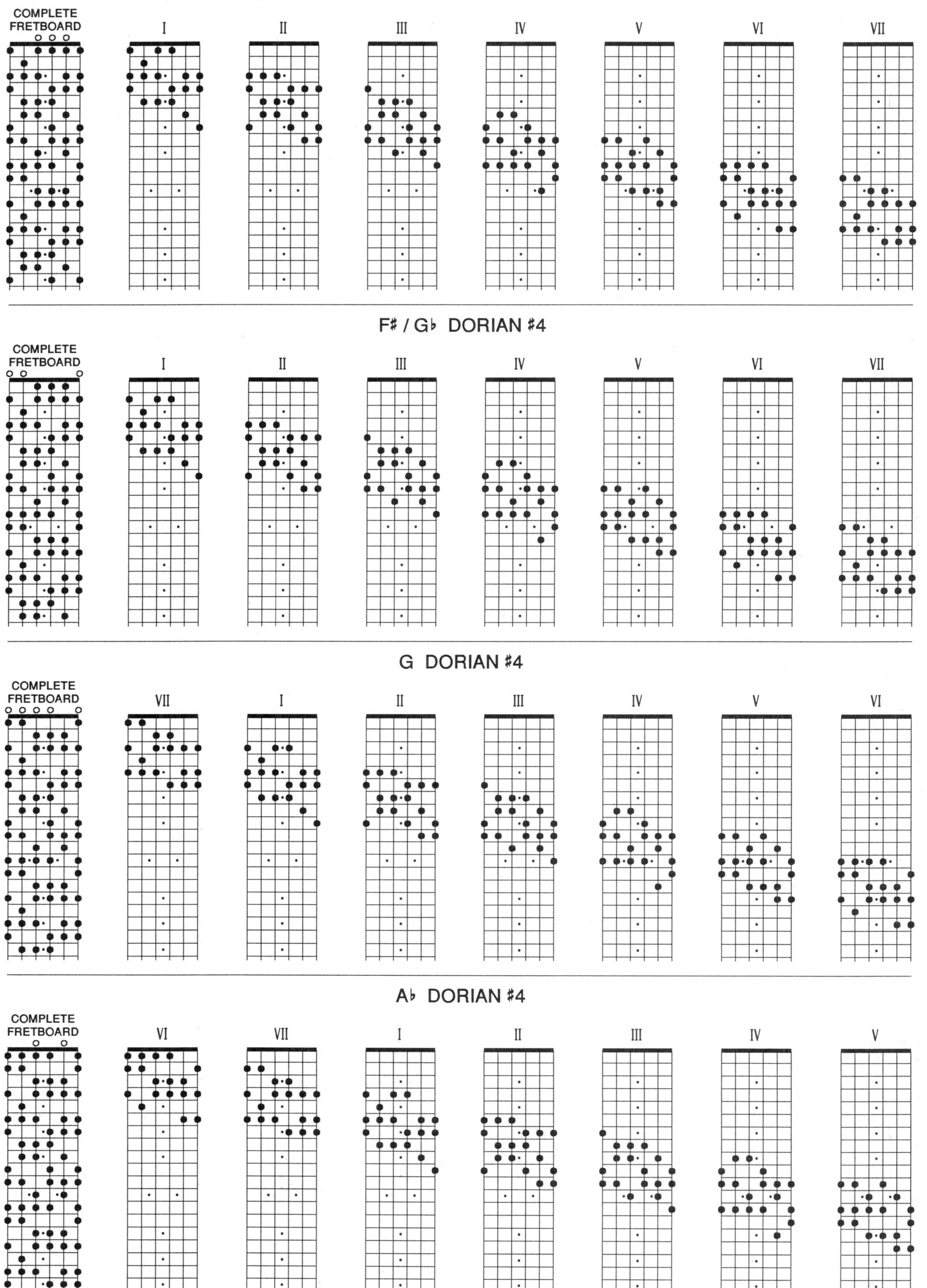

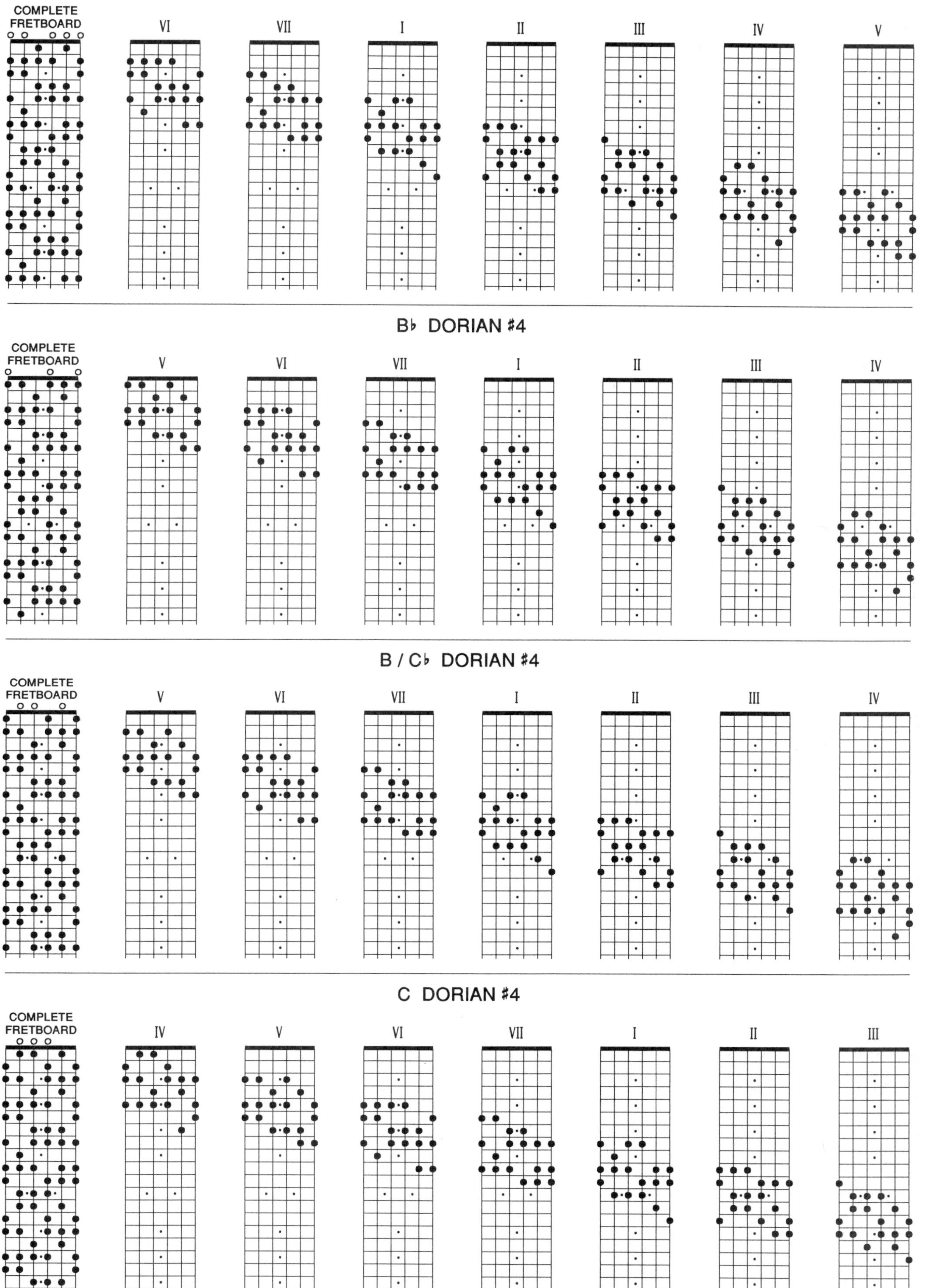
A DORIAN #4
COMPLETE FRETBOARD
VI
VII
I
II
III
IV
V
B♭ DORIAN #4
COMPLETE FRETBOARD
V
VI
VII
I
II
III
IV
B / C♭ DORIAN #4
COMPLETE FRETBOARD
V
VI
VII
I
II
III
IV
C DORIAN #4
COMPLETE FRETBOARD
IV
V
VI
VII
I
II
III

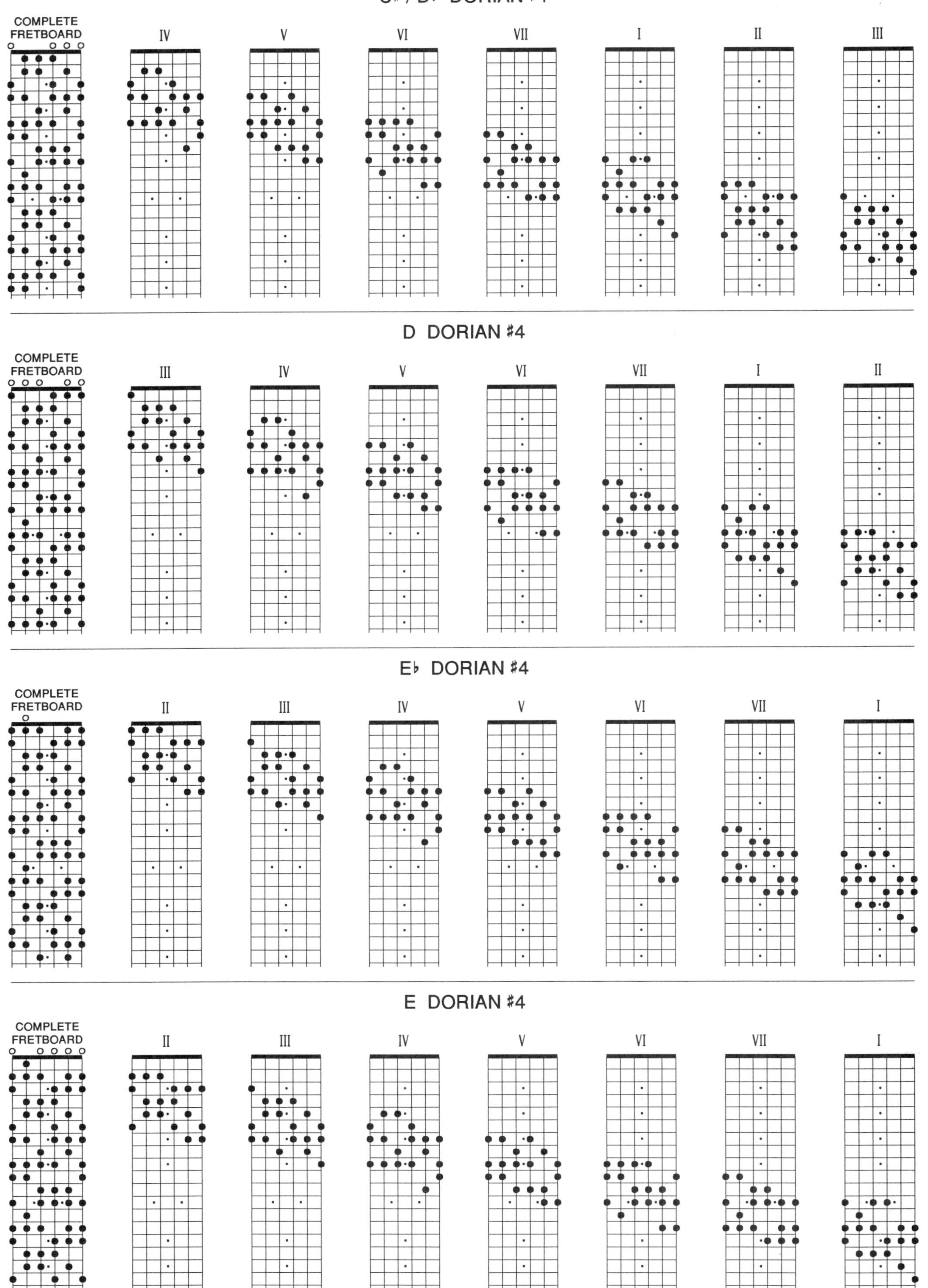
C♯ / D♭ DORIAN ♯4
COMPLETE FRETBOARD
IV V VI VII I II III
D DORIAN ♯4
COMPLETE FRETBOARD
III IV V VI VII I II
E♭ DORIAN ♯4
COMPLETE FRETBOARD
II III IV V VI VII I
E DORIAN ♯4
COMPLETE FRETBOARD
II III IV V VI VII I

F PHRYGIAN MAJOR

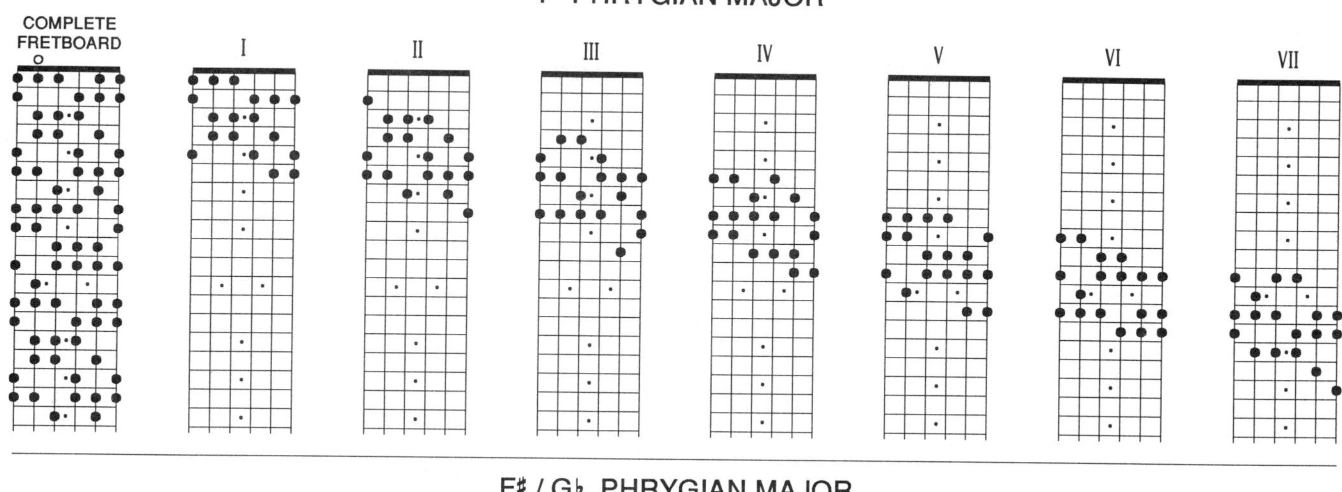

F♯ / G♭ PHRYGIAN MAJOR

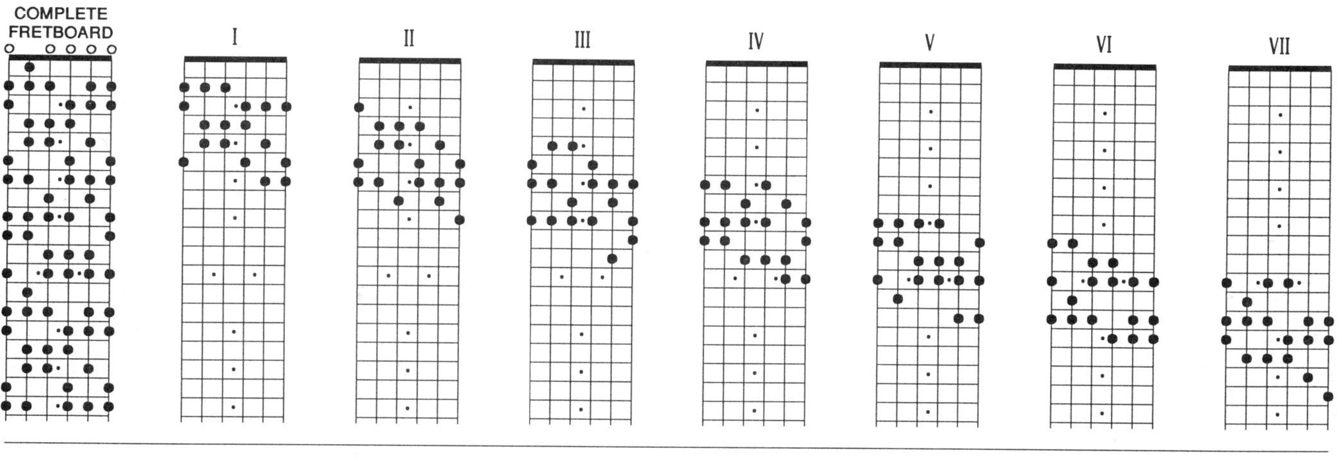

G PHRYGIAN MAJOR

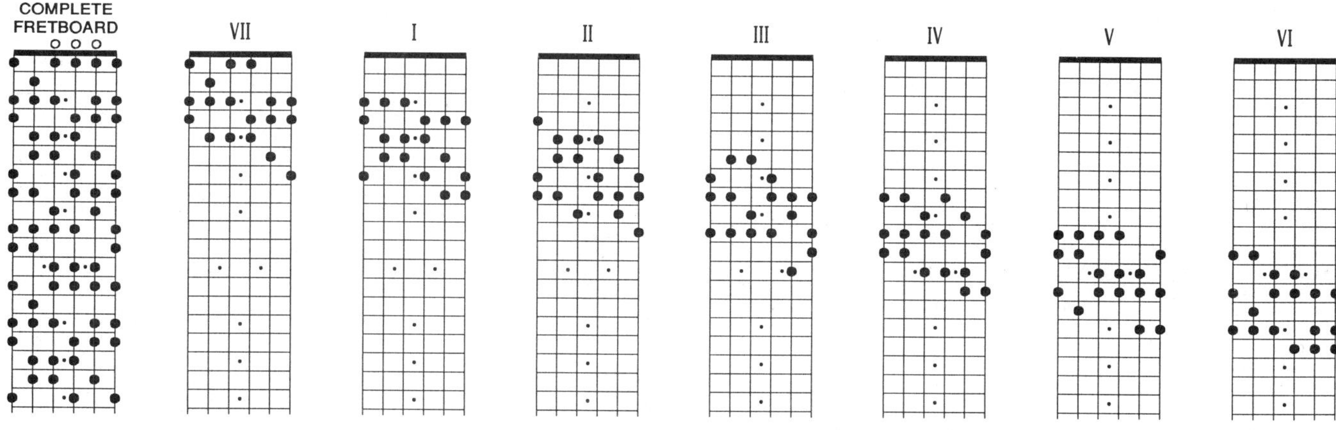

A♭ PHRYGIAN MAJOR

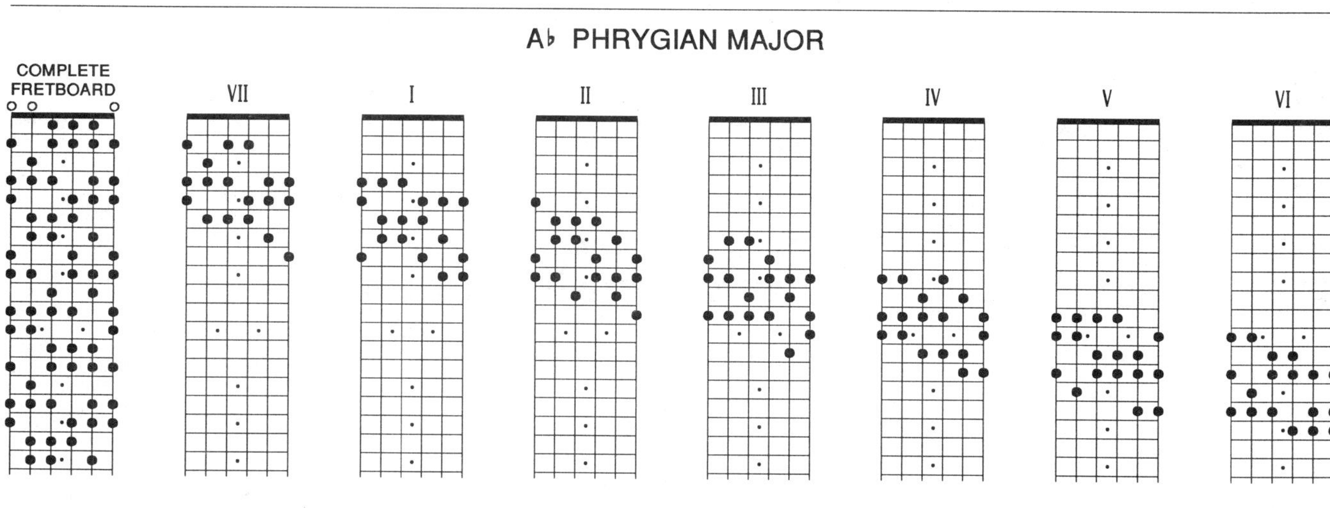

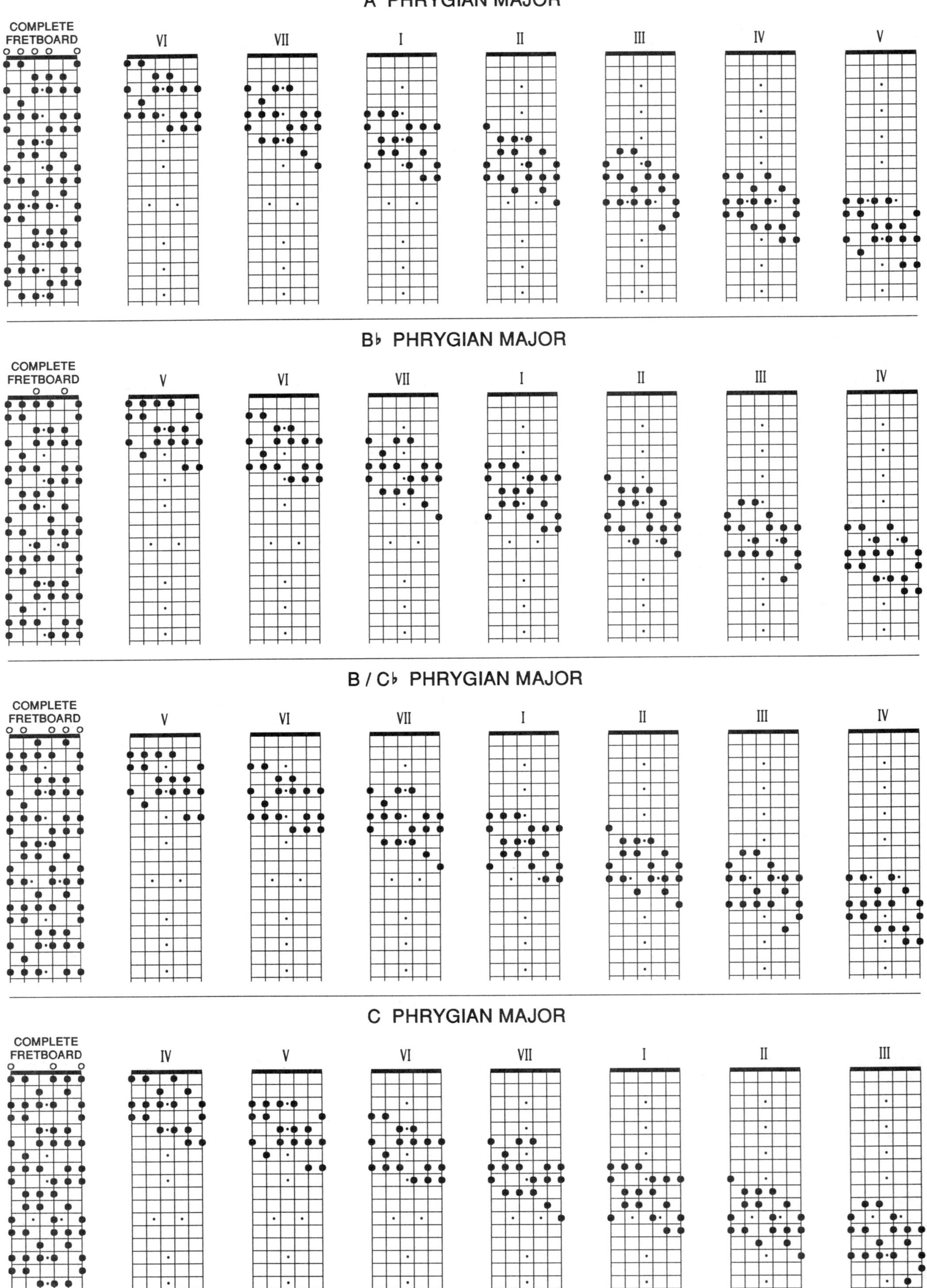
A PHRYGIAN MAJOR
COMPLETE FRETBOARD
VI
VII
I
II
III
IV
V
B♭ PHRYGIAN MAJOR
COMPLETE FRETBOARD
V
VI
VII
I
II
III
IV
B / C♭ PHRYGIAN MAJOR
COMPLETE FRETBOARD
V
VI
VII
I
II
III
IV
C PHRYGIAN MAJOR
COMPLETE FRETBOARD
IV
V
VI
VII
I
II
III

C♯ / D♭ PHRYGIAN MAJOR

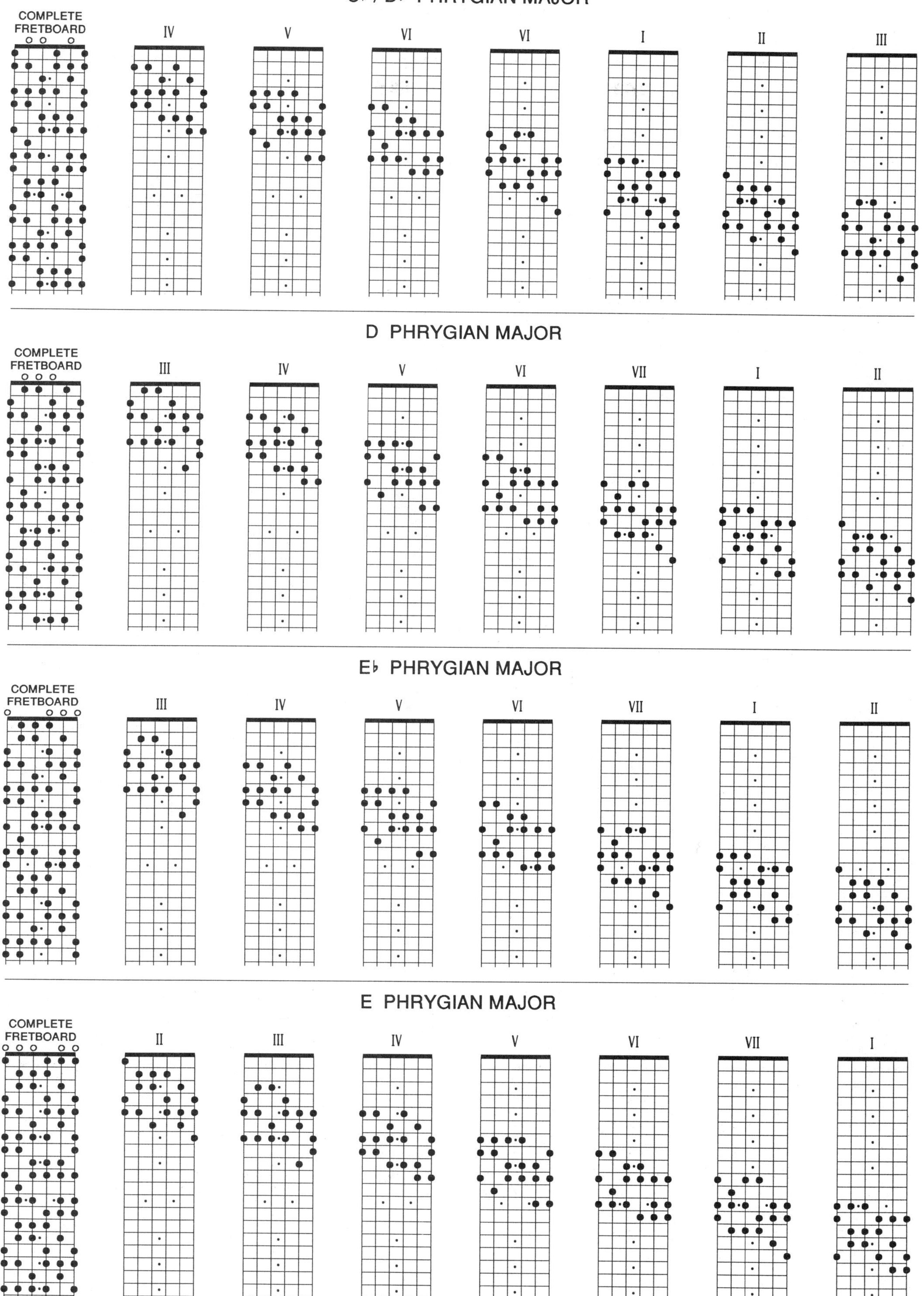

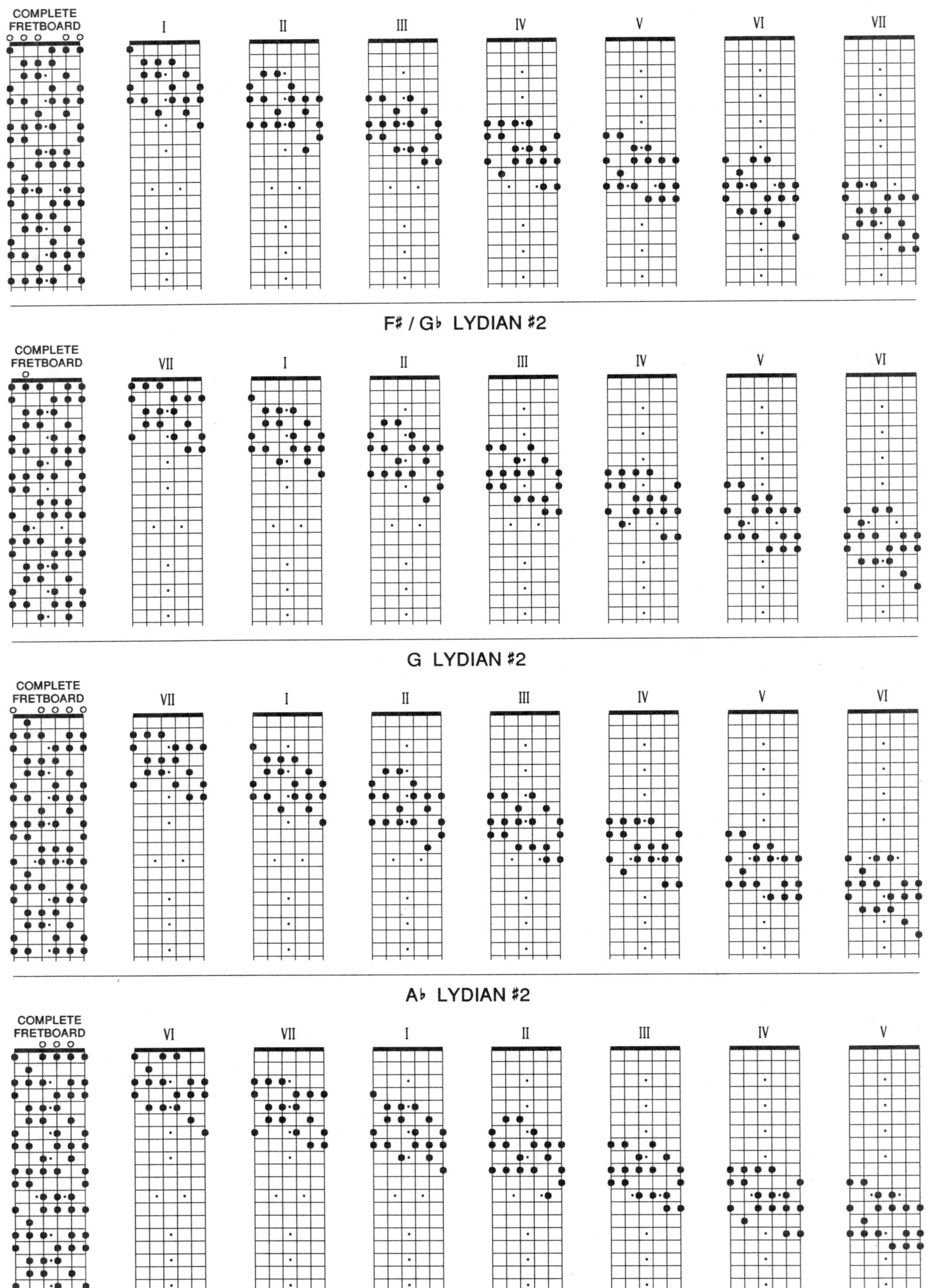
F LYDIAN #2
COMPLETE FRETBOARD
I
II
III
IV
V
VI
VII
F# / G♭ LYDIAN #2
COMPLETE FRETBOARD
VII
I
II
III
IV
V
VI
G LYDIAN #2
COMPLETE FRETBOARD
VII
I
II
III
IV
V
VI
A♭ LYDIAN #2
COMPLETE FRETBOARD
VI
VII
I
II
III
IV
V

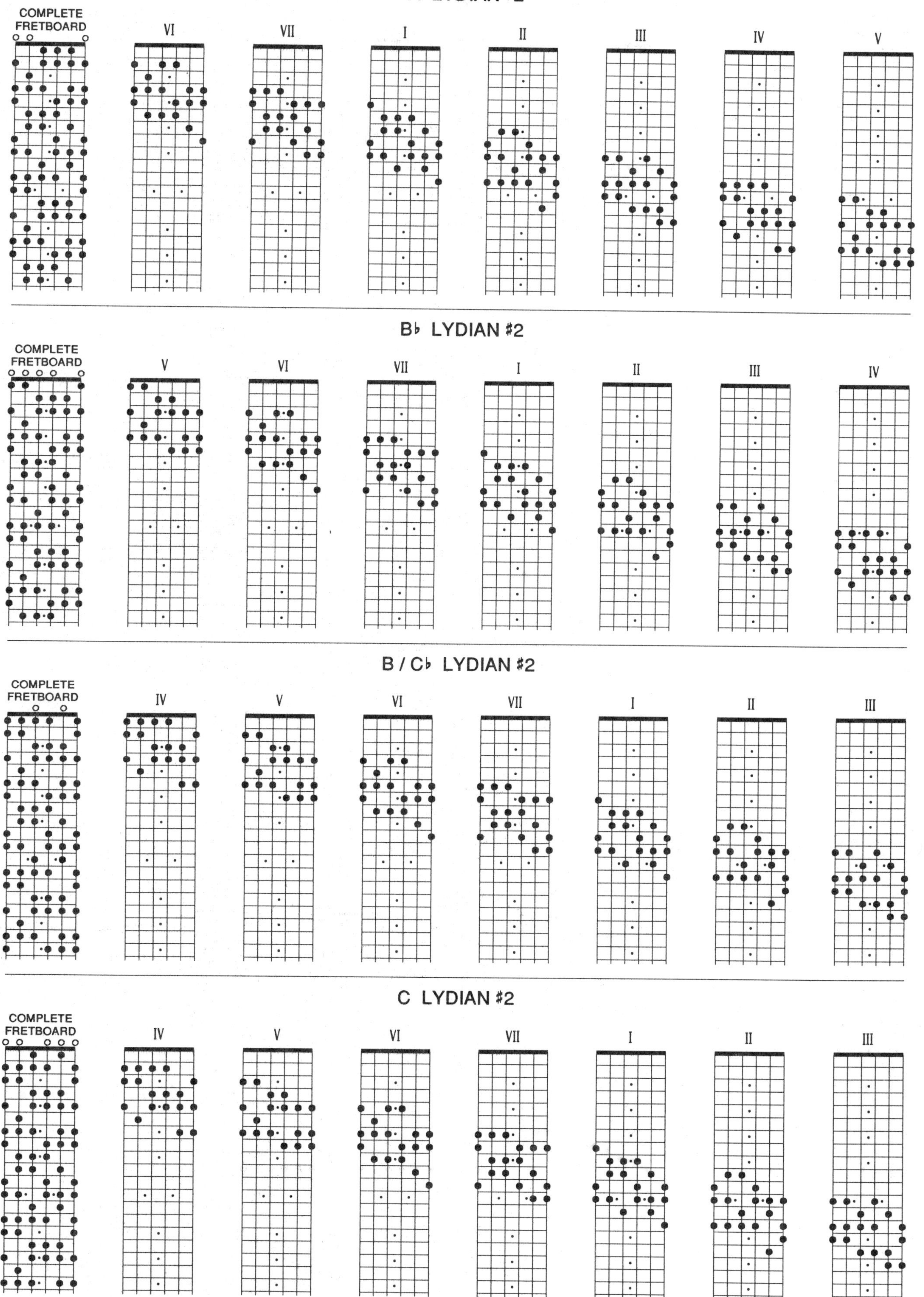
A LYDIAN #2
COMPLETE FRETBOARD
VI
VII
I
II
III
IV
V
B♭ LYDIAN #2
COMPLETE FRETBOARD
V
VI
VII
I
II
III
IV
B / C♭ LYDIAN #2
COMPLETE FRETBOARD
IV
V
VI
VII
I
II
III
C LYDIAN #2
COMPLETE FRETBOARD
IV
V
VI
VII
I
II
III

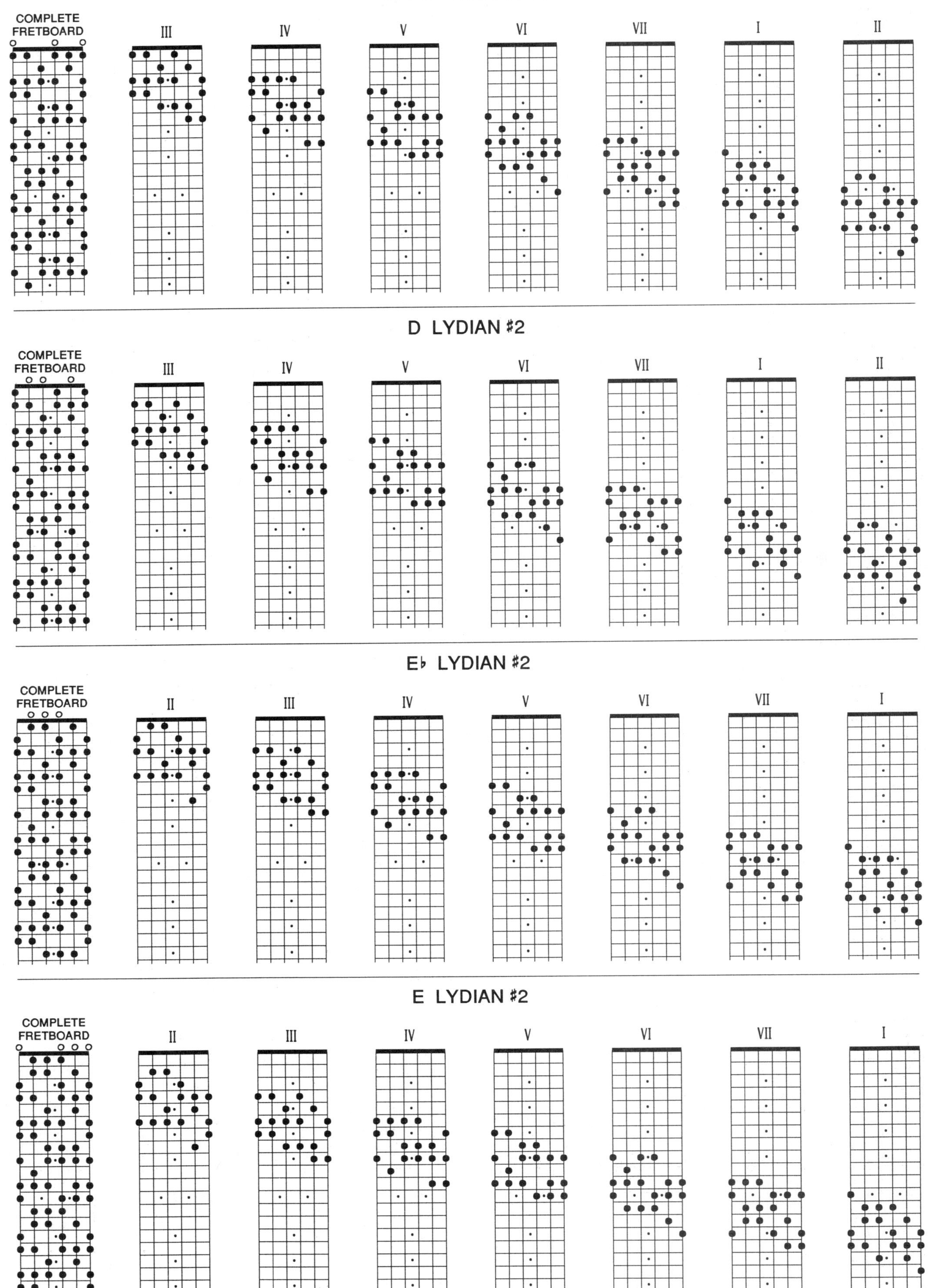
C♯ / D♭ LYDIAN ♯2
COMPLETE FRETBOARD
III
IV
V
VI
VII
I
II
D LYDIAN ♯2
COMPLETE FRETBOARD
III
IV
V
VI
VII
I
II
E♭ LYDIAN ♯2
COMPLETE FRETBOARD
II
III
IV
V
VI
VII
I
E LYDIAN ♯2
COMPLETE FRETBOARD
II
III
IV
V
VI
VII
I

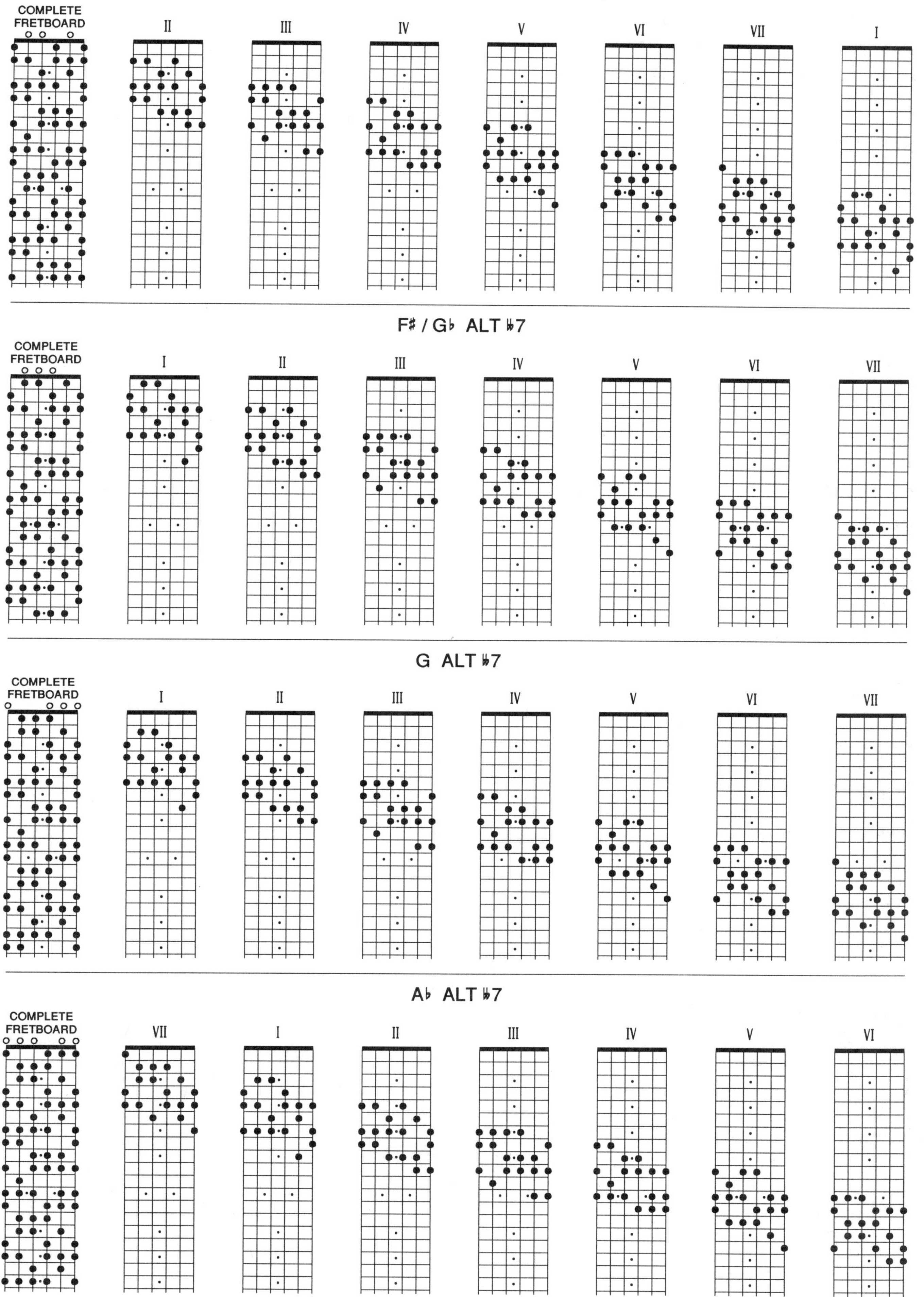
F ALT 𝄫7
COMPLETE FRETBOARD
II
III
IV
V
VI
VII
I
F♯ / G♭ ALT 𝄫7
COMPLETE FRETBOARD
I
II
III
IV
V
VI
VII
G ALT 𝄫7
COMPLETE FRETBOARD
I
II
III
IV
V
VI
VII
A♭ ALT 𝄫7
COMPLETE FRETBOARD
VII
I
II
III
IV
V
VI

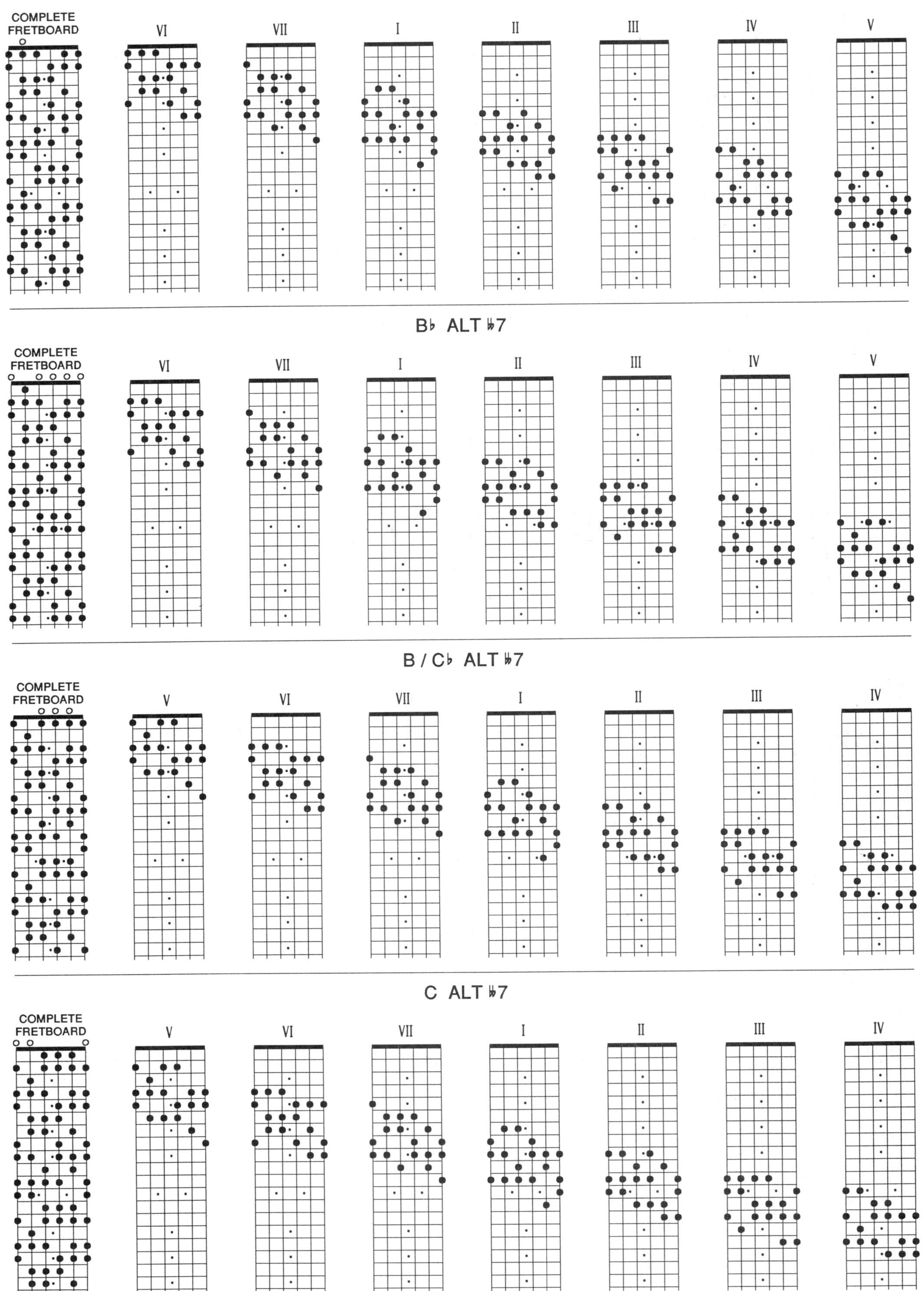
A ALT 𝄫7
COMPLETE FRETBOARD
VI
VII
I
II
III
IV
V
B♭ ALT 𝄫7
COMPLETE FRETBOARD
VI
VII
I
II
III
IV
V
B / C♭ ALT 𝄫7
COMPLETE FRETBOARD
V
VI
VII
I
II
III
IV
C ALT 𝄫7
COMPLETE FRETBOARD
V
VI
VII
I
II
III
IV

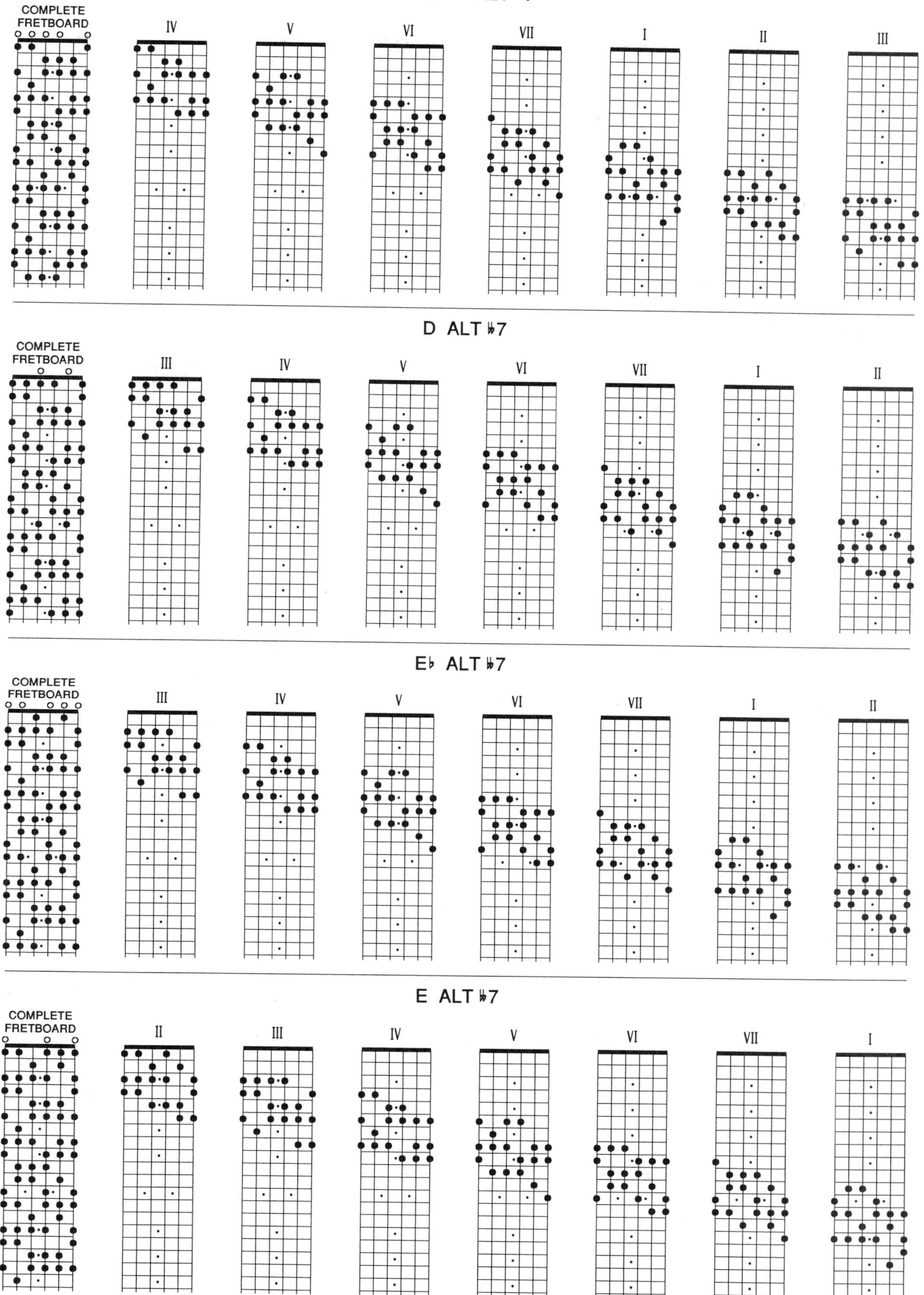
C♯ / D♭ ALT 𝄫7
COMPLETE FRETBOARD
IV
V
VI
VII
I
II
III
D ALT 𝄫7
COMPLETE FRETBOARD
III
IV
V
VI
VII
I
II
E♭ ALT 𝄫7
COMPLETE FRETBOARD
III
IV
V
VI
VII
I
II
E ALT 𝄫7
COMPLETE FRETBOARD
II
III
IV
V
VI
VII
I

HARMONIC MAJOR

KEYBOARD PATTERNS

QUICK MODE GENERATOR CHART

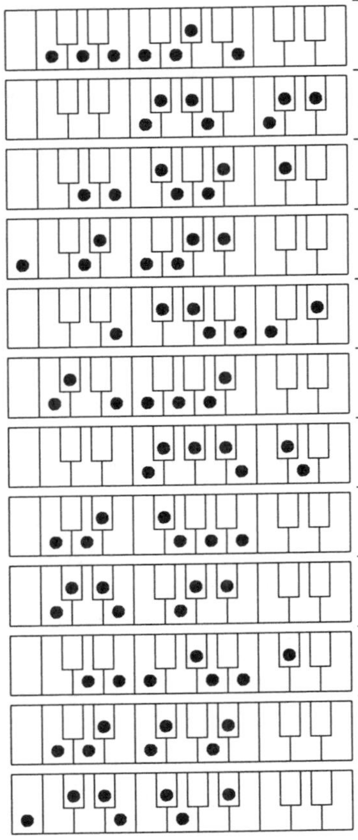

I	II	III	IV	V	VI	VII
C	B♭	A♭	G	F	E	C♯/D♭
C♯/D♭	B/C♭	A	A♭	F♯/G♭	F	D
D	C	B♭	A	G	F♯/G♭	E♭
E♭	C♯/D♭	B/C♭	B♭	A♭	G	E
E	D	C	B/C♭	A	A♭	F
F	E♭	C♯/D♭	C	B♭	A	F♯/G♭
F♯/G♭	E	D	C♯/D♭	B/C♭	B♭	G
G	F	E♭	D	C	B/C♭	A♭
A♭	F♯/G♭	E	E♭	C♯/D♭	C	A
A	G	F	E	D	C♯/D♭	B♭
B♭	A♭	F♯/G♭	F	E♭	D	B/C♭
B/C♭	A	G	F♯/G♭	E	E♭	C

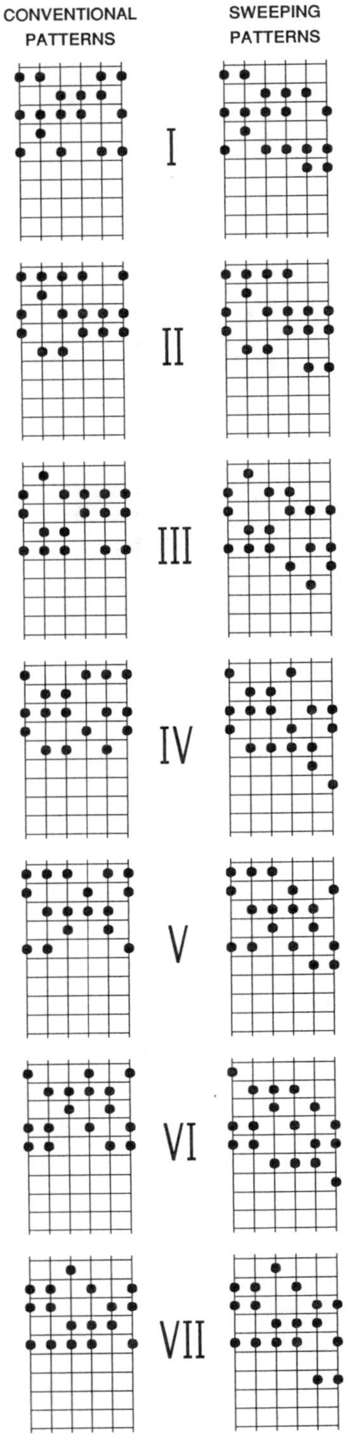

CONVENTIONAL PATTERNS

SWEEPING PATTERNS

I

II

III

IV

V

VI

VII

SCALE / MODE - CHORD CHART

I	HARMONIC MAJOR	△, △+, △sus2, △sus, ♭6
II	DORIAN ♭5	∅, °7, °9
III	PHRYGIAN ♭4	7, 7+, -7, ♭9, ♯9, ♭13
IV	LYDIAN ♭3	-△, △°, -6, °7
V	DOMINANT ♭2	7, 6, 7sus, ♭9, 11, 13
VI	LYDIAN AUGMENTED ♯2	△+, -△+, △♭5
VII	LOCRIAN 𝄫7	○, °7

NUMERIC SCALE / MODE CHART

		1		2		3	4		5		6		7	1		2		3	4		5		6		7
I	HARMONIC MAJOR	1		2		3	4		5	♭6			7	1		2		3	4		5	♭6			7
II	DORIAN ♭5			1		2	♭3		4	♭5			6	♭7											
III	PHRYGIAN ♭4					1	♭2		♭3	♭4			5	♭6		♭7									
IV	LYDIAN ♭3						1		2	♭3			♯4	5		6		7							
V	DOMINANT ♭2								1	♭2			3	4		5		6	♭7						
VI	LYDIAN AUG ♯2									1			♯2	3		♯4		♯5	6		7				
VII	LOCRIAN 𝄫7												1	♭2		♭3		4	♭5		♭6	𝄫7			

F HARMONIC MAJOR

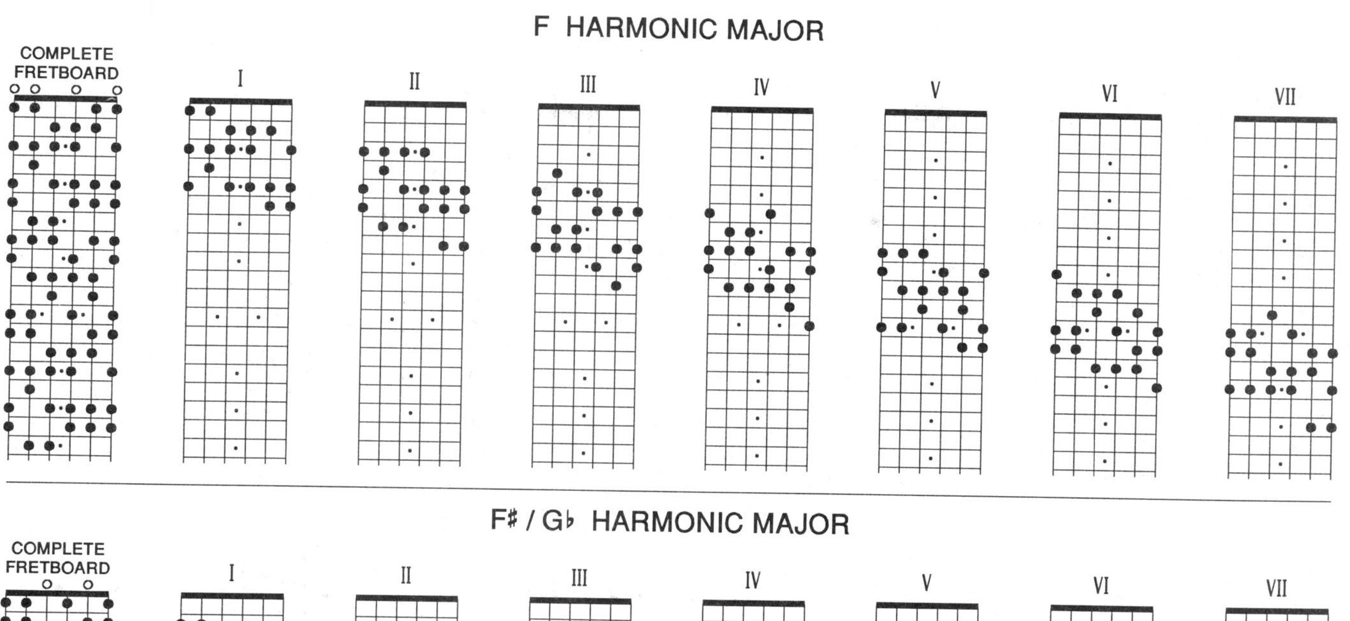

COMPLETE FRETBOARD
I
II
III
IV
V
VI
VII

F♯ / G♭ HARMONIC MAJOR

COMPLETE FRETBOARD
I
II
III
IV
V
VI
VII

G HARMONIC MAJOR

COMPLETE FRETBOARD
VII
I
II
III
IV
V
VI

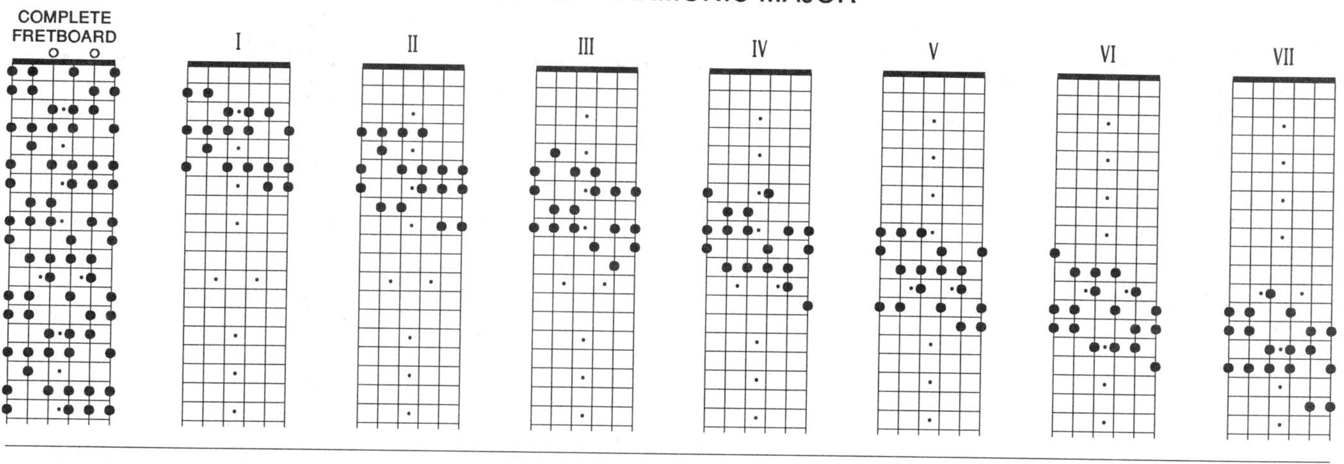

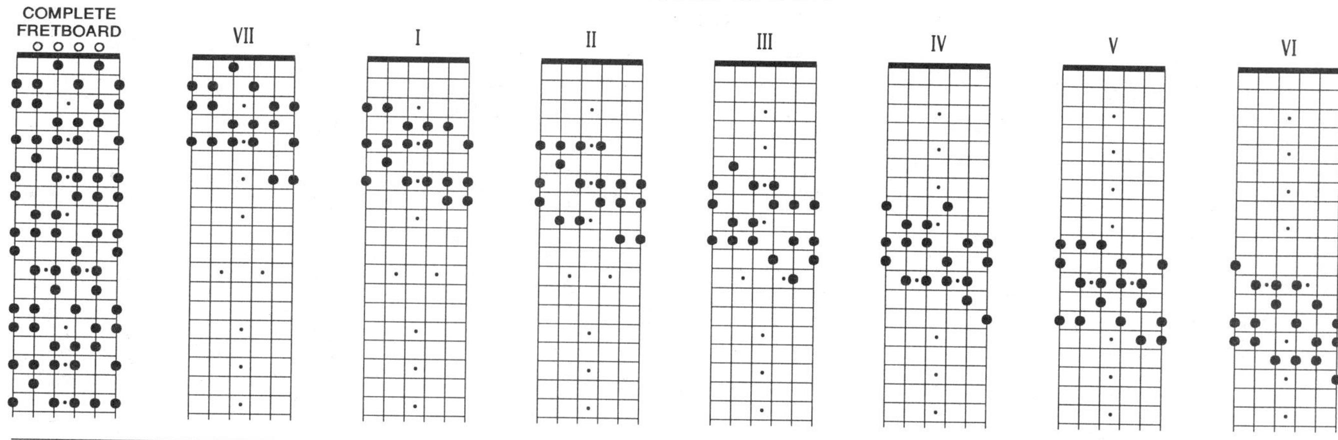

A♭ HARMONIC MAJOR

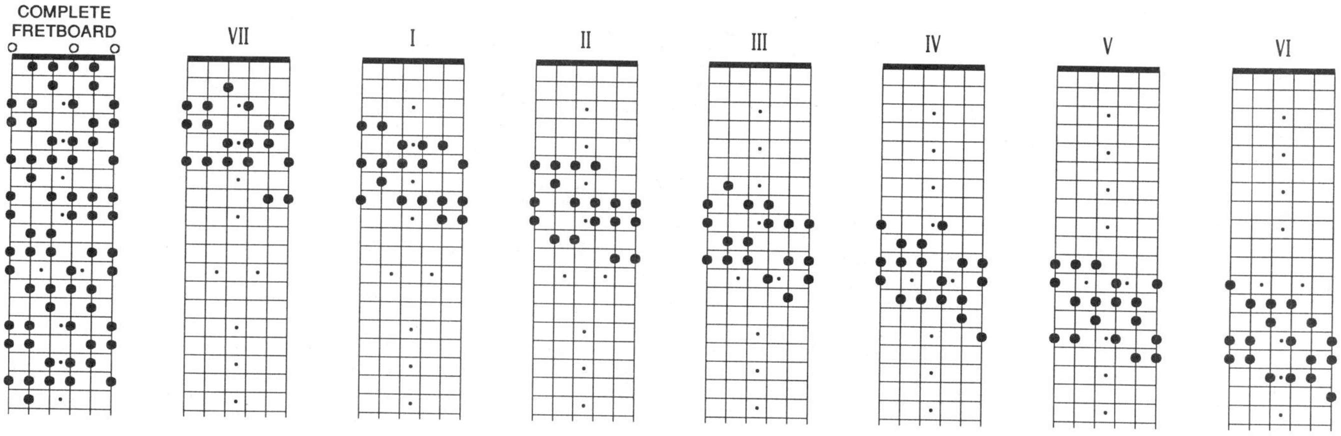

COMPLETE FRETBOARD
VII
I
II
III
IV
V
VI

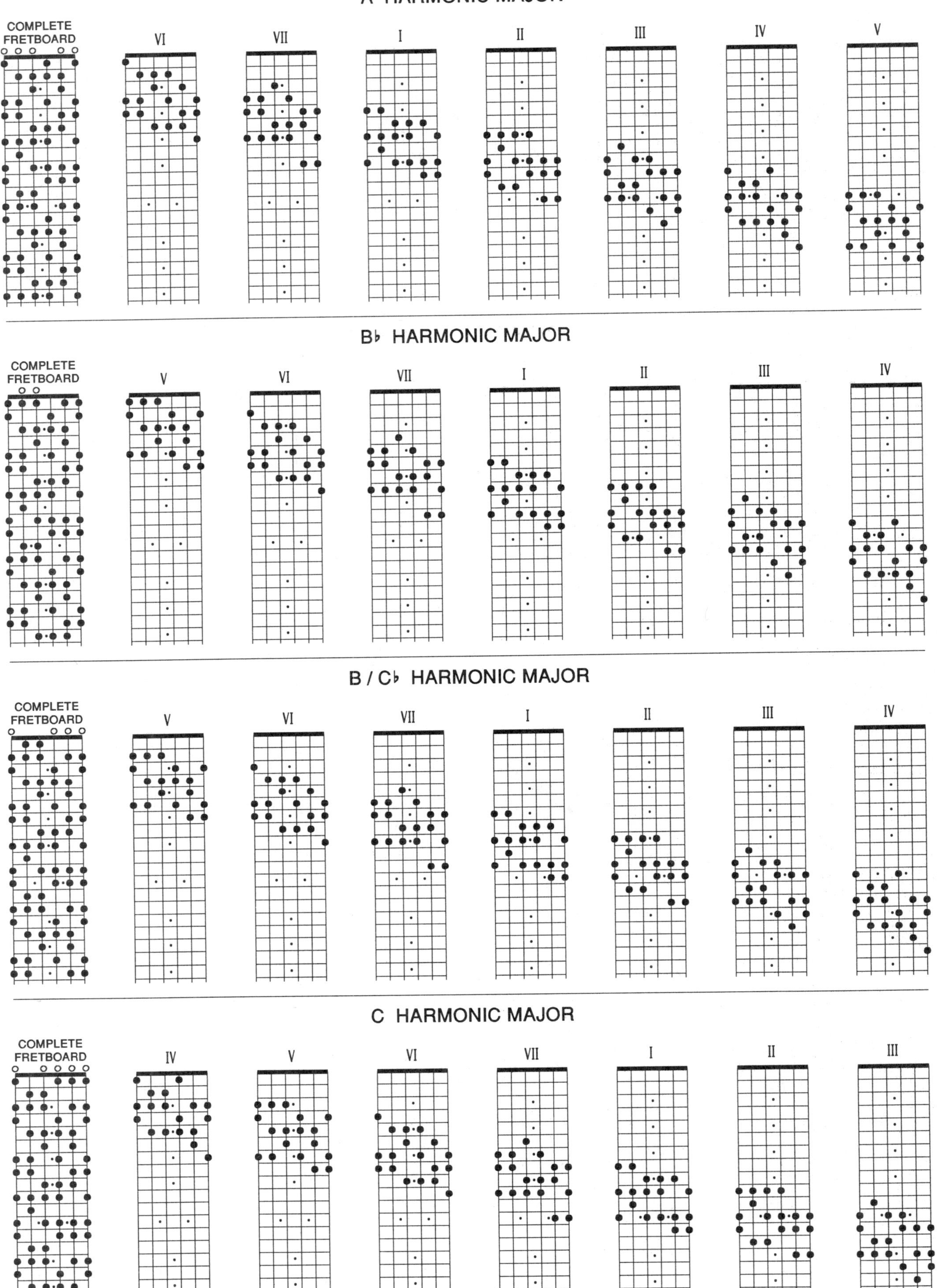
A HARMONIC MAJOR
COMPLETE FRETBOARD
VI
VII
I
II
III
IV
V
B♭ HARMONIC MAJOR
COMPLETE FRETBOARD
V
VI
VII
I
II
III
IV
B / C♭ HARMONIC MAJOR
COMPLETE FRETBOARD
V
VI
VII
I
II
III
IV
C HARMONIC MAJOR
COMPLETE FRETBOARD
IV
V
VI
VII
I
II
III

C♯ / D♭ HARMONIC MAJOR

D HARMONIC MAJOR

E♭ HARMONIC MAJOR

E HARMONIC MAJOR

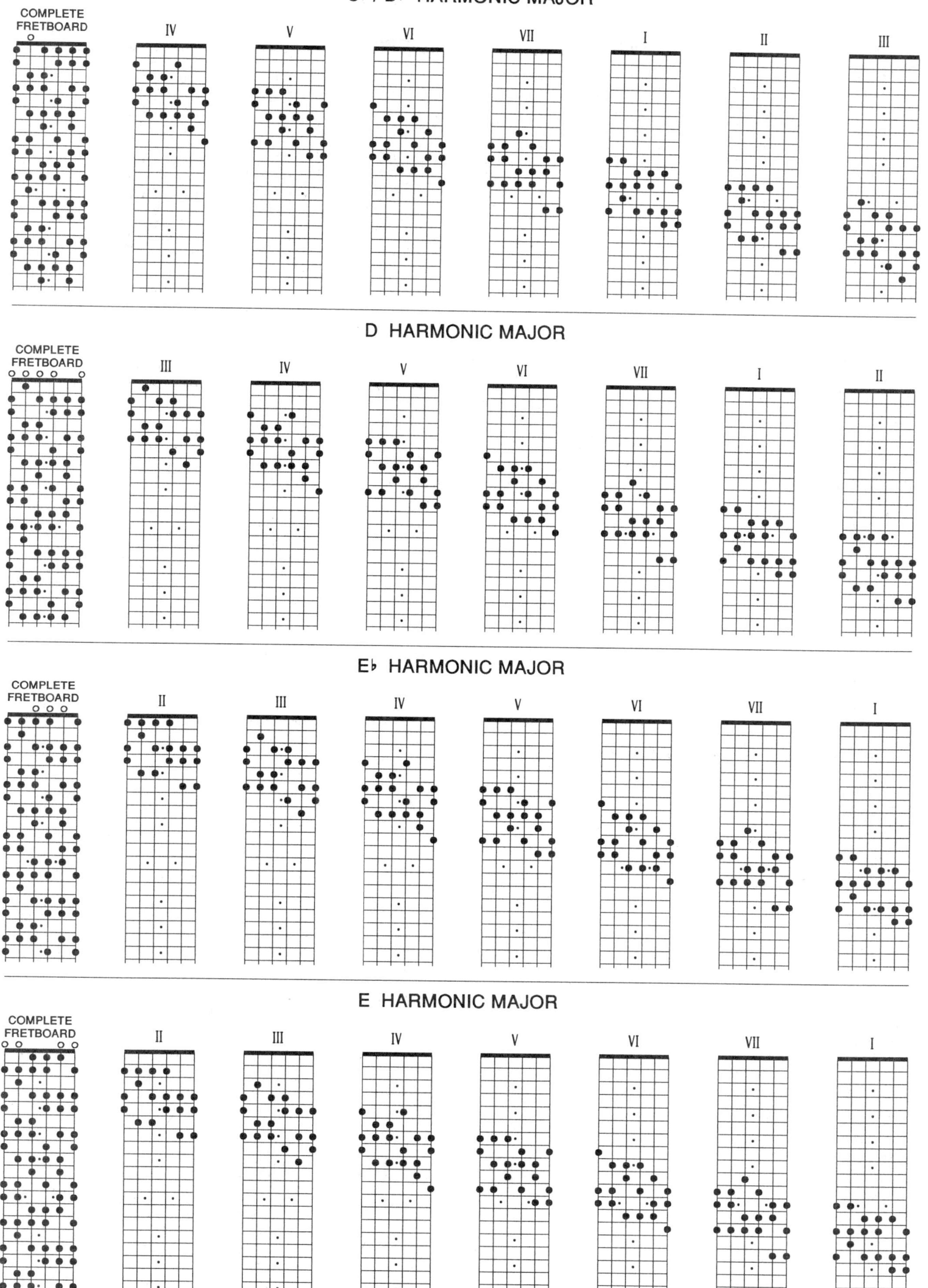

F DORIAN ♭5

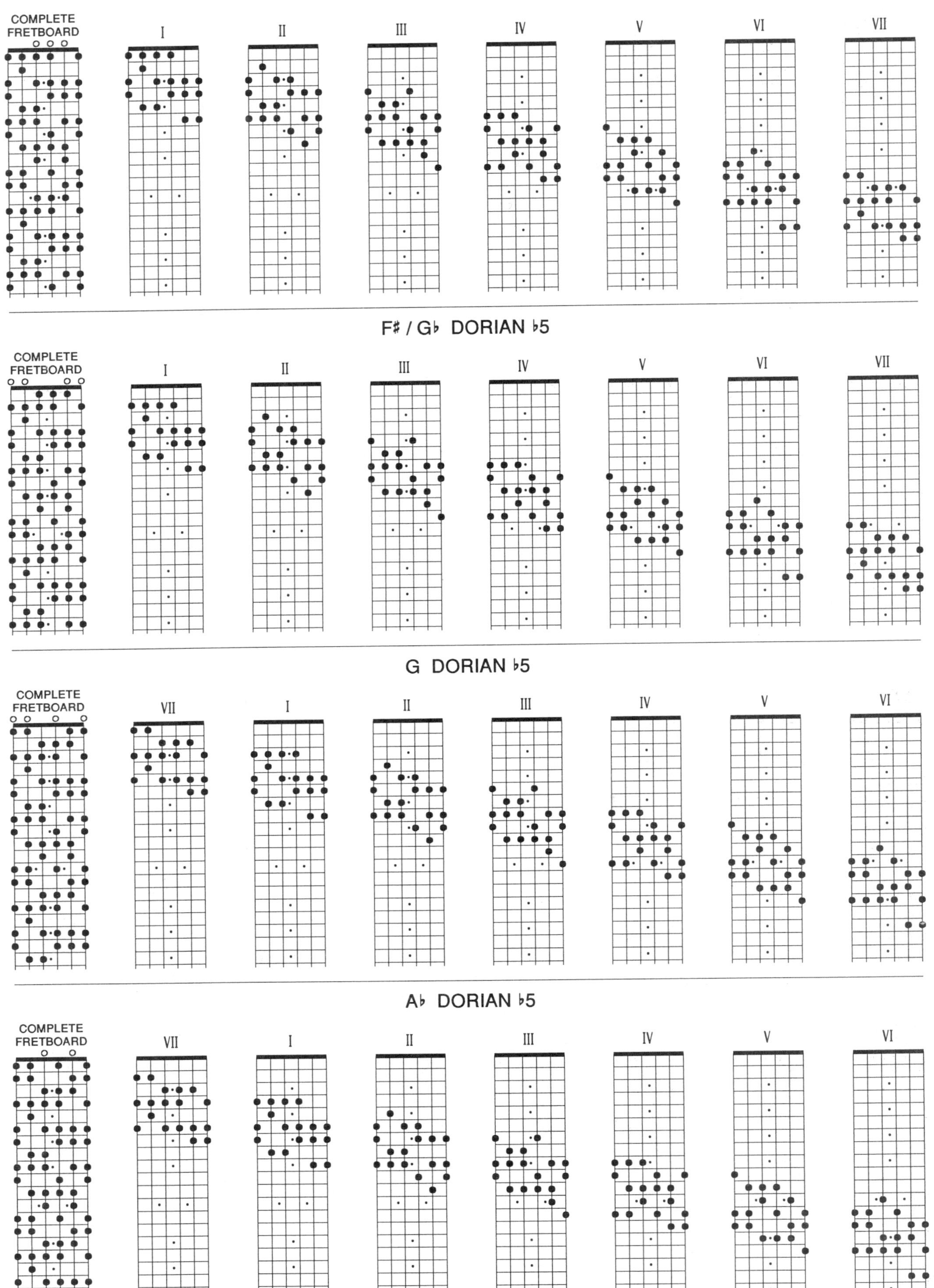

F♯ / G♭ DORIAN ♭5

G DORIAN ♭5

A♭ DORIAN ♭5

A DORIAN ♭5

B♭ DORIAN ♭5

B / C♭ DORIAN ♭5

C DORIAN ♭5

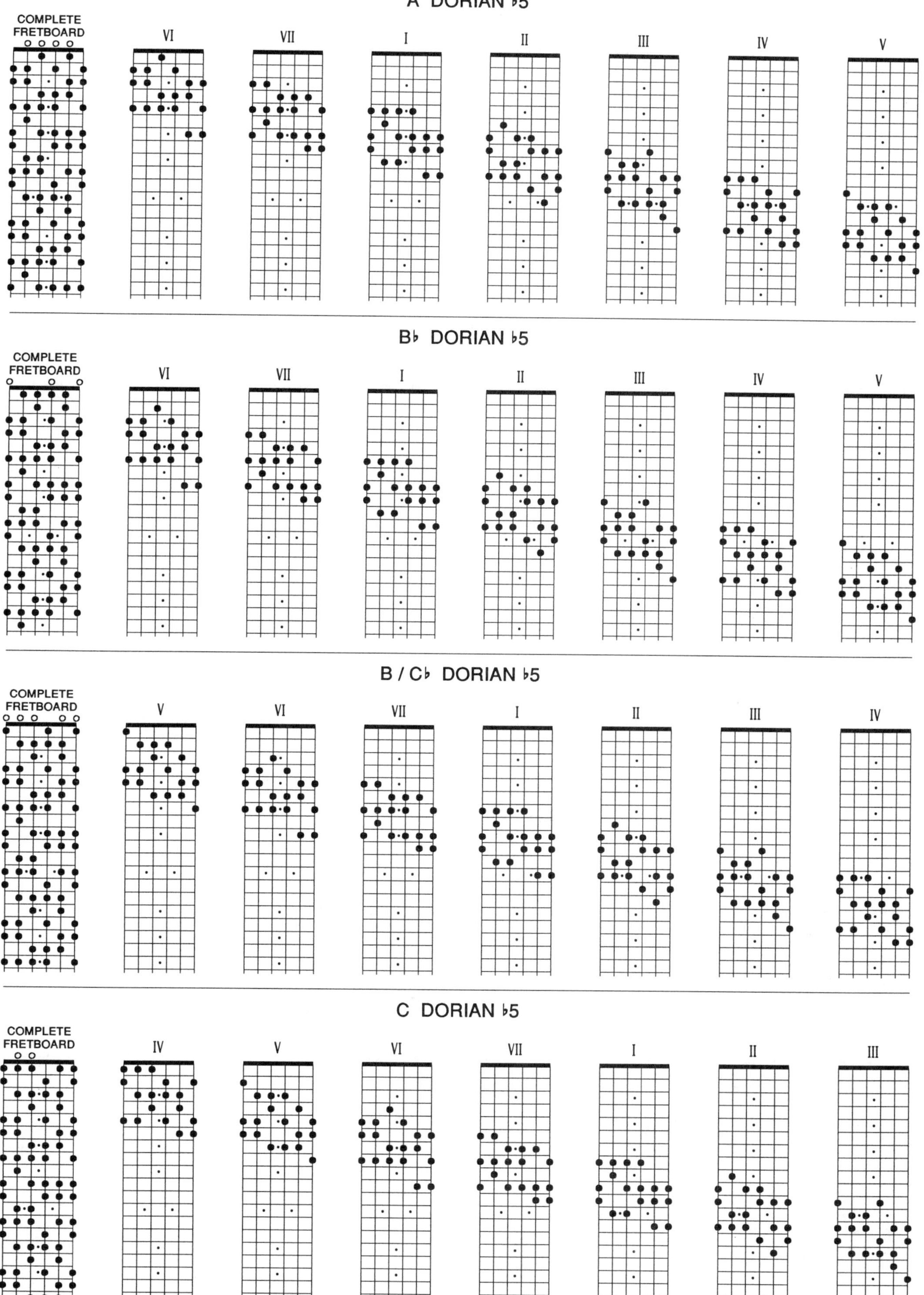

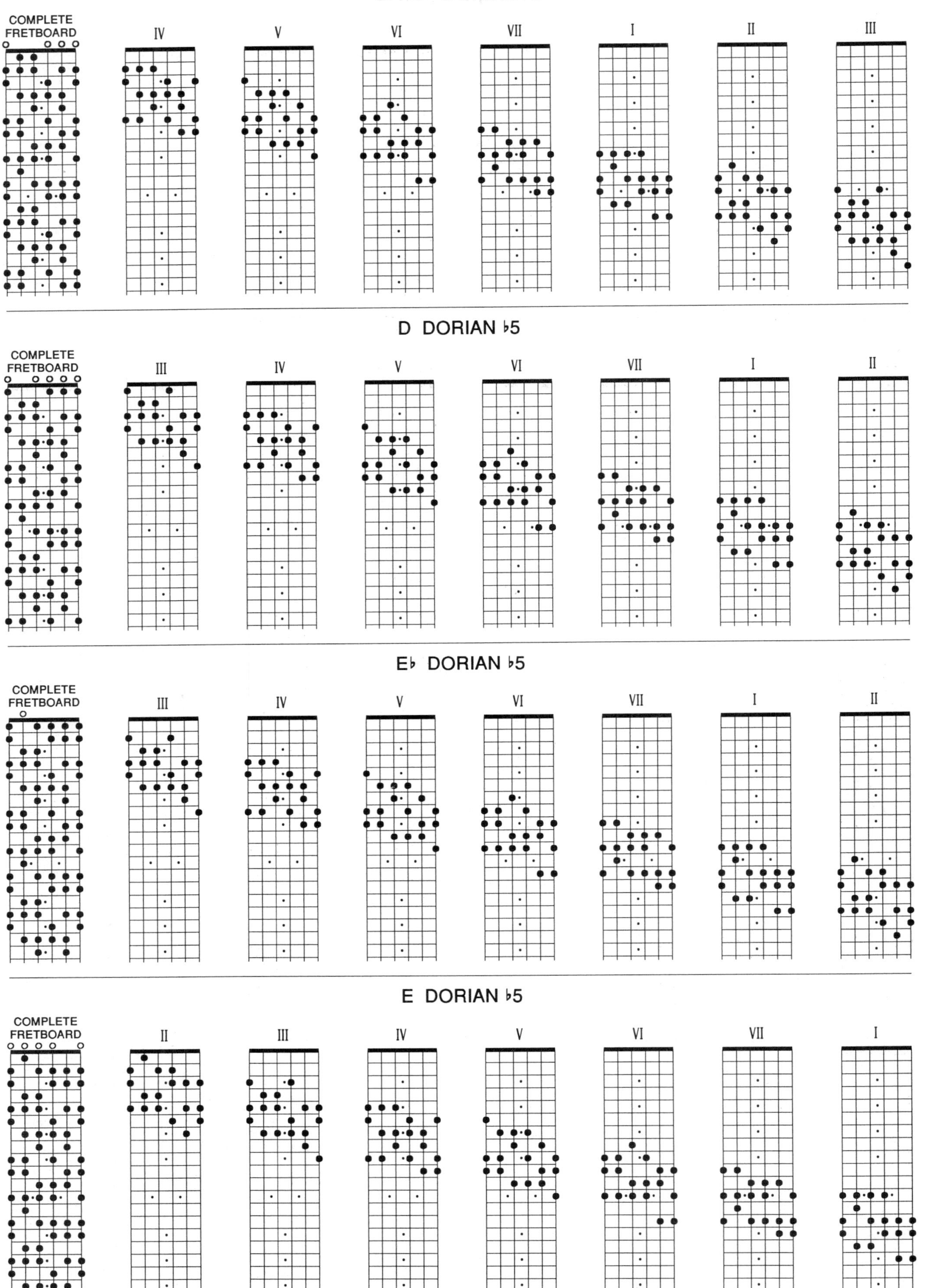
C♯ / D♭ DORIAN ♭5
COMPLETE FRETBOARD
IV
V
VI
VII
I
II
III
D DORIAN ♭5
COMPLETE FRETBOARD
III
IV
V
VI
VII
I
II
E♭ DORIAN ♭5
COMPLETE FRETBOARD
III
IV
V
VI
VII
I
II
E DORIAN ♭5
COMPLETE FRETBOARD
II
III
IV
V
VI
VII
I

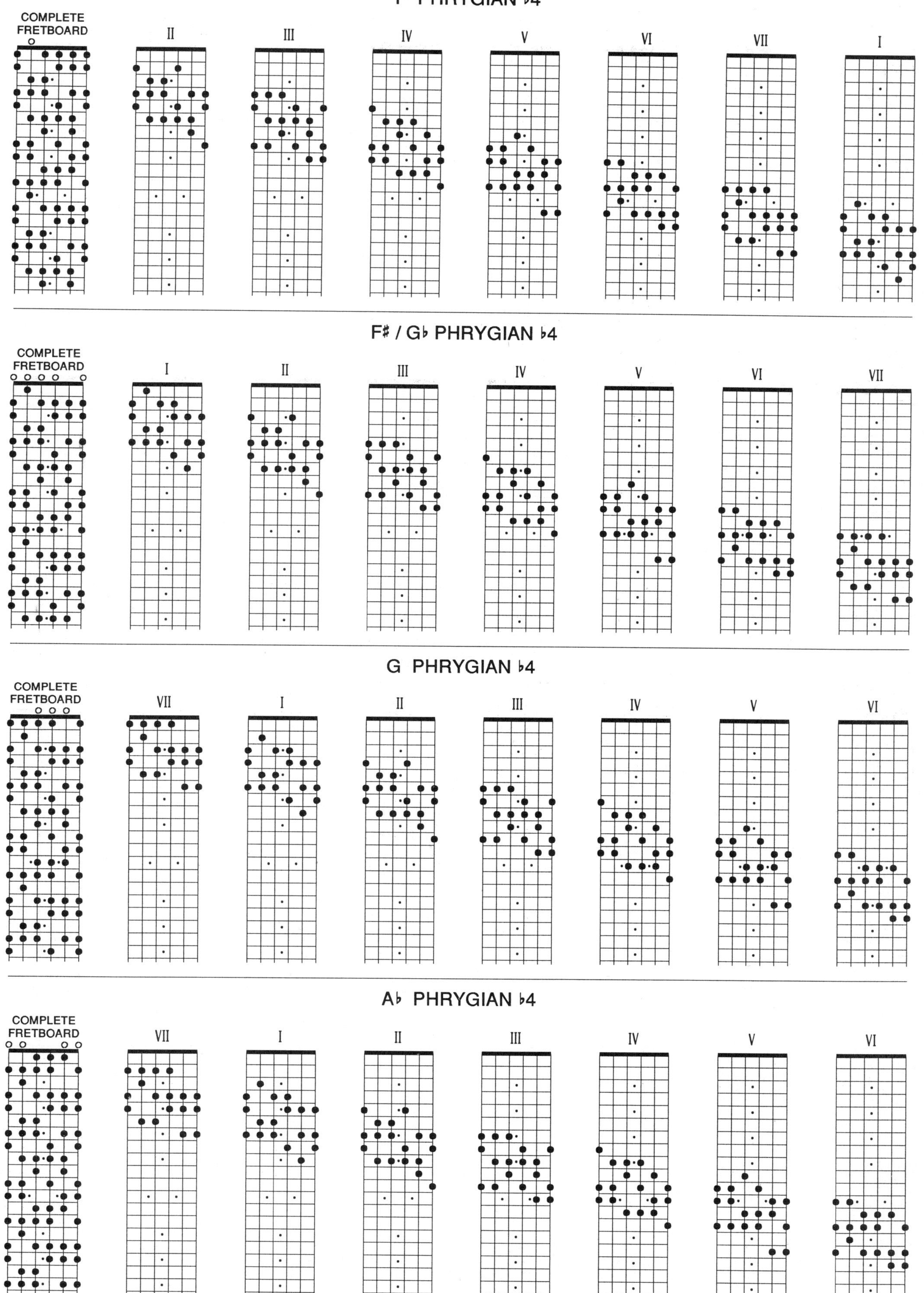
F PHRYGIAN ♭4
COMPLETE FRETBOARD
II
III
IV
V
VI
VII
I
F♯ / G♭ PHRYGIAN ♭4
COMPLETE FRETBOARD
I
II
III
IV
V
VI
VII
G PHRYGIAN ♭4
COMPLETE FRETBOARD
VII
I
II
III
IV
V
VI
A♭ PHRYGIAN ♭4
COMPLETE FRETBOARD
VII
I
II
III
IV
V
VI

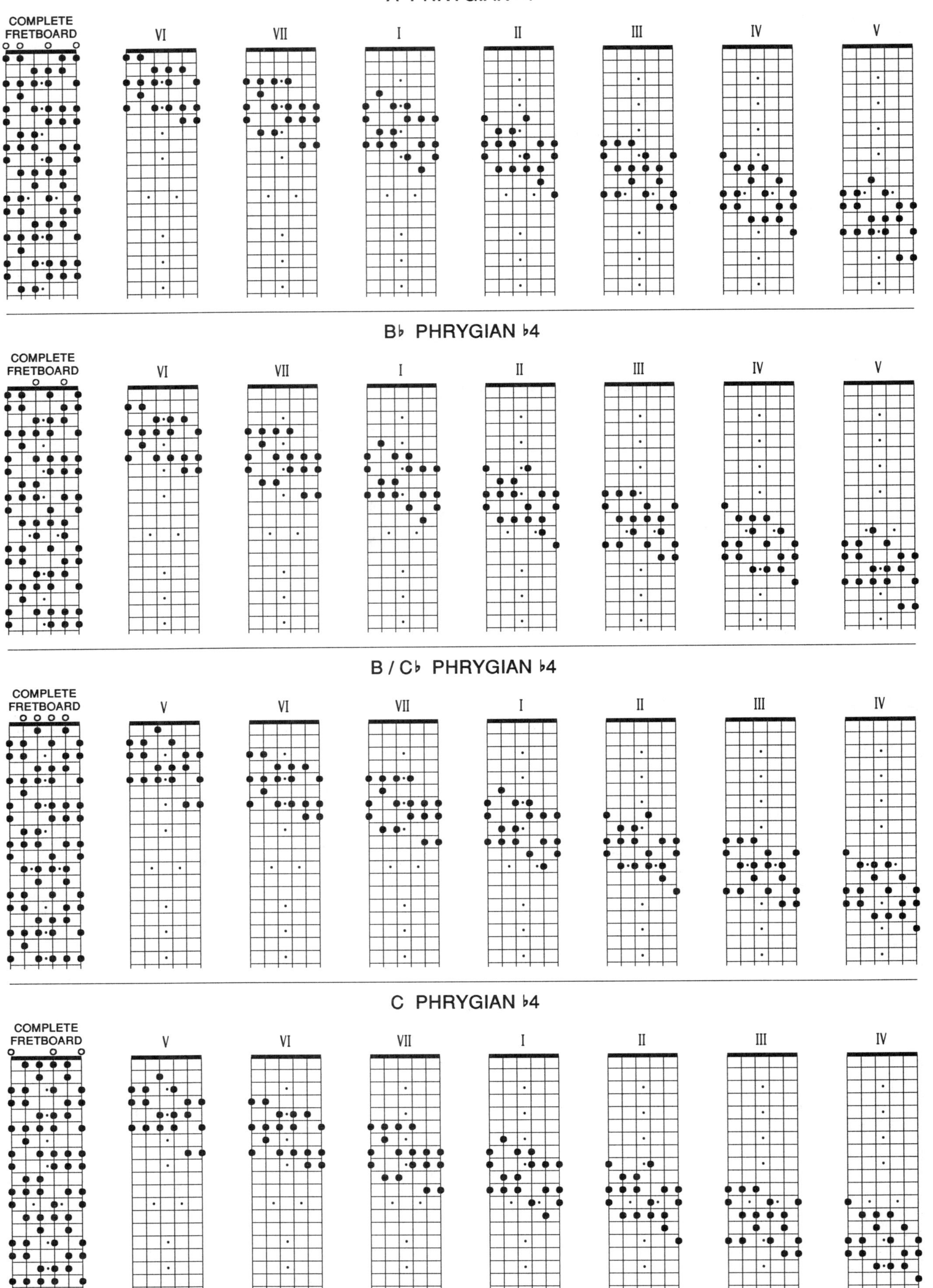
A PHRYGIAN ♭4
COMPLETE FRETBOARD
VI
VII
I
II
III
IV
V
B♭ PHRYGIAN ♭4
COMPLETE FRETBOARD
VI
VII
I
II
III
IV
V
B / C♭ PHRYGIAN ♭4
COMPLETE FRETBOARD
V
VI
VII
I
II
III
IV
C PHRYGIAN ♭4
COMPLETE FRETBOARD
V
VI
VII
I
II
III
IV

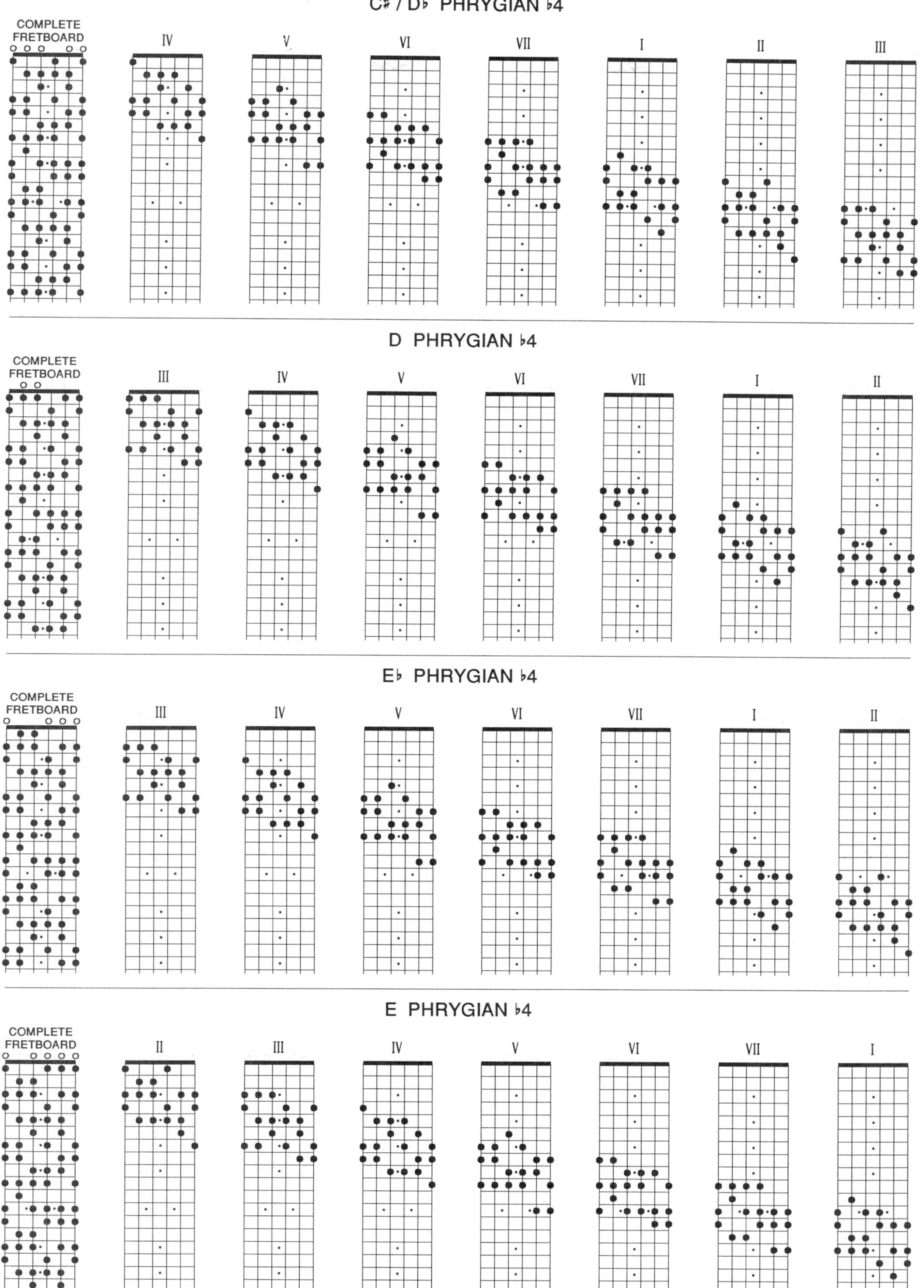
C♯ / D♭ PHRYGIAN ♭4
COMPLETE FRETBOARD
IV
V
VI
VII
I
II
III
D PHRYGIAN ♭4
COMPLETE FRETBOARD
III
IV
V
VI
VII
I
II
E♭ PHRYGIAN ♭4
COMPLETE FRETBOARD
III
IV
V
VI
VII
I
II
E PHRYGIAN ♭4
COMPLETE FRETBOARD
II
III
IV
V
VI
VII
I

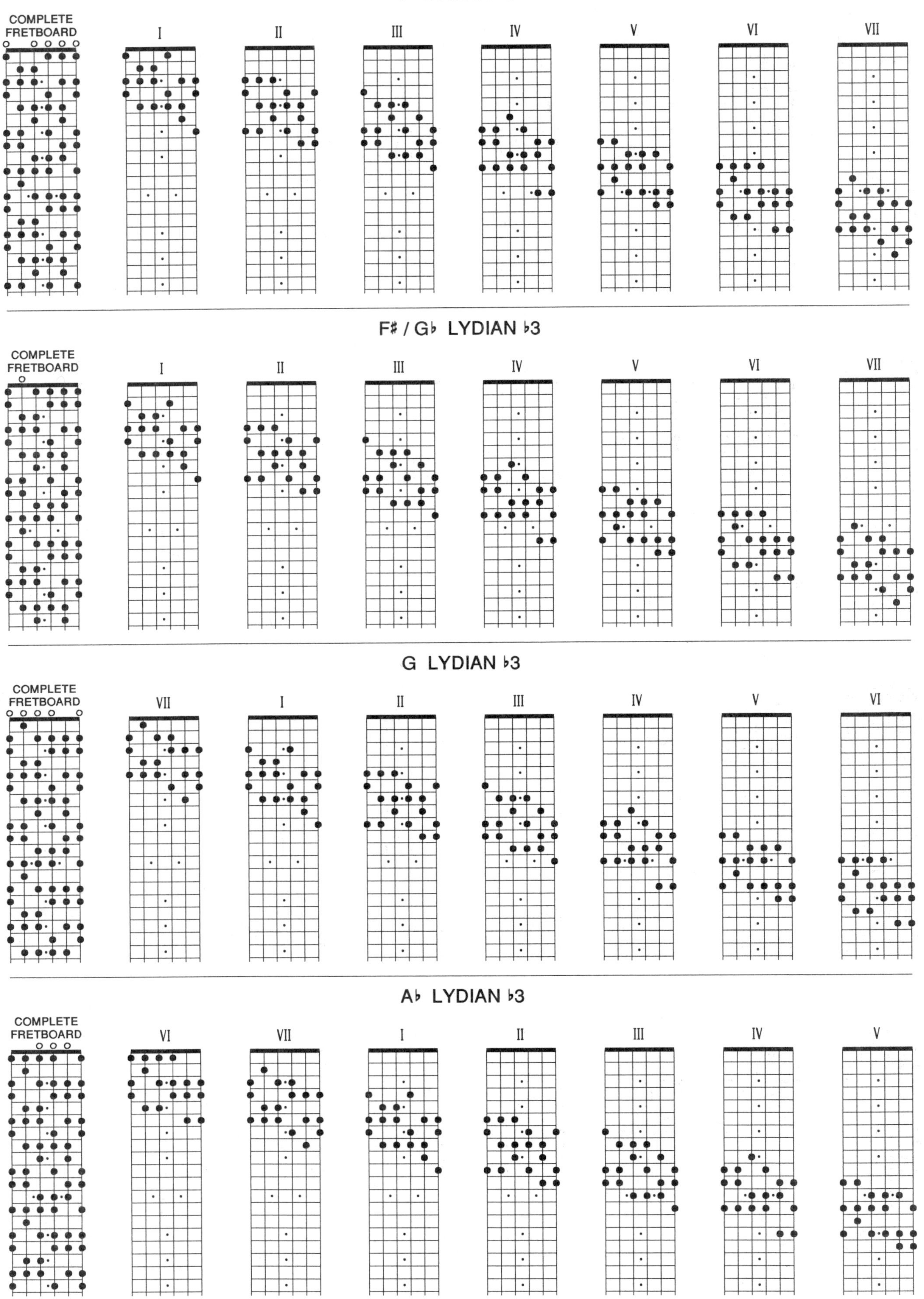
F LYDIAN ♭3
COMPLETE FRETBOARD
I
II
III
IV
V
VI
VII
F♯ / G♭ LYDIAN ♭3
COMPLETE FRETBOARD
I
II
III
IV
V
VI
VII
G LYDIAN ♭3
COMPLETE FRETBOARD
VII
I
II
III
IV
V
VI
A♭ LYDIAN ♭3
COMPLETE FRETBOARD
VI
VII
I
II
III
IV
V

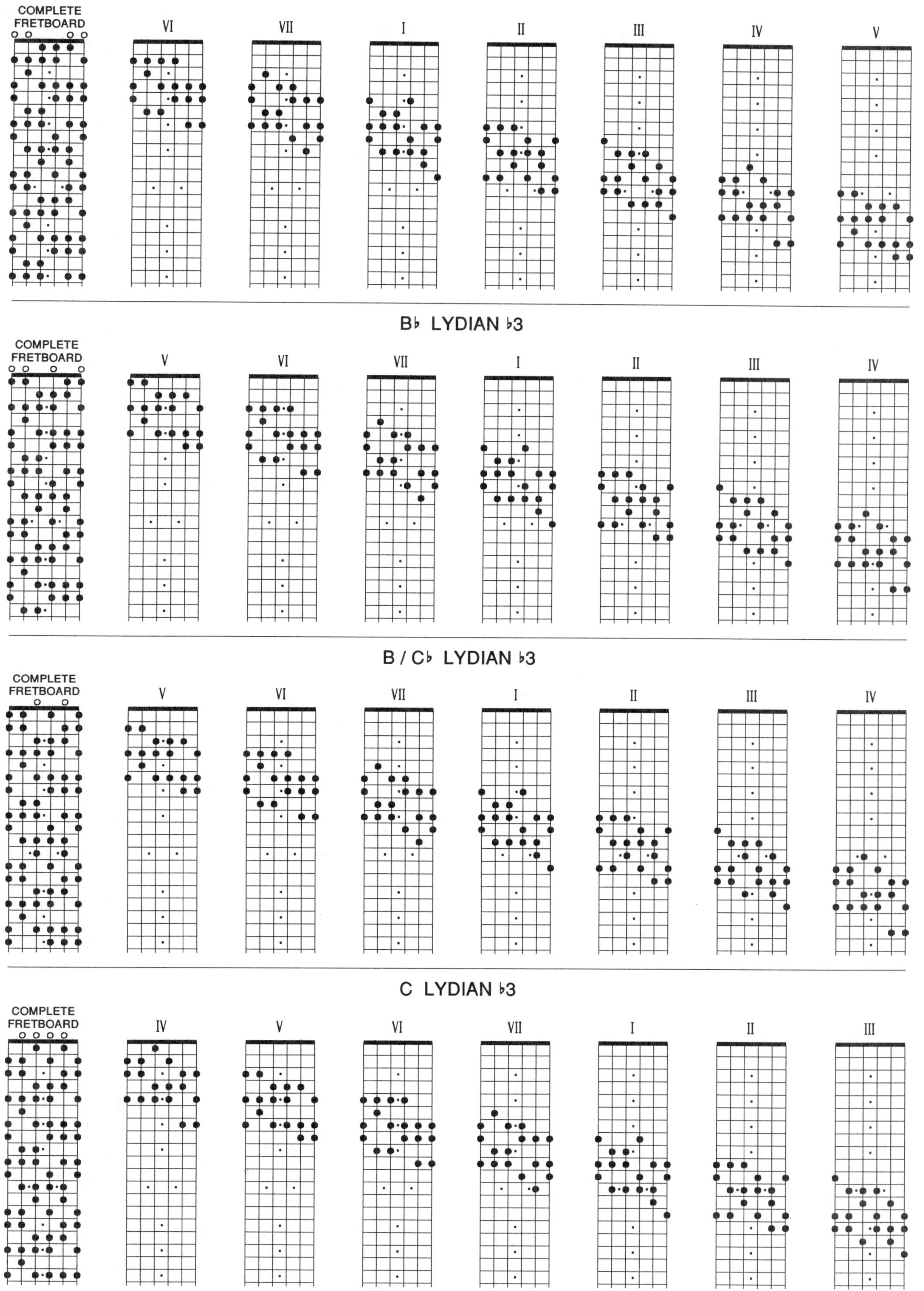
A LYDIAN ♭3
COMPLETE FRETBOARD
VI
VII
I
II
III
IV
V
B♭ LYDIAN ♭3
COMPLETE FRETBOARD
V
VI
VII
I
II
III
IV
B / C♭ LYDIAN ♭3
COMPLETE FRETBOARD
V
VI
VII
I
II
III
IV
C LYDIAN ♭3
COMPLETE FRETBOARD
IV
V
VI
VII
I
II
III

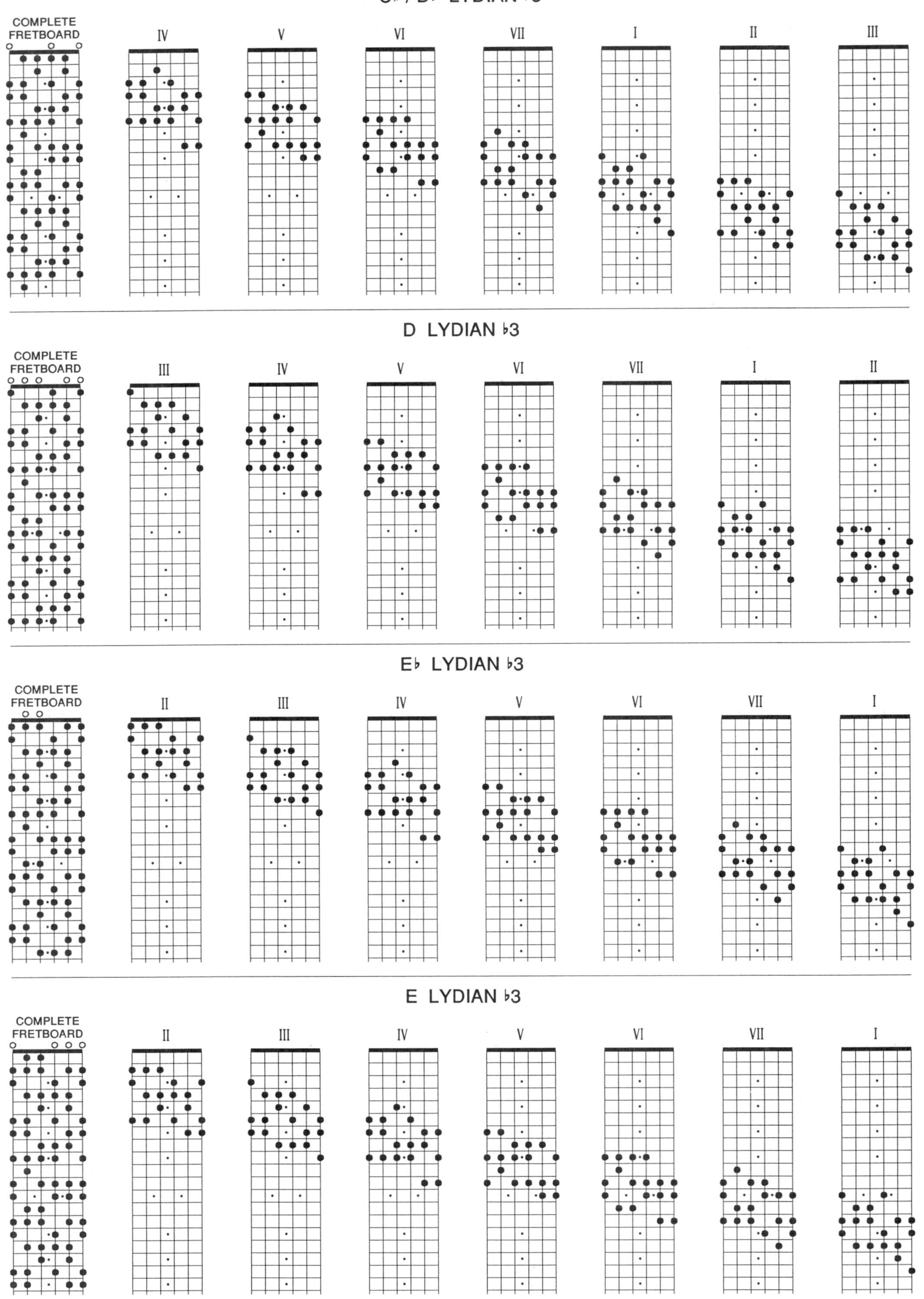
C♯ / D♭ LYDIAN ♭3
COMPLETE FRETBOARD
IV
V
VI
VII
I
II
III
D LYDIAN ♭3
COMPLETE FRETBOARD
III
IV
V
VI
VII
I
II
E♭ LYDIAN ♭3
COMPLETE FRETBOARD
II
III
IV
V
VI
VII
I
E LYDIAN ♭3
COMPLETE FRETBOARD
II
III
IV
V
VI
VII
I

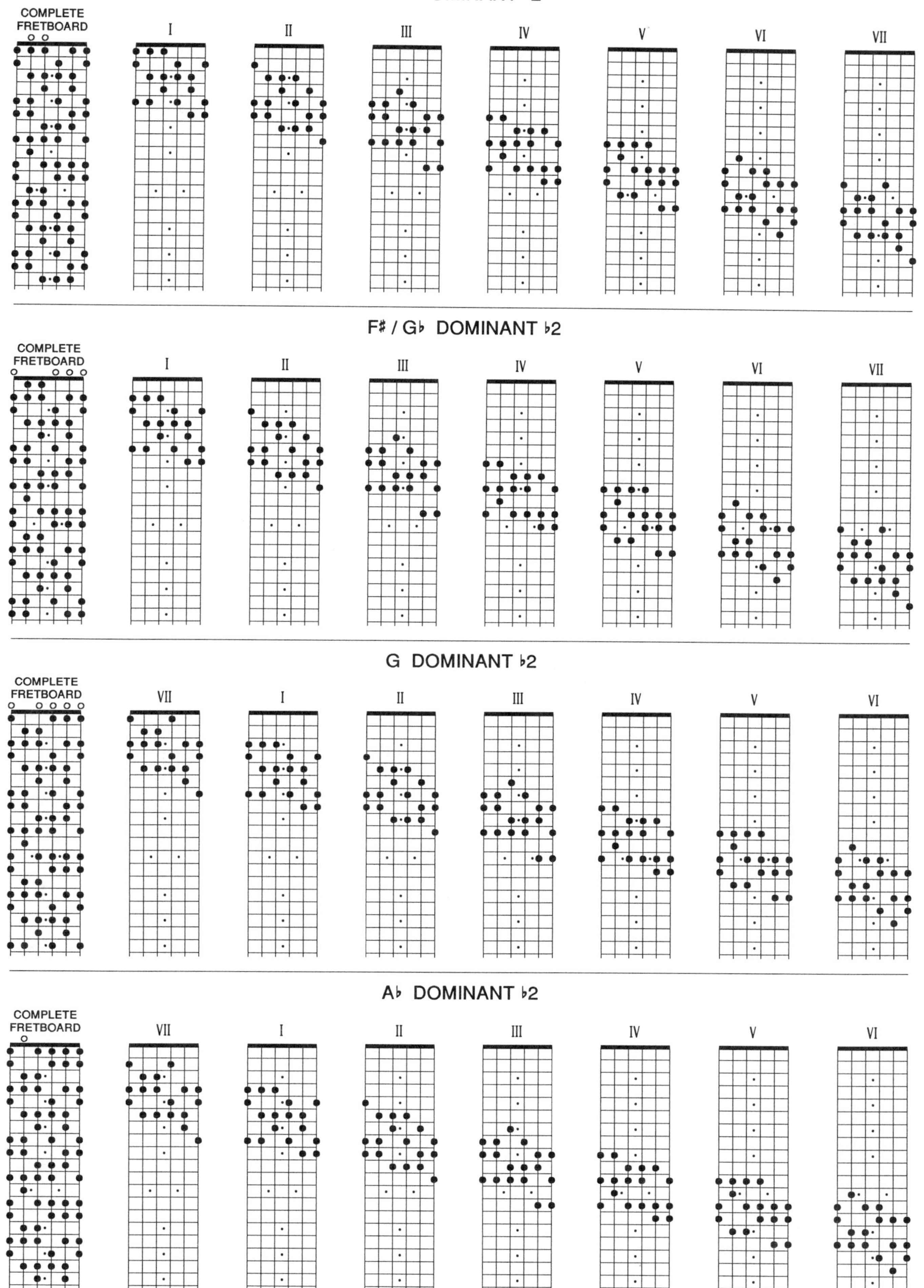
F DOMINANT ♭2
COMPLETE FRETBOARD
I
II
III
IV
V
VI
VII
F♯ / G♭ DOMINANT ♭2
COMPLETE FRETBOARD
I
II
III
IV
V
VI
VII
G DOMINANT ♭2
COMPLETE FRETBOARD
VII
I
II
III
IV
V
VI
A♭ DOMINANT ♭2
COMPLETE FRETBOARD
VII
I
II
III
IV
V
VI

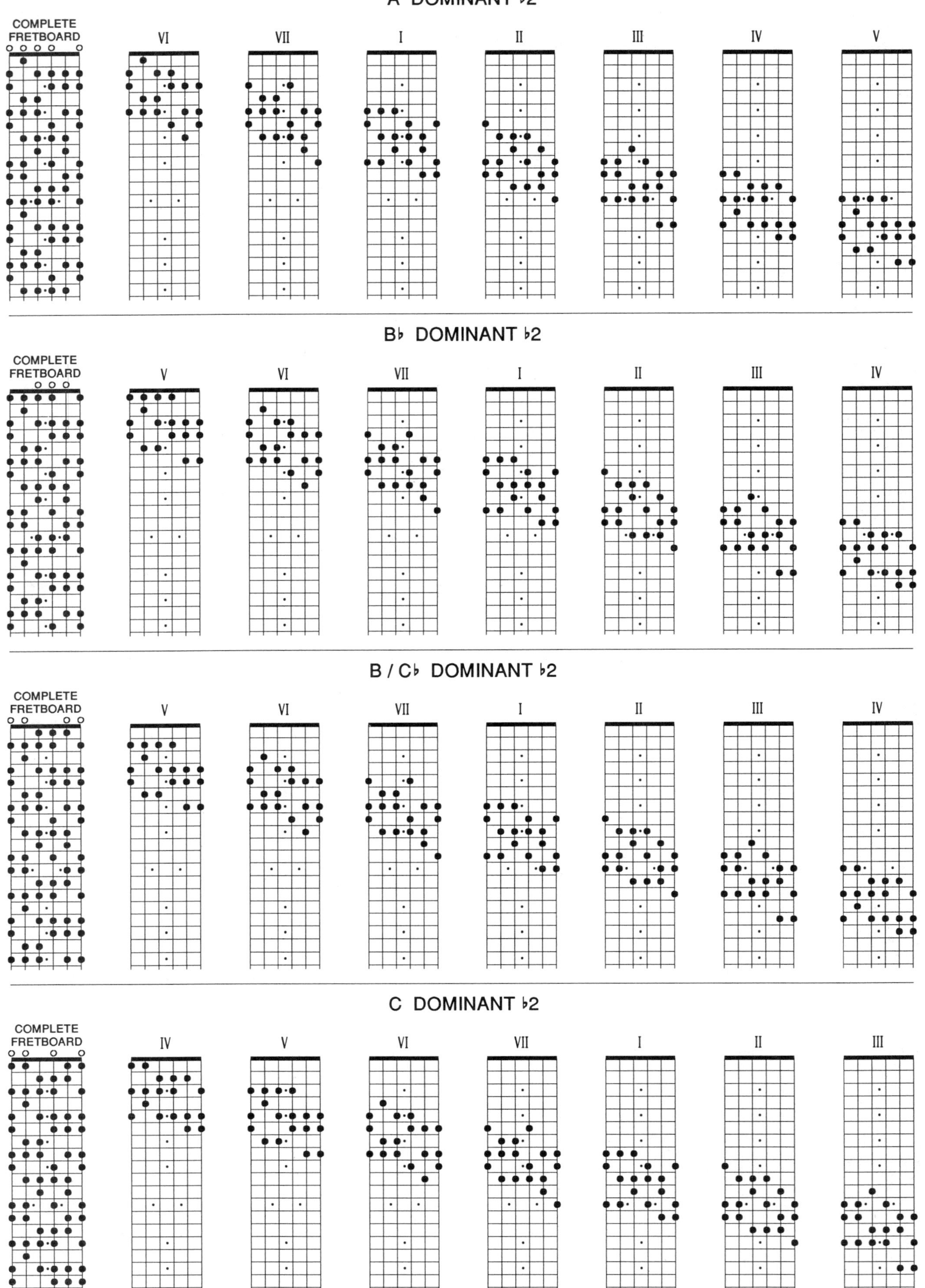
A DOMINANT ♭2
COMPLETE FRETBOARD
VI
VII
I
II
III
IV
V
B♭ DOMINANT ♭2
COMPLETE FRETBOARD
V
VI
VII
I
II
III
IV
B / C♭ DOMINANT ♭2
COMPLETE FRETBOARD
V
VI
VII
I
II
III
IV
C DOMINANT ♭2
COMPLETE FRETBOARD
IV
V
VI
VII
I
II
III

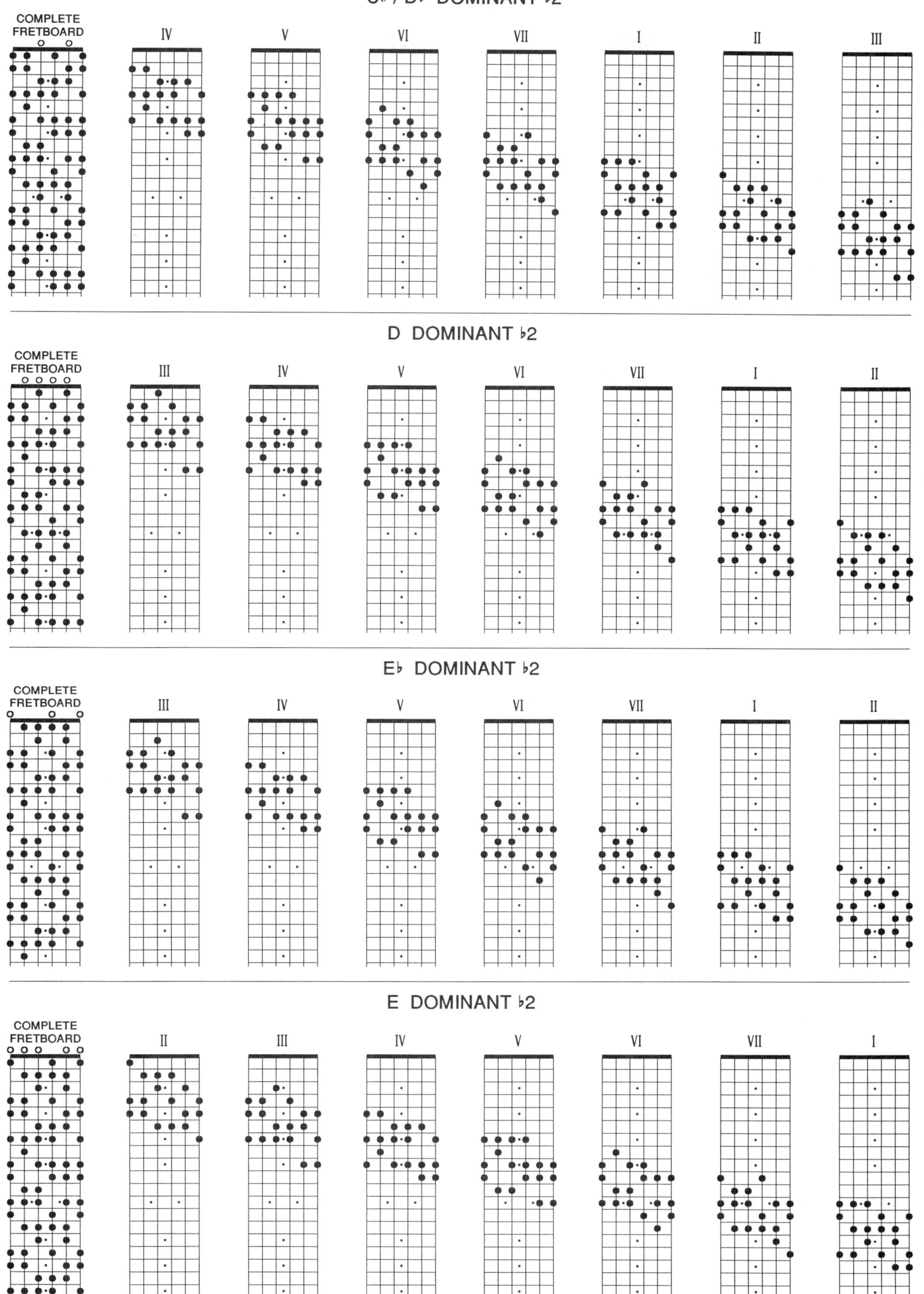
C♯ / D♭ DOMINANT ♭2
COMPLETE FRETBOARD
IV
V
VI
VII
I
II
III
D DOMINANT ♭2
COMPLETE FRETBOARD
III
IV
V
VI
VII
I
II
E♭ DOMINANT ♭2
COMPLETE FRETBOARD
III
IV
V
VI
VII
I
II
E DOMINANT ♭2
COMPLETE FRETBOARD
II
III
IV
V
VI
VII
I

F LYDIAN AUGMENTED #2

F♯ / G♭ LYDIAN AUGMENTED #2

G LYDIAN AUGMENTED #2

A♭ LYDIAN AUGMENTED #2

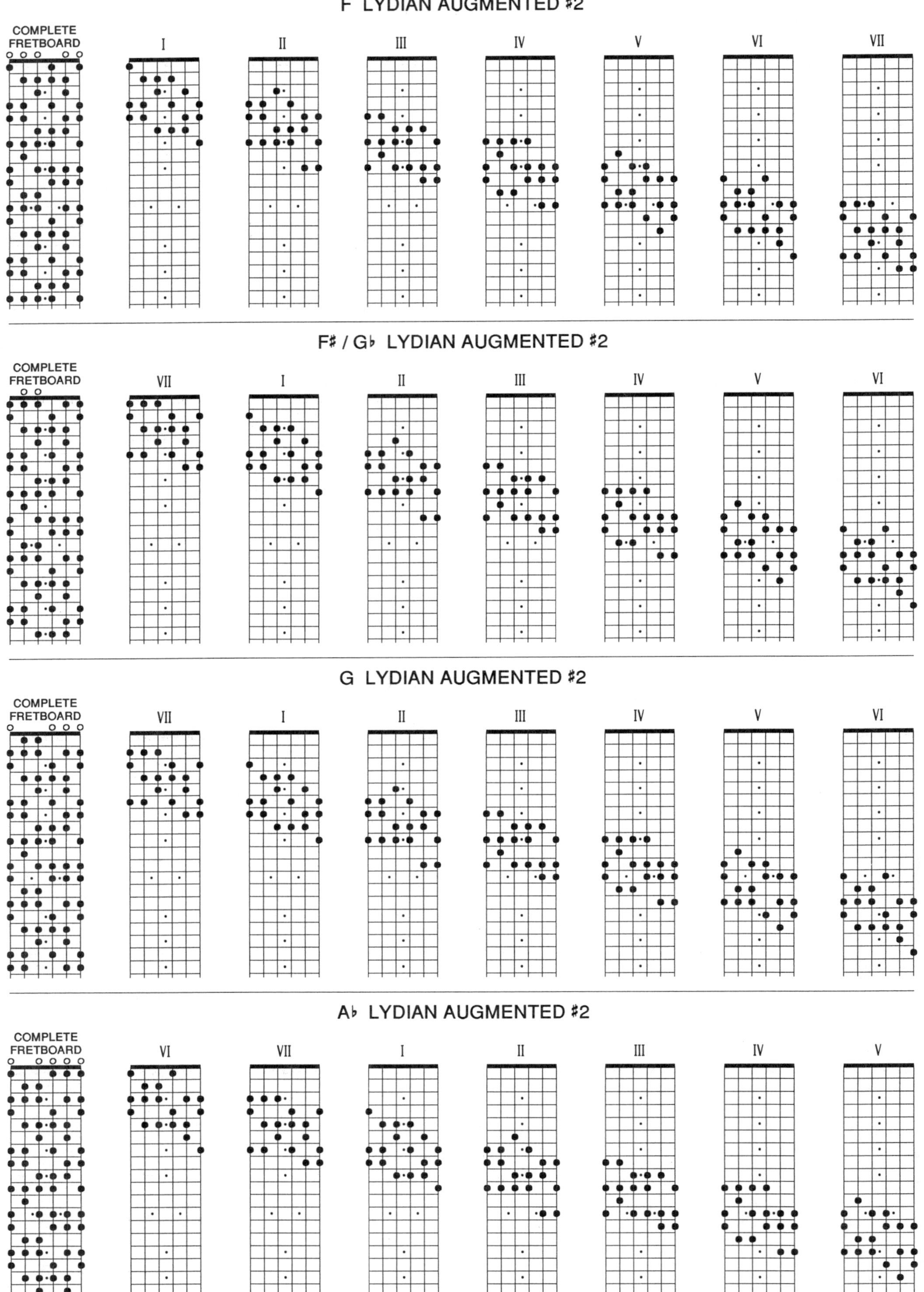

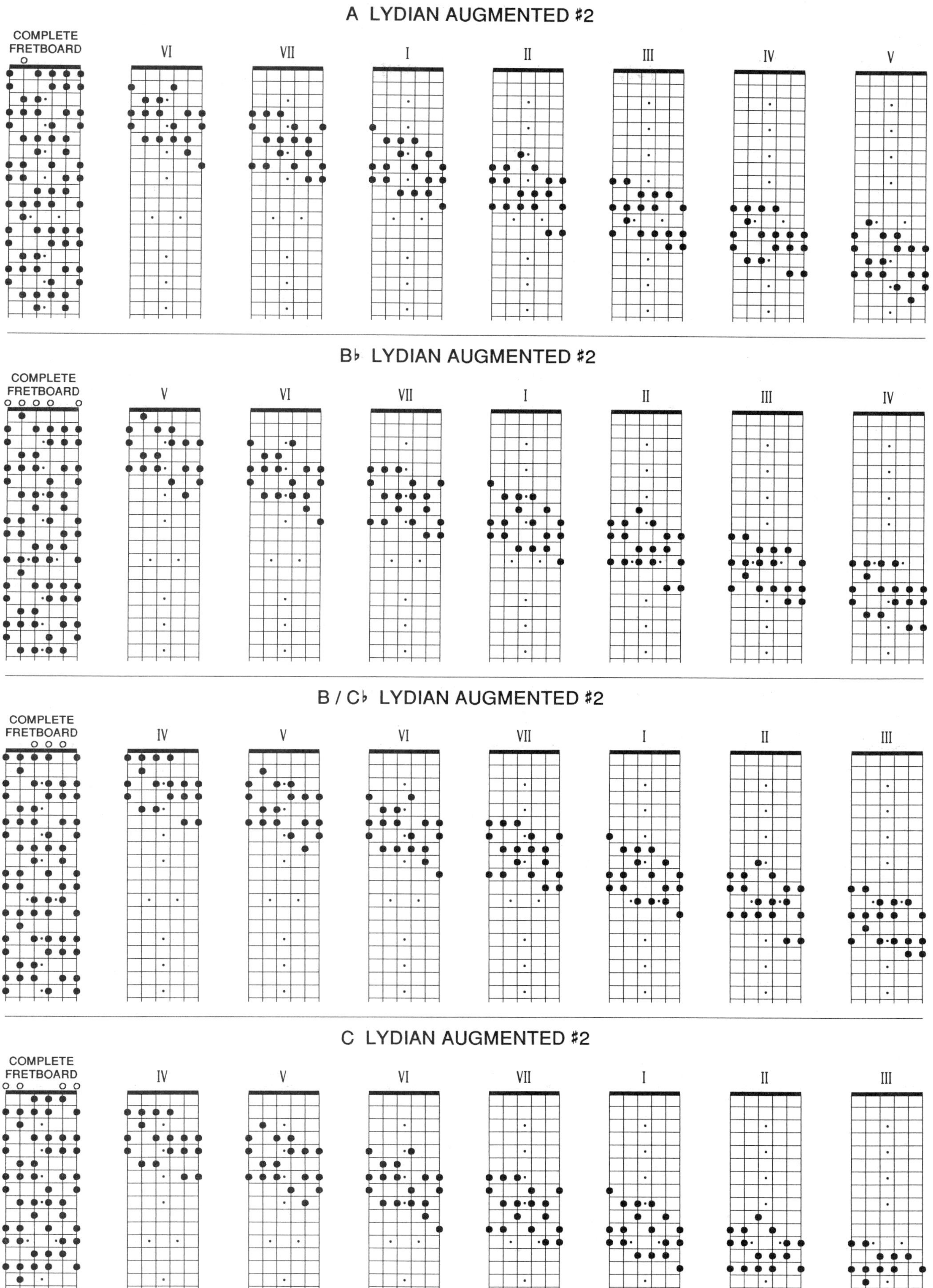
A LYDIAN AUGMENTED #2
COMPLETE FRETBOARD
VI
VII
I
II
III
IV
V
B♭ LYDIAN AUGMENTED #2
COMPLETE FRETBOARD
V
VI
VII
I
II
III
IV
B / C♭ LYDIAN AUGMENTED #2
COMPLETE FRETBOARD
IV
V
VI
VII
I
II
III
C LYDIAN AUGMENTED #2
COMPLETE FRETBOARD
IV
V
VI
VII
I
II
III

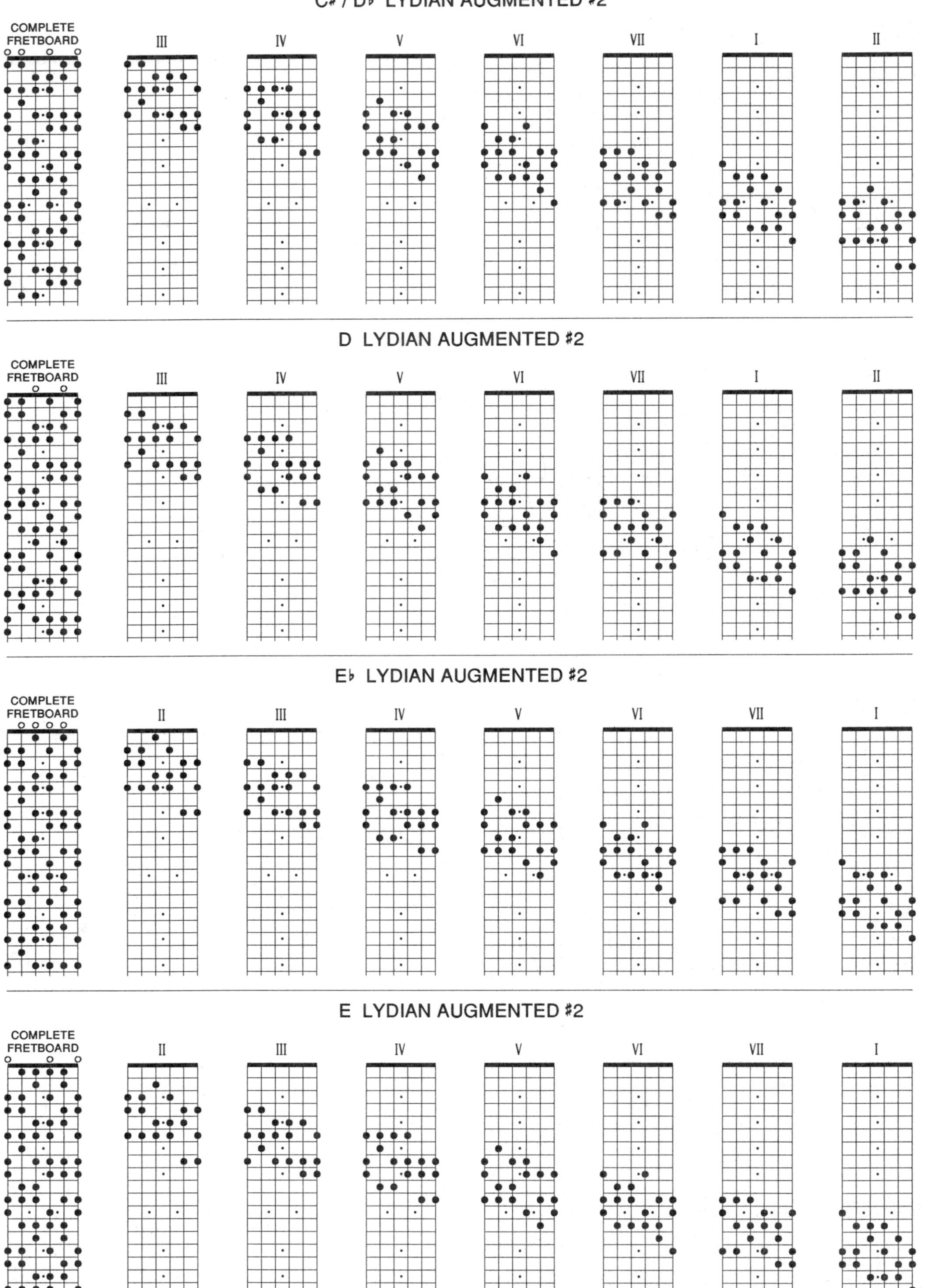
C# / D♭ LYDIAN AUGMENTED #2
COMPLETE FRETBOARD
III
IV
V
VI
VII
I
II
D LYDIAN AUGMENTED #2
COMPLETE FRETBOARD
III
IV
V
VI
VII
I
II
E♭ LYDIAN AUGMENTED #2
COMPLETE FRETBOARD
II
III
IV
V
VI
VII
I
E LYDIAN AUGMENTED #2
COMPLETE FRETBOARD
II
III
IV
V
VI
VII
I

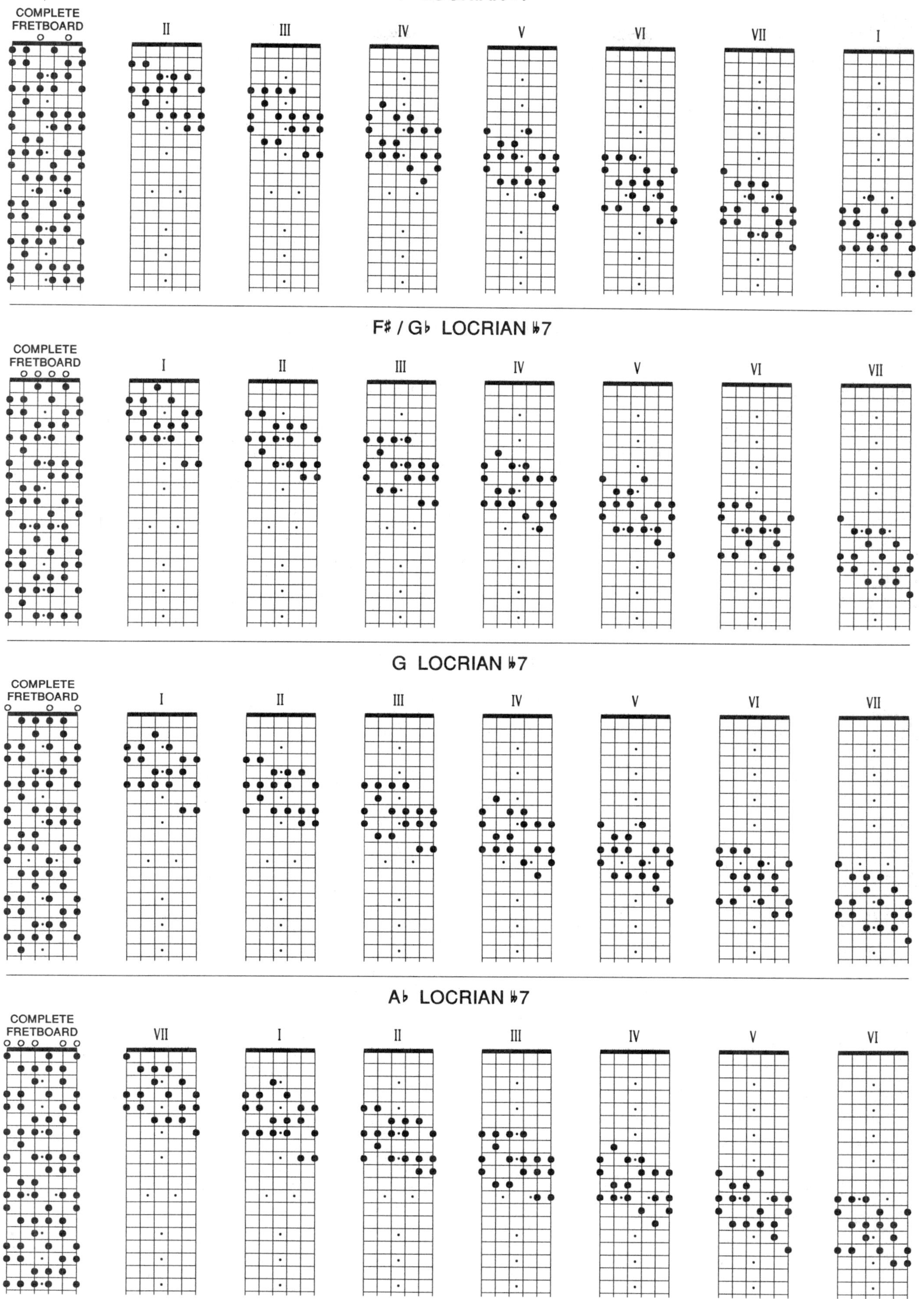
F LOCRIAN 𝄫7
COMPLETE FRETBOARD
II
III
IV
V
VI
VII
I
F♯ / G♭ LOCRIAN 𝄫7
COMPLETE FRETBOARD
I
II
III
IV
V
VI
VII
G LOCRIAN 𝄫7
COMPLETE FRETBOARD
I
II
III
IV
V
VI
VII
A♭ LOCRIAN 𝄫7
COMPLETE FRETBOARD
VII
I
II
III
IV
V
VI

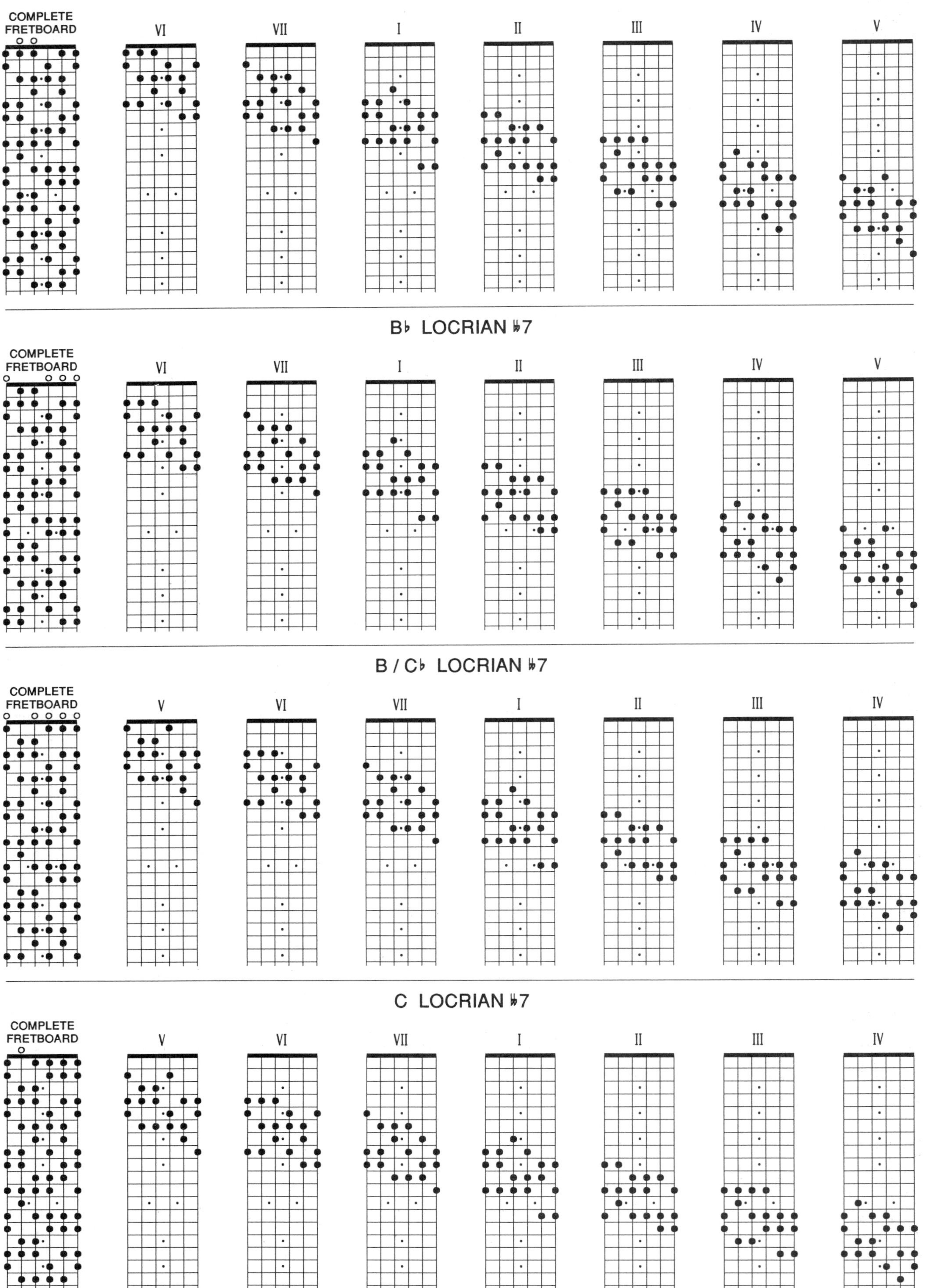
A LOCRIAN 𝄫7
COMPLETE FRETBOARD
VI
VII
I
II
III
IV
V
B♭ LOCRIAN 𝄫7
COMPLETE FRETBOARD
VI
VII
I
II
III
IV
V
B / C♭ LOCRIAN 𝄫7
COMPLETE FRETBOARD
V
VI
VII
I
II
III
IV
C LOCRIAN 𝄫7
COMPLETE FRETBOARD
V
VI
VII
I
II
III
IV

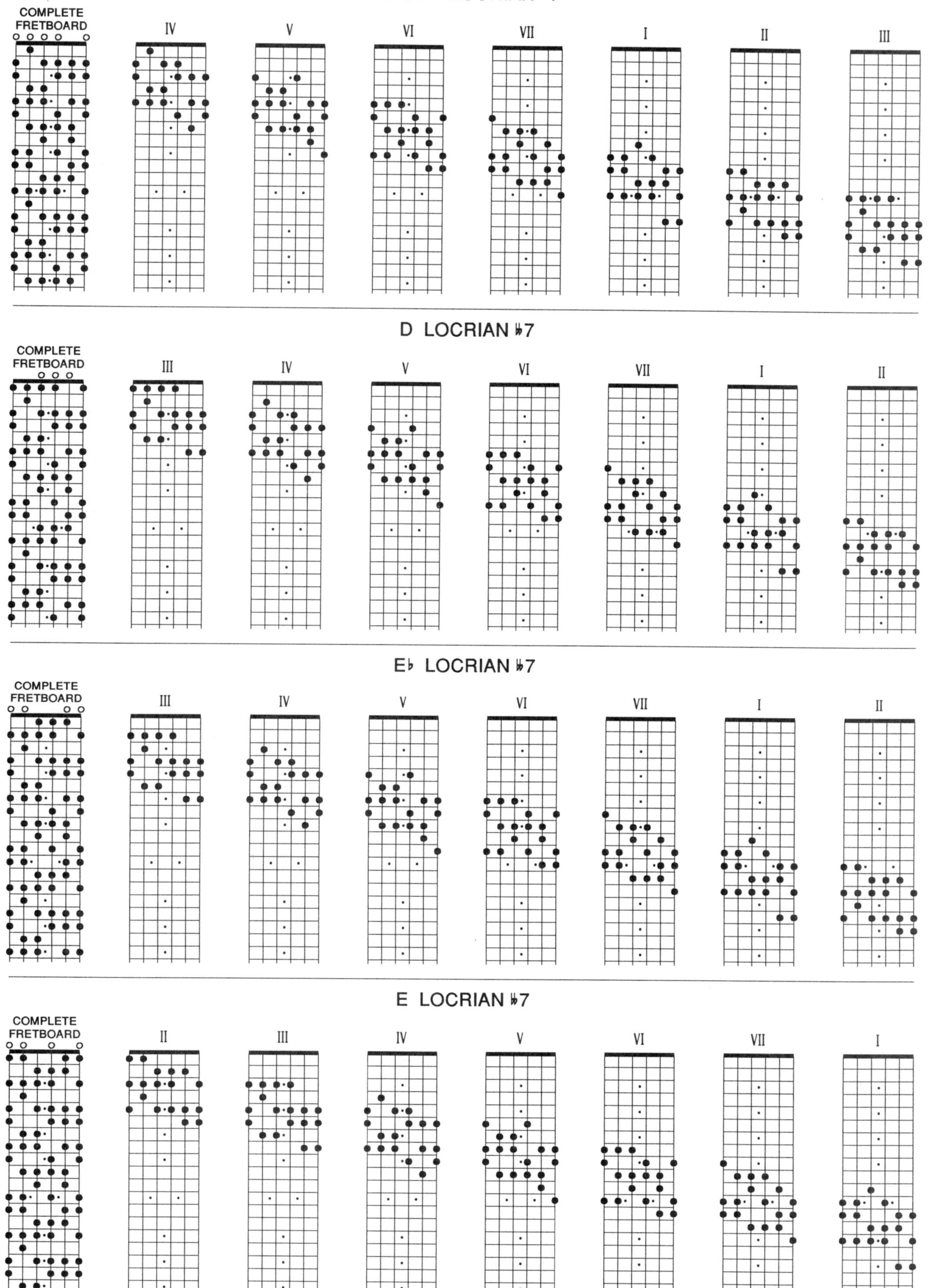
C♯ / D♭ LOCRIAN 𝄫7
COMPLETE FRETBOARD
IV
V
VI
VII
I
II
III
D LOCRIAN 𝄫7
COMPLETE FRETBOARD
III
IV
V
VI
VII
I
II
E♭ LOCRIAN 𝄫7
COMPLETE FRETBOARD
III
IV
V
VI
VII
I
II
E LOCRIAN 𝄫7
COMPLETE FRETBOARD
II
III
IV
V
VI
VII
I

KEYBOARD PATTERNS

QUICK MODE GENERATOR CHART

HUNGARIAN MINOR	I	II	III	IV	V	VI	VII
	C	B♭	A	F♯/G♭	F	E	C♯/D♭
	C♯/D♭	B/C♭	B♭	G	F♯/G♭	F	D
	D	C	B/C♭	A♭	G	F♯/G♭	E♭
	E♭	C♯/D♭	C	A	A♭	G	E
	E	D	C♯/D♭	B♭	A	A♭	F
	F	E♭	D	B/C♭	B♭	A	F♯/G♭
	F♯/G♭	E	E♭	C	B/C♭	B♭	G
	G	F	E	C♯/D♭	C	B/C♭	A♭
	A♭	F♯/G♭	F	D	C♯/D♭	C	A
	A	G	F♯/G♭	E♭	D	C♯/D♭	B♭
	B♭	A♭	G	E	E♭	D	B/C♭
	B/C♭	A	A♭	F	E	E♭	C

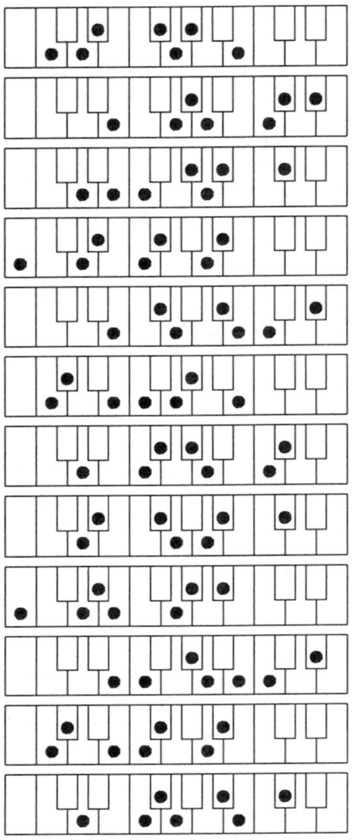

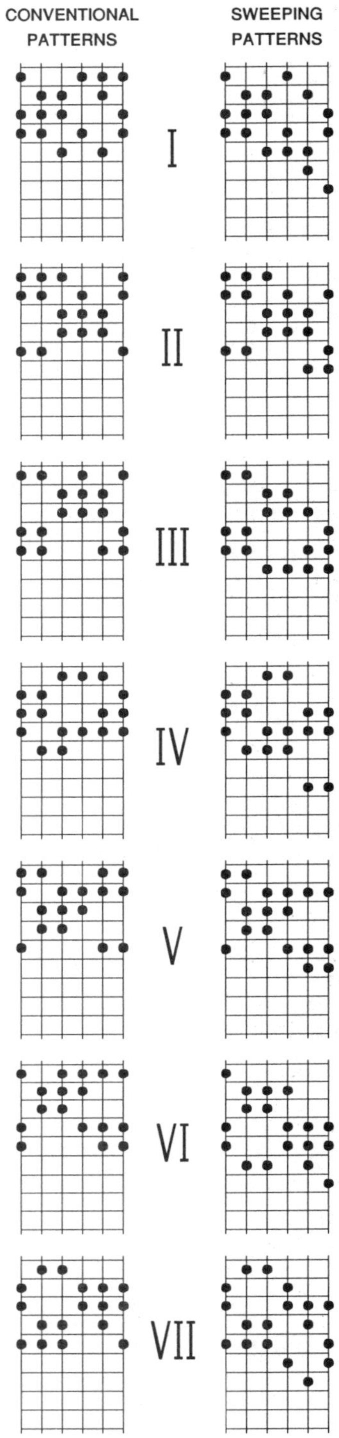

CONVENTIONAL PATTERNS

SWEEPING PATTERNS

I

II

III

IV

V

VI

VII

SCALE / MODE - CHORD CHART

I	HUNGARIAN MINOR	⁻△, △°, ⁻△⁺
II	ORIENTAL	$7^{\flat 5}$
III	IONIAN AUGMENTED ♯2	△⁺, ⁻△⁺
IV	LOCRIAN 𝄫3 𝄫7	$\text{sus}2^{\flat 5}$
V	DOUBLE HARMONIC	△, $△^{\text{sus}}$, ♭6
VI	LYDIAN ♯6 ♯2	7, ⁻7, ∅, $7^{\flat 5}$, △, ⁻△, △°, $△^{\flat 5}$
VII	ALT ♮5 𝄫7	6, ⁻6, ♭6, ⁻♭6, ♭9, ♯9, 13

NUMERIC SCALE / MODE CHART

		1		2		3	4		5		6		7	1		2		3	4		5		6		7
I	HUNGAR MINOR	1		2	♭3			♯4	5	♭6			7												
II	ORIENTAL			1	♭2			3	4	♭5			6	♭7											
III	IONIAN AUG ♯2				1			♯2	3	4			♯5	6		7									
IV	LOCRIAN 𝄫3 𝄫7							1	♭2	𝄫3			4	♭5		♭6	𝄫7								
V	DOUBLE HARMONIC								1	♭2			3	4		5	♭6			7					
VI	LYDIAN ♯6 ♯2									1			♯2	3		♯4	5			♯6	7				
VII	ALT ♮5𝄫7												1	♭2		♭3	♭4			5	♭6	𝄫7			

F HUNGARIAN MINOR

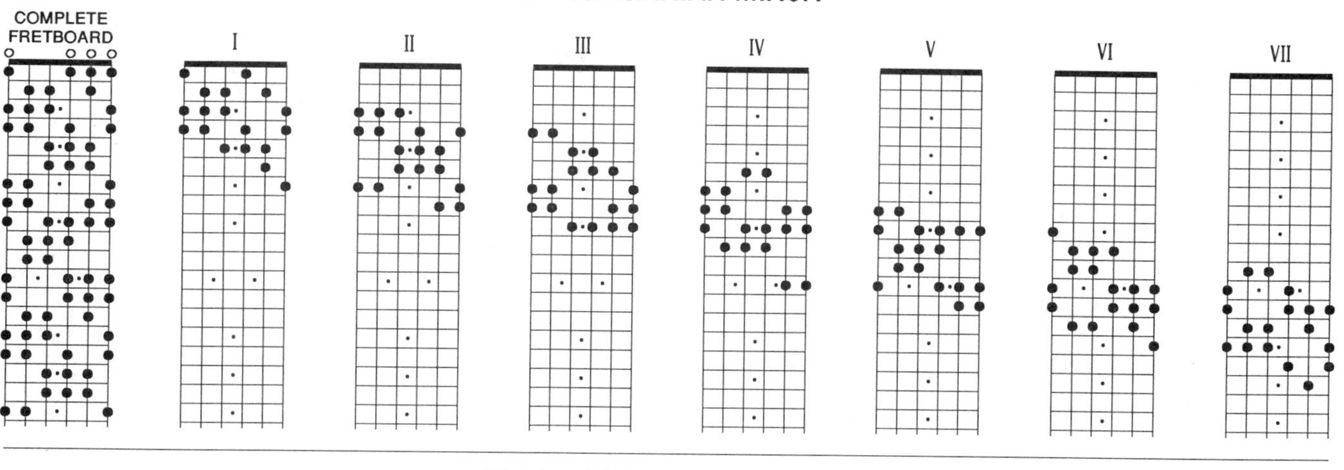

F♯ / G♭ HUNGARIAN MINOR

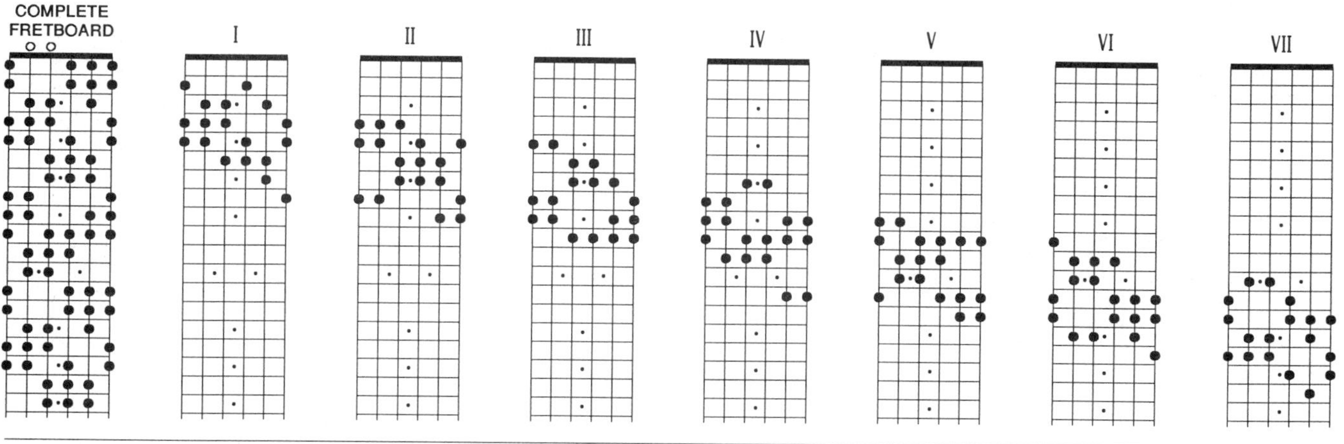

G HUNGARIAN MINOR

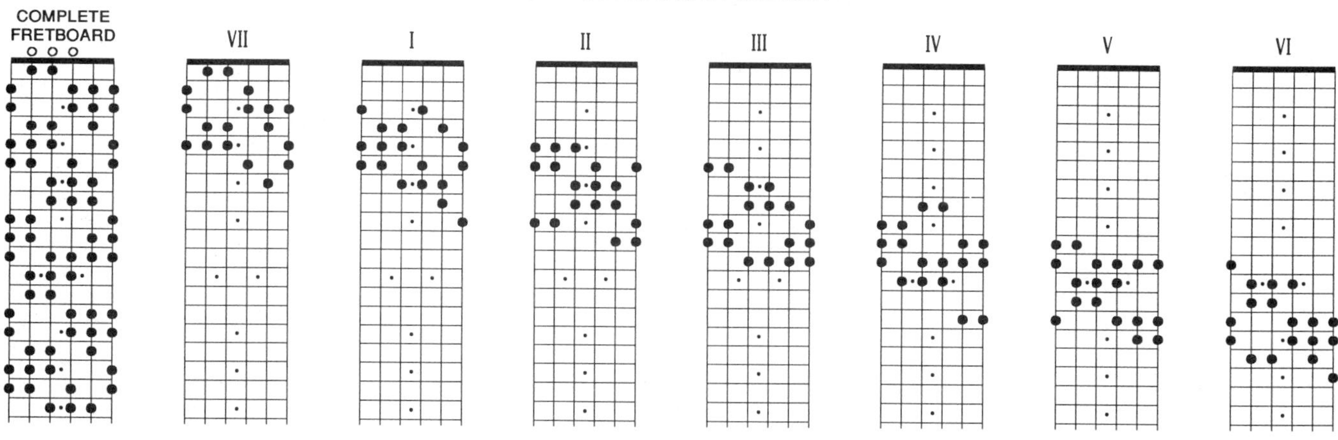

A♭ HUNGARIAN MINOR

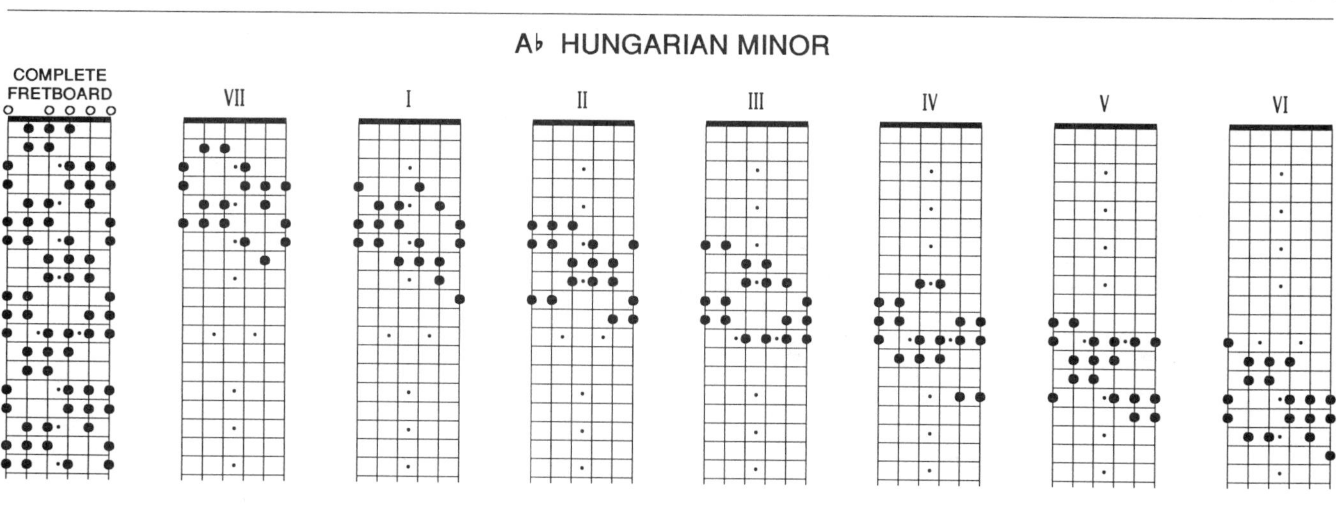

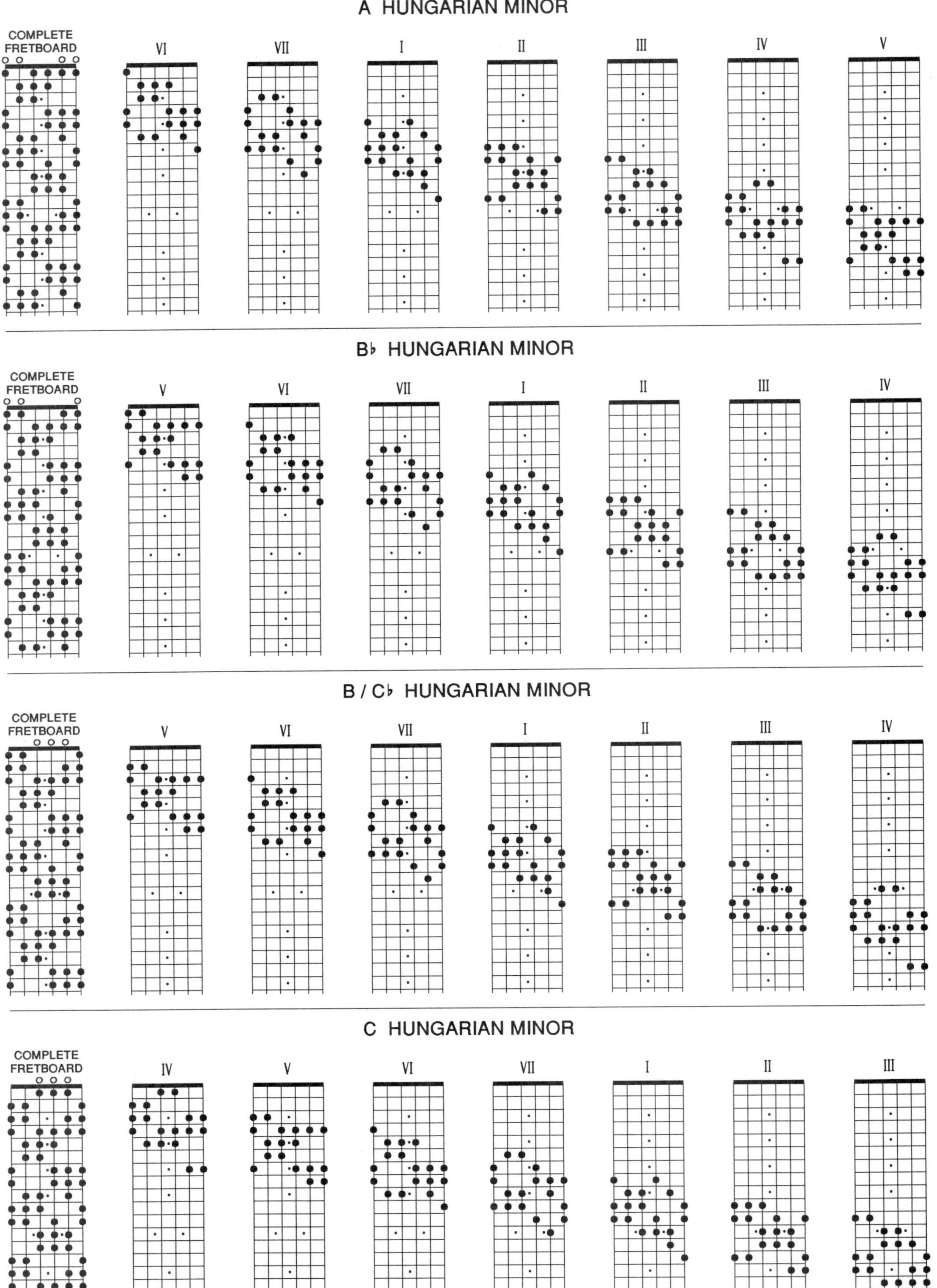
A HUNGARIAN MINOR
COMPLETE FRETBOARD
VI
VII
I
II
III
IV
V
B♭ HUNGARIAN MINOR
COMPLETE FRETBOARD
V
VI
VII
I
II
III
IV
B / C♭ HUNGARIAN MINOR
COMPLETE FRETBOARD
V
VI
VII
I
II
III
IV
C HUNGARIAN MINOR
COMPLETE FRETBOARD
IV
V
VI
VII
I
II
III

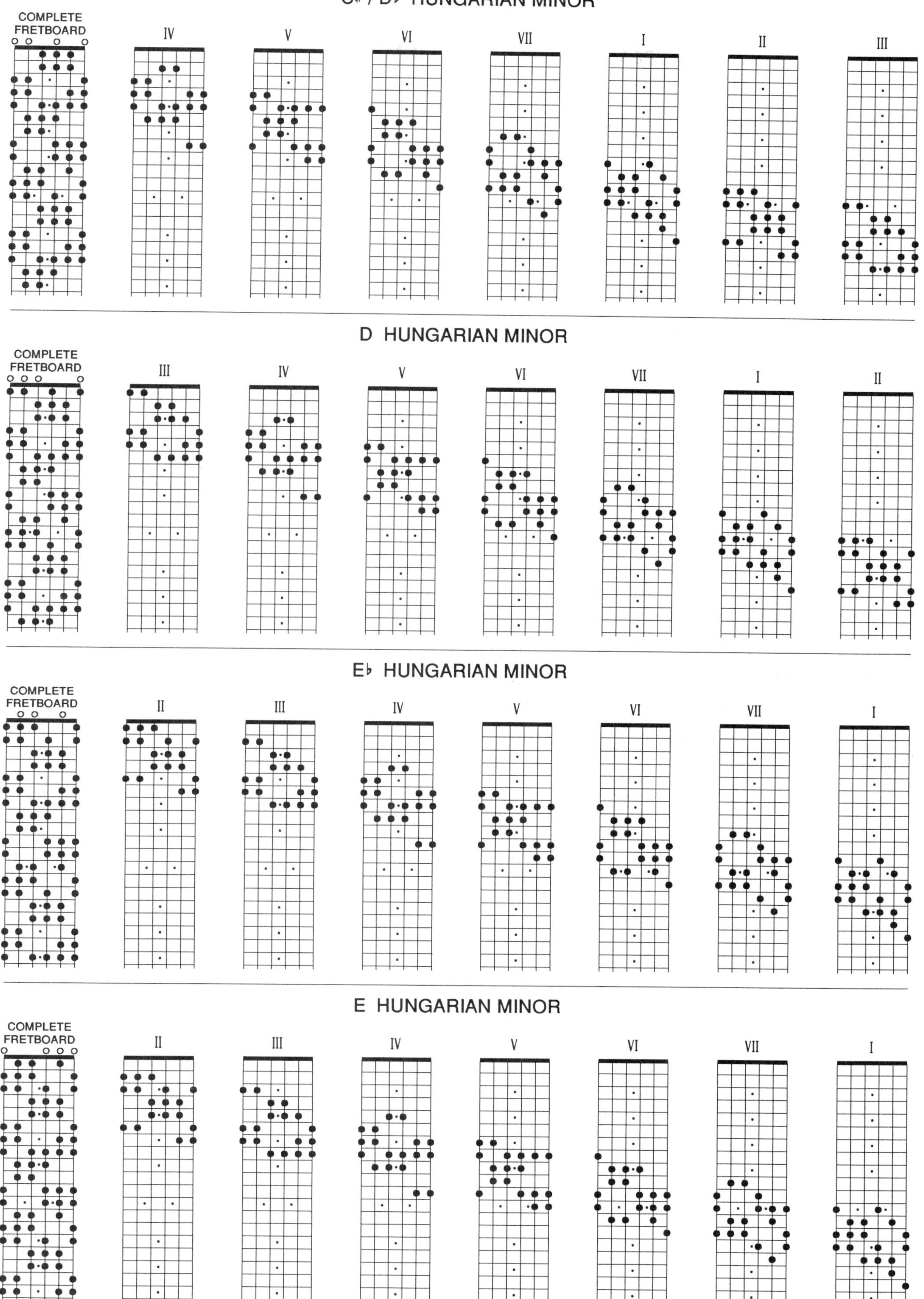
C♯ / D♭ HUNGARIAN MINOR
COMPLETE FRETBOARD
IV
V
VI
VII
I
II
III
D HUNGARIAN MINOR
COMPLETE FRETBOARD
III
IV
V
VI
VII
I
II
E♭ HUNGARIAN MINOR
COMPLETE FRETBOARD
II
III
IV
V
VI
VII
I
E HUNGARIAN MINOR
COMPLETE FRETBOARD
II
III
IV
V
VI
VII
I

KEYBOARD PATTERNS

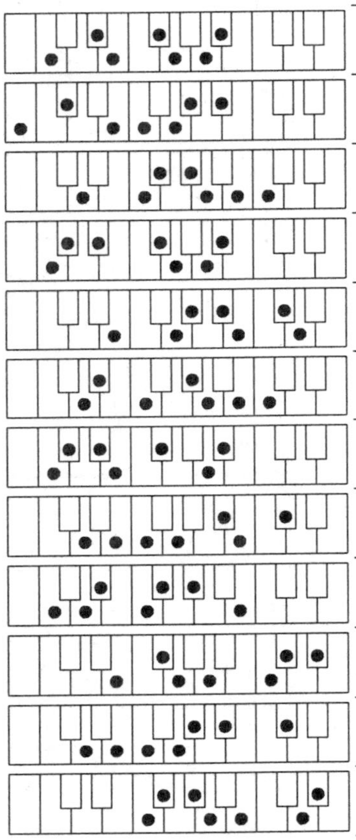

QUICK MODE GENERATOR CHART

HUNGARIAN MAJOR

I	II	III	IV	V	VI	VII
C	A	A♭	F#/G♭	F	E♭	D
C#/D♭	B♭	A	G	F#/G♭	E	E♭
D	B/C♭	B♭	A♭	G	F	E
E♭	C	B/C♭	A	A♭	F#/G♭	F
E	C#/D♭	C	B♭	A	G	F#/G♭
F	D	C#/D♭	B/C♭	B♭	A♭	G
F#/G♭	E♭	D	C	B/C♭	A	A♭
G	E	E♭	C#/D♭	C	B♭	A
A♭	F	E	D	C#/D♭	B/C♭	B♭
A	F#/G♭	F	E♭	D	C	B/C♭
B♭	G	F#/G♭	E	E♭	C#/D♭	C
B/C♭	A♭	G	F	E	D	C#/D♭

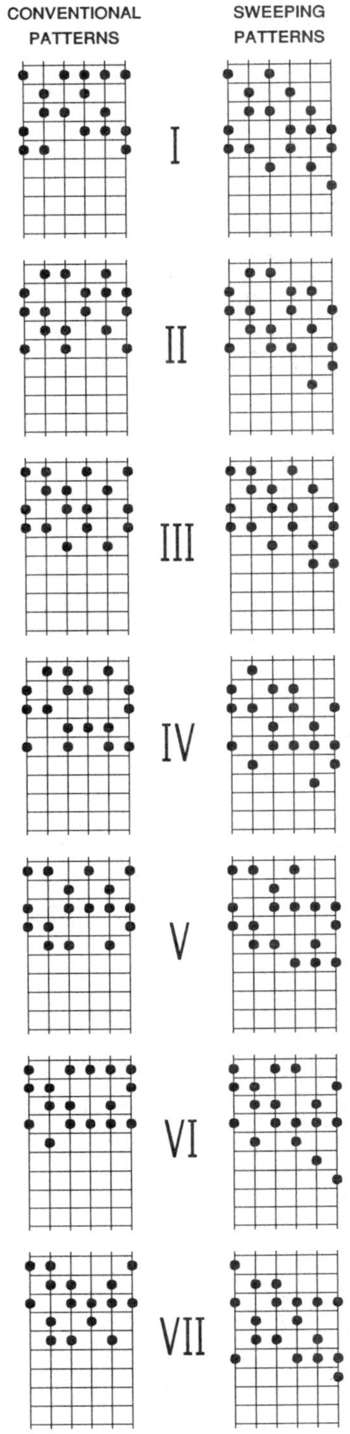

CONVENTIONAL PATTERNS

SWEEPING PATTERNS

I

II

III

IV

V

VI

VII

SCALE / MODE - CHORD CHART

I	HUNGARIAN MAJOR	7, $7^{\flat 5}$, ∅, °7, ⁻7, 6, #9, #11, 13
II	ALT 𝄫6 𝄫7	°7, 6
III	LOCRIAN ♮2 ♮7	△°, ⁻△⁺
IV	ALT ♮6	°7, $7^{\flat 5}$, ∅
V	MELODIC AUGMENTED	⁻△⁺
VI	DORIAN ♭2 #4	∅, ⁻7, ⁻6, °7
VII	LYDIAN AUGMENTED #3	$\triangle^{\#11}$ (NO 3,5)

NUMERIC SCALE / MODE CHART

		1		2		3	4		5		6		7	1		2		3	4		5		6		7
I	HUNGAR MAJOR	1			#2	3		#4	5		6	♭7		1			#2	3		#4	5		6	♭7	
II	ALT 𝄫6 𝄫7				1	♭2		♭3	♭4		♭5	𝄫6		𝄫7											
III	LOCRIAN ♮2 ♮7					1		2	♭3		4	♭5		♭6			7								
IV	ALT ♮6							1	♭2		♭3	♭4		♭5			6	♭7							
V	MELODIC AUG								1		2	♭3		4			#5	6		7					
VI	DORIAN ♭2 #4										1	♭2		♭3			#4	5		6	♭7				
VII	LYDIAN AUG #3											1		2			#3	#4		#5	6		7		

F HUNGARIAN MAJOR

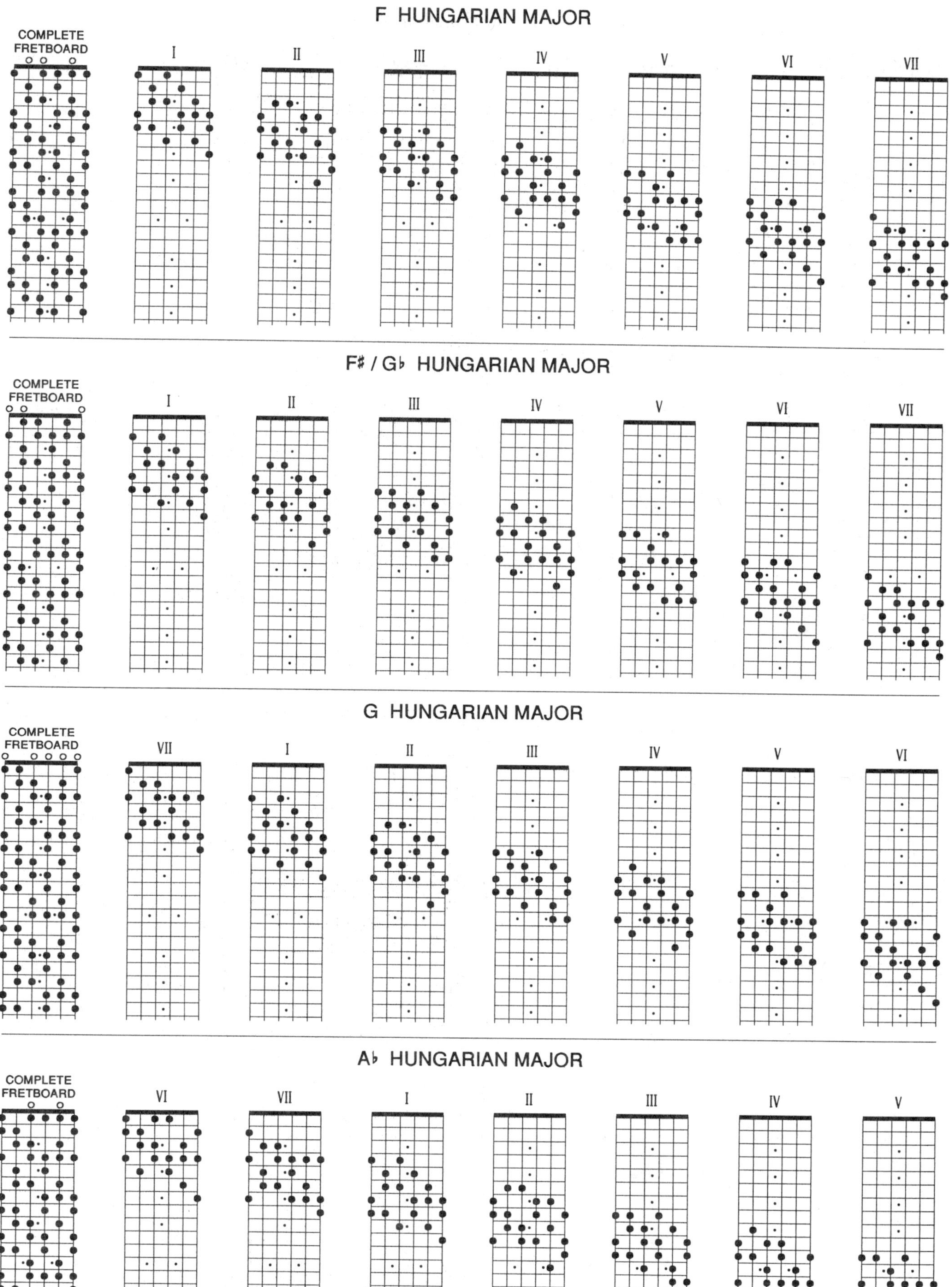

F♯ / G♭ HUNGARIAN MAJOR

G HUNGARIAN MAJOR

A♭ HUNGARIAN MAJOR

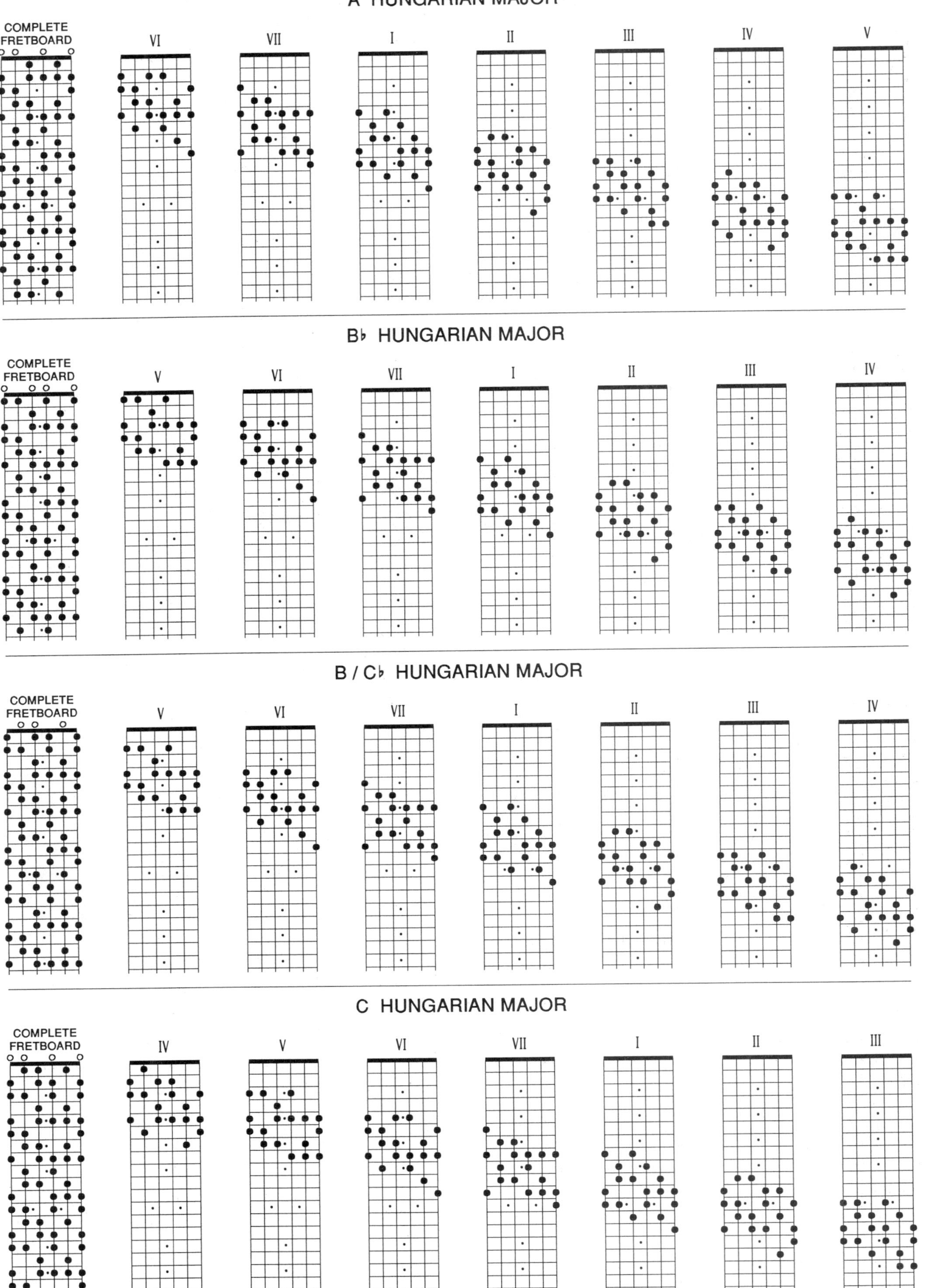
A HUNGARIAN MAJOR
COMPLETE FRETBOARD
VI
VII
I
II
III
IV
V
B♭ HUNGARIAN MAJOR
COMPLETE FRETBOARD
V
VI
VII
I
II
III
IV
B / C♭ HUNGARIAN MAJOR
COMPLETE FRETBOARD
V
VI
VII
I
II
III
IV
C HUNGARIAN MAJOR
COMPLETE FRETBOARD
IV
V
VI
VII
I
II
III

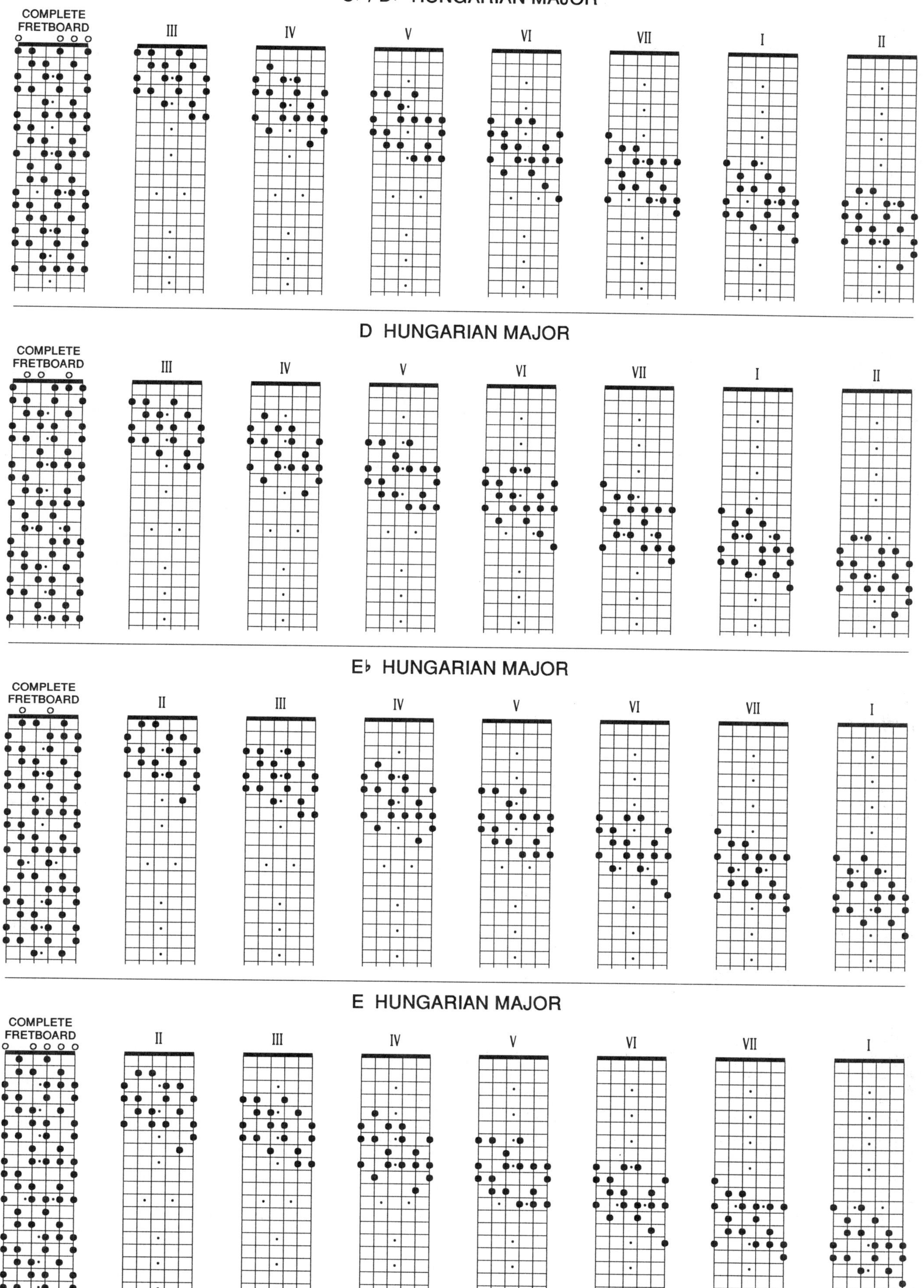
C♯ / D♭ HUNGARIAN MAJOR
COMPLETE FRETBOARD
III
IV
V
VI
VII
I
II
D HUNGARIAN MAJOR
COMPLETE FRETBOARD
III
IV
V
VI
VII
I
II
E♭ HUNGARIAN MAJOR
COMPLETE FRETBOARD
II
III
IV
V
VI
VII
I
E HUNGARIAN MAJOR
COMPLETE FRETBOARD
II
III
IV
V
VI
VII
I

KEYBOARD PATTERNS

QUICK MODE GENERATOR CHART

CONVENTIONAL PATTERNS

SWEEPING PATTERNS

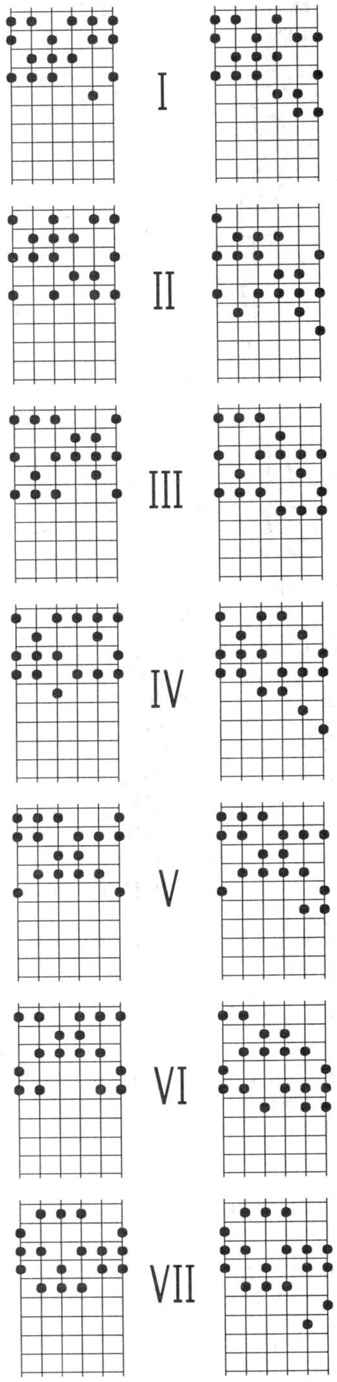

NEAPOLITAN MINOR

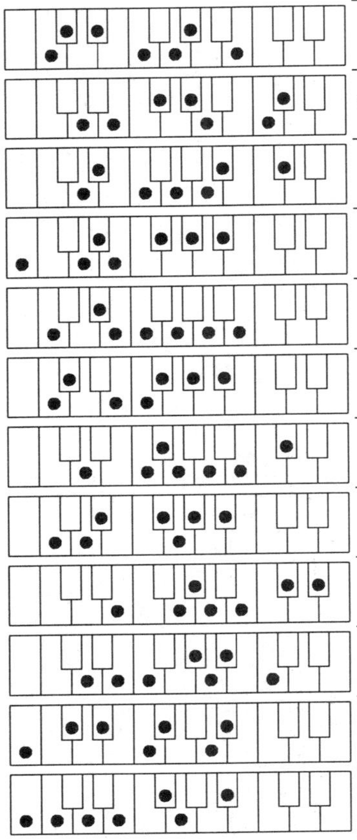

I	II	III	IV	V	VI	VII
C	B/C♭	A	G	F	E	C#/D♭
C#/D♭	C	B♭	A♭	F#/G♭	F	D
D	C#/D♭	B/C♭	A	G	F#/G♭	E♭
E♭	D	C	B♭	A♭	G	E
E	E♭	C#/D♭	B/C♭	A	A♭	F
F	E	D	C	B♭	A	F#/G♭
F#/G♭	F	E♭	C#/D♭	B/C♭	B♭	G
G	F#/G♭	E	D	C	B/C♭	A♭
A♭	G	F	E♭	C#/D♭	C	A
A	A♭	F#/G♭	E	D	C#/D♭	B♭
B♭	A	G	F	E♭	D	B/C♭
B/C♭	B♭	A♭	F#/G♭	E	E♭	C

SCALE / MODE - CHORD CHART

I	NEAPOLITAN MINOR	$^{-}\triangle$, $^{-}\triangle^{+}$
II	LYDIAN #6	$(\triangle, 7, \triangle^{\flat 5}, 7^{\flat 5})^{sus4}$, 9, #11
III	DOMINANT AUGMENTED	7^{+sus}, 7^{+sus2}
IV	HUNGARIAN GYPSY	∅, −7, −♭6, 7^{sus2}, 9, #9, #11, ♭13
V	LOCRIAN ♮3	7^{+}, $7^{\flat 5}$, ♭9, 11, #11, ♭13
VI	IONIAN #2	△, $\triangle^{sus}$, −△, 6, −6
VII	ALT 𝄫3 𝄫7	+, ♭5

NUMERIC SCALE / MODE CHART

		1		2		3	4		5		6		7	1		2		3	4		5		6		7
I	NEAPOL MINOR	1	♭2		♭3		4		5	♭6			7	1	♭2		♭3		4		5	♭6			7
II	LYDIAN #6		1		2		3		#4	5			#6	7											
III	DOMINANT AUG				1		2		3	4			#5	6	♭7										
IV	HUNGAR GYPSY						1		2	♭3			#4	5	♭6		♭7								
V	LOCRIAN ♮3								1	♭2			3	4	♭5		♭6		♭7						
VI	IONIAN #2									1			#2	3	4		5		6		7				
VII	ALT 𝄫3 𝄫7												1	♭2	𝄫3		♭4		♭5		♭6	𝄫7			

F NEAPOLITAN MINOR

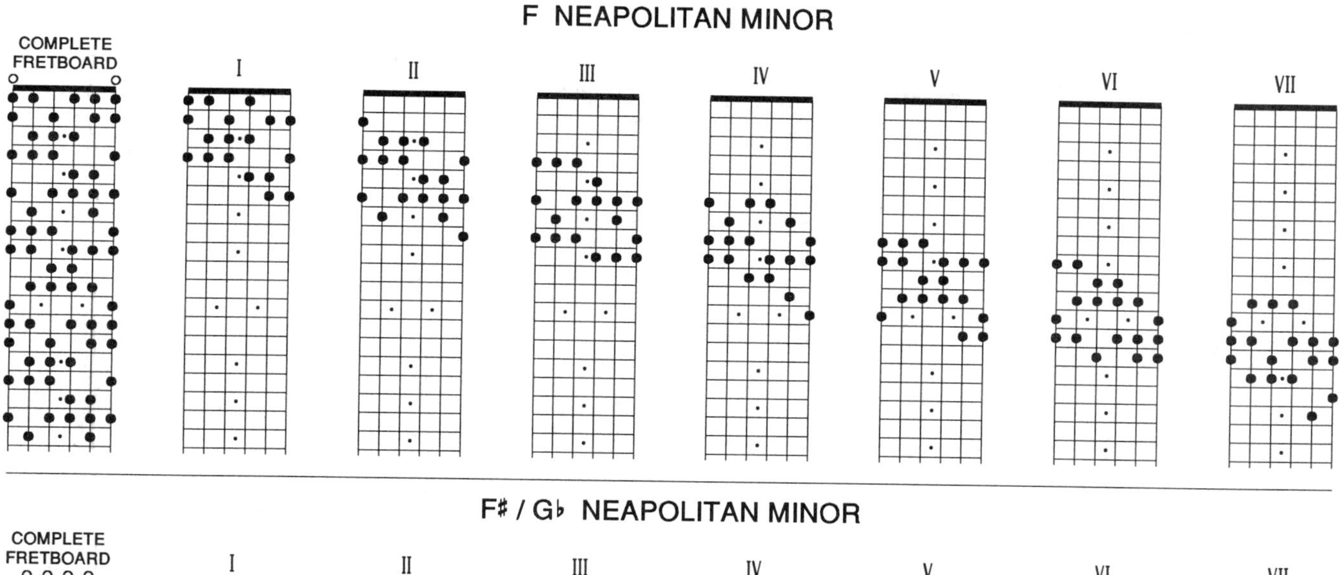

F♯ / G♭ NEAPOLITAN MINOR

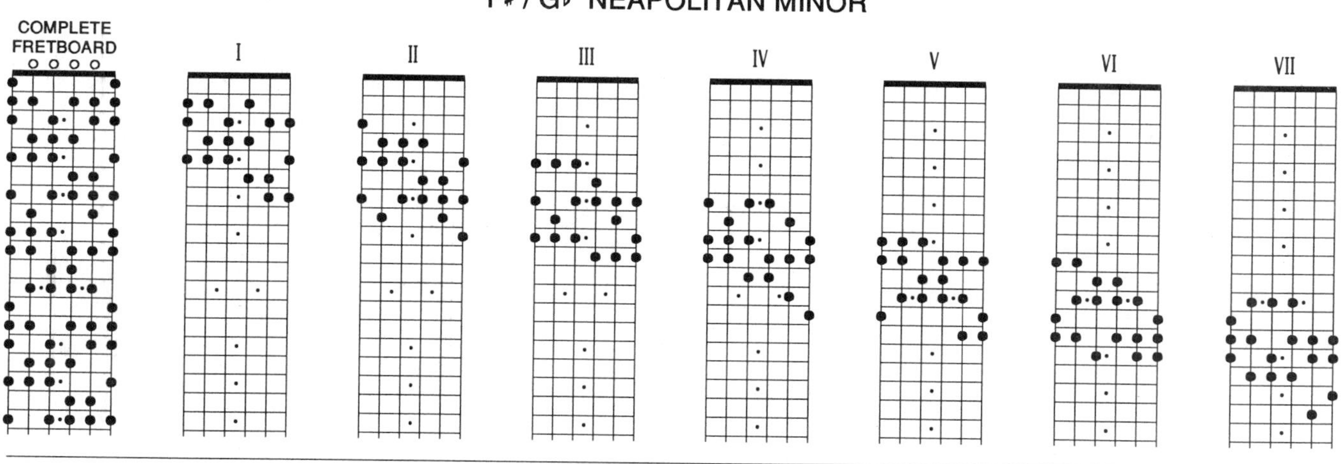

G NEAPOLITAN MINOR

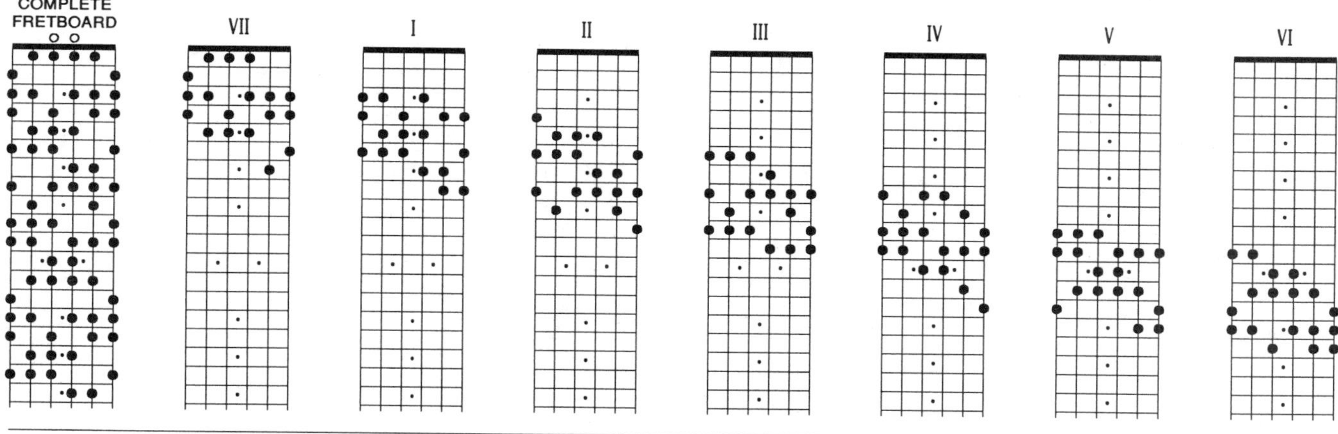

A♭ NEAPOLITAN MINOR

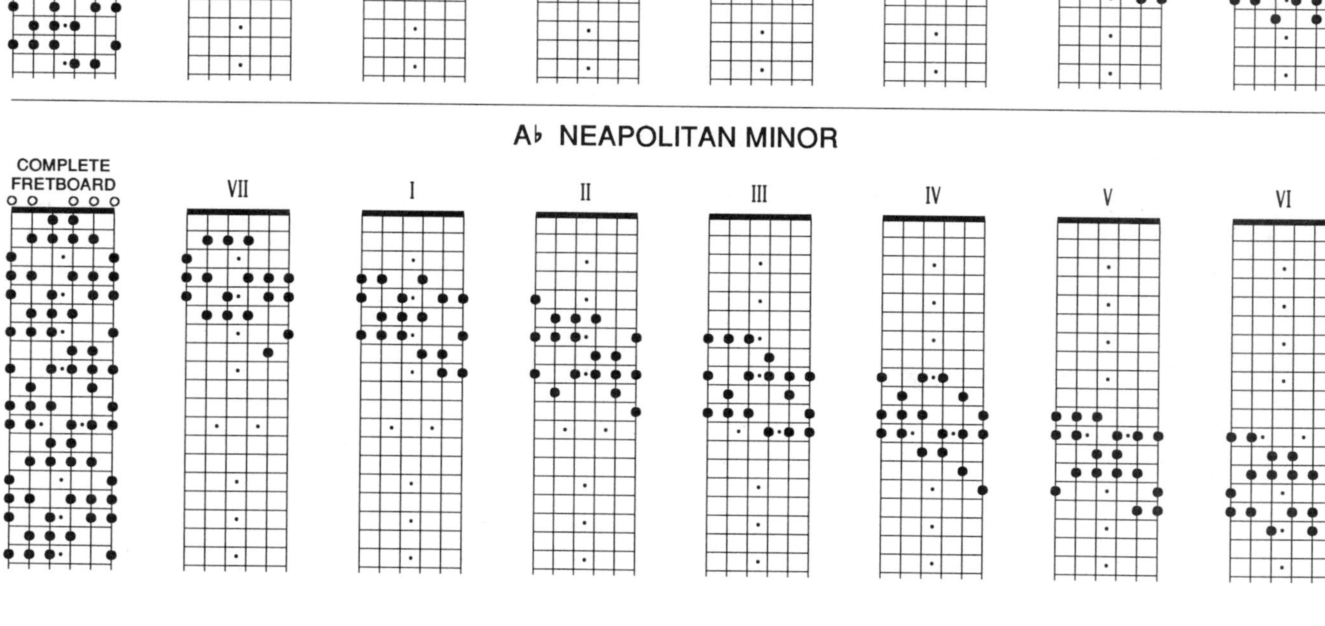

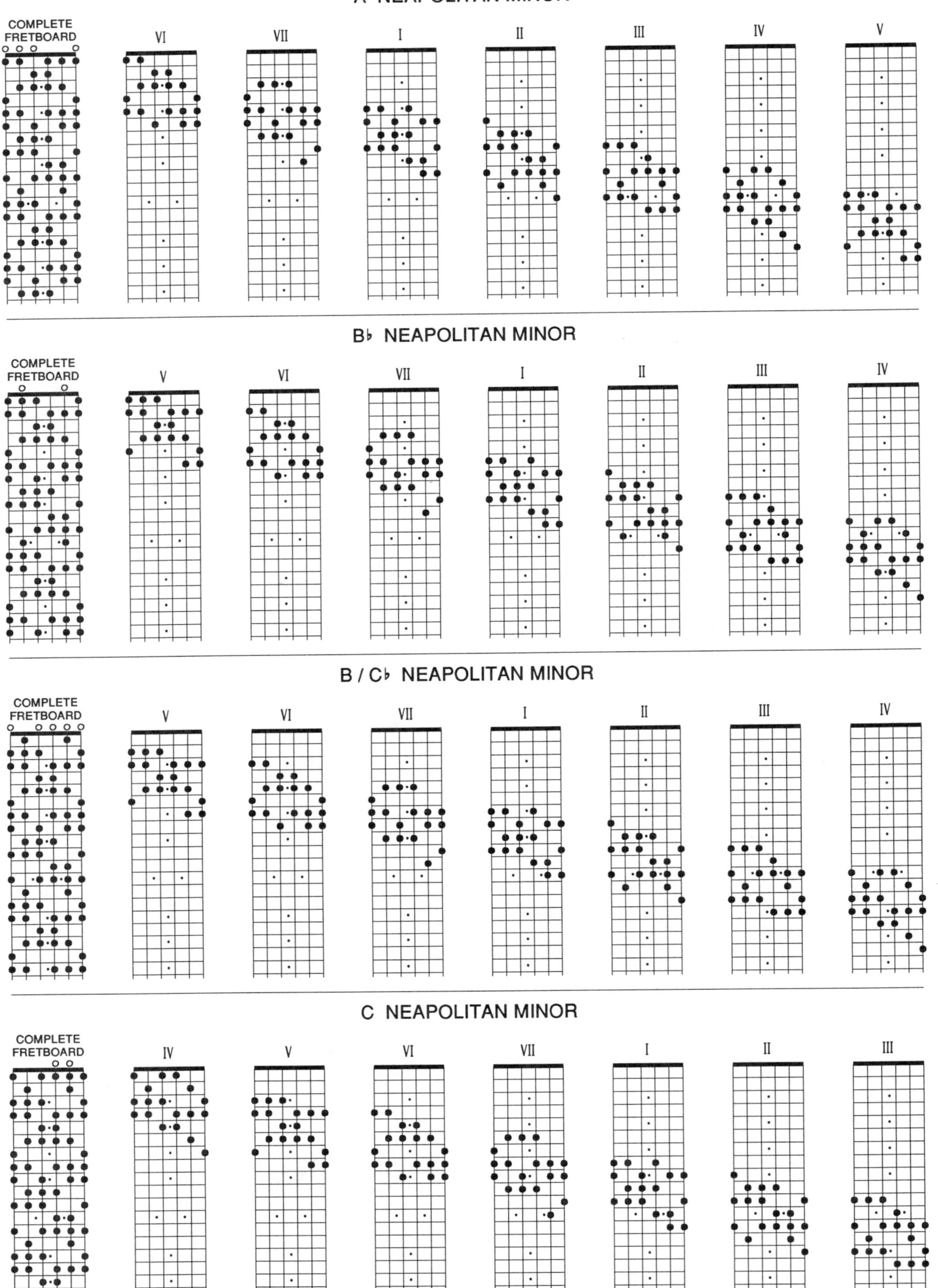
A NEAPOLITAN MINOR
COMPLETE FRETBOARD
VI
VII
I
II
III
IV
V
B♭ NEAPOLITAN MINOR
COMPLETE FRETBOARD
V
VI
VII
I
II
III
IV
B / C♭ NEAPOLITAN MINOR
COMPLETE FRETBOARD
V
VI
VII
I
II
III
IV
C NEAPOLITAN MINOR
COMPLETE FRETBOARD
IV
V
VI
VII
I
II
III

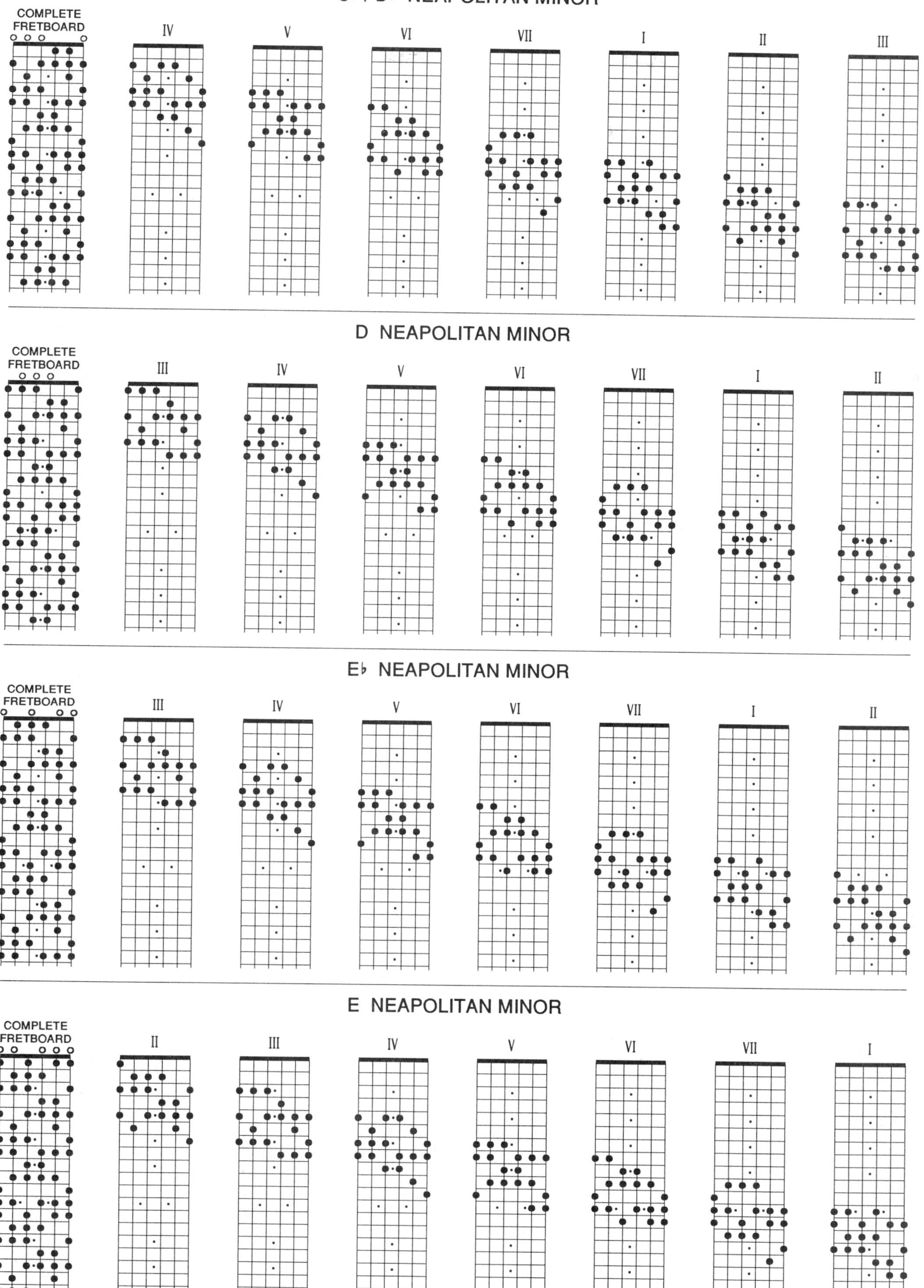
C♯ / D♭ NEAPOLITAN MINOR
COMPLETE FRETBOARD
IV
V
VI
VII
I
II
III
D NEAPOLITAN MINOR
COMPLETE FRETBOARD
III
IV
V
VI
VII
I
II
E♭ NEAPOLITAN MINOR
COMPLETE FRETBOARD
III
IV
V
VI
VII
I
II
E NEAPOLITAN MINOR
COMPLETE FRETBOARD
II
III
IV
V
VI
VII
I

KEYBOARD PATTERNS

QUICK MODE GENERATOR CHART

NEAPOLITAN MAJOR

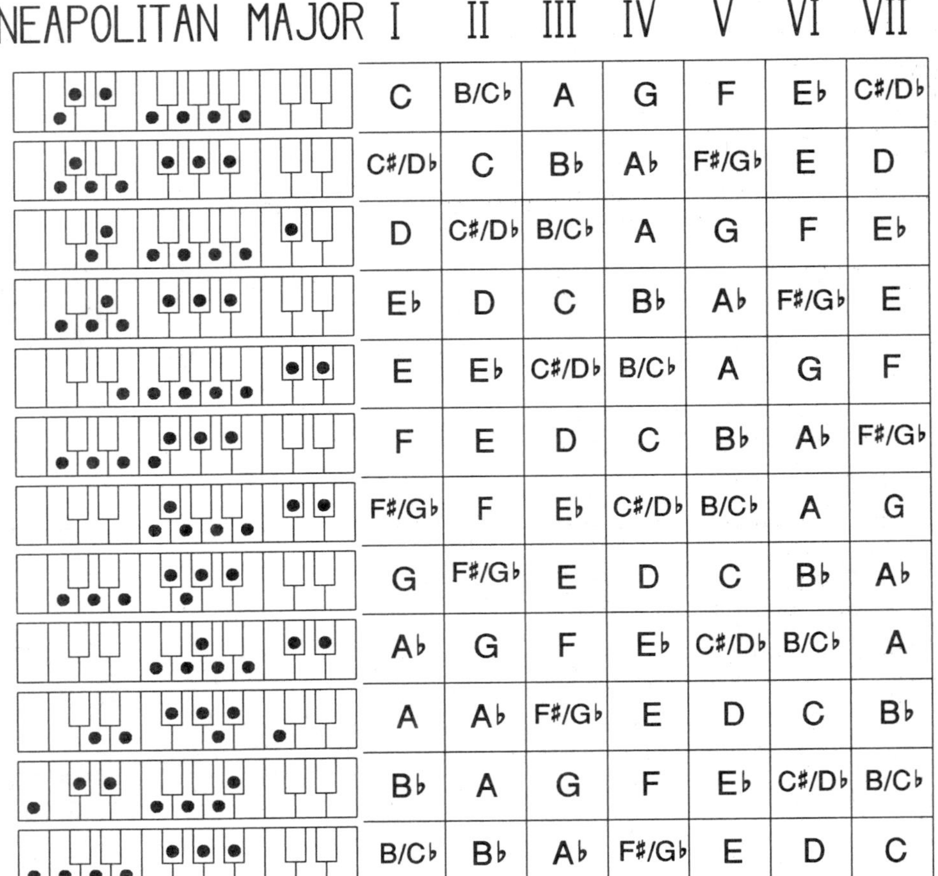

I	II	III	IV	V	VI	VII
C	B/C♭	A	G	F	E♭	C♯/D♭
C♯/D♭	C	B♭	A♭	F♯/G♭	E	D
D	C♯/D♭	B/C♭	A	G	F	E♭
E♭	D	C	B♭	A♭	F♯/G♭	E
E	E♭	C♯/D♭	B/C♭	A	G	F
F	E	D	C	B♭	A♭	F♯/G♭
F♯/G♭	F	E♭	C♯/D♭	B/C♭	A	G
G	F♯/G♭	E	D	C	B♭	A♭
A♭	G	F	E♭	C♯/D♭	B/C♭	A
A	A♭	F♯/G♭	E	D	C	B♭
B♭	A	G	F	E♭	C♯/D♭	B/C♭
B/C♭	B♭	A♭	F♯/G♭	E	D	C

CONVENTIONAL PATTERNS

SWEEPING PATTERNS

I

II

III

IV

V

VI

VII

SCALE / MODE - CHORD CHART

I	NEAPOLITAN MAJOR	$^{-}\triangle$, $\triangle^{sus}$, $^{-}6$
II	LYDIAN AUGMENTED ♯6	7^{+}, $\triangle^{+}$, $7^{\flat 5}$, $\triangle^{\flat 5}$
III	LYDIAN DOMINANT AUGMENTED	7^{+}, $7^{\flat 5}$
IV	LYDIAN MINOR	7, 7^{+}, $7^{\flat 5}$, 7^{sus2}, 9, ♯11, ♭13
V	MAJOR LOCRIAN	7^{+}, $7^{\flat 5}$, 9, 11, ♯11, ♭13
VI	ALT ♮2	7^{+}, $7^{\flat 5}$, ⌀
VII	ALT 𝄫3	7^{+}, $7^{\flat 5}$

NUMERIC SCALE / MODE CHART

		1		2		3	4		5		6		7	1		2		3	4		5		6		7
I	NEAPOL MAJOR	1	♭2		♭3		4		5		6		7	1	♭2		♭3		4		5		6		7
II	LYDIAN AUG ♯6		1		2		3		♯4		♯5		♯6	7											
III	LYD DOM AUG				1		2		3		♯4		♯5	6	♭7										
IV	LYDIAN MINOR						1		2		3		♯4	5	♭6		♭7								
V	MAJOR LOCRIAN								1		2		3	4	♭5		♭6		♭7						
VI	ALT ♮2										1		2	♭3	♭4		♭5		♭6		♭7				
VII	ALT 𝄫3												1	♭2	𝄫3		♭4		♭5		♭6		♭7		

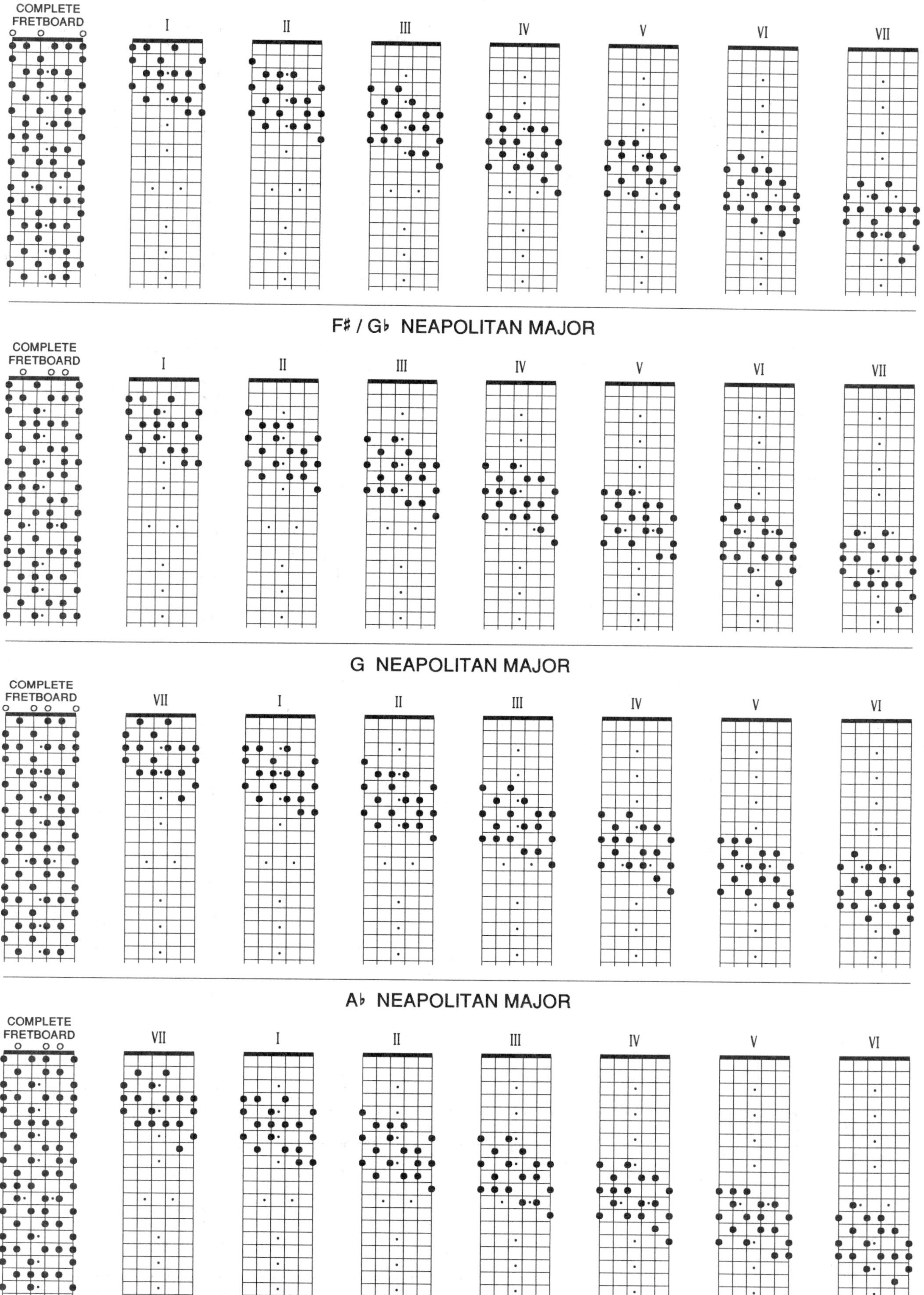
F NEAPOLITAN MAJOR
COMPLETE FRETBOARD
I
II
III
IV
V
VI
VII
F♯ / G♭ NEAPOLITAN MAJOR
COMPLETE FRETBOARD
I
II
III
IV
V
VI
VII
G NEAPOLITAN MAJOR
COMPLETE FRETBOARD
VII
I
II
III
IV
V
VI
A♭ NEAPOLITAN MAJOR
COMPLETE FRETBOARD
VII
I
II
III
IV
V
VI

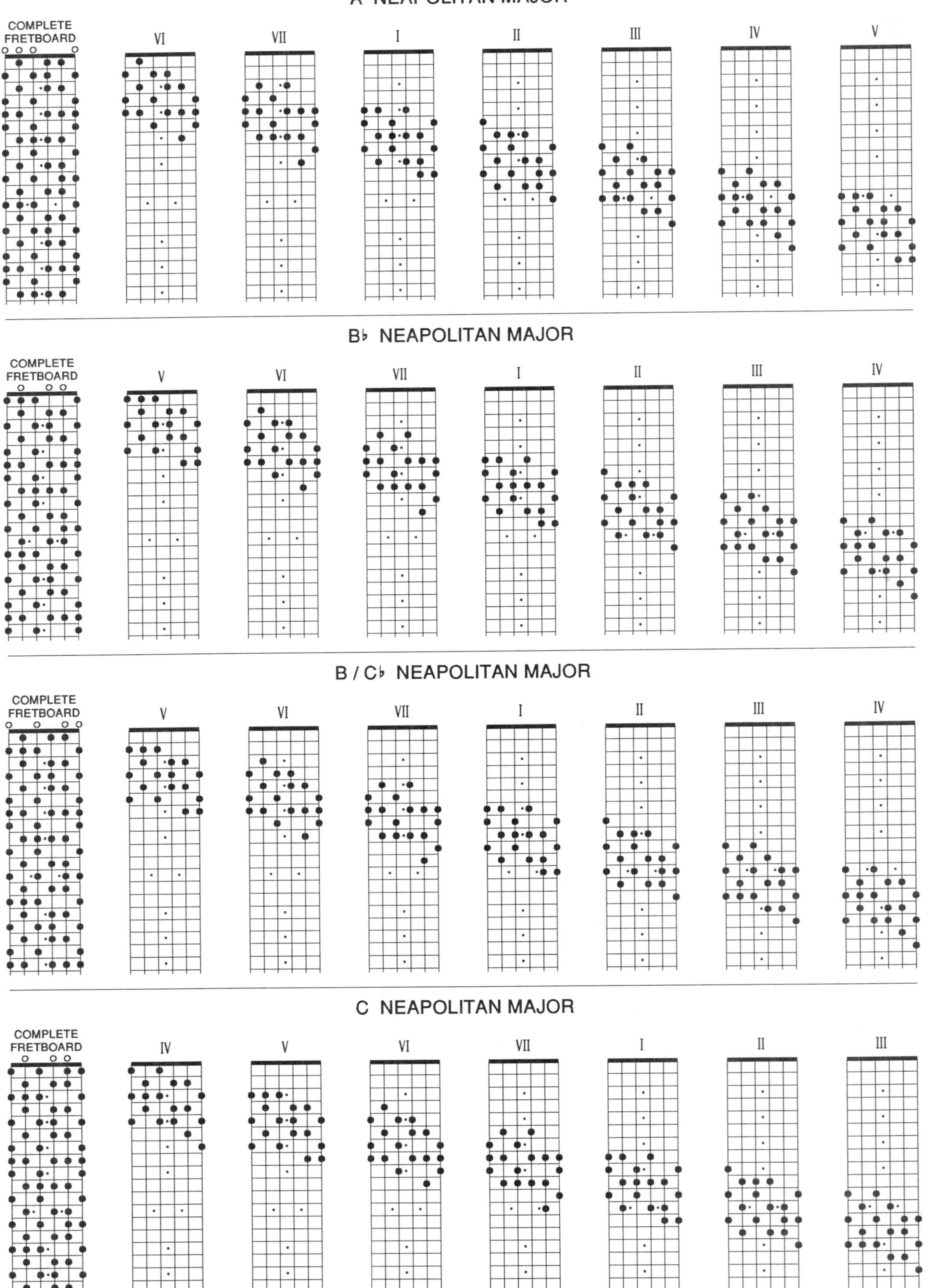
A NEAPOLITAN MAJOR
COMPLETE FRETBOARD
VI
VII
I
II
III
IV
V
B♭ NEAPOLITAN MAJOR
COMPLETE FRETBOARD
V
VI
VII
I
II
III
IV
B / C♭ NEAPOLITAN MAJOR
COMPLETE FRETBOARD
V
VI
VII
I
II
III
IV
C NEAPOLITAN MAJOR
COMPLETE FRETBOARD
IV
V
VI
VII
I
II
III

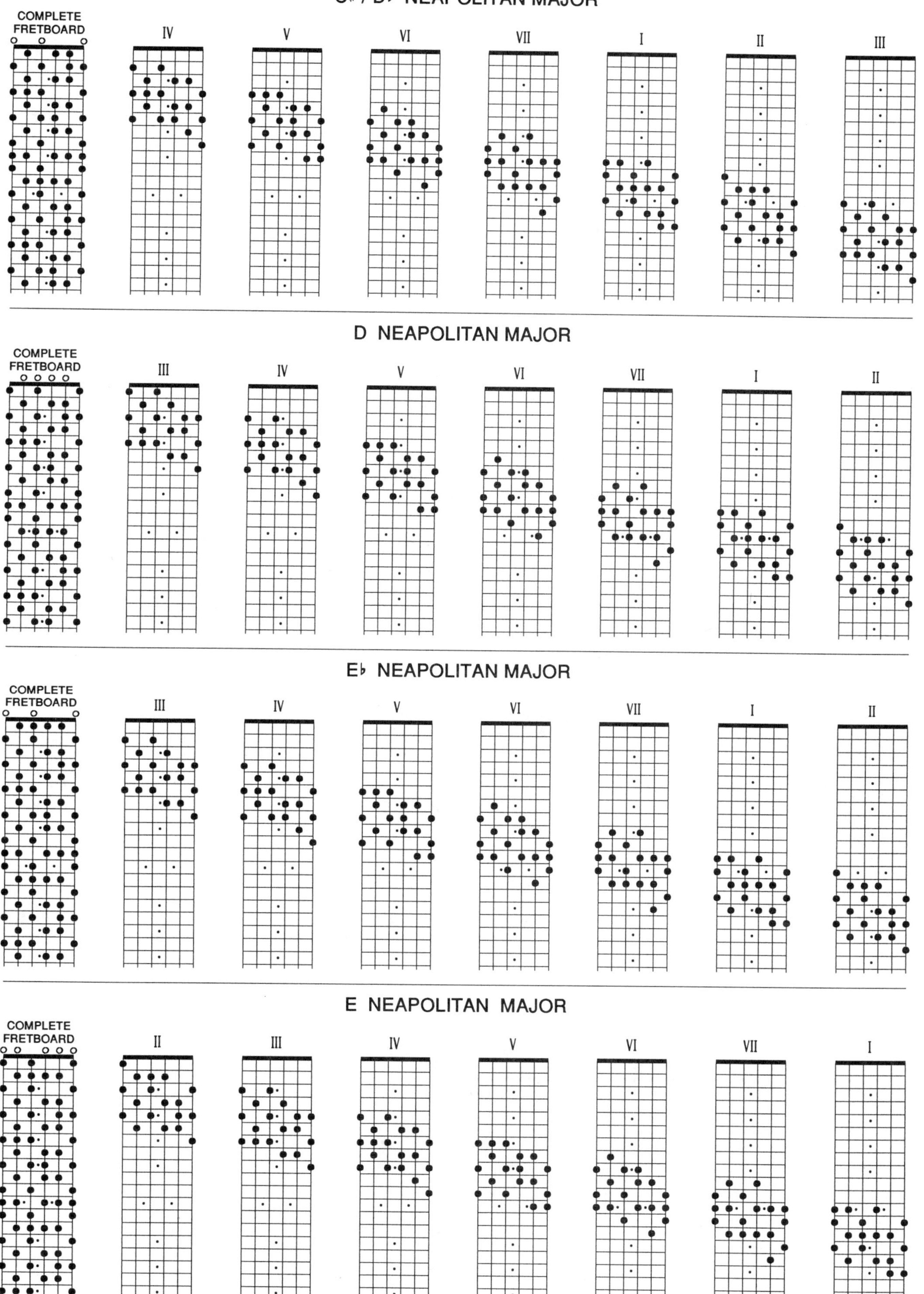
C♯ / D♭ NEAPOLITAN MAJOR
COMPLETE FRETBOARD
IV
V
VI
VII
I
II
III
D NEAPOLITAN MAJOR
COMPLETE FRETBOARD
III
IV
V
VI
VII
I
II
E♭ NEAPOLITAN MAJOR
COMPLETE FRETBOARD
III
IV
V
VI
VII
I
II
E NEAPOLITAN MAJOR
COMPLETE FRETBOARD
II
III
IV
V
VI
VII
I

KEYBOARD PATTERNS

QUICK MODE GENERATOR CHART

ENIGMATIC MINOR

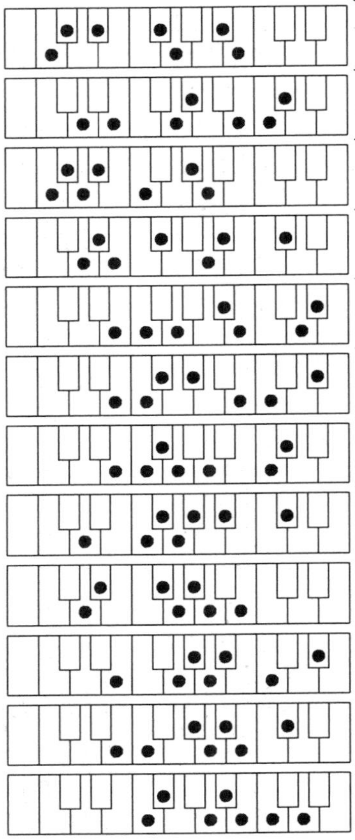

I	II	III	IV	V	VI	VII
C	B/C♭	A	F♯/G♭	F	D	C♯/D♭
C♯/D♭	C	B♭	G	F♯/G♭	E♭	D
D	C♯/D♭	B/C♭	A♭	G	E	E♭
E♭	D	C	A	A♭	F	E
E	E♭	C♯/D♭	B♭	A	F♯/G♭	F
F	E	D	B/C♭	B♭	G	F♯/G♭
F♯/G♭	F	E♭	C	B/C♭	A♭	G
G	F♯/G♭	E	C♯/D♭	C	A	A♭
A♭	G	F	D	C♯/D♭	B♭	A
A	A♭	F♯/G♭	E♭	D	B/C♭	B♭
B♭	A	G	E	E♭	C	B/C♭
B/C♭	B♭	A♭	F	E	C♯/D♭	C

CONVENTIONAL PATTERNS

SWEEPING PATTERNS

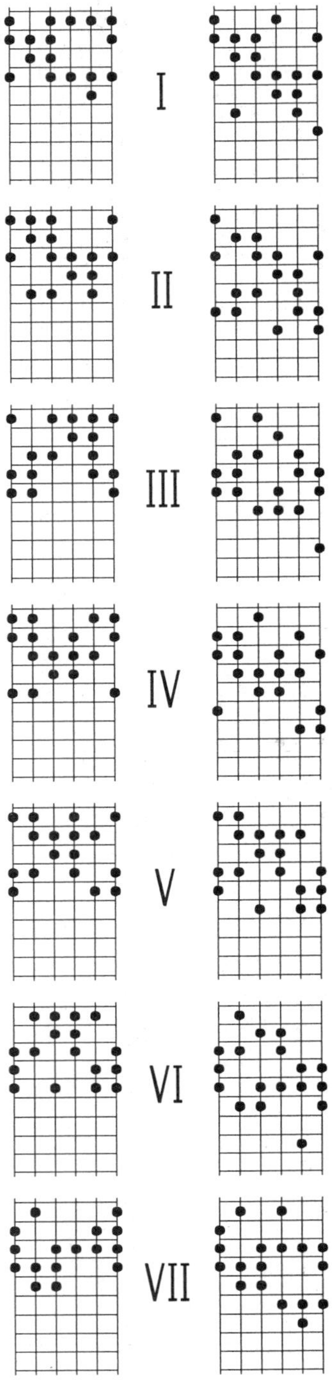

I

II

III

IV

V

VI

VII

SCALE / MODE - CHORD CHART

I	ENIGMATIC MINOR	-△, ∅, -7, △°, -♭9, -♯9
II	MODE 2	△sus2 (NO 5)
III	MODE 3	7, 7+, ♭6, 6, ♯9
IV	MODE 4	sus, 6, -6
V	MODE 5	△+, △, -△, -△+
VI	MODE 6	sus2 (NO 5)
VII	MODE 7	△, ♭6

NUMERIC SCALE / MODE CHART

		1		2		3	4		5		6		7	1		2		3	4		5		6		7
I	ENIGMATIC MINOR	1	♭2		♭3			♯4	5			♯6	7	1	♭2		♭3			♯4	5			♯6	7
II	MODE 2		1		2			♯3	♯4			𝄪5	♯6	7											
III	MODE 3				1			♯2	3			𝄪4	♯5	6	♭7										
IV	MODE 4							1	♭2			3	4	♭5	𝄫6		𝄫7								
V	MODE 5								1			♯2	3	4	♭5		♭6			7					
VI	MODE 6											1	♭2	𝄫3	𝄫4		𝄫5			♭6	𝄫7				
VII	MODE 7												1	♭2	𝄫3		♭4			5	♭6			7	

F ENIGMATIC MINOR

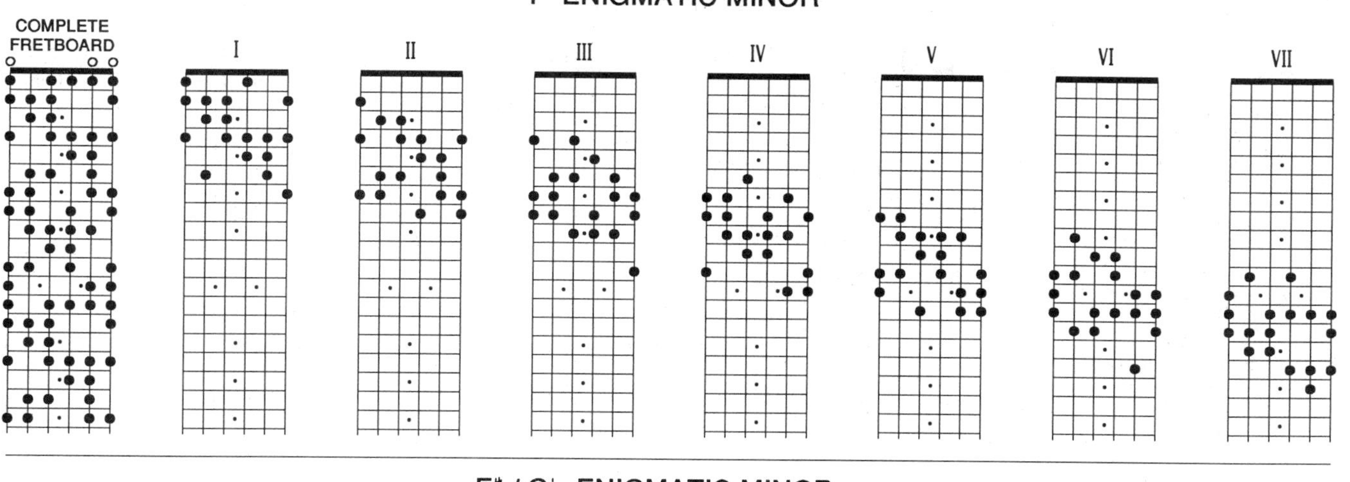

F♯ / G♭ ENIGMATIC MINOR

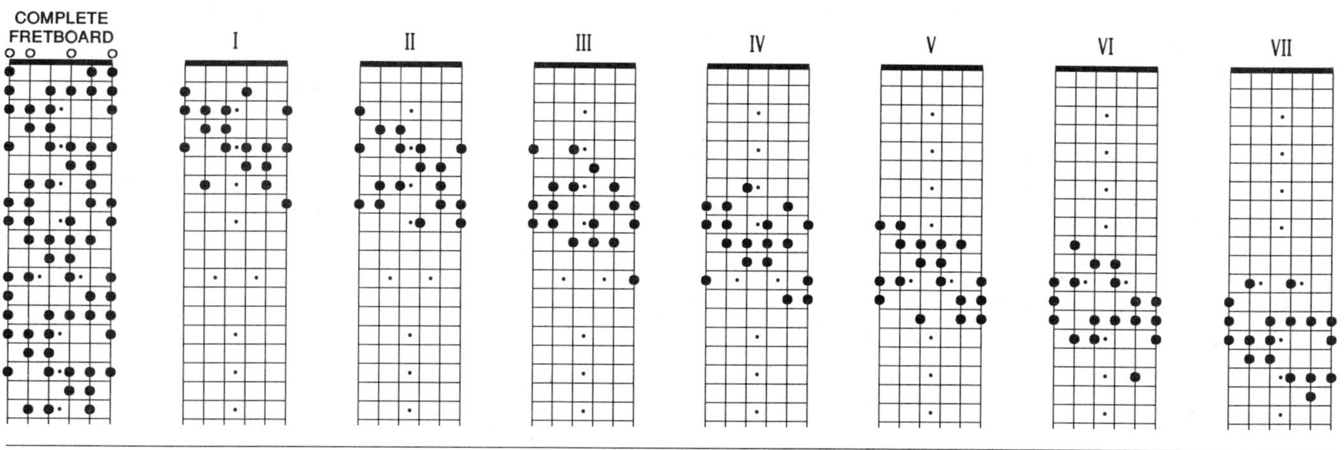

G ENIGMATIC MINOR

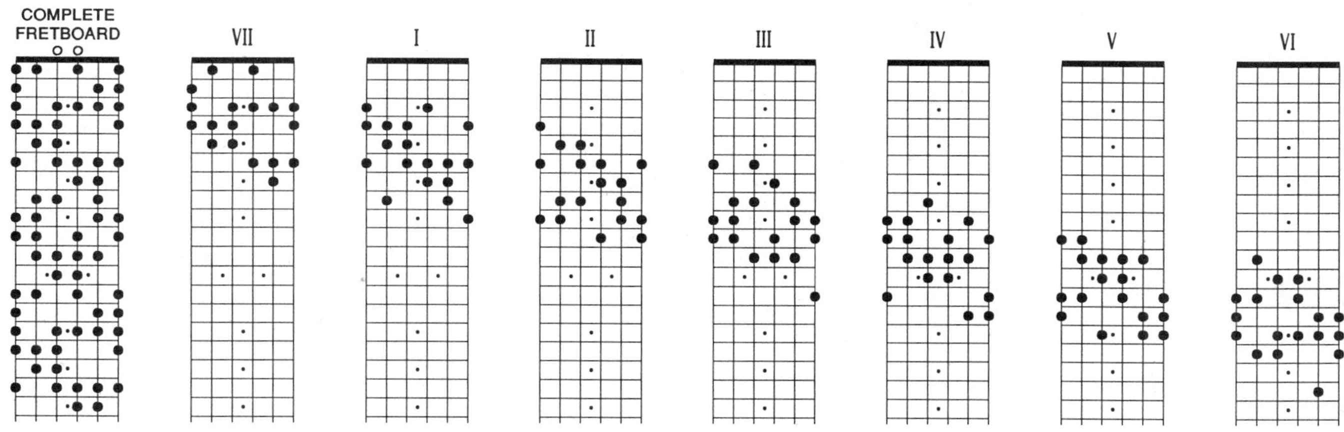

A♭ ENIGMATIC MINOR

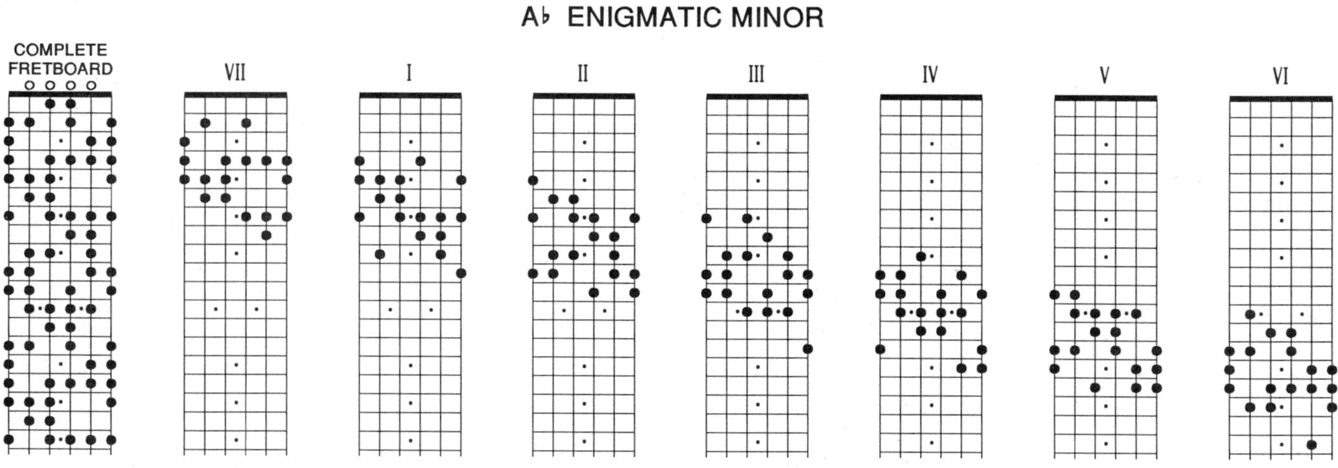

A ENIGMATIC MINOR

B♭ ENIGMATIC MINOR

B / C♭ ENIGMATIC MINOR

C ENIGMATIC MINOR

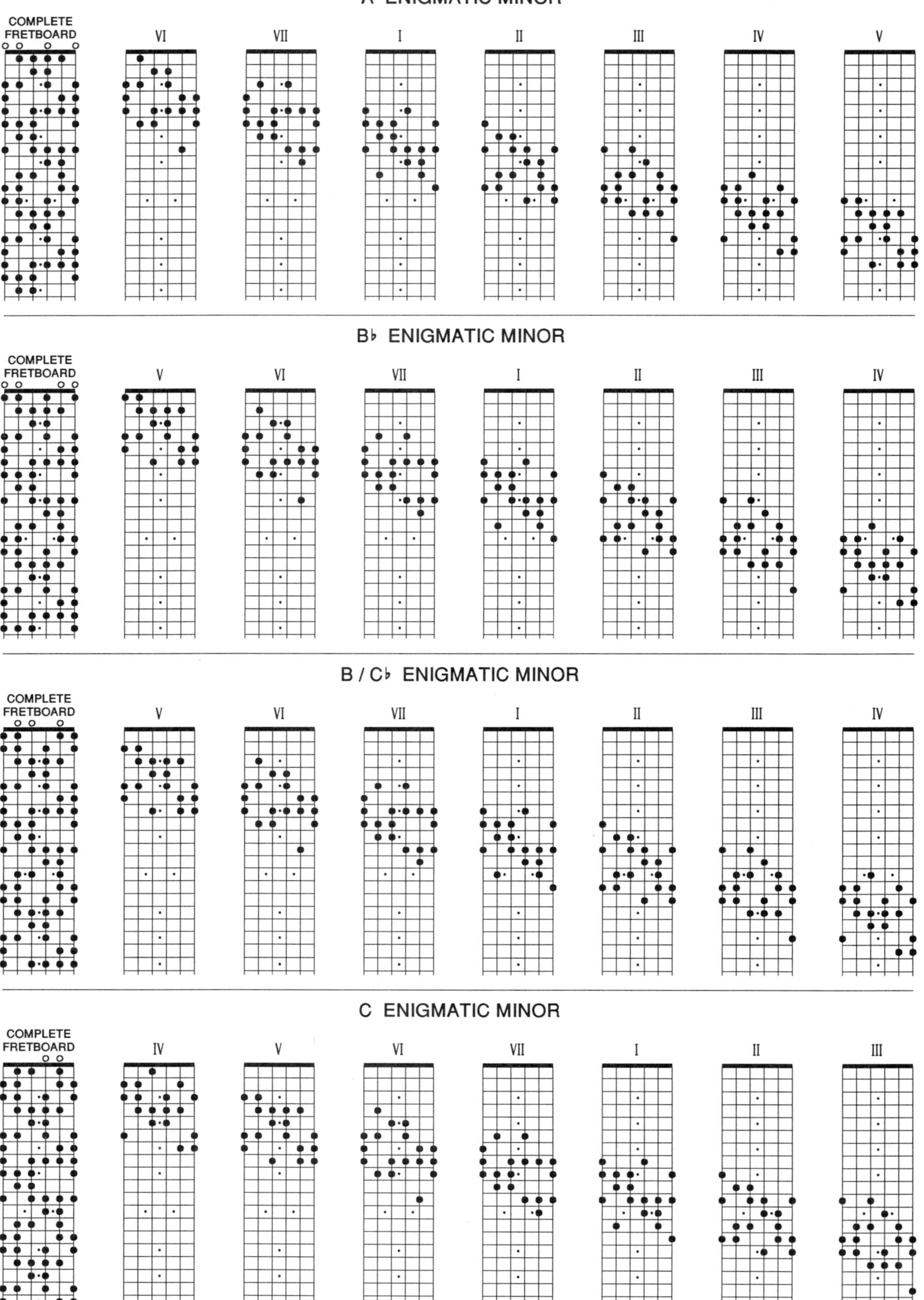

C♯ / D♭ ENIGMATIC MINOR

D ENIGMATIC MINOR

E♭ ENIGMATIC MINOR

E ENIGMATIC MINOR

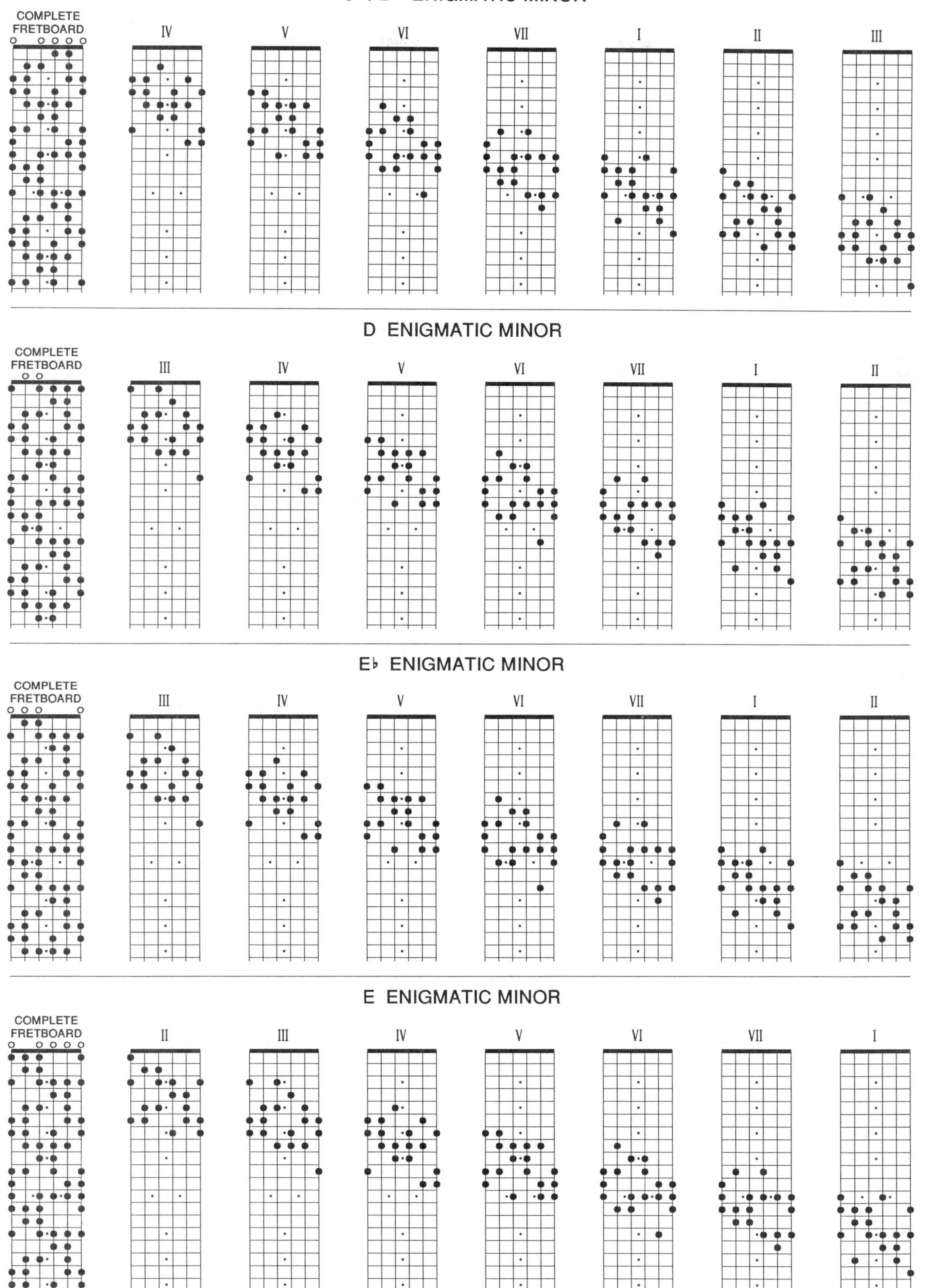

KEYBOARD PATTERNS

ENIGMATIC

QUICK MODE GENERATOR CHART

I	II	III	IV	V	VI	VII
C	B/C♭	A♭	F♯/G♭	E	D	C♯/D♭
C♯/D♭	C	A	G	F	E♭	D
D	C♯/D♭	B♭	A♭	F♯/G♭	E	E♭
E♭	D	B/C♭	A	G	F	E
E	E♭	C	B♭	A♭	F♯/G♭	F
F	E	C♯/D♭	B/C♭	A	G	F♯/G♭
F♯/G♭	F	D	C	B♭	A♭	G
G	F♯/G♭	E♭	C♯/D♭	B/C♭	A	A♭
A♭	G	E	D	C	B♭	A
A	A♭	F	E♭	C♯/D♭	B/C♭	B♭
B♭	A	F♯/G♭	E	D	C	B/C♭
B/C♭	B♭	G	F	E♭	C♯/D♭	C

CONVENTIONAL PATTERNS

SWEEPING PATTERNS

I

II

III

IV

V

VI

VII

SCALE / MODE - CHORD CHART

I	ENIGMATIC	△+, △♭5, 7+, ♭9
II	MODE 2	-△, -7, -6, 7sus, △sus
III	MODE 3	6, ♭6, 9
IV	MODE 4	7, 7♭5
V	MODE 5	7+
VI	MODE 6	ø
VII	MODE 7	△sus2, △sus

NUMERIC SCALE / MODE CHART

		1		2		3	4		5		6		7	1		2		3	4		5		6		7
I	ENIGMATIC	1	♭2			3		♯4		♯5		♯6	7	1	♭2			3		♯4		♯5		♯6	7
II	MODE 2		1			♯2		♯3		x4		x5	♯6	7											
III	MODE 3					1		2		3		♯4	5	♭6	𝄫7										
IV	MODE 4							1		2		3	4	♭5	𝄫6			♭7							
V	MODE 5									1		2	♭3	♭4	𝄫5			♭6		♭7					
VI	MODE 6											1	♭2	𝄫3	♭4			♭5		♭6		♭7			
VII	MODE 7												1	♭2	𝄫3			4		5		6		7	

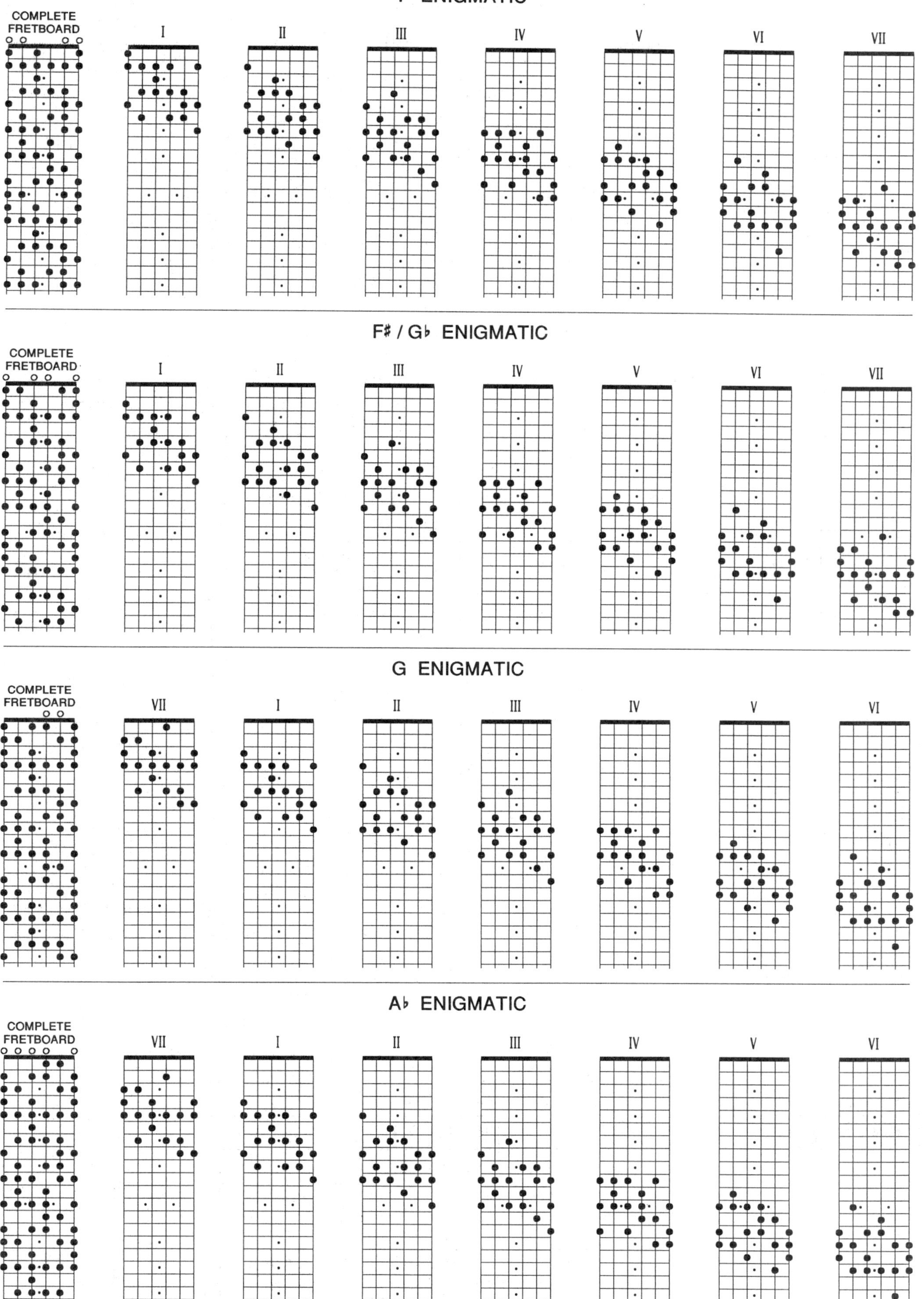

F ENIGMATIC
COMPLETE FRETBOARD
I
II
III
IV
V
VI
VII
F♯ / G♭ ENIGMATIC
COMPLETE FRETBOARD
I
II
III
IV
V
VI
VII
G ENIGMATIC
COMPLETE FRETBOARD
VII
I
II
III
IV
V
VI
A♭ ENIGMATIC
COMPLETE FRETBOARD
VII
I
II
III
IV
V
VI

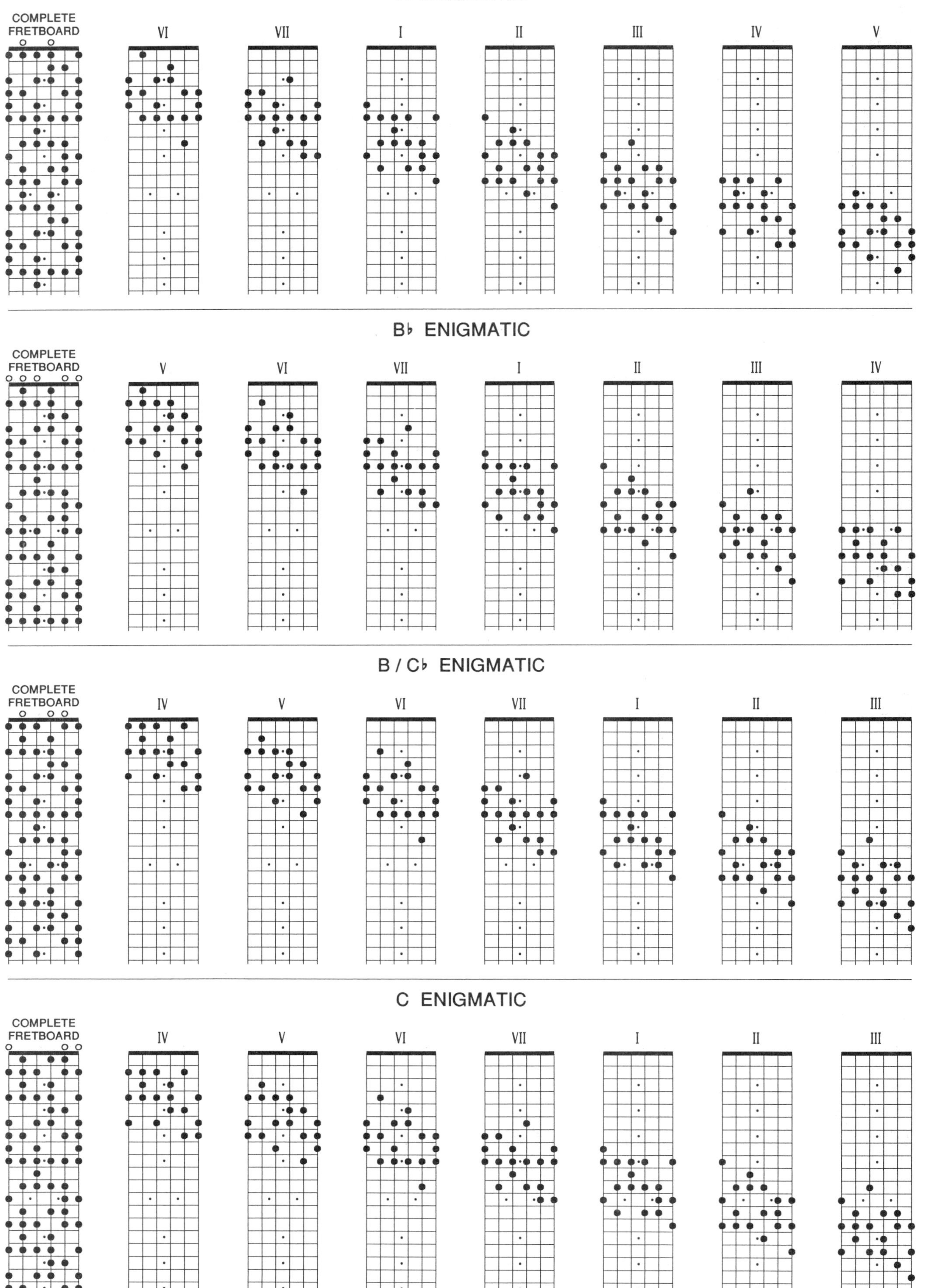
A ENIGMATIC
COMPLETE FRETBOARD
VI
VII
I
II
III
IV
V
B♭ ENIGMATIC
COMPLETE FRETBOARD
V
VI
VII
I
II
III
IV
B / C♭ ENIGMATIC
COMPLETE FRETBOARD
IV
V
VI
VII
I
II
III
C ENIGMATIC
COMPLETE FRETBOARD
IV
V
VI
VII
I
II
III

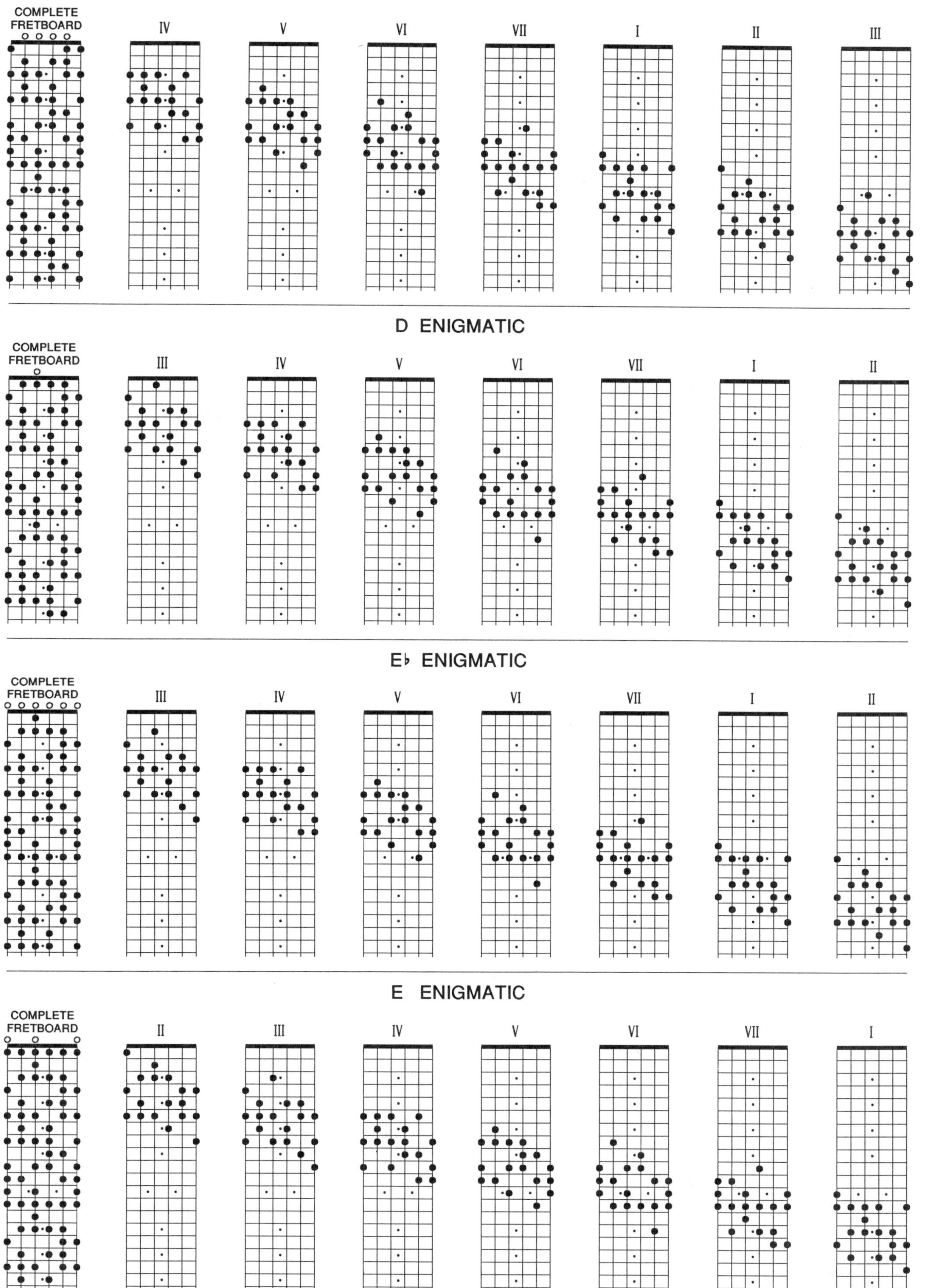
C♯ / D♭ ENIGMATIC
COMPLETE FRETBOARD
IV
V
VI
VII
I
II
III
D ENIGMATIC
COMPLETE FRETBOARD
III
IV
V
VI
VII
I
II
E♭ ENIGMATIC
COMPLETE FRETBOARD
III
IV
V
VI
VII
I
II
E ENIGMATIC
COMPLETE FRETBOARD
II
III
IV
V
VI
VII
I

KEYBOARD PATTERNS

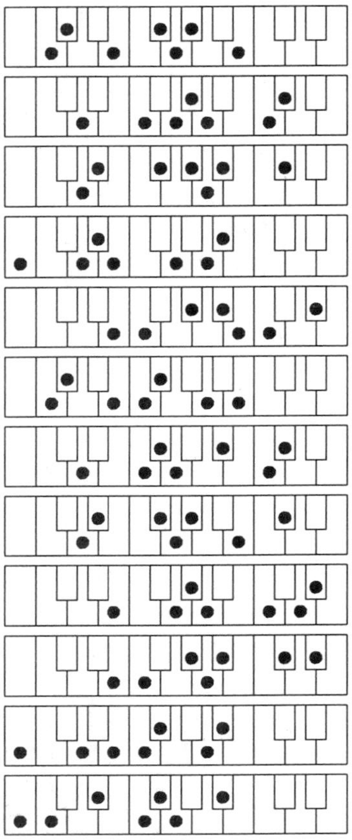

QUICK MODE GENERATOR CHART

COMPOSITE II

I	II	III	IV	V	VI	VII
C	B/C♭	A♭	F#/G♭	F	E	C#/D♭
C#/D♭	C	A	G	F#/G♭	F	D
D	C#/D♭	B♭	A♭	G	F#/G♭	E♭
E♭	D	B/C♭	A	A♭	G	E
E	E♭	C	B♭	A	A♭	F
F	E	C#/D♭	B/C♭	B♭	A	F#/G♭
F#/G♭	F	D	C	B/C♭	B♭	G
G	F#/G♭	E♭	C#/D♭	C	B/C♭	A♭
A♭	G	E	D	C#/D♭	C	A
A	A♭	F	E♭	D	C#/D♭	B♭
B♭	A	F#/G♭	E	E♭	D	B/C♭
B/C♭	B♭	G	F	E	E♭	C

CONVENTIONAL PATTERNS

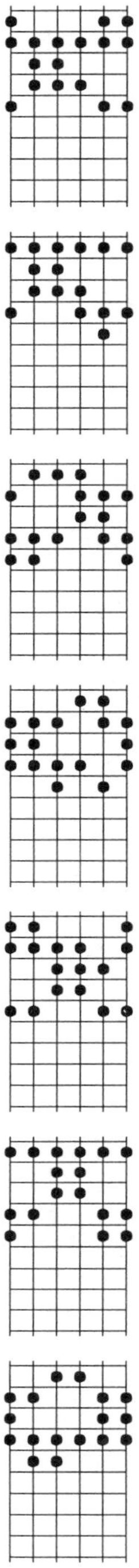

SWEEPING PATTERNS

I

II

III

IV

V

VI

VII

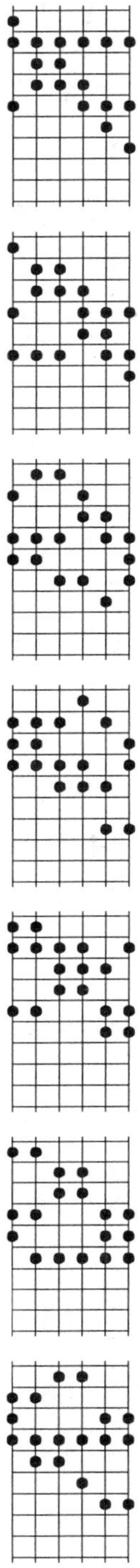

SCALE / MODE - CHORD CHART

I	COMPOSITE II	△, △♭5, △♭9, ♭6
II	MODE 2	⁻△, ø, △°, ⁻7
III	MODE 3	6, ⁻6, ⁻♭6
IV	MODE 4	7sus, 7sus2
V	MODE 5	△♭5
VI	MODE 6	△+, ⁻△+
VII	MODE 7	sus2, sus4

NUMERIC SCALE / MODE CHART

		1		2		3	4		5		6		7	1		2		3	4		5		6		7
I	COMPOS II	1	♭2			3		#4	5	♭6			7	1	♭2			3		#4	5	♭6			7
II	MODE 2		1			#2		#3	#4	5			#6	7											
III	MODE 3					1		2	♭3	♭4			5	♭6	♭7										
IV	MODE 4							1	♭2	𝄫3			4	♭5	𝄫6			♭7							
V	MODE 5								1	♭2			3	4	♭5			6		7					
VI	MODE 6									1			#2	3	4			#5		#6	7				
VII	MODE 7												1	♭2	𝄫3			4		5	♭6	𝄫7			

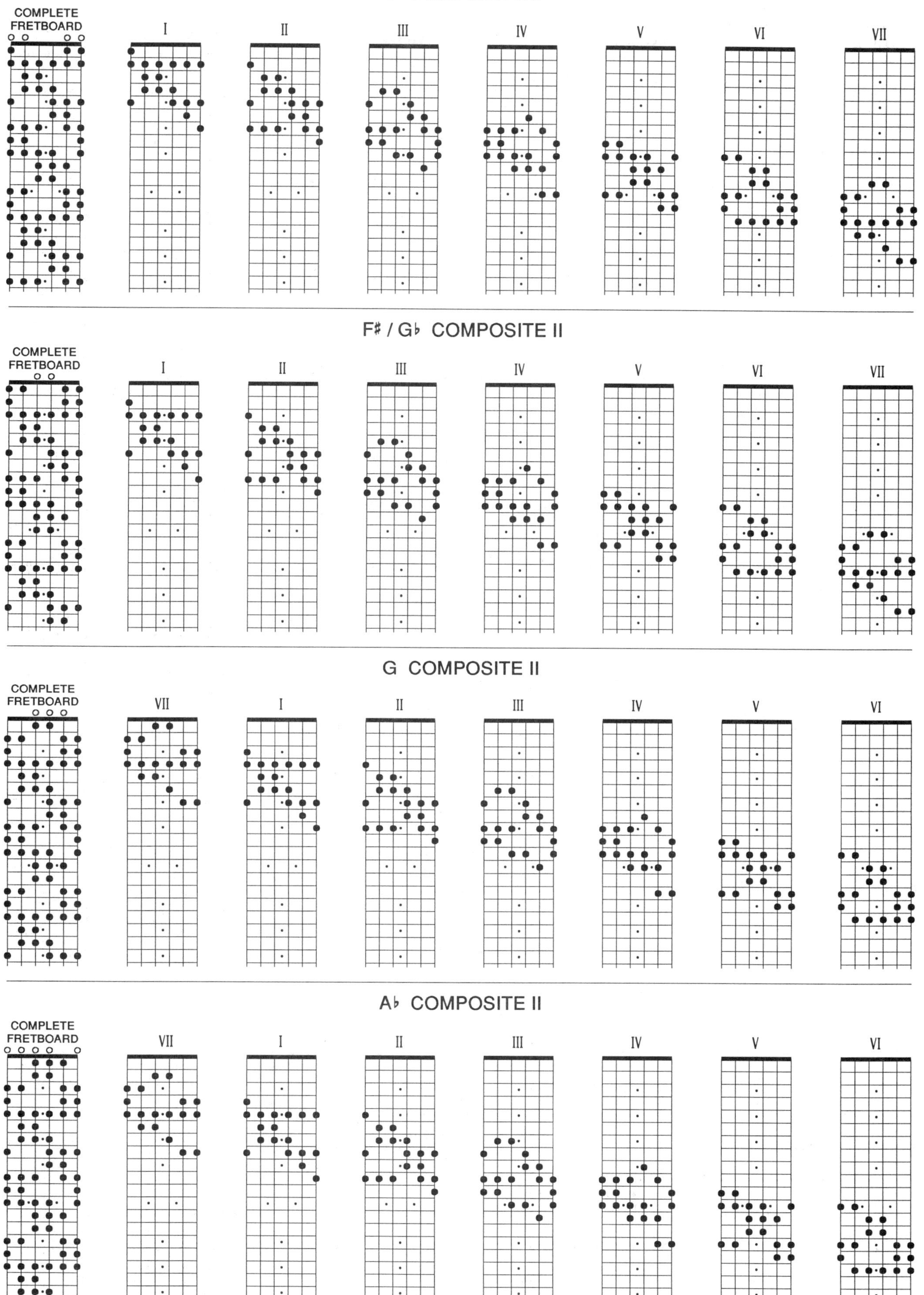
F COMPOSITE II
COMPLETE FRETBOARD
I
II
III
IV
V
VI
VII
F♯ / G♭ COMPOSITE II
COMPLETE FRETBOARD
I
II
III
IV
V
VI
VII
G COMPOSITE II
COMPLETE FRETBOARD
VII
I
II
III
IV
V
VI
A♭ COMPOSITE II
COMPLETE FRETBOARD
VII
I
II
III
IV
V
VI

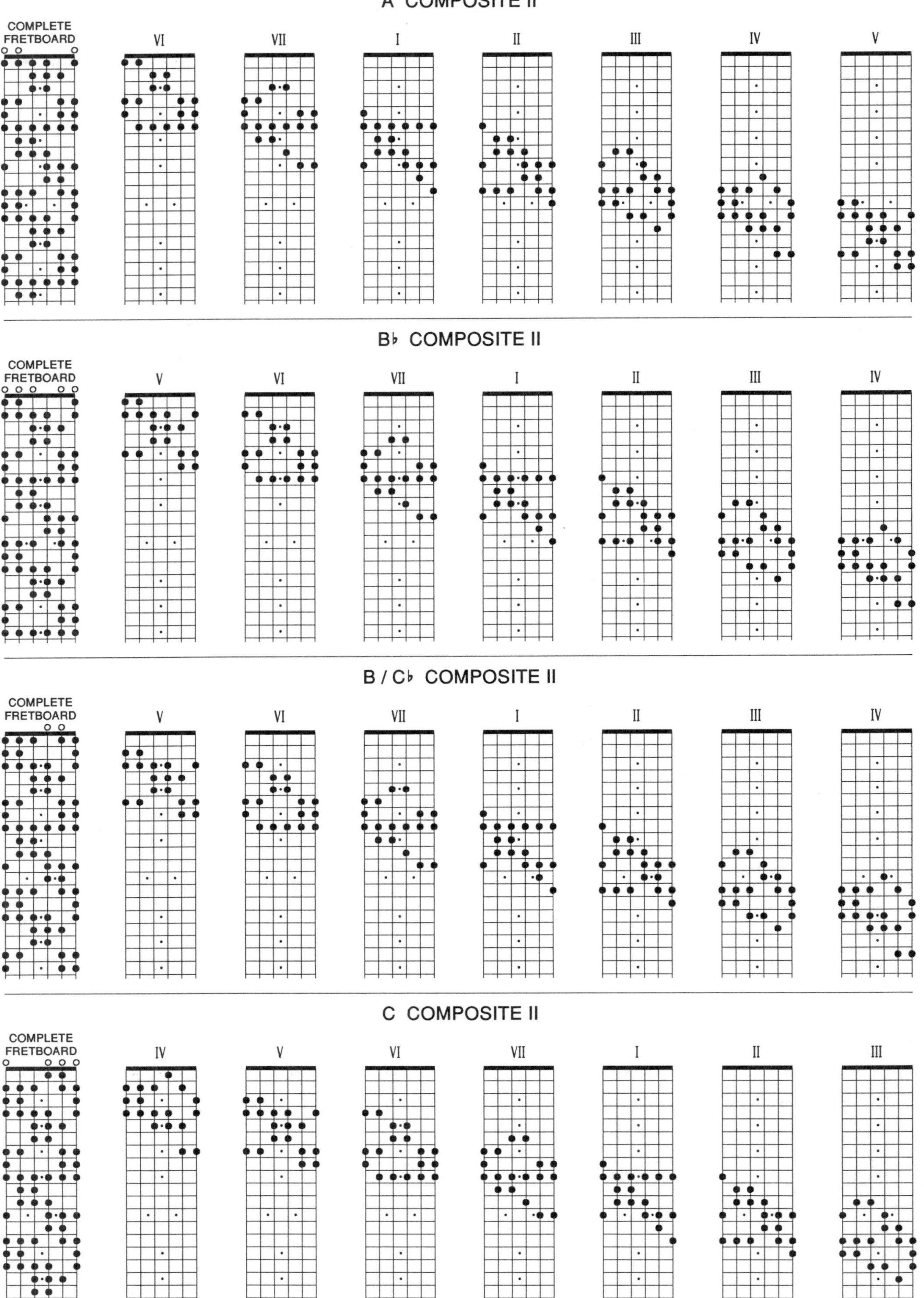
A COMPOSITE II
COMPLETE FRETBOARD
VI
VII
I
II
III
IV
V
B♭ COMPOSITE II
COMPLETE FRETBOARD
V
VI
VII
I
II
III
IV
B / C♭ COMPOSITE II
COMPLETE FRETBOARD
V
VI
VII
I
II
III
IV
C COMPOSITE II
COMPLETE FRETBOARD
IV
V
VI
VII
I
II
III

C♯ / D♭ COMPOSITE II

D COMPOSITE II

E♭ COMPOSITE II

E COMPOSITE II

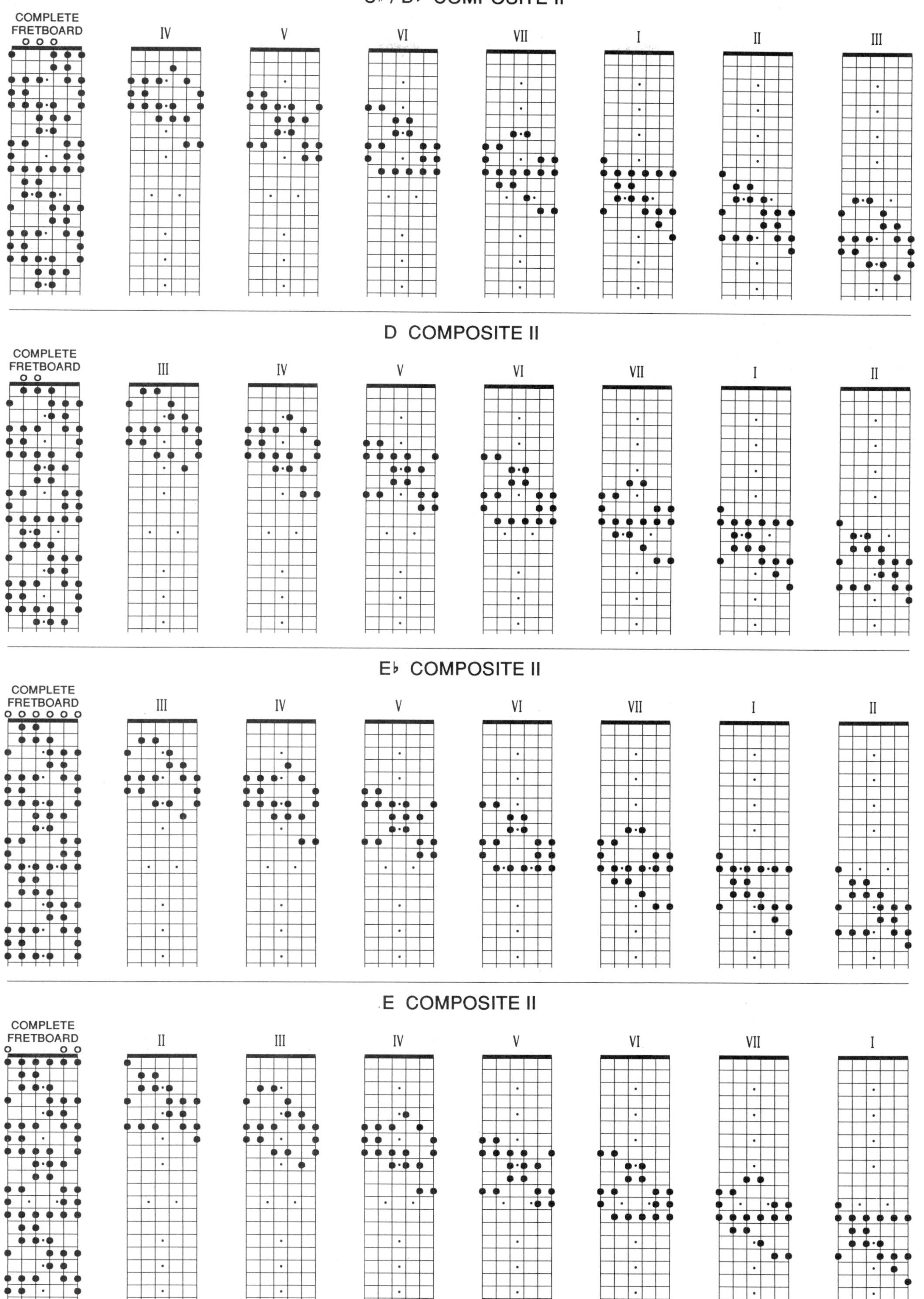

KEYBOARD PATTERNS

QUICK MODE GENERATOR CHART

IONIAN ♭5

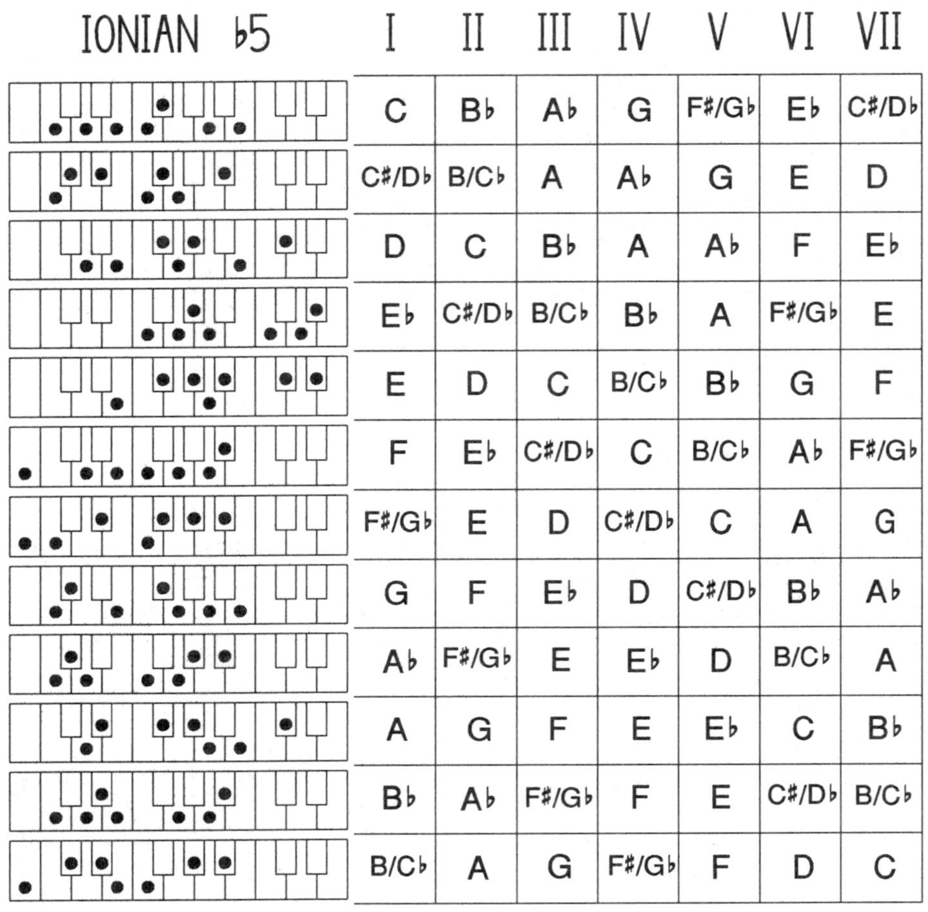

I	II	III	IV	V	VI	VII
C	B♭	A♭	G	F♯/G♭	E♭	C♯/D♭
C♯/D♭	B/C♭	A	A♭	G	E	D
D	C	B♭	A	A♭	F	E♭
E♭	C♯/D♭	B/C♭	B♭	A	F♯/G♭	E
E	D	C	B/C♭	B♭	G	F
F	E♭	C♯/D♭	C	B/C♭	A♭	F♯/G♭
F♯/G♭	E	D	C♯/D♭	C	A	G
G	F	E♭	D	C♯/D♭	B♭	A♭
A♭	F♯/G♭	E	E♭	D	B/C♭	A
A	G	F	E	E♭	C	B♭
B♭	A♭	F♯/G♭	F	E	C♯/D♭	B/C♭
B/C♭	A	G	F♯/G♭	F	D	C

CONVENTIONAL PATTERNS

SWEEPING PATTERNS

I

II

III

IV

V

VI

VII

SCALE / MODE - CHORD CHART

I	IONIAN ♭5	$\triangle^{\flat 5}$
II	DORIAN ♭4	⁻6, 6, ⁻7, 7^{sus2}
III	PHRYGIAN 𝄫3	7^{sus}, 7^{sus2}
IV	LYDIAN ♭2	△, $\triangle^{\flat 5}$
V	SUPER LYDIAN AUGMENTED	∅, △°
VI	AEOLIAN 𝄫7	⁻6, ⁻♭6, ⁻9
VII	LOCRIAN 𝄫6	∅, ⁻7

NUMERIC SCALE / MODE CHART

		1		2		3	4		5		6		7	1		2		3	4		5		6		7
I	IONIAN ♭5	1		2		3	4	♭5			6		7	1		2		3	4	♭5			6		7
II	DORIAN ♭4			1		2	♭3	♭4			5		6	♭7											
III	PHRYGIAN 𝄫3					1	♭2	𝄫3			4		5	♭6		♭7									
IV	LYDIAN ♭2						1	♭2			3		♯4	5		6		7							
V	SUPER LYD AUG							1			♯2		♯3	♯4		♯5		♯6	7						
VI	AEOLIAN 𝄫7										1		2	♭3		4		5	♭6	𝄫7					
VII	LOCRIAN 𝄫6												1	♭2		♭3		4	♭5	𝄫6			♭7		

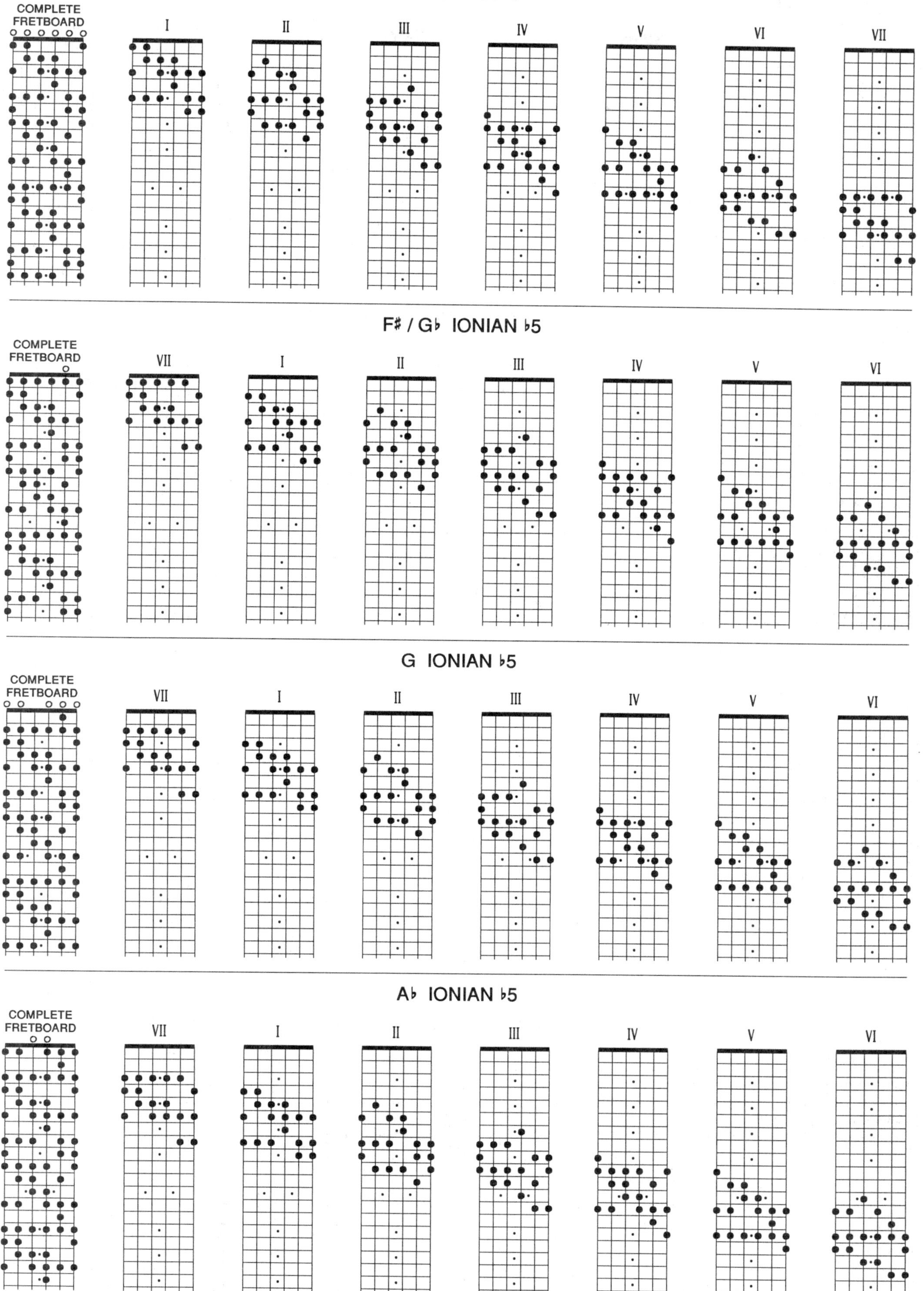
F IONIAN ♭5
COMPLETE FRETBOARD
I
II
III
IV
V
VI
VII
F♯ / G♭ IONIAN ♭5
COMPLETE FRETBOARD
VII
I
II
III
IV
V
VI
G IONIAN ♭5
COMPLETE FRETBOARD
VII
I
II
III
IV
V
VI
A♭ IONIAN ♭5
COMPLETE FRETBOARD
VII
I
II
III
IV
V
VI

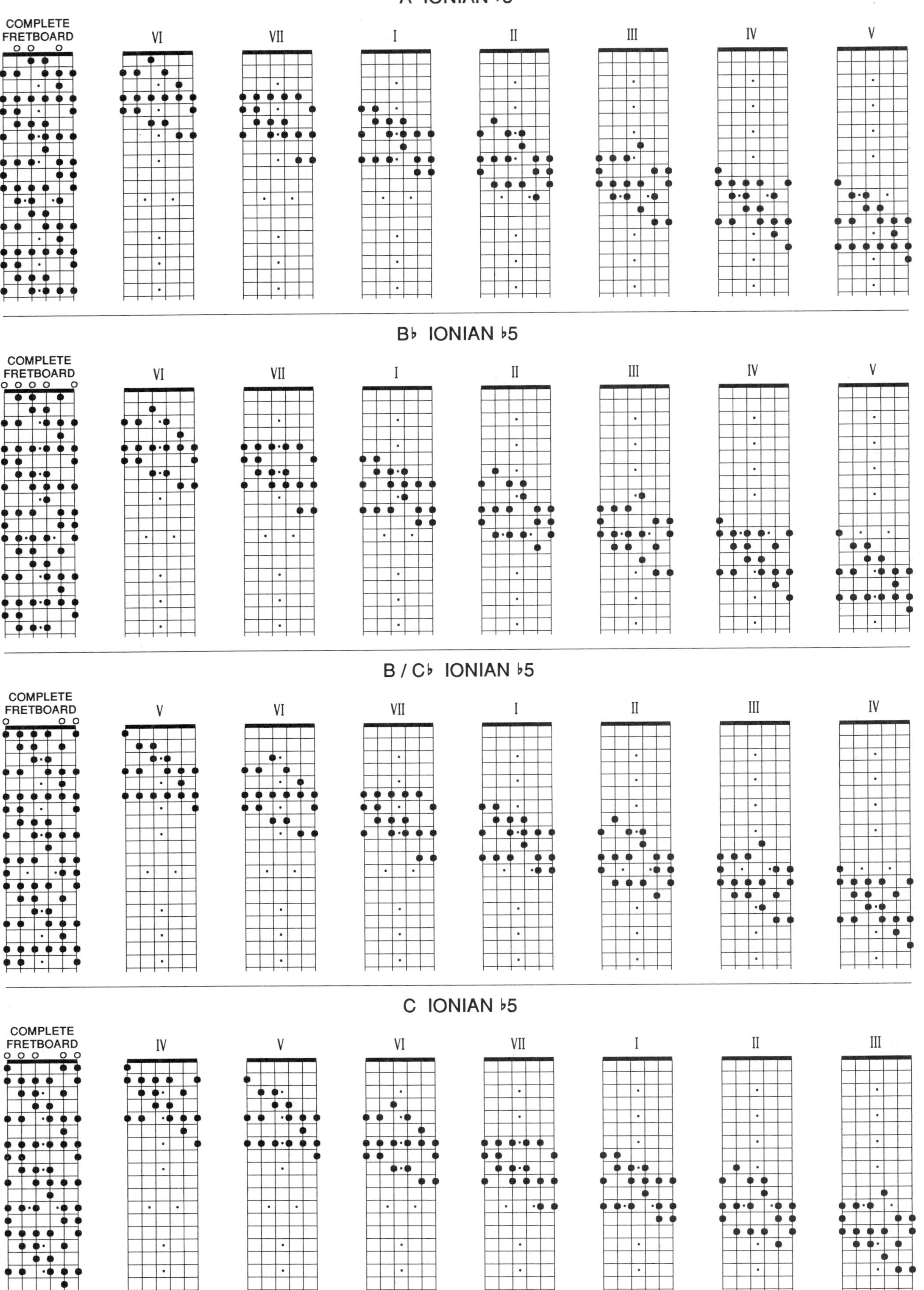
A IONIAN ♭5
COMPLETE FRETBOARD
VI
VII
I
II
III
IV
V
B♭ IONIAN ♭5
COMPLETE FRETBOARD
VI
VII
I
II
III
IV
V
B / C♭ IONIAN ♭5
COMPLETE FRETBOARD
V
VI
VII
I
II
III
IV
C IONIAN ♭5
COMPLETE FRETBOARD
IV
V
VI
VII
I
II
III

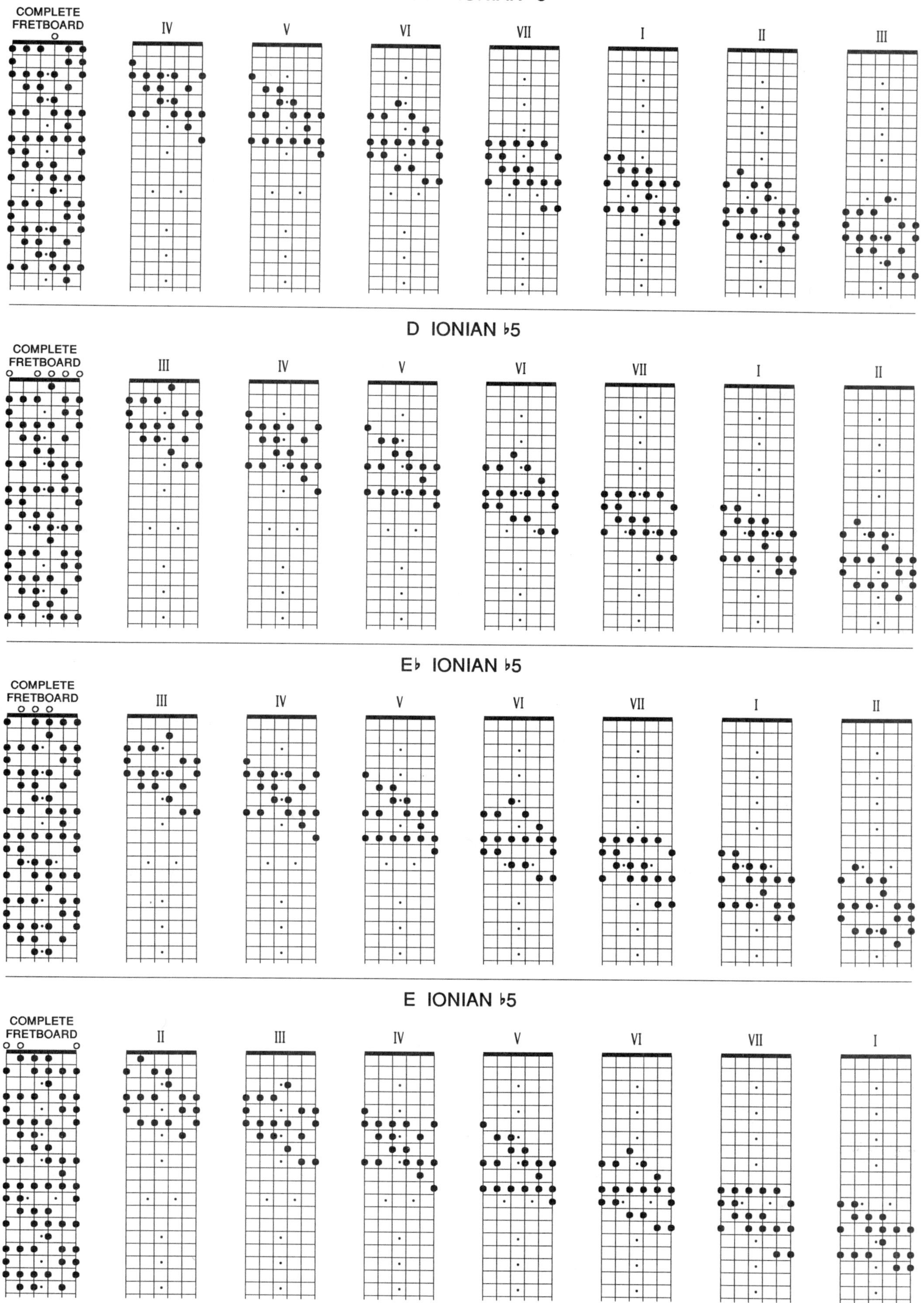
C♯ / D♭ IONIAN ♭5
COMPLETE FRETBOARD
IV
V
VI
VII
I
II
III
D IONIAN ♭5
COMPLETE FRETBOARD
III
IV
V
VI
VII
I
II
E♭ IONIAN ♭5
COMPLETE FRETBOARD
III
IV
V
VI
VII
I
II
E IONIAN ♭5
COMPLETE FRETBOARD
II
III
IV
V
VI
VII
I

KEYBOARD PATTERNS

LOCRIAN ♮7

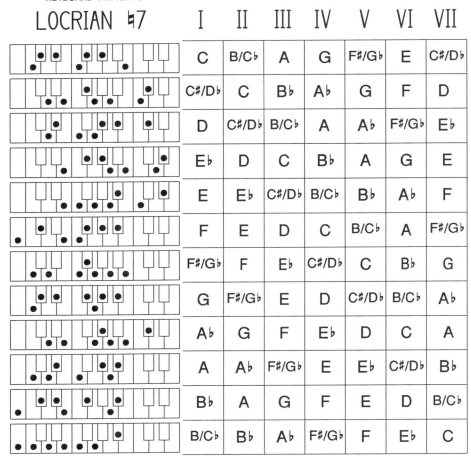

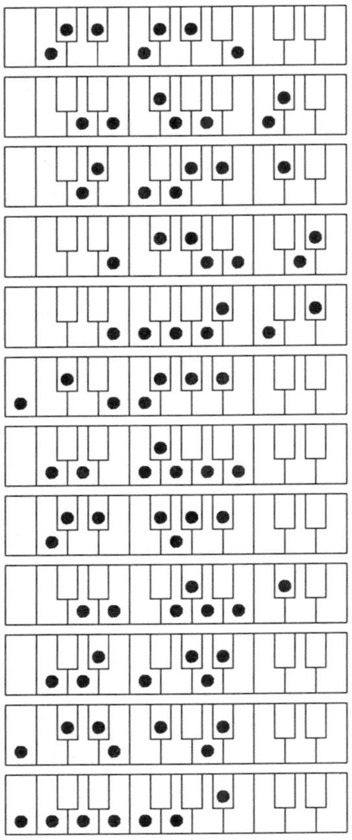

QUICK MODE GENERATOR CHART

I	II	III	IV	V	VI	VII
C	B/C♭	A	G	F♯/G♭	E	C♯/D♭
C♯/D♭	C	B♭	A♭	G	F	D
D	C♯/D♭	B/C♭	A	A♭	F♯/G♭	E♭
E♭	D	C	B♭	A	G	E
E	E♭	C♯/D♭	B/C♭	B♭	A♭	F
F	E	D	C	B/C♭	A	F♯/G♭
F♯/G♭	F	E♭	C♯/D♭	C	B♭	G
G	F♯/G♭	E	D	C♯/D♭	B/C♭	A♭
A♭	G	F	E♭	D	C	A
A	A♭	F♯/G♭	E	E♭	C♯/D♭	B♭
B♭	A	G	F	E	D	B/C♭
B/C♭	B♭	A♭	F♯/G♭	F	E♭	C

CONVENTIONAL PATTERNS

SWEEPING PATTERNS

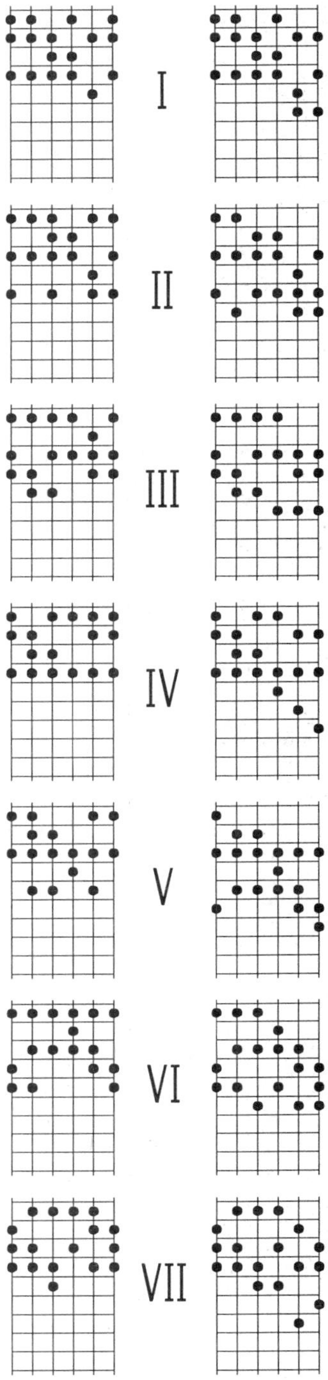

I

II

III

IV

V

VI

VII

SCALE / MODE - CHORD CHART

I	LOCRIAN ♮7	$\triangle^{\circ}$, $^{-}\triangle^{+}$
II	IONIAN ♯6	$\triangle$, 7, $\triangle^{sus2}$, 7^{sus2}, 9, 11
III	DORIAN AUG	$sus2^{+}$
IV	PHYRGIAN ♯4	ø, $^{-}7$
V	LYDIAN ♯3	$\triangle^{sus2}$, $\triangle^{sus}$
VI	DOMINANT ♯2	$^{-}6$, 6, 7, $^{-}7$, 7^{sus}
VII	ALT ALT	6

NUMERIC SCALE / MODE CHART

		1		2		3	4		5		6		7	1		2		3	4		5		6		7
I	LOCRIAN ♮7	1	♭2		♭3		4	♭5		♭6			7	1	♭2		♭3		4	♭5		♭6			7
II	IONIAN ♯6		1		2		3	4		5			♯6	7											
III	DORIAN AUG				1		2	♭3		4			♯5	6	♭7										
IV	PHRYGIAN ♯4						1	♭2		♭3			♯4	5	♭6		♭7								
V	LYDIAN ♯3							1		2			♯3	♯4	5		6		7						
VI	DOMINANT ♯2									1			♯2	3	4		5		6	♭7					
VII	ALT ALT												1	♭2	𝄫3		♭4		♭5	𝄫6		𝄫7			

F LOCRIAN ♮7

F♯ / G♭ LOCRIAN ♮7

G LOCRIAN ♮7

A♭ LOCRIAN ♮7

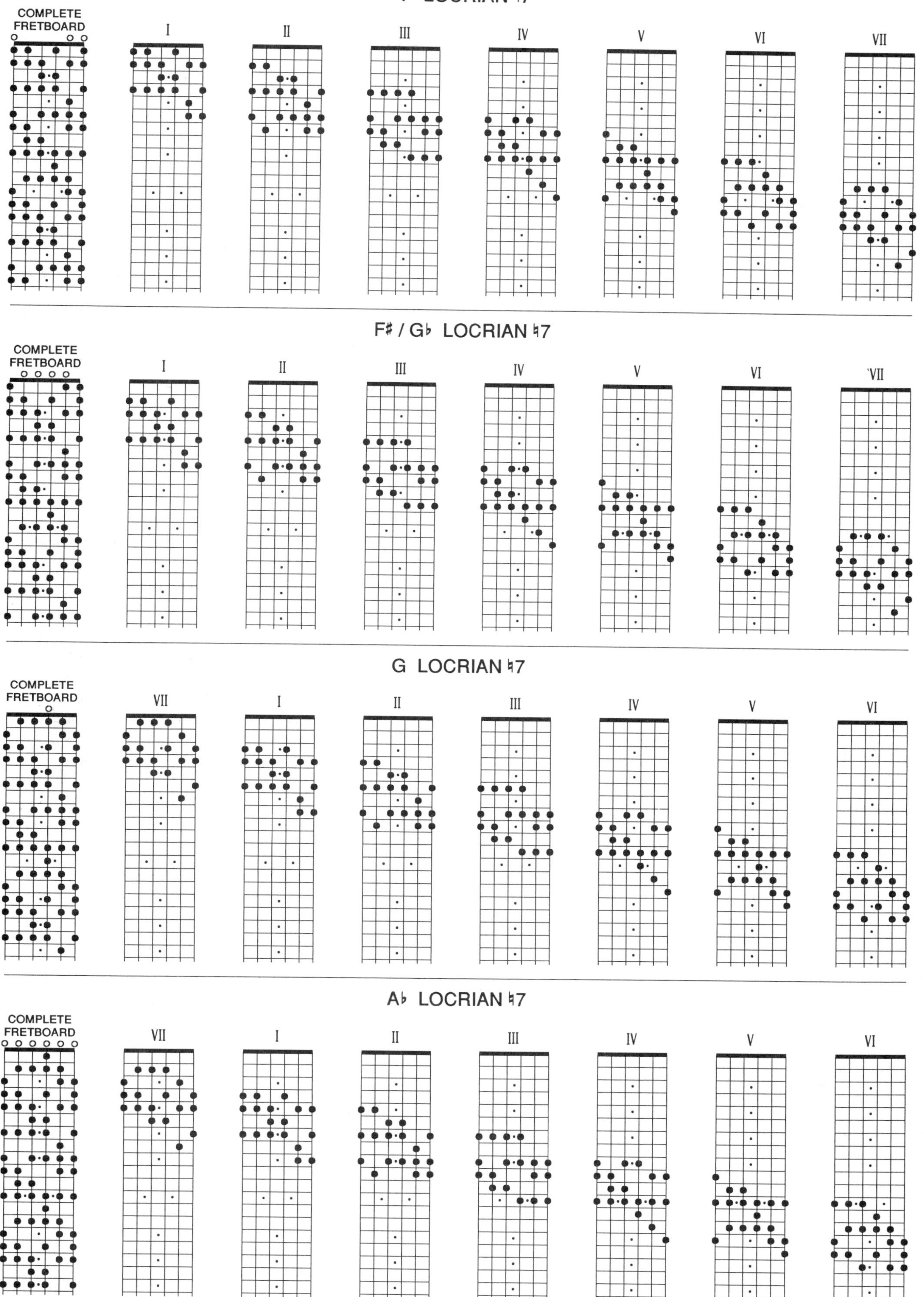

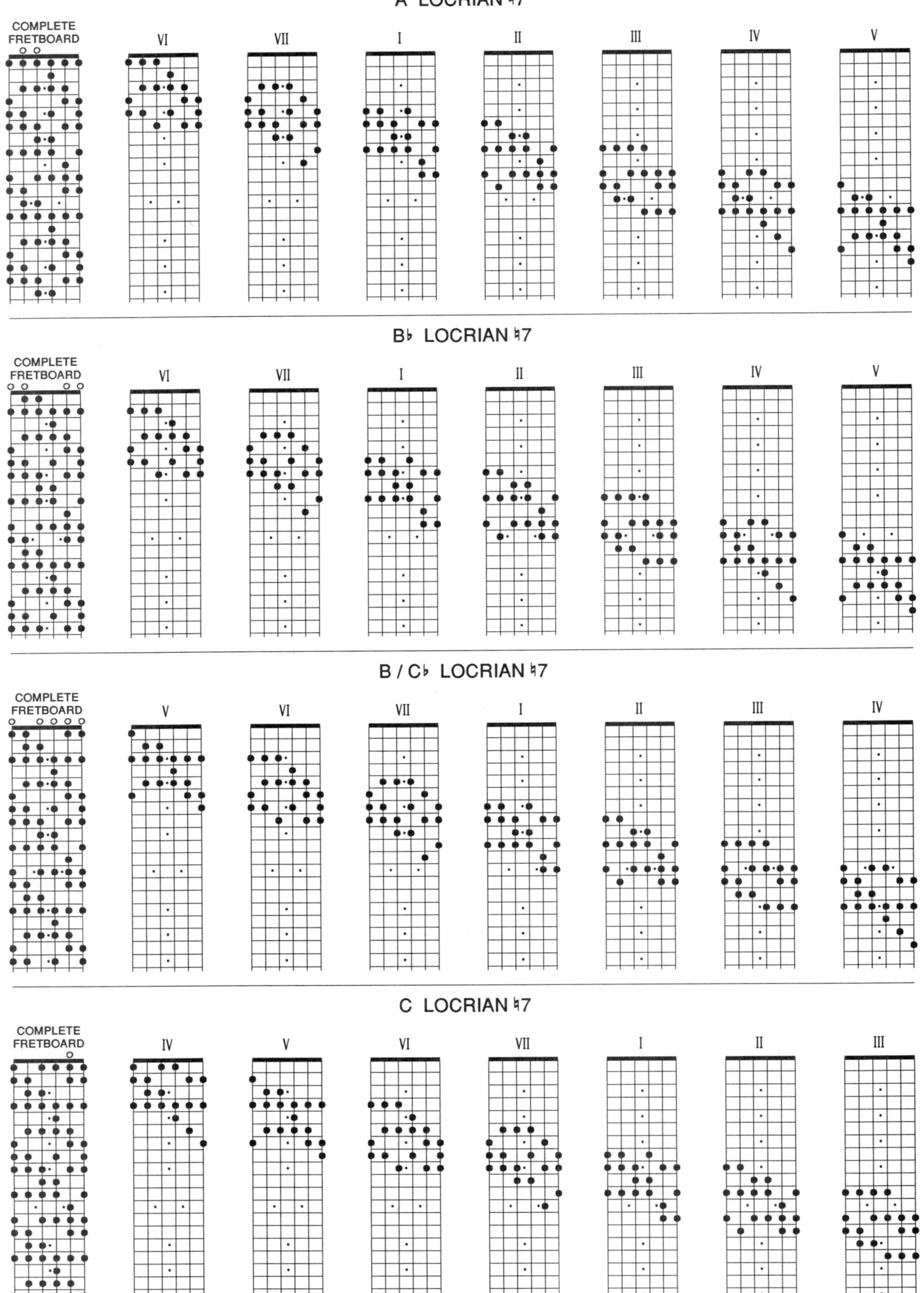
A LOCRIAN ♮7
COMPLETE FRETBOARD
VI
VII
I
II
III
IV
V
B♭ LOCRIAN ♮7
COMPLETE FRETBOARD
VI
VII
I
II
III
IV
V
B / C♭ LOCRIAN ♮7
COMPLETE FRETBOARD
V
VI
VII
I
II
III
IV
C LOCRIAN ♮7
COMPLETE FRETBOARD
IV
V
VI
VII
I
II
III

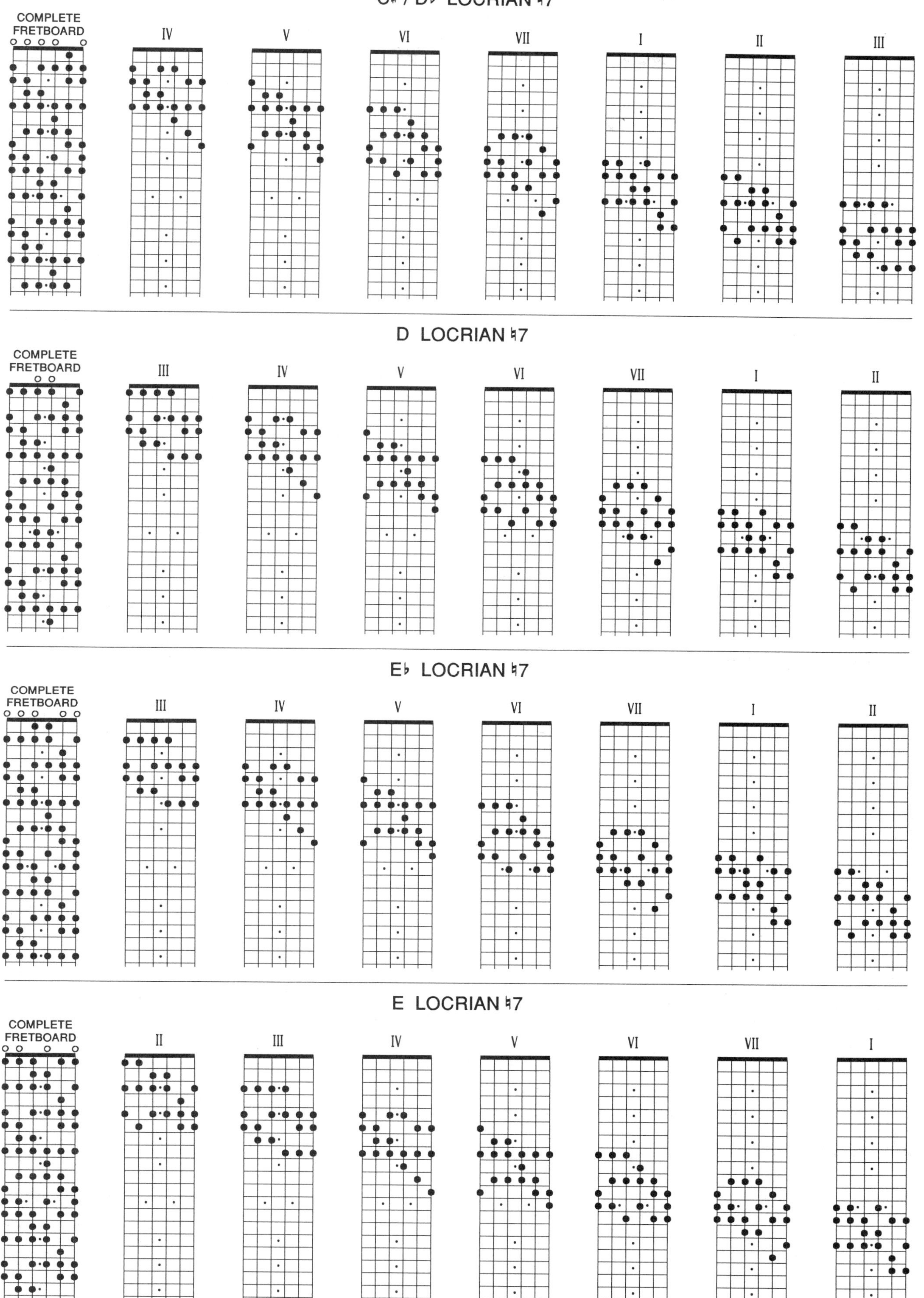
C♯ / D♭ LOCRIAN ♮7
COMPLETE FRETBOARD
IV
V
VI
VII
I
II
III
D LOCRIAN ♮7
COMPLETE FRETBOARD
III
IV
V
VI
VII
I
II
E♭ LOCRIAN ♮7
COMPLETE FRETBOARD
III
IV
V
VI
VII
I
II
E LOCRIAN ♮7
COMPLETE FRETBOARD
II
III
IV
V
VI
VII
I

KEYBOARD PATTERNS

PERSIAN

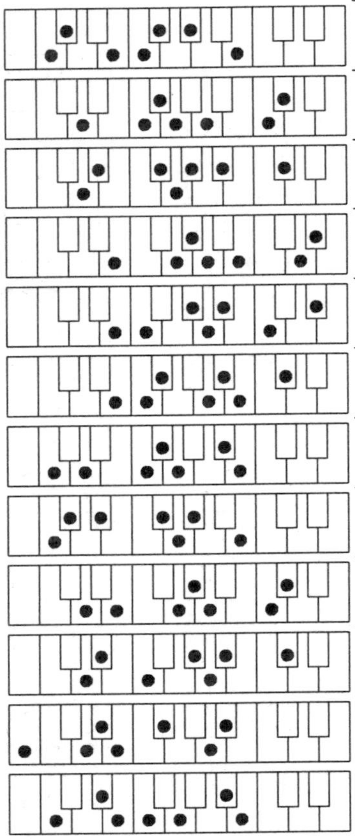

QUICK MODE GENERATOR CHART

I	II	III	IV	V	VI	VII
C	B/C♭	A♭	G	F♯/G♭	E	C♯/D♭
C♯/D♭	C	A	A♭	G	F	D
D	C♯/D♭	B♭	A	A♭	F♯/G♭	E♭
E♭	D	B/C♭	B♭	A	G	E
E	E♭	C	B/C♭	B♭	A♭	F
F	E	C♯/D♭	C	B/C♭	A	F♯/G♭
F♯/G♭	F	D	C♯/D♭	C	B♭	G
G	F♯/G♭	E♭	D	C♯/D♭	B/C♭	A♭
A♭	G	E	E♭	D	C	A
A	A♭	F	E	E♭	C♯/D♭	B♭
B♭	A	F♯/G♭	F	E	D	B/C♭
B/C♭	B♭	G	F♯/G♭	F	E♭	C

CONVENTIONAL PATTERNS

SWEEPING PATTERNS

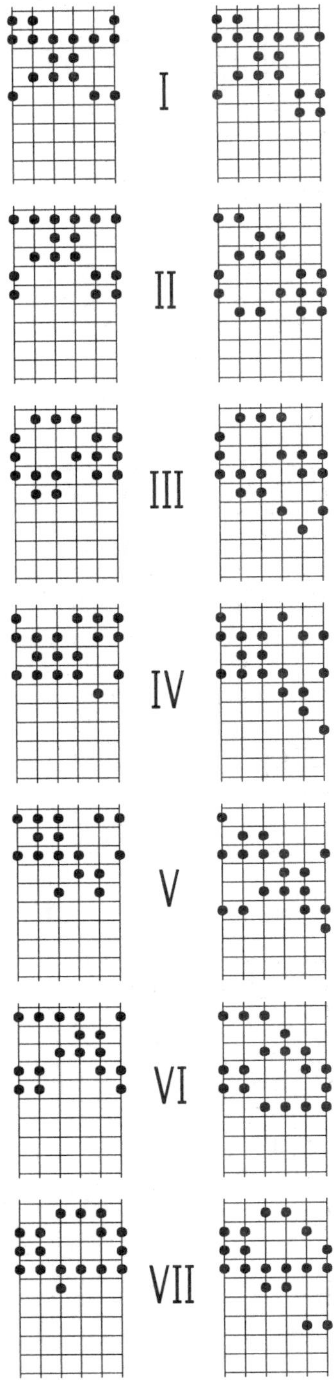

I

II

III

IV

V

VI

VII

SCALE / MODE - CHORD CHART

I	PERSIAN	♭5, $\triangle^{\flat 5}$
II	MODE 2	△, 7, $^{-}$7, ♯9, 11
III	MODE 3	– , sus2, ♭6, 6
IV	MODE 4	$^{-}\triangle$, $^{-}$♭6
V	MODE 5	sus2, sus, $\triangle^{sus2}$, $\triangle^{sus}$
VI	MODE 6	+ , 7^{+}
VII	MODE 7	sus2, sus

NUMERIC SCALE / MODE CHART

		1		2		3	4		5		6		7	1		2		3	4		5		6		7
I	PERSIAN	1	♭2			3	4	♭5		♭6			7	1	♭2			3	4	♭5		♭6			7
II	MODE 2		1			♯2	3	4		5			♯6	7											
III	MODE 3					1	♭2	𝄫3		♭4			5	♭6	𝄫7										
IV	MODE 4						1	♭2		♭3			♯4	5	♭6			7							
V	MODE 5							1		2			♯3	♯4	5			♯6	7						
VI	MODE 6									1			♯2	3	4			♯5	6	♭7					
VII	MODE 7												1	♭2	𝄫3			4	♭5	𝄫6		𝄫7			

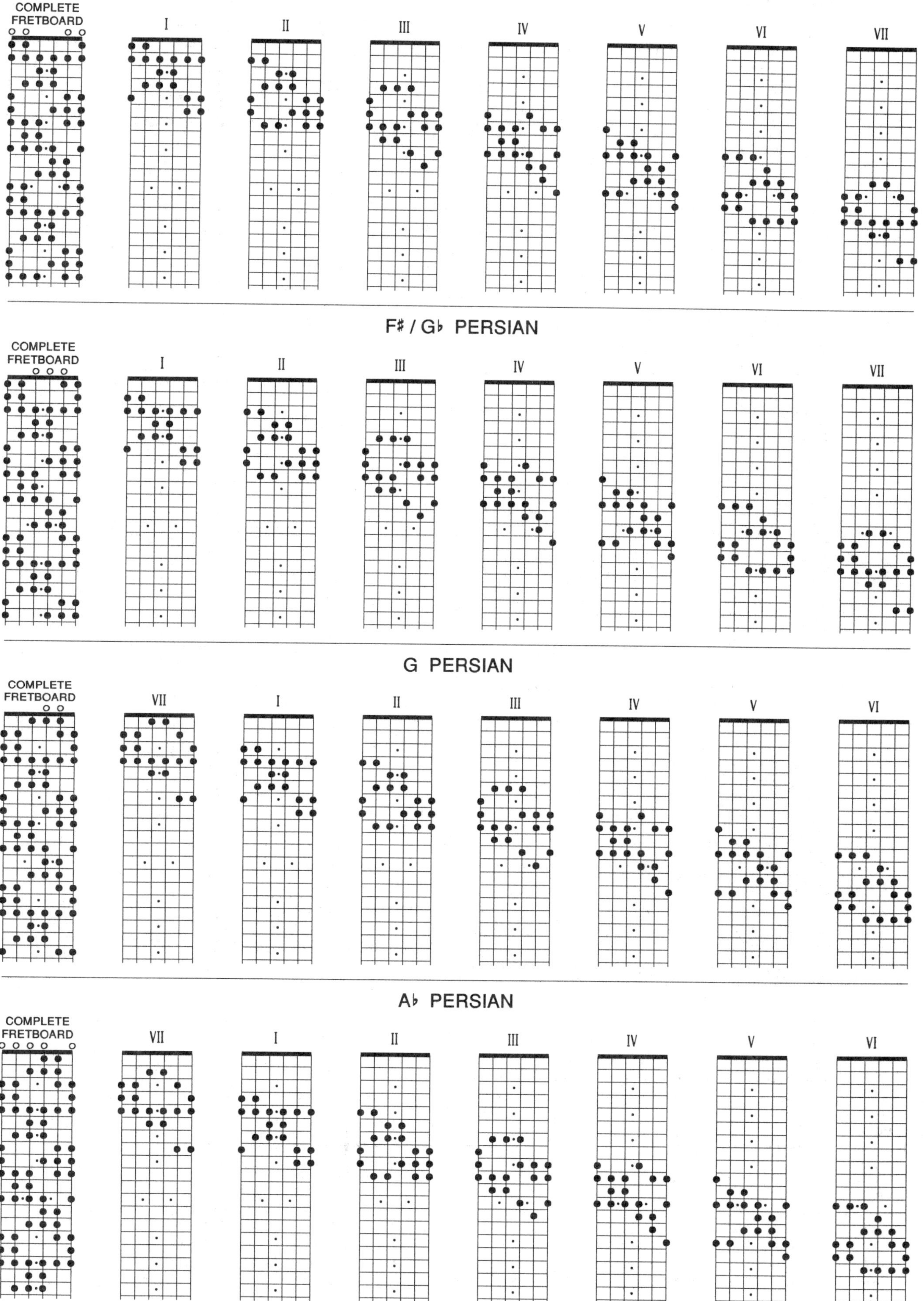
F PERSIAN
COMPLETE FRETBOARD
I
II
III
IV
V
VI
VII
F♯ / G♭ PERSIAN
COMPLETE FRETBOARD
I
II
III
IV
V
VI
VII
G PERSIAN
COMPLETE FRETBOARD
VII
I
II
III
IV
V
VI
A♭ PERSIAN
COMPLETE FRETBOARD
VII
I
II
III
IV
V
VI

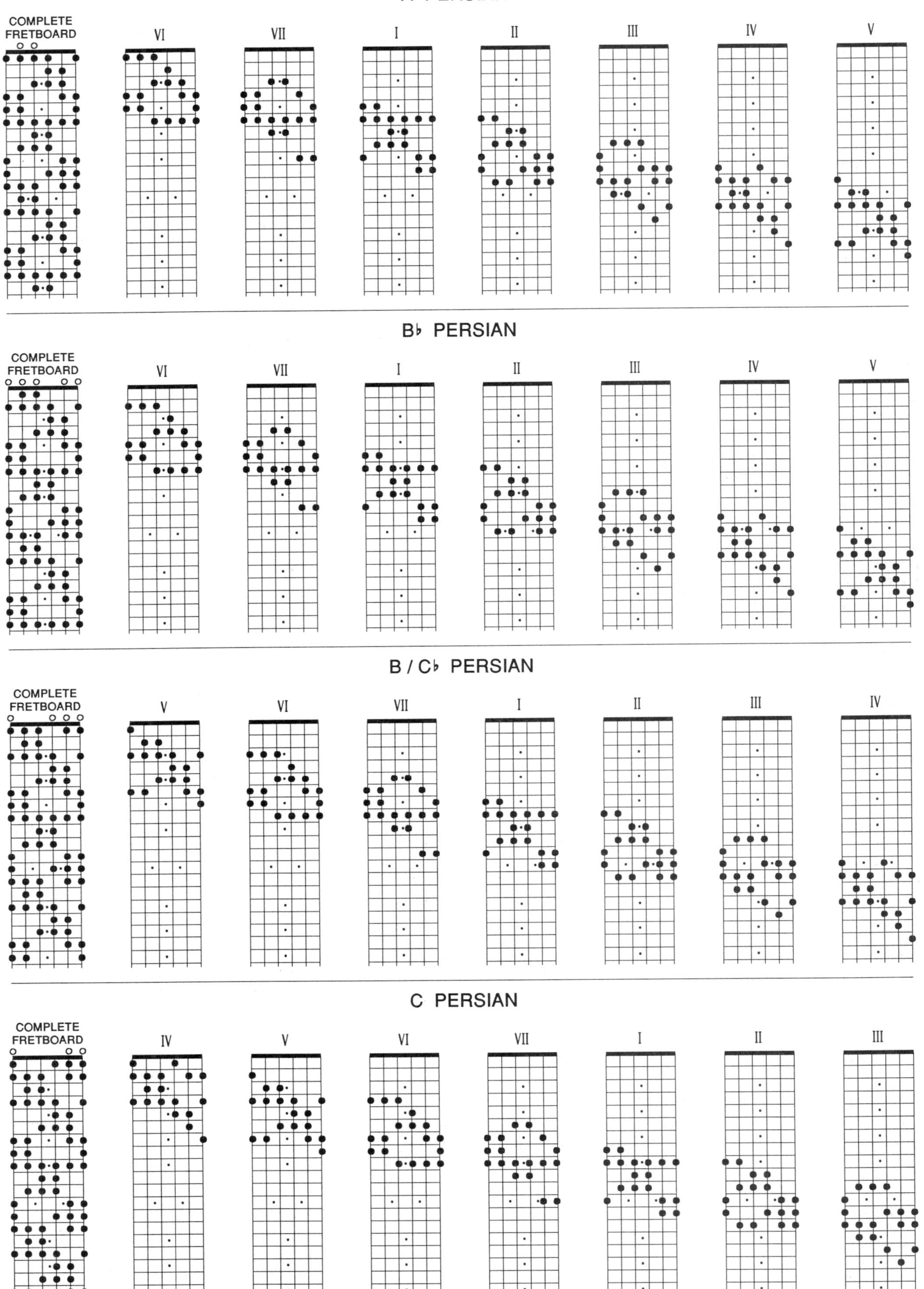
A PERSIAN
COMPLETE FRETBOARD
VI
VII
I
II
III
IV
V
B♭ PERSIAN
COMPLETE FRETBOARD
VI
VII
I
II
III
IV
V
B / C♭ PERSIAN
COMPLETE FRETBOARD
V
VI
VII
I
II
III
IV
C PERSIAN
COMPLETE FRETBOARD
IV
V
VI
VII
I
II
III

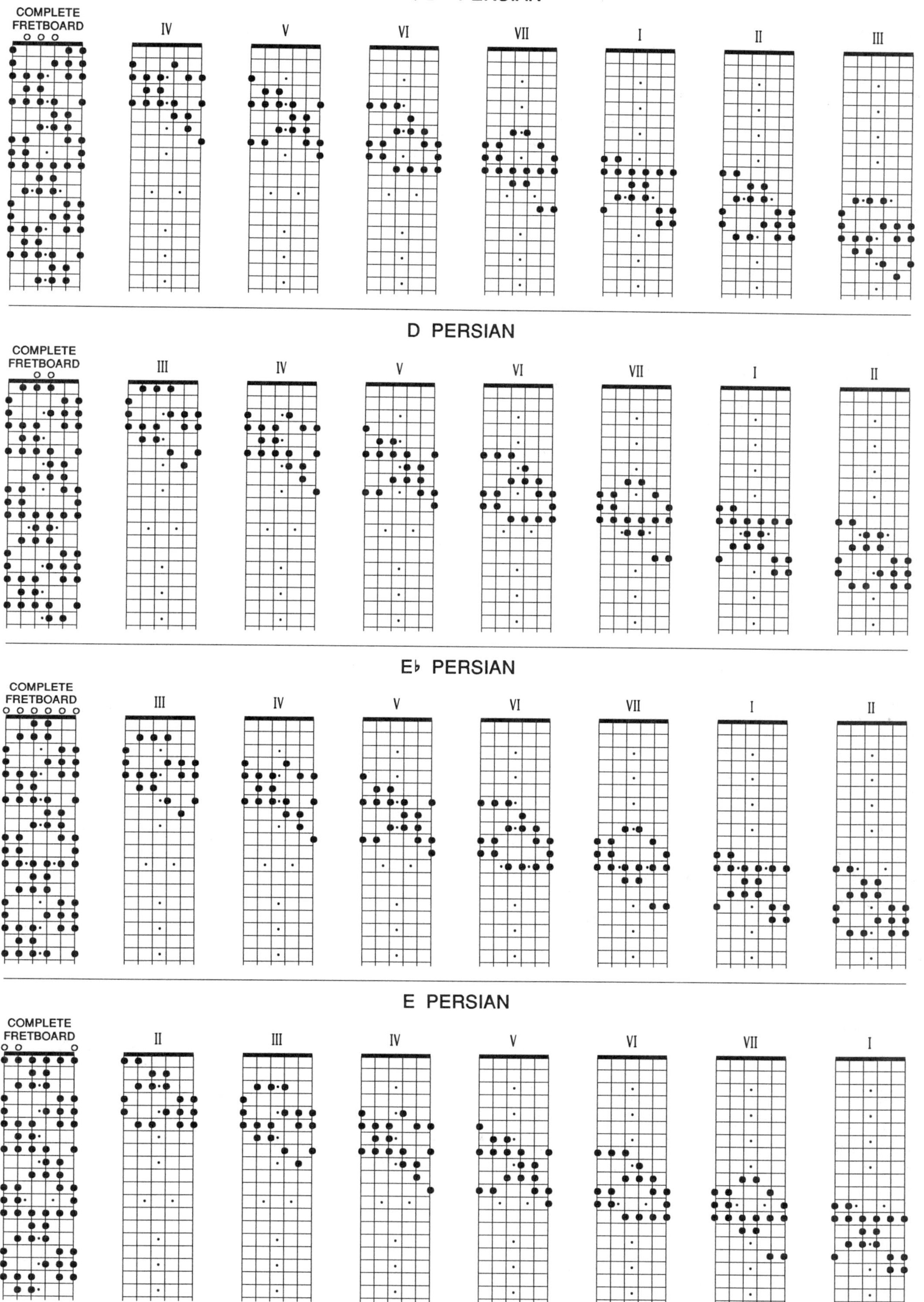
C♯ / D♭ PERSIAN
COMPLETE FRETBOARD
IV
V
VI
VII
I
II
III
D PERSIAN
COMPLETE FRETBOARD
III
IV
V
VI
VII
I
II
E♭ PERSIAN
COMPLETE FRETBOARD
III
IV
V
VI
VII
I
II
E PERSIAN
COMPLETE FRETBOARD
II
III
IV
V
VI
VII
I

5 TONE SCALES

A 5 tone scale, otherwise known as a pentatonic scale, is merely a 7 tone scale with 2 tones omitted. The chart to the right will allow you to turn any 7 tone scale into a pentatonic. By a systematic process of elimination, you can derive 15 pentatonics from any 7 tone scale (fig. 44).

PENTATONIC SCALE FORMULA CHART

1	2	3	4	5	6	7
	X	X				
	X		X			
	X			X		
	X				X	
	X					X
		X	X			
		X		X		
		X			X	
		X				X
			X	X		
			X		X	
			X			X
				X	X	
				X		X
					X	X

fig. 44

→→→→→→→→→→→→→→

- The **X** in the boxes of *this* chart indicate tones of the scale which have been **deleted•**
- **The tones or numbers at the top are "generic" meaning they could be either** ♭ 𝄫 ♯ 𝄪 ♮•
  Ex•♭2 𝄫2 ♯2 𝄪2 2
- If we were to give you all the possible combinations with alterations there would be 98 such charts— try it if you like•

In summary:

Step 1 Pick any 7 tone scale or mode•

Step 2 Delete any 2 tones•

The 4 other mini-patterns used for sweeping the pentatonics along with the 8 mini-patterns given in the introduction to the 7 tone scales, are as follows (fig. 45):

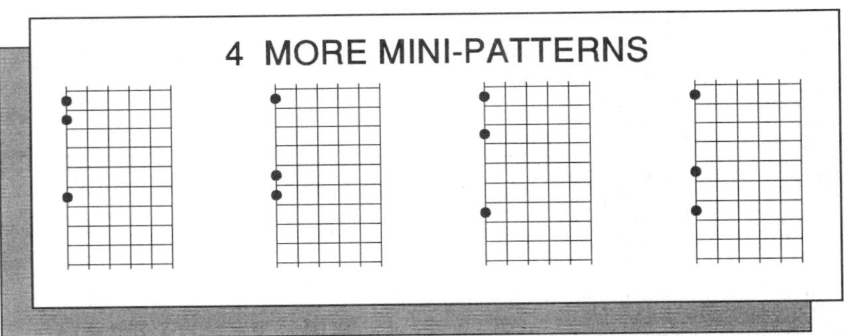

fig. 45

The sweeping patterns break down into patterns A and B. That is because the *sweep* takes place on different combinations of strings depending on whether you are in set A or set B.

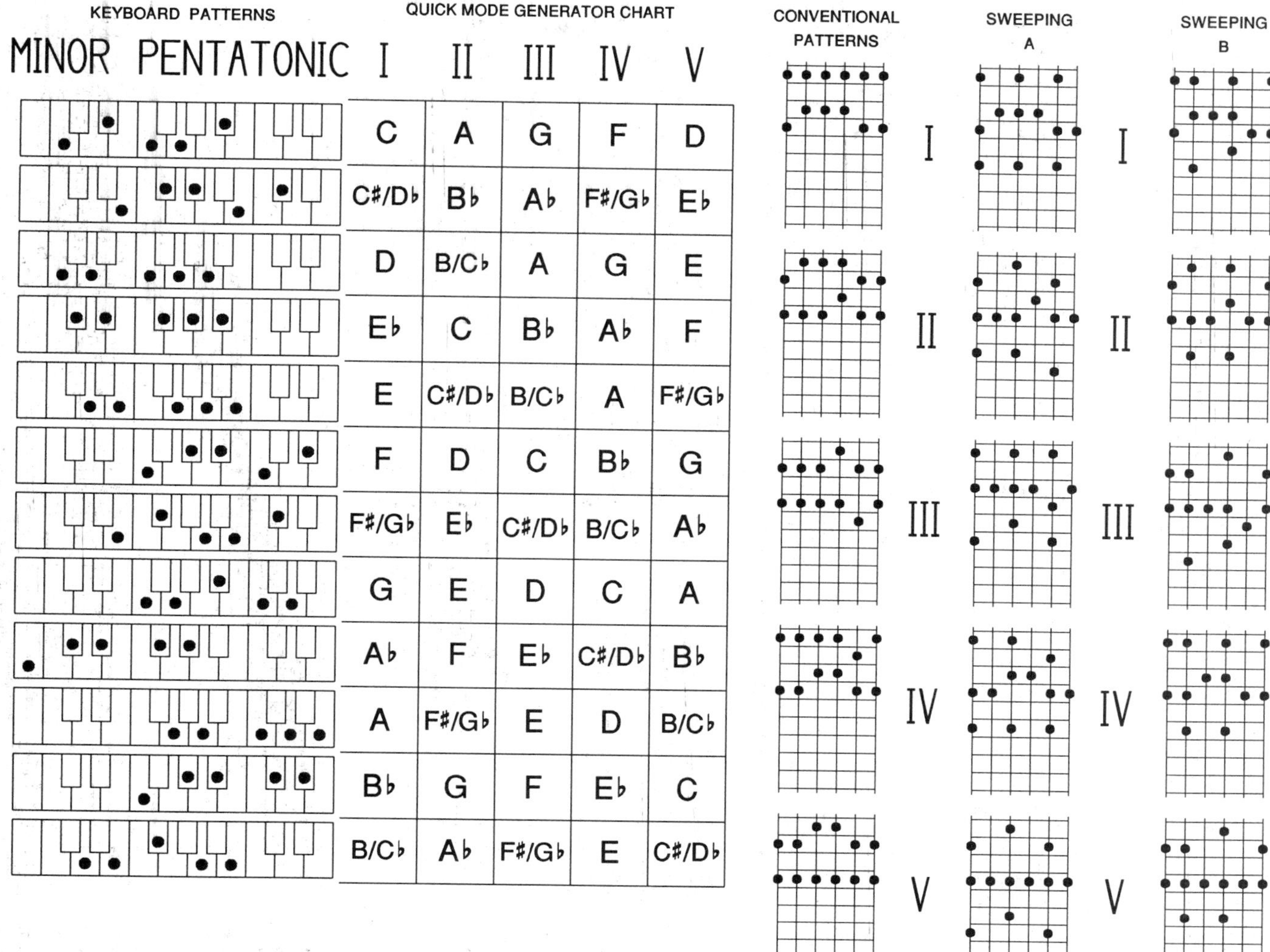

MINOR PENTATONIC	I	II	III	IV	V
	C	A	G	F	D
	C#/Db	Bb	Ab	F#/Gb	Eb
	D	B/Cb	A	G	E
	Eb	C	Bb	Ab	F
	E	C#/Db	B/Cb	A	F#/Gb
	F	D	C	Bb	G
	F#/Gb	Eb	C#/Db	B/Cb	Ab
	G	E	D	C	A
	Ab	F	Eb	C#/Db	Bb
	A	F#/Gb	E	D	B/Cb
	Bb	G	F	Eb	C
	B/Cb	Ab	F#/Gb	E	C#/Db

SCALE / MODE - CHORD CHART

I	MINOR PENTATONIC	-7
II	MAJOR PENTATONIC	sus2, M, 6
III	MODE 3	sus2, sus
IV	MODE 4	Q3
V	MODE 5	sus2, sus

The Minor Pentatonic is the most common pentatonic scale. The Minor Pentatonic can be interspersed with the Dorian, Phyrgian, and Aeolian (of the Major scale), because the tones of the Minor Pentatonic are contained in all 3 modes, as well as other scales.

NUMERIC SCALE / MODE CHART

		1		2		3	4		5		6		7	1		2		3	4		5		6		7
I	MINOR PENT	1			b3		4		5			b7		1			b3		4		5			b7	
II	MAJOR PENT				1		2		3			5		6											
III	MODE 3						1		2			4		5			b7								
IV	MODE 4								1			b3		4			#5		b7						
V	MODE 5											1		2			4		5		6				

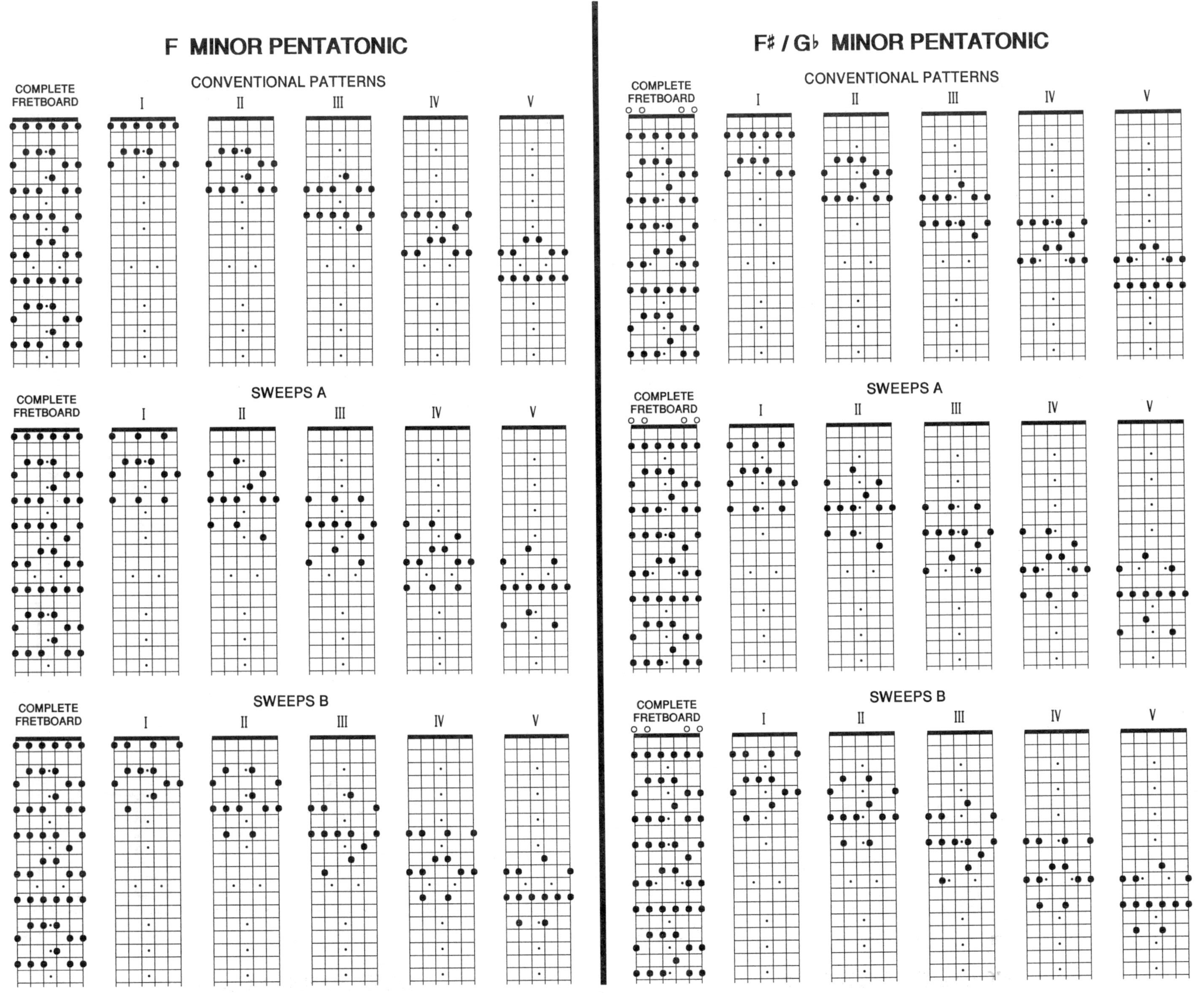
F MINOR PENTATONIC
CONVENTIONAL PATTERNS
COMPLETE FRETBOARD
I
II
III
IV
V
SWEEPS A
COMPLETE FRETBOARD
I
II
III
IV
V
SWEEPS B
COMPLETE FRETBOARD
I
II
III
IV
V
F♯ / G♭ MINOR PENTATONIC
CONVENTIONAL PATTERNS
COMPLETE FRETBOARD
I
II
III
IV
V
SWEEPS A
COMPLETE FRETBOARD
I
II
III
IV
V
SWEEPS B
COMPLETE FRETBOARD
I
II
III
IV
V

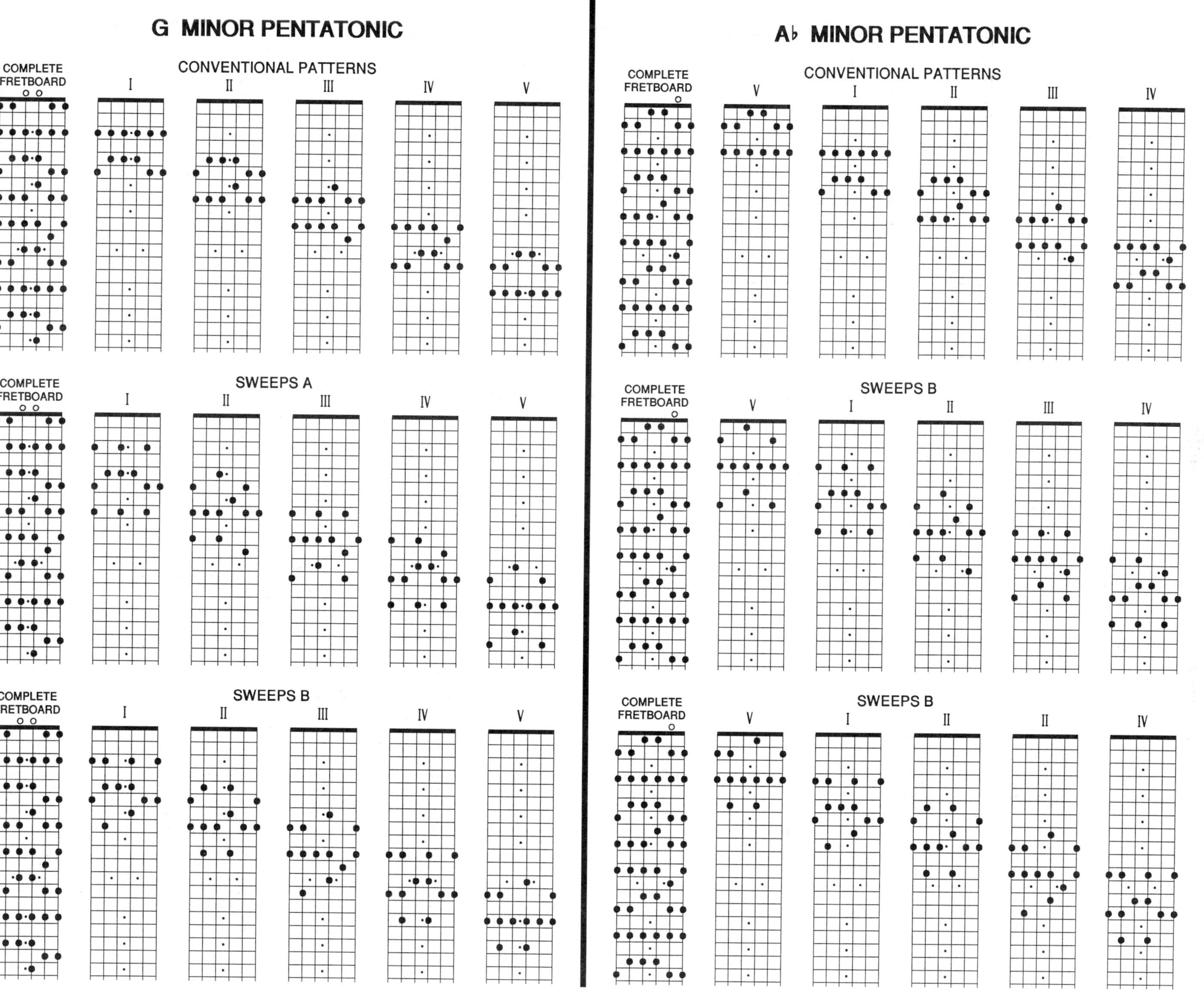

G MINOR PENTATONIC
COMPLETE FRETBOARD
CONVENTIONAL PATTERNS
I
II
III
IV
V
COMPLETE FRETBOARD
SWEEPS A
I
II
III
IV
V
COMPLETE FRETBOARD
SWEEPS B
I
II
III
IV
V
A♭ MINOR PENTATONIC
COMPLETE FRETBOARD
CONVENTIONAL PATTERNS
V
I
II
III
IV
COMPLETE FRETBOARD
SWEEPS B
V
I
II
III
IV
COMPLETE FRETBOARD
SWEEPS B
V
I
II
II
IV

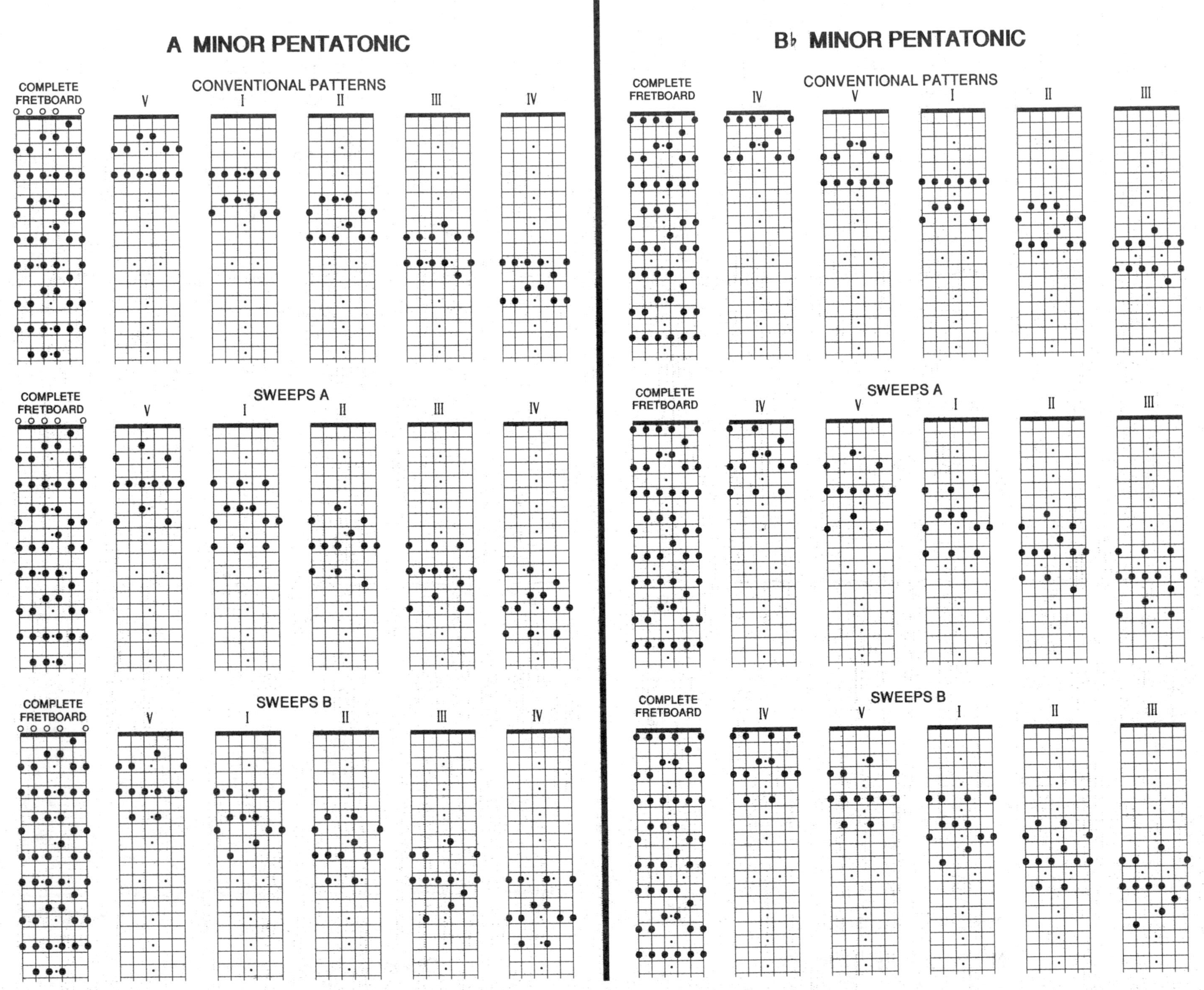
A MINOR PENTATONIC
COMPLETE FRETBOARD
CONVENTIONAL PATTERNS
V
I
II
III
IV
COMPLETE FRETBOARD
SWEEPS A
V
I
II
III
IV
COMPLETE FRETBOARD
SWEEPS B
V
I
II
III
IV
B♭ MINOR PENTATONIC
COMPLETE FRETBOARD
CONVENTIONAL PATTERNS
IV
V
I
II
III
COMPLETE FRETBOARD
SWEEPS A
IV
V
I
II
III
COMPLETE FRETBOARD
SWEEPS B
IV
V
I
II
III

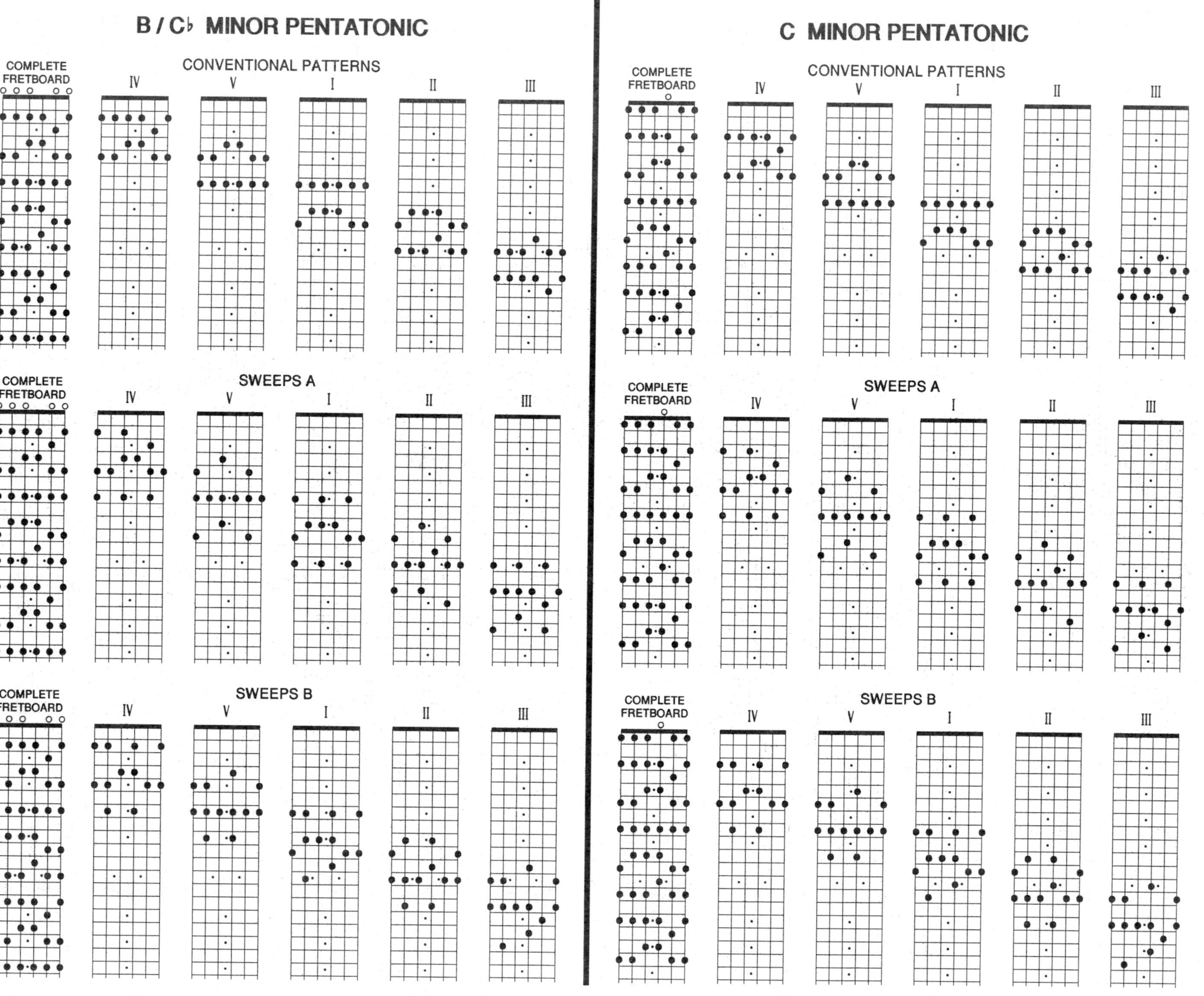
B / C♭ MINOR PENTATONIC
CONVENTIONAL PATTERNS
COMPLETE FRETBOARD
IV
V
I
II
III
SWEEPS A
COMPLETE FRETBOARD
IV
V
I
II
III
SWEEPS B
COMPLETE FRETBOARD
IV
V
I
II
III
C MINOR PENTATONIC
CONVENTIONAL PATTERNS
COMPLETE FRETBOARD
IV
V
I
II
III
SWEEPS A
COMPLETE FRETBOARD
IV
V
I
II
III
SWEEPS B
COMPLETE FRETBOARD
IV
V
I
II
III

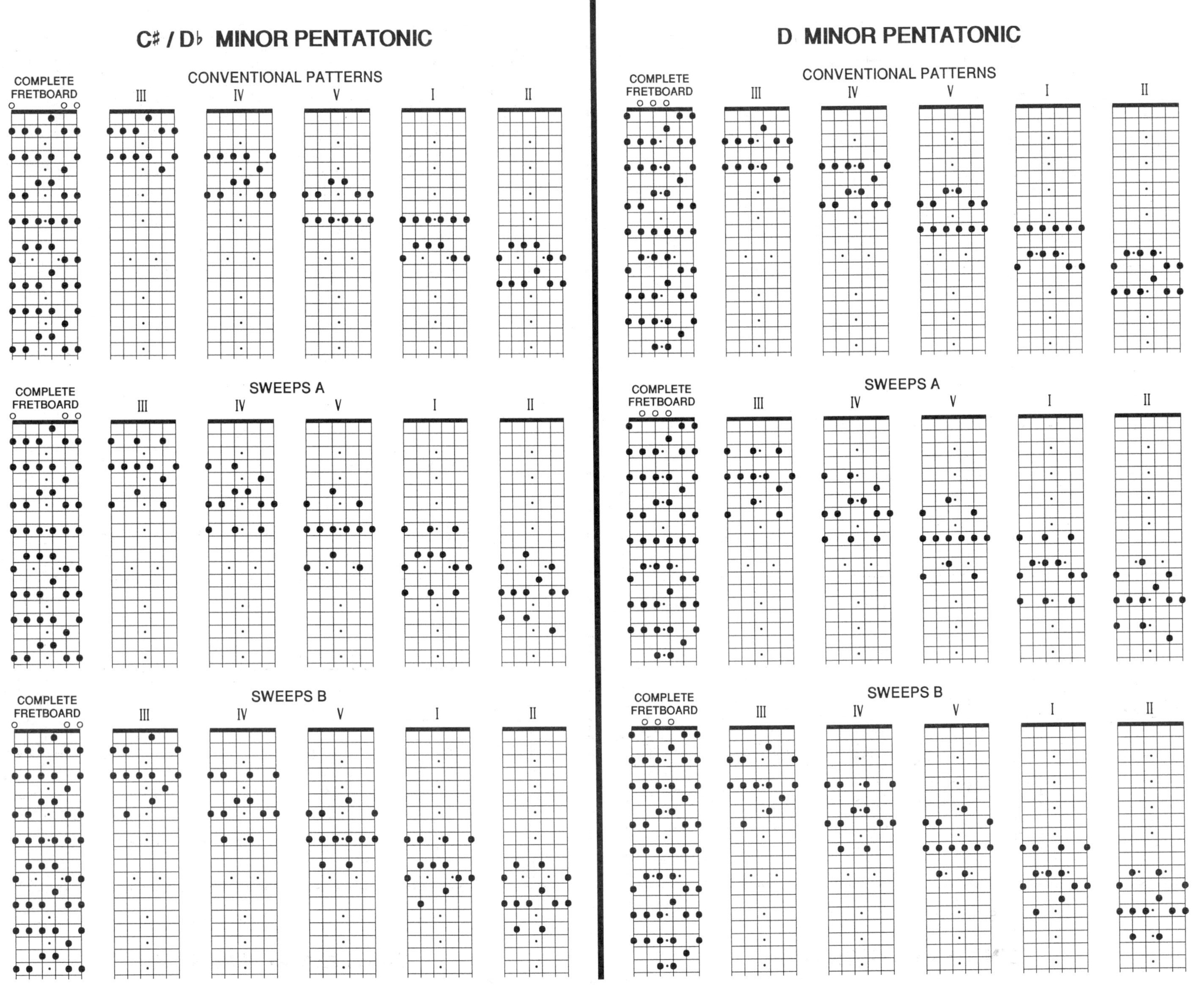
C♯ / D♭ MINOR PENTATONIC
COMPLETE FRETBOARD
CONVENTIONAL PATTERNS
III
IV
V
I
II
COMPLETE FRETBOARD
SWEEPS A
III
IV
V
I
II
COMPLETE FRETBOARD
SWEEPS B
III
IV
V
I
II
D MINOR PENTATONIC
COMPLETE FRETBOARD
CONVENTIONAL PATTERNS
III
IV
V
I
II
COMPLETE FRETBOARD
SWEEPS A
III
IV
V
I
II
COMPLETE FRETBOARD
SWEEPS B
III
IV
V
I
II

E♭ MINOR PENTATONIC

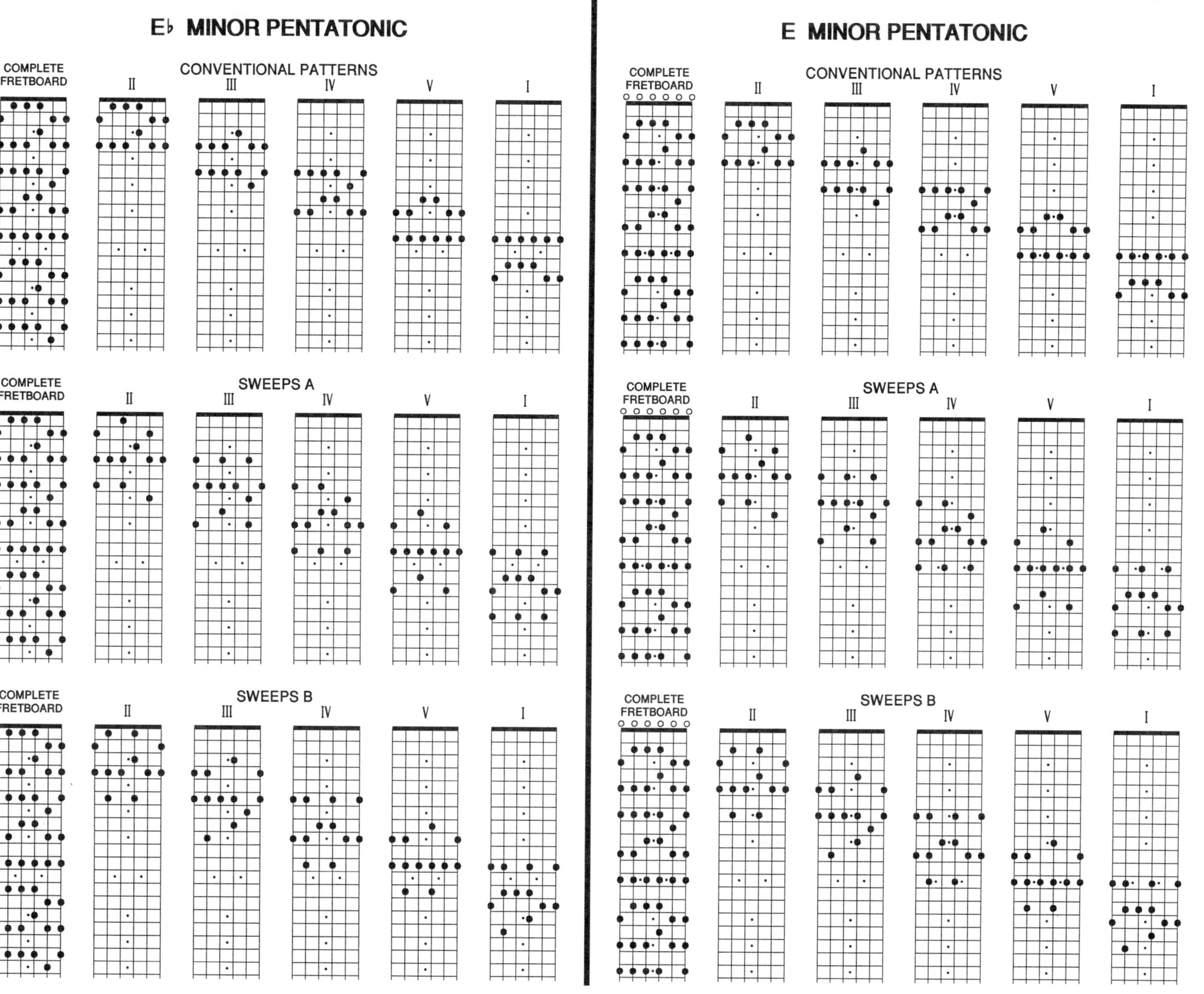

E MINOR PENTATONIC

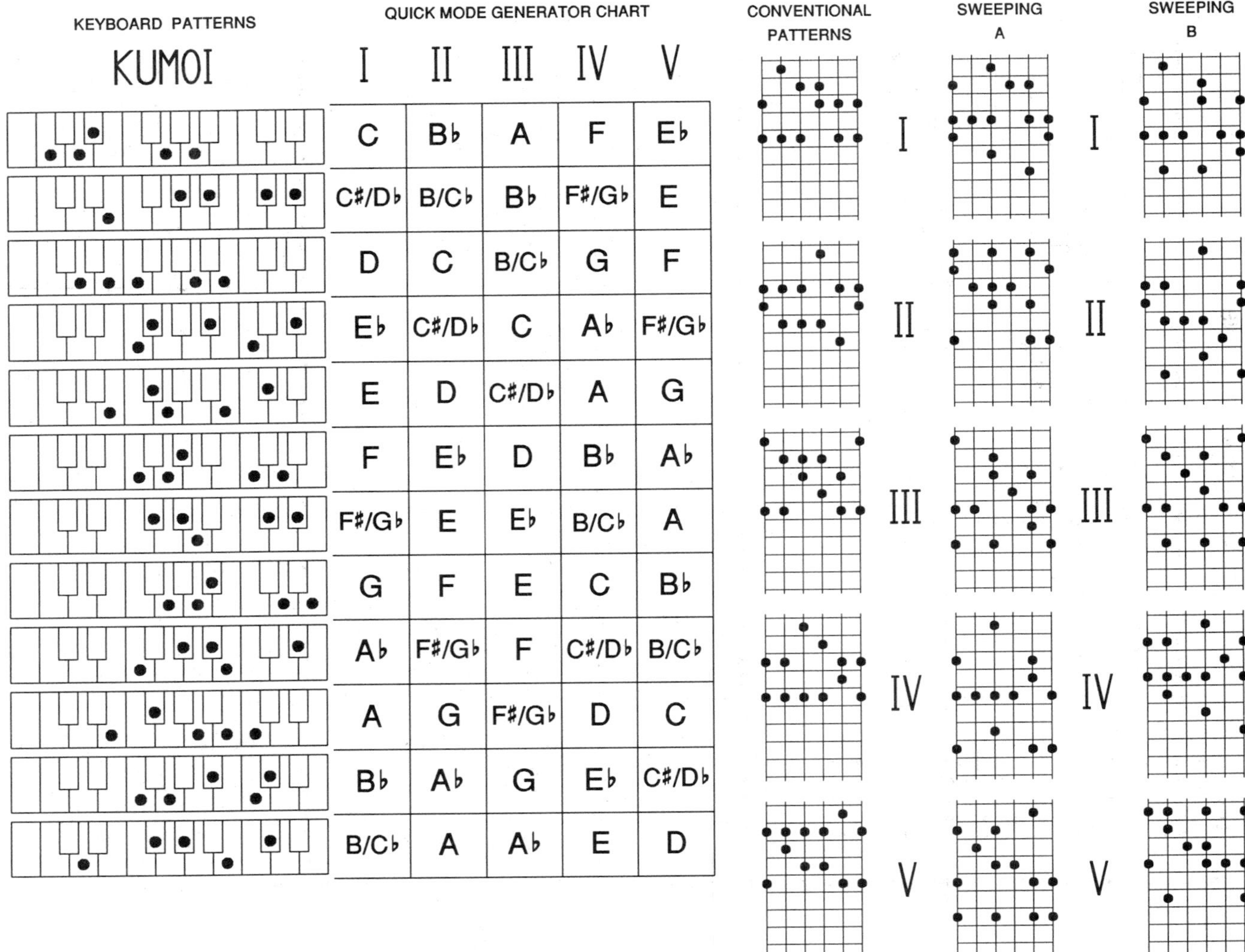

I	II	III	IV	V
C	B♭	A	F	E♭
C♯/D♭	B/C♭	B♭	F♯/G♭	E
D	C	B/C♭	G	F
E♭	C♯/D♭	C	A♭	F♯/G♭
E	D	C♯/D♭	A	G
F	E♭	D	B♭	A♭
F♯/G♭	E	E♭	B/C♭	A
G	F	E	C	B♭
A♭	F♯/G♭	F	C♯/D♭	B/C♭
A	G	F♯/G♭	D	C
B♭	A♭	G	E♭	C♯/D♭
B/C♭	A	A♭	E	D

SCALE / MODE - CHORD CHART

I	KUMOI	–, –6, sus2
II	MODE 2	sus, 7sus
III	MODE 3	△♭5
IV	MODE 4	sus2, sus
V	MODE 5	∅

The Kumoi can be used in place of the Melodic, IV mode of the Harmonic Major, as well as any scale that contains the same notes as the Kumoi.

NUMERIC SCALE / MODE CHART

		1		2		3	4		5		6		7	1		2		3	4		5		6		7
I	KUMOI	1		2	♭3				5		6			1		2	♭3				5		6		
II	MODE 2			1	♭2				4		5			♭7											
III	MODE 3				1				3		♭5			6		7									
IV	MODE 4								1		2			4		5	♭6								
V	MODE 5										1			♭3		4	♭5				♭7				

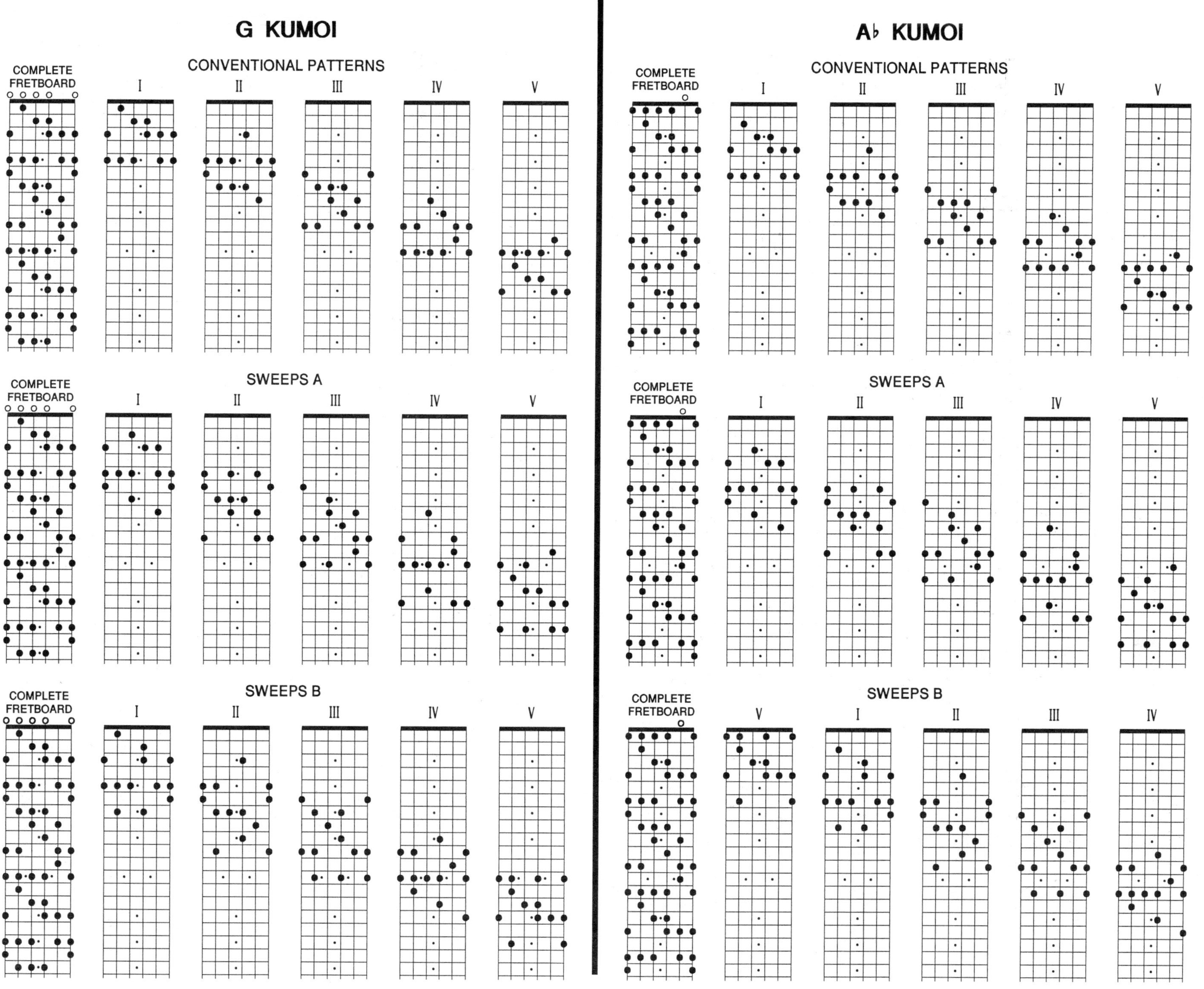

G KUMOI
CONVENTIONAL PATTERNS
COMPLETE FRETBOARD
I
II
III
IV
V
SWEEPS A
COMPLETE FRETBOARD
I
II
III
IV
V
SWEEPS B
COMPLETE FRETBOARD
I
II
III
IV
V
A♭ KUMOI
CONVENTIONAL PATTERNS
COMPLETE FRETBOARD
I
II
III
IV
V
SWEEPS A
COMPLETE FRETBOARD
I
II
III
IV
V
SWEEPS B
COMPLETE FRETBOARD
V
I
II
III
IV

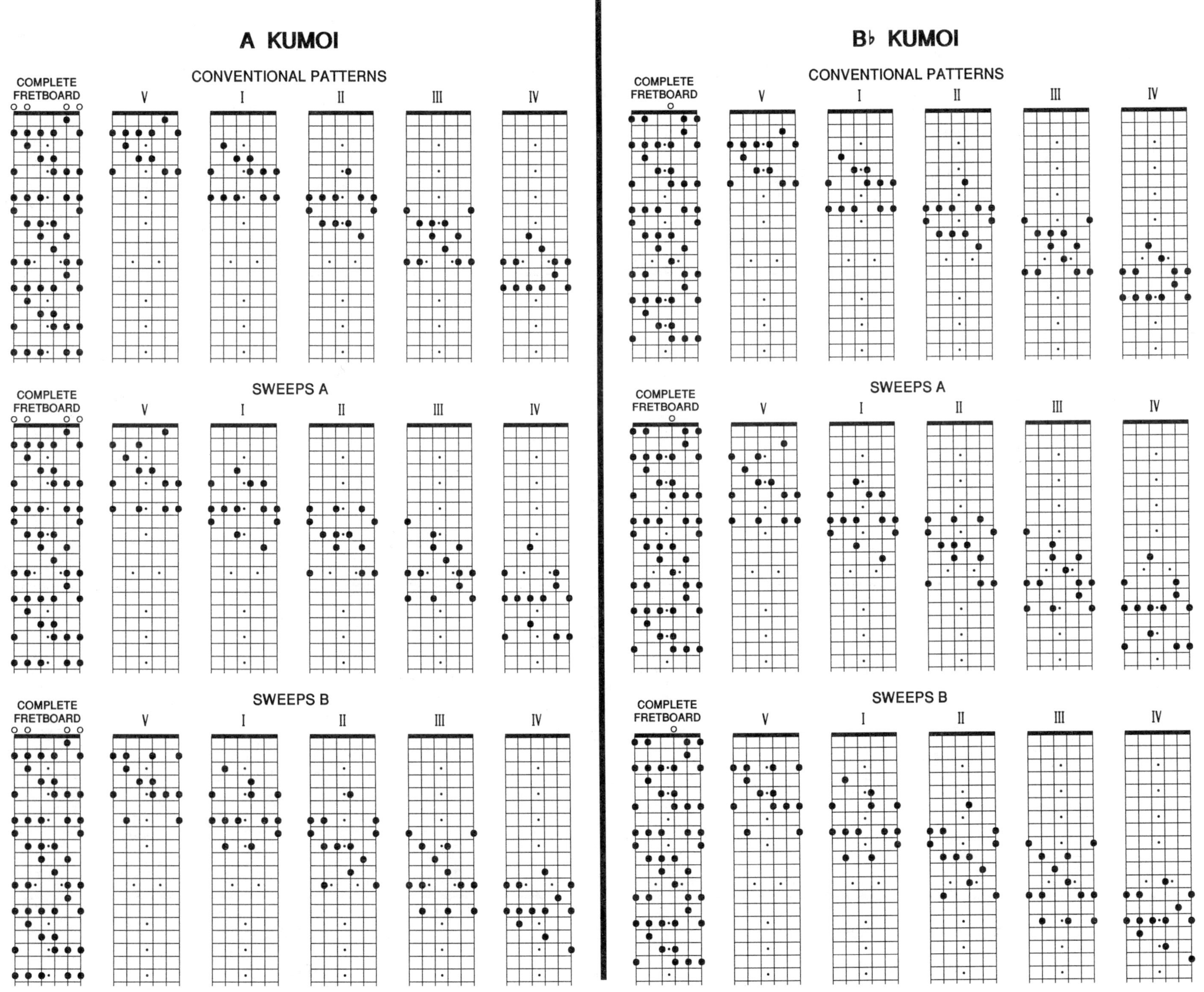
A KUMOI
CONVENTIONAL PATTERNS
COMPLETE FRETBOARD
V
I
II
III
IV
SWEEPS A
COMPLETE FRETBOARD
V
I
II
III
IV
SWEEPS B
COMPLETE FRETBOARD
V
I
II
III
IV
B♭ KUMOI
CONVENTIONAL PATTERNS
COMPLETE FRETBOARD
V
I
II
III
IV
SWEEPS A
COMPLETE FRETBOARD
V
I
II
III
IV
SWEEPS B
COMPLETE FRETBOARD
V
I
II
III
IV

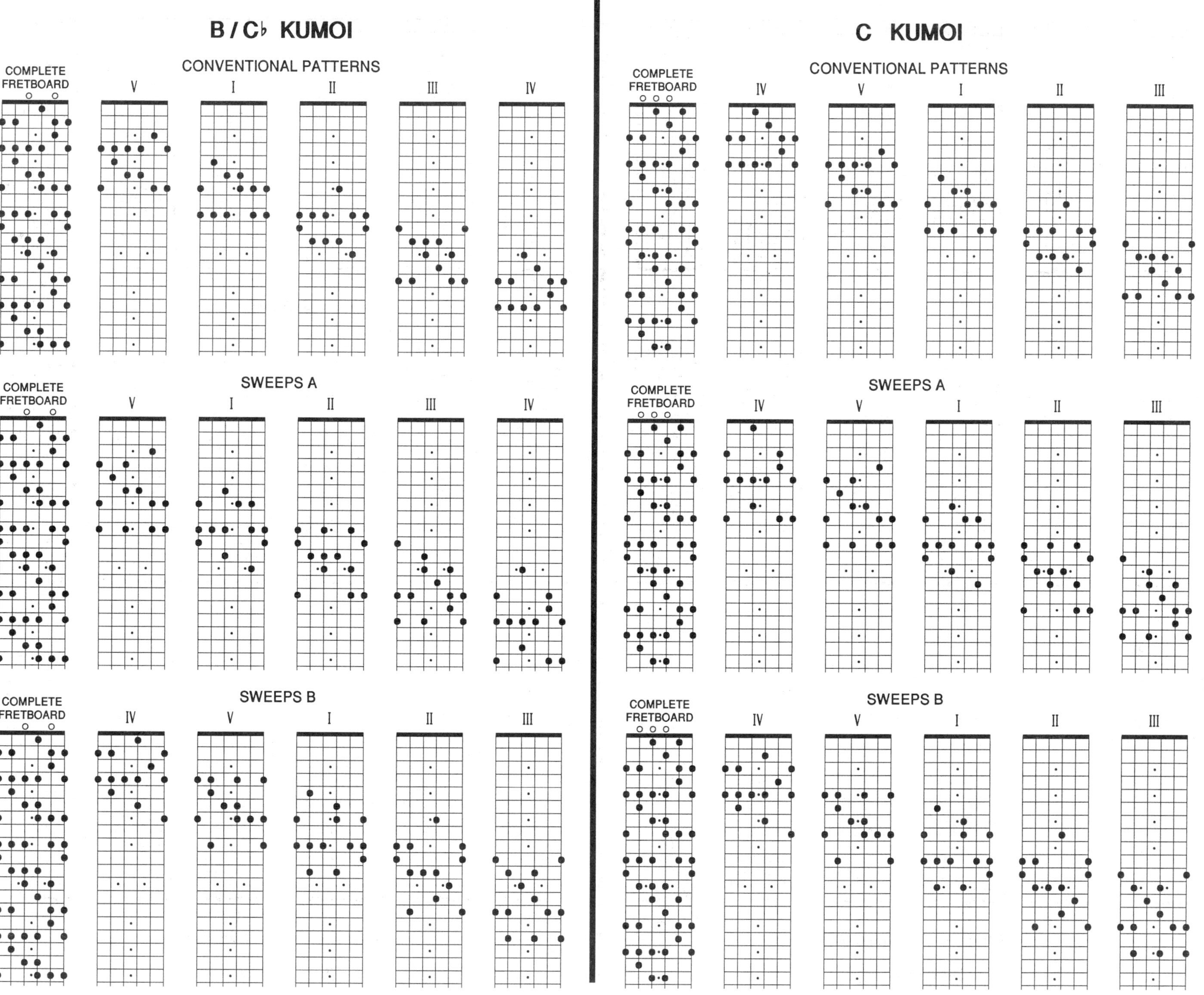
B / C♭ KUMOI
CONVENTIONAL PATTERNS
COMPLETE FRETBOARD
V
I
II
III
IV
SWEEPS A
COMPLETE FRETBOARD
V
I
II
III
IV
SWEEPS B
COMPLETE FRETBOARD
IV
V
I
II
III
C KUMOI
CONVENTIONAL PATTERNS
COMPLETE FRETBOARD
IV
V
I
II
III
SWEEPS A
COMPLETE FRETBOARD
IV
V
I
II
III
SWEEPS B
COMPLETE FRETBOARD
IV
V
I
II
III

C♯ / D♭ KUMOI

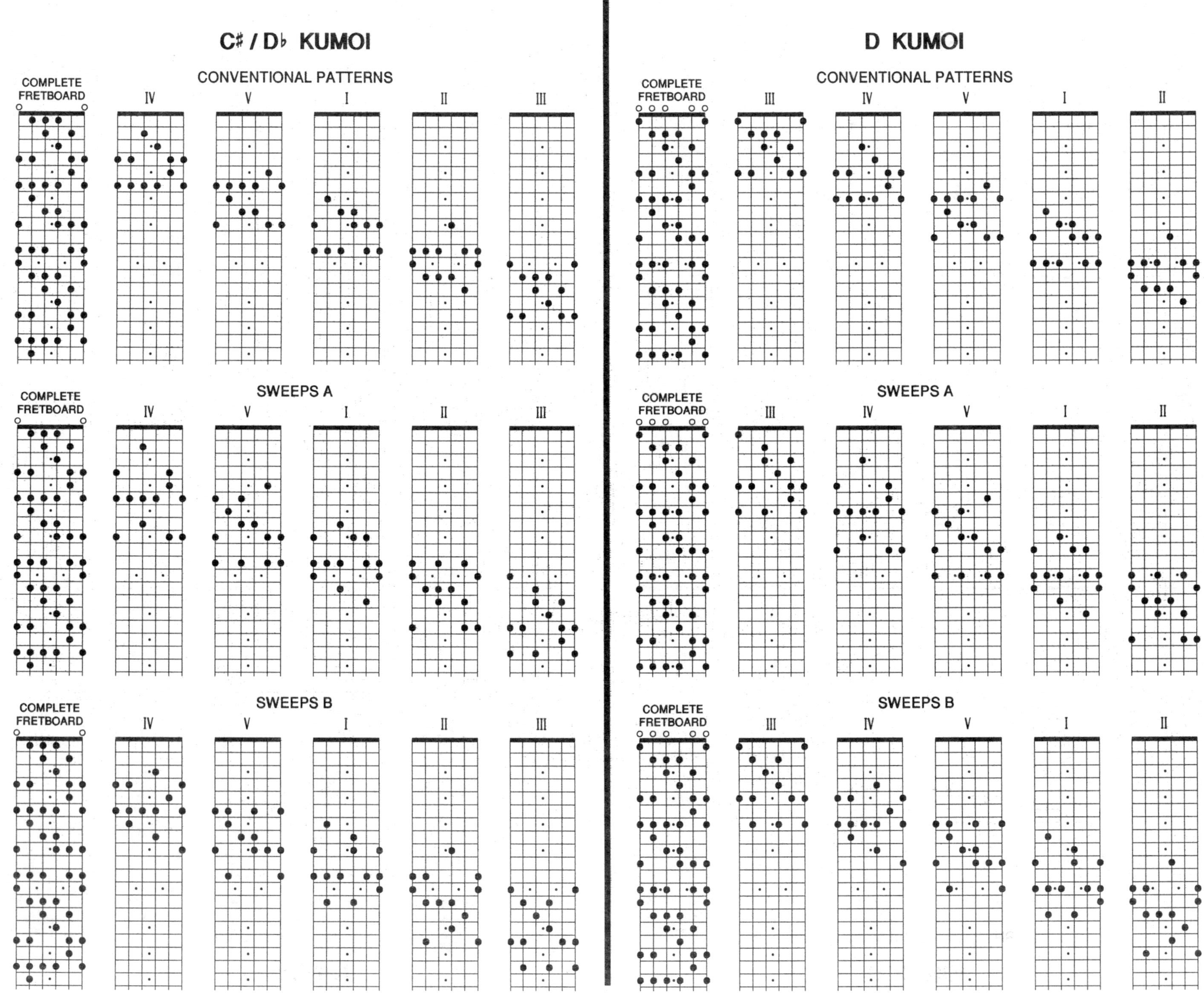

D KUMOI

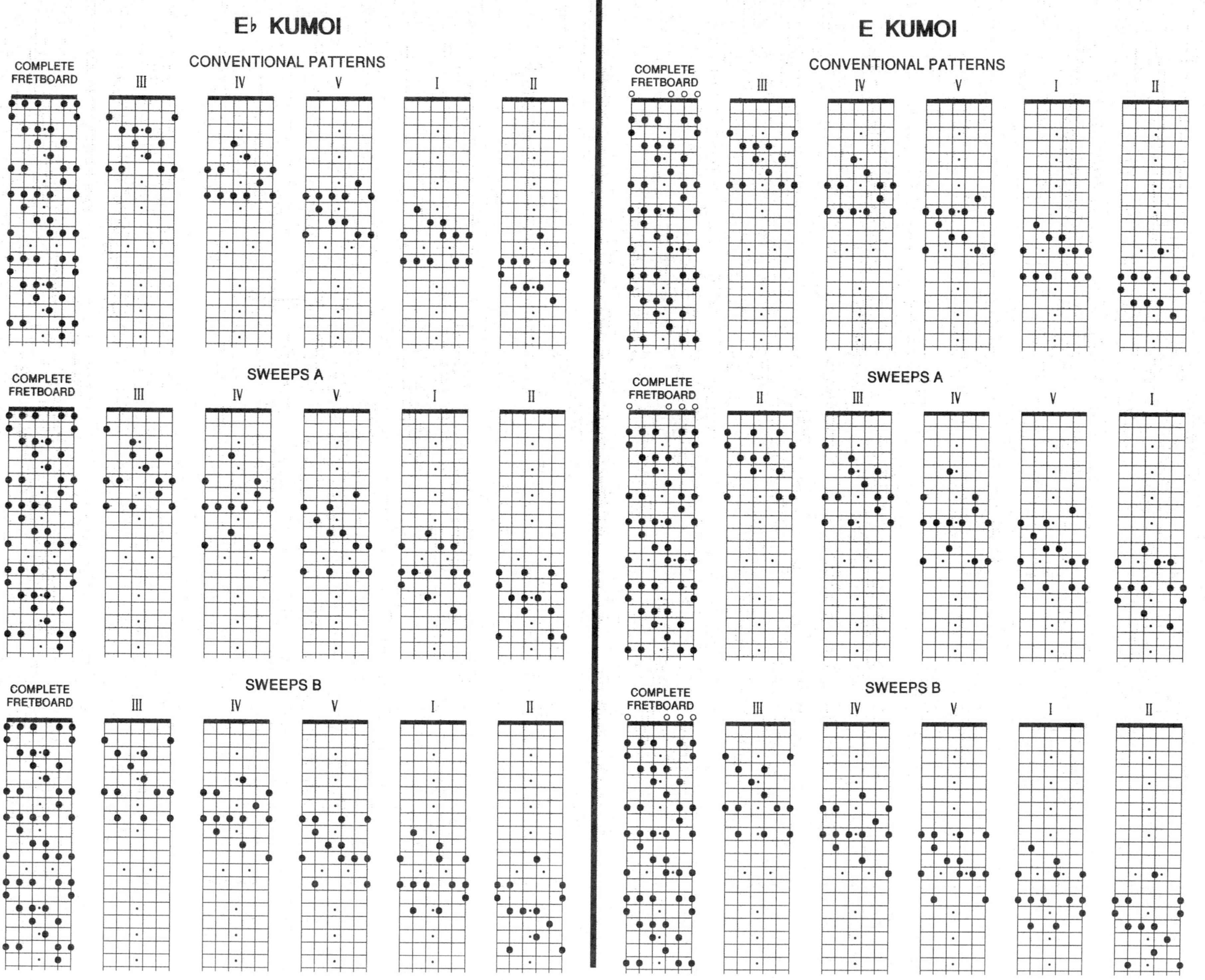
E♭ KUMOI
CONVENTIONAL PATTERNS
COMPLETE FRETBOARD
III
IV
V
I
II
SWEEPS A
COMPLETE FRETBOARD
III
IV
V
I
II
SWEEPS B
COMPLETE FRETBOARD
III
IV
V
I
II
E KUMOI
CONVENTIONAL PATTERNS
COMPLETE FRETBOARD
III
IV
V
I
II
SWEEPS A
COMPLETE FRETBOARD
II
III
IV
V
I
SWEEPS B
COMPLETE FRETBOARD
III
IV
V
I
II

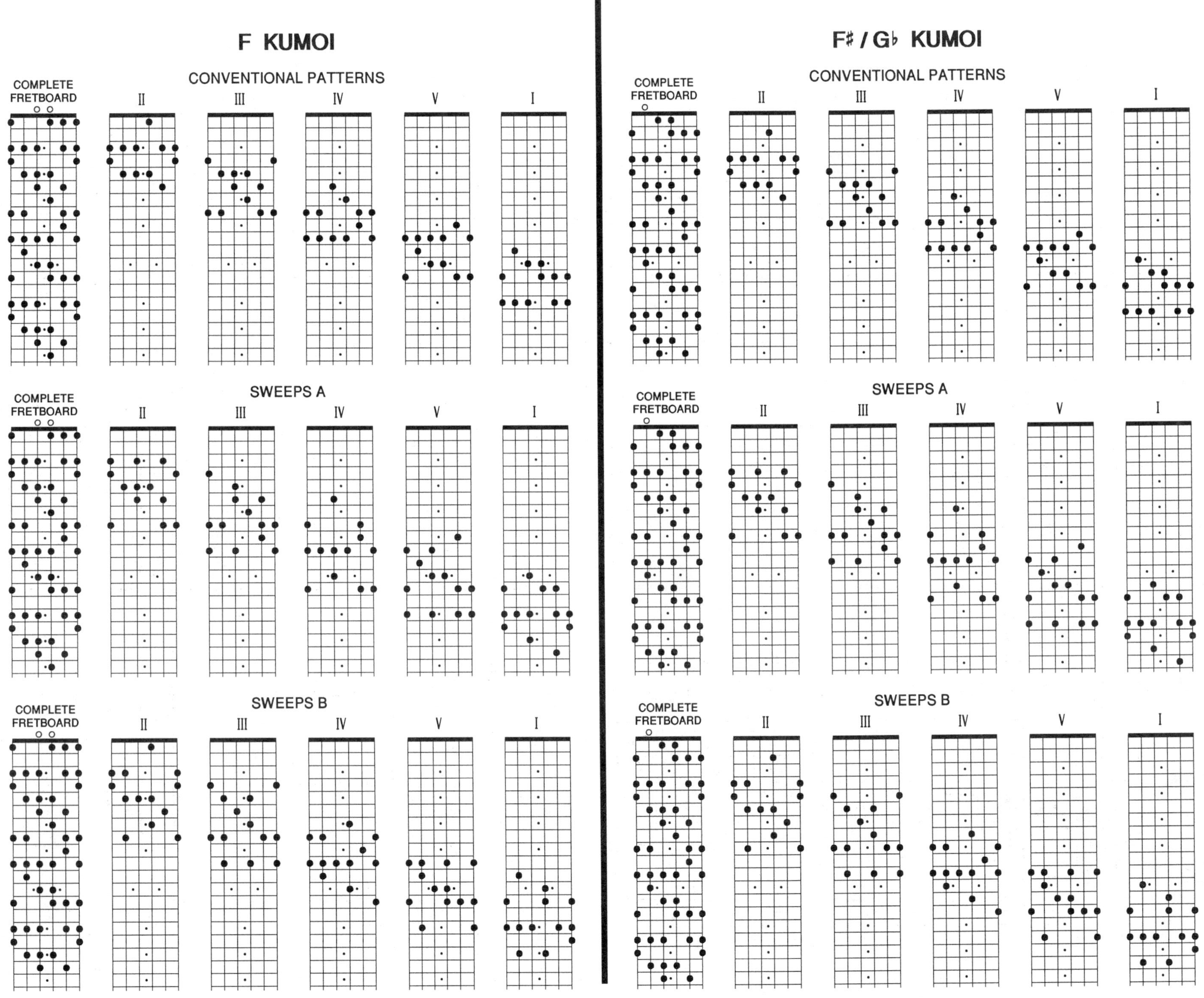

F KUMOI
CONVENTIONAL PATTERNS
COMPLETE FRETBOARD
II
III
IV
V
I
SWEEPS A
COMPLETE FRETBOARD
II
III
IV
V
I
SWEEPS B
COMPLETE FRETBOARD
II
III
IV
V
I
F♯ / G♭ KUMOI
CONVENTIONAL PATTERNS
COMPLETE FRETBOARD
II
III
IV
V
I
SWEEPS A
COMPLETE FRETBOARD
II
III
IV
V
I
SWEEPS B
COMPLETE FRETBOARD
II
III
IV
V
I

KEYBOARD PATTERNS

HIROJOSHI

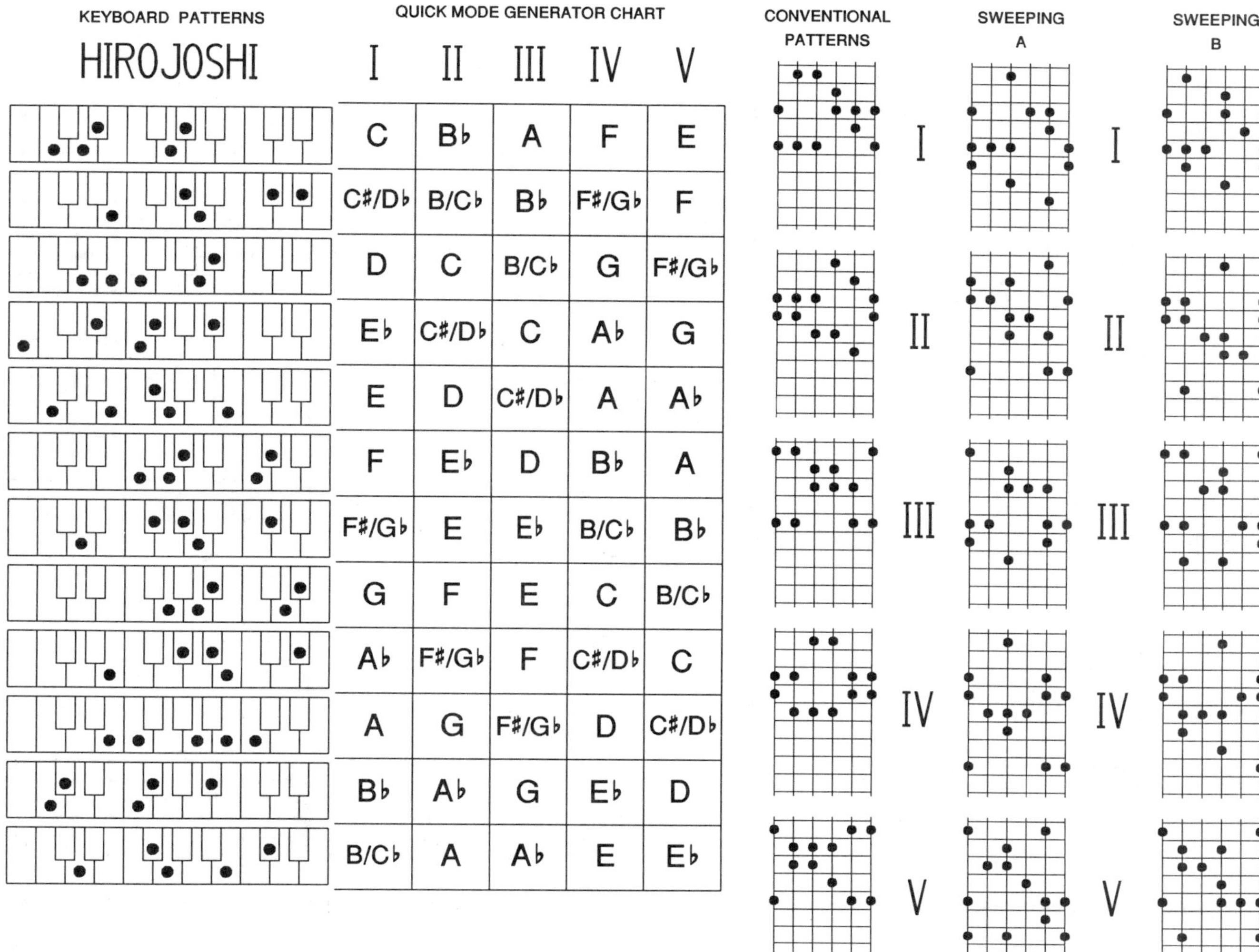

I	II	III	IV	V
C	B♭	A	F	E
C♯/D♭	B/C♭	B♭	F♯/G♭	F
D	C	B/C♭	G	F♯/G♭
E♭	C♯/D♭	C	A♭	G
E	D	C♯/D♭	A	A♭
F	E♭	D	B♭	A
F♯/G♭	E	E♭	B/C♭	B♭
G	F	E	C	B/C♭
A♭	F♯/G♭	F	C♯/D♭	C
A	G	F♯/G♭	D	C♯/D♭
B♭	A♭	G	E♭	D
B/C♭	A	A♭	E	E♭

SCALE / MODE - CHORD CHART

I	HIROJOSHI	–, –♭6
II	MODE 2	Q3
III	MODE 3	△sus
IV	MODE 4	sus
V	MODE 5	△, △♭5

The Hirojoshi can be used in place of the Harmonic Minor and the Hungarian Minor, as well as any scale that contains those tones.

NUMERIC SCALE / MODE CHART

		1		2		3	4		5		6		7	1		2		3	4		5		6		7
I	HIROJOSHI	1		2	♭3				5	♭6				1		2	♭3				5	♭6			
II	MODE 2			1	♭2				4	♭5				♭7											
III	MODE 3				1				3	4				6		7									
IV	MODE 4								1	♭2				4		5	♭6								
V	MODE 5									1				3		♯4	5				7				

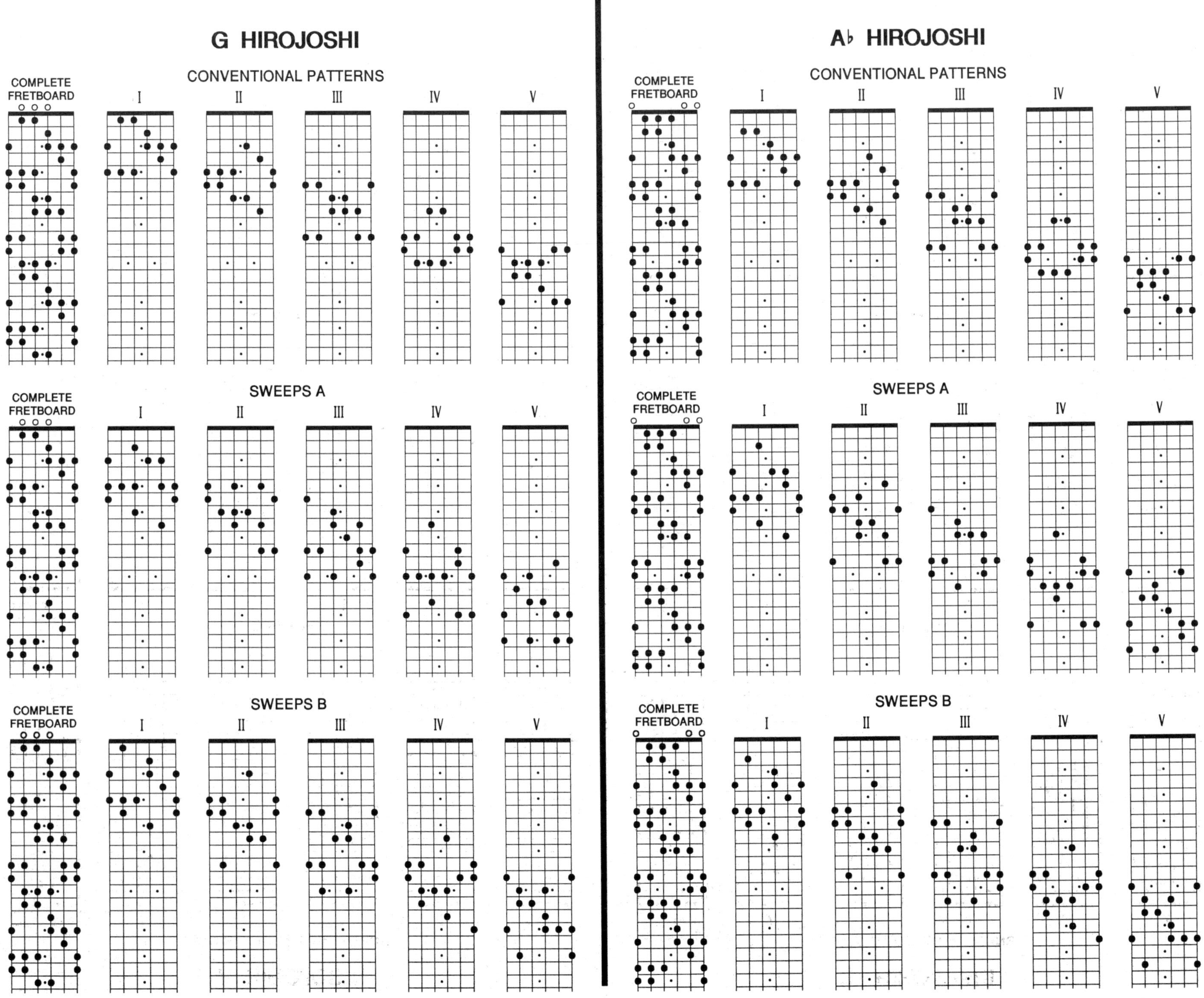
G HIROJOSHI
CONVENTIONAL PATTERNS
COMPLETE FRETBOARD
I
II
III
IV
V
SWEEPS A
COMPLETE FRETBOARD
I
II
III
IV
V
SWEEPS B
COMPLETE FRETBOARD
I
II
III
IV
V
A♭ HIROJOSHI
CONVENTIONAL PATTERNS
COMPLETE FRETBOARD
I
II
III
IV
V
SWEEPS A
COMPLETE FRETBOARD
I
II
III
IV
V
SWEEPS B
COMPLETE FRETBOARD
I
II
III
IV
V

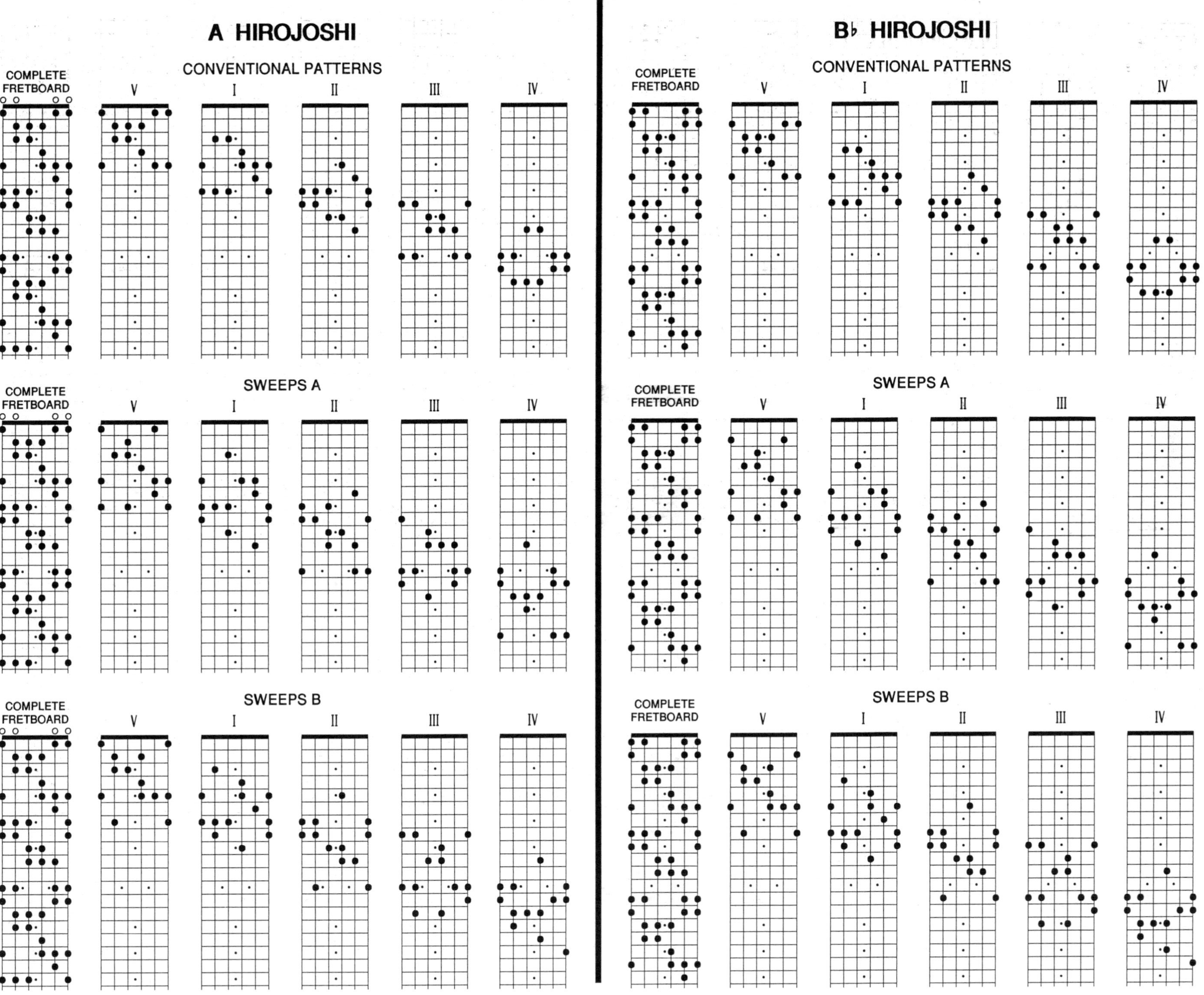
A HIROJOSHI
CONVENTIONAL PATTERNS
COMPLETE FRETBOARD
V
I
II
III
IV
SWEEPS A
SWEEPS B
B♭ HIROJOSHI

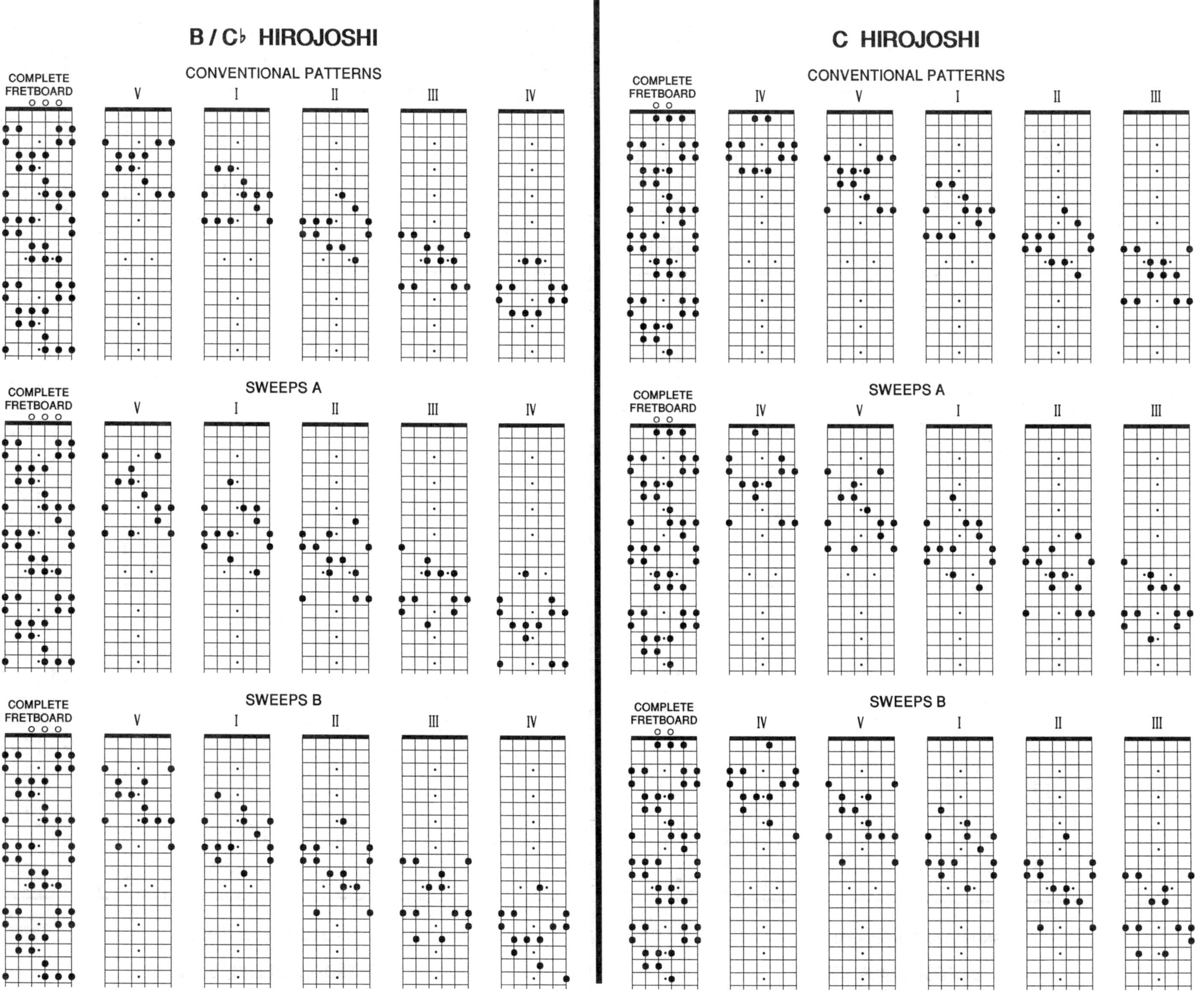
B / C♭ HIROJOSHI
CONVENTIONAL PATTERNS
COMPLETE FRETBOARD
V
I
II
III
IV
SWEEPS A
COMPLETE FRETBOARD
V
I
II
III
IV
SWEEPS B
COMPLETE FRETBOARD
V
I
II
III
IV
C HIROJOSHI
CONVENTIONAL PATTERNS
COMPLETE FRETBOARD
IV
V
I
II
III
SWEEPS A
COMPLETE FRETBOARD
IV
V
I
II
III
SWEEPS B
COMPLETE FRETBOARD
IV
V
I
II
III

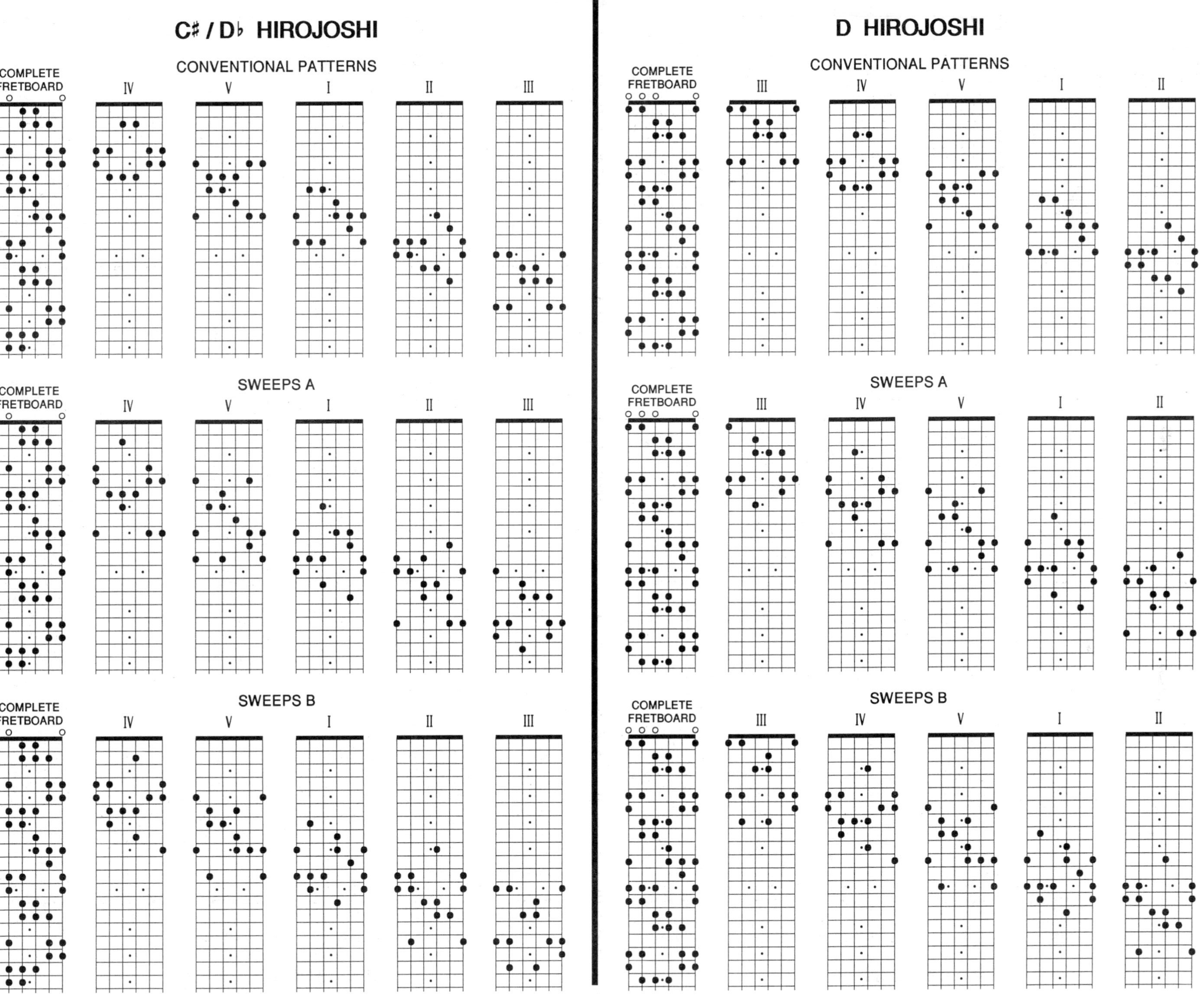
C♯ / D♭ HIROJOSHI
CONVENTIONAL PATTERNS
COMPLETE FRETBOARD
IV
V
I
II
III
SWEEPS A
COMPLETE FRETBOARD
IV
V
I
II
III
SWEEPS B
COMPLETE FRETBOARD
IV
V
I
II
III
D HIROJOSHI
CONVENTIONAL PATTERNS
COMPLETE FRETBOARD
III
IV
V
I
II
SWEEPS A
COMPLETE FRETBOARD
III
IV
V
I
II
SWEEPS B
COMPLETE FRETBOARD
III
IV
V
I
II

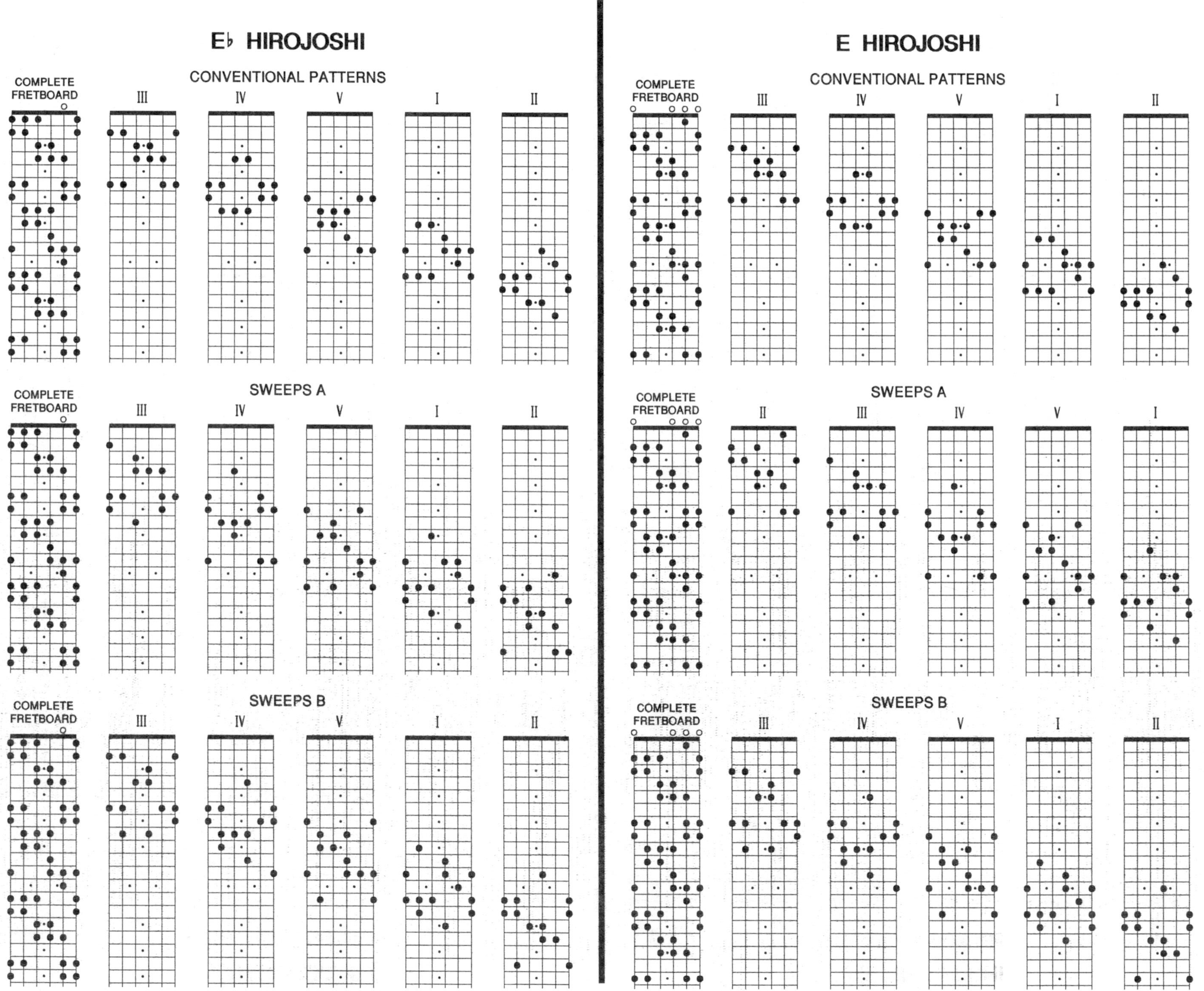

E♭ HIROJOSHI
CONVENTIONAL PATTERNS
COMPLETE FRETBOARD
III
IV
V
I
II
SWEEPS A
COMPLETE FRETBOARD
III
IV
V
I
II
SWEEPS B
COMPLETE FRETBOARD
III
IV
V
I
II
E HIROJOSHI
CONVENTIONAL PATTERNS
COMPLETE FRETBOARD
III
IV
V
I
II
SWEEPS A
COMPLETE FRETBOARD
II
III
IV
V
I
SWEEPS B
COMPLETE FRETBOARD
III
IV
V
I
II

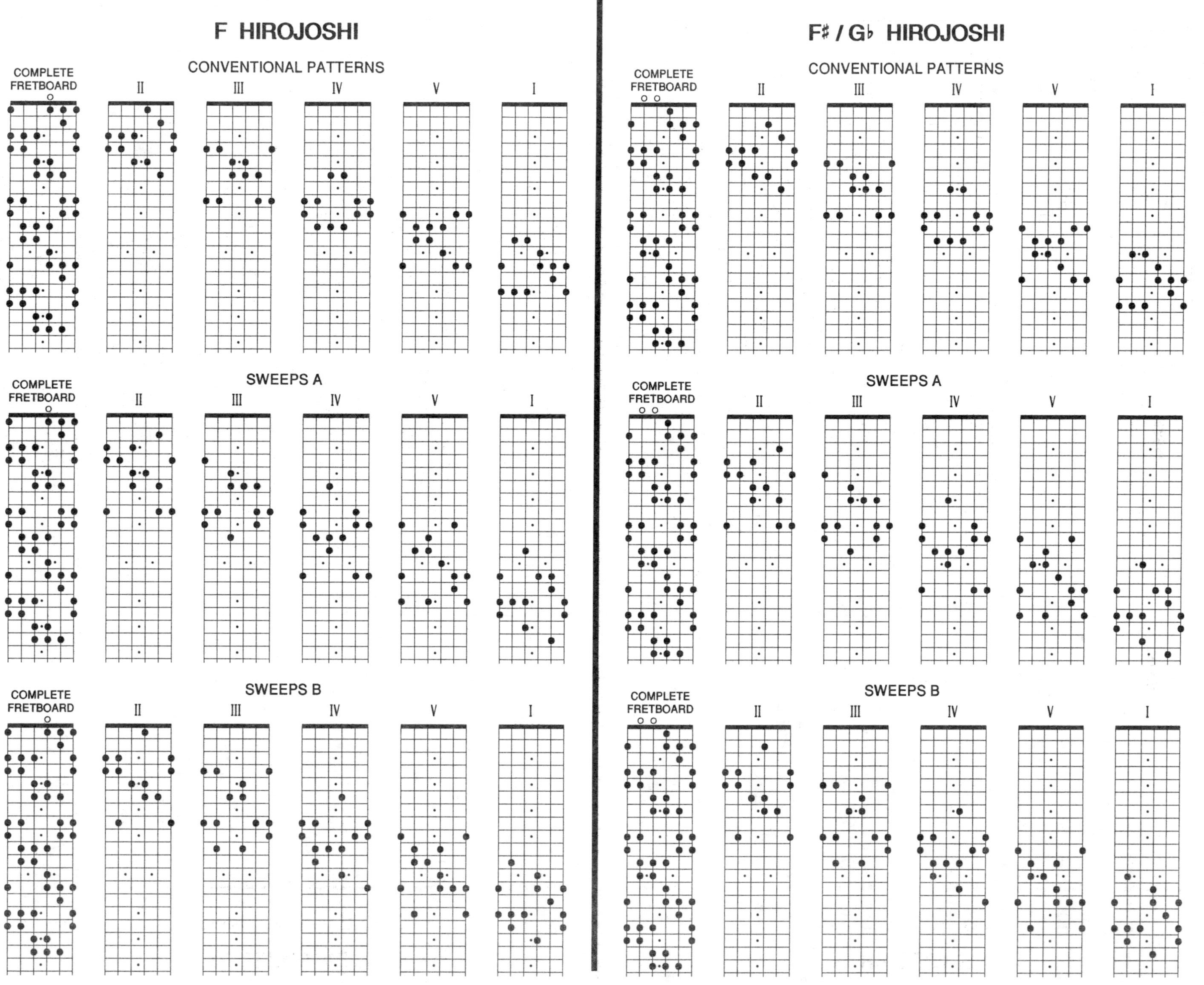
F HIROJOSHI
CONVENTIONAL PATTERNS
COMPLETE FRETBOARD
II
III
IV
V
I
SWEEPS A
COMPLETE FRETBOARD
II
III
IV
V
I
SWEEPS B
COMPLETE FRETBOARD
II
III
IV
V
I
F♯ / G♭ HIROJOSHI
CONVENTIONAL PATTERNS
COMPLETE FRETBOARD
II
III
IV
V
I
SWEEPS A
COMPLETE FRETBOARD
II
III
IV
V
I
SWEEPS B
COMPLETE FRETBOARD
II
III
IV
V
I

6 TONE SCALES

6 tone scales are merely 7 tones scales with 1 tone omitted. The 6 tone scales utilize the same mini-patterns as the 7 and 5 tone scales, making a total of 12 mini-patterns: 8 from the 7 tone scale and 4 from the 5 tone scales.

The most popular of the 6 tone scales would be the Whole-Tone Diminished and the Augmented Scale. The formulas in fig. 46 are based upon the Augmented Chord: 1 - ♭3 - ♯5. 3 tones are added to the chord, making 6 tone scales.

→ → → → → → → → →

- The **X** in the boxes along with the numbers of *this* chart indicate the tones which are to be played.
- The * *Augmented* scale is the most common of all the scales listed.→

AUGMENTED SCALE FORMULAS

	1		2		3	4		5		6		7
	1	X	X	X	**3**	X	X	X	**♯5**	X	X	X
A	1	X			3	X			♯5	X		
B	1	X			3	X			♯5		X	
C	1	X			3	X			♯5			X
D	1	X			3		X		♯5	X		
E	1	X			3		X		♯5		X	
F	1	X			3		X		♯5			X
G	1	X			3			X	♯5	X		
H	1	X			3			X	♯5		X	
I	1	X			3			X	♯5			X
J	1		X		3	X			♯5	X		
K	1		X		3	X			♯5		X	
L	1		X		3	X			♯5			X
M	1		X		3		X		♯5	X		
N	1		X		3		X		♯5		X	
O	1		X		3		X		♯5			X
P	1		X		3			X	♯5	X		
Q	1		X		3			X	♯5		X	
R	1		X		3			X	♯5			X
S	1			X	3	X			♯5	X		
T	1			X	3	X			♯5		X	
U	1			X	3	X			♯5			X
V	1			X	3		X		♯5	X		
W	1			X	3		X		♯5		X	
X	1			X	3		X		♯5			X
Y	1			X	3			X	♯5	X		
Z	1			X	3			X	♯5		X	
*	1			X	3			X	♯5			X

fig. 46

KEYBOARD PATTERNS

QUICK MODE GENERATOR CHART

WHOLE TONE

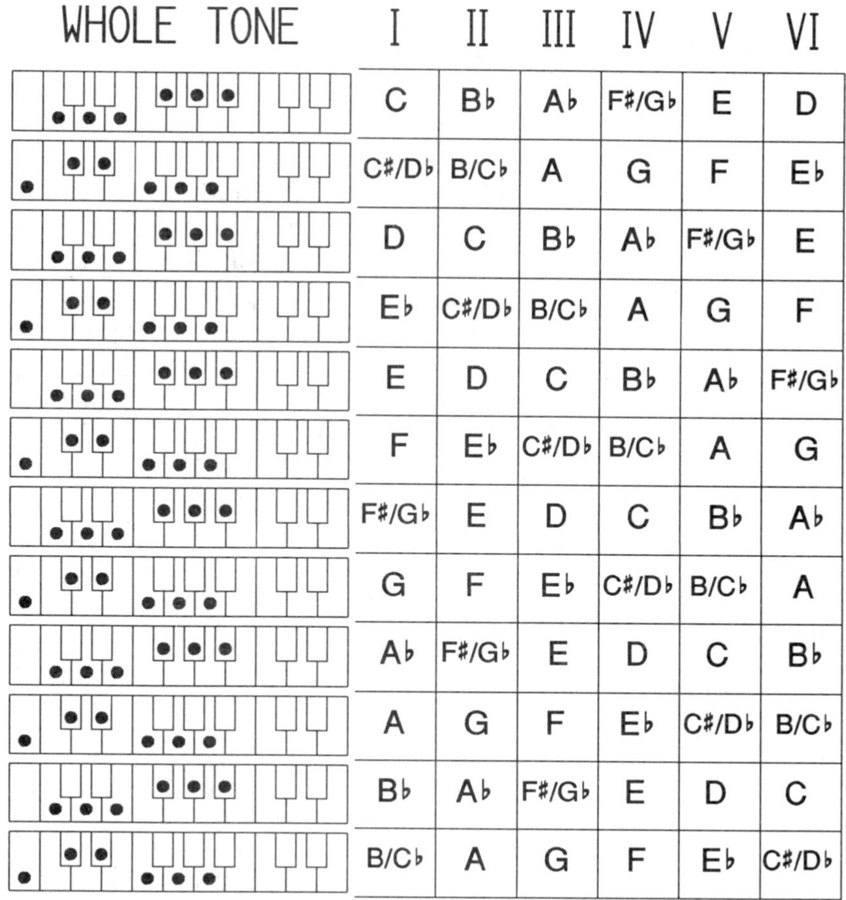

I	II	III	IV	V	VI
C	B♭	A♭	F#/G♭	E	D
C#/D♭	B/C♭	A	G	F	E♭
D	C	B♭	A♭	F#/G♭	E
E♭	C#/D♭	B/C♭	A	G	F
E	D	C	B♭	A♭	F#/G♭
F	E♭	C#/D♭	B/C♭	A	G
F#/G♭	E	D	C	B♭	A♭
G	F	E♭	C#/D♭	B/C♭	A
A♭	F#/G♭	E	D	C	B♭
A	G	F	E♭	C#/D♭	B/C♭
B♭	A♭	F#/G♭	E	D	C
B/C♭	A	G	F	E♭	C#/D♭

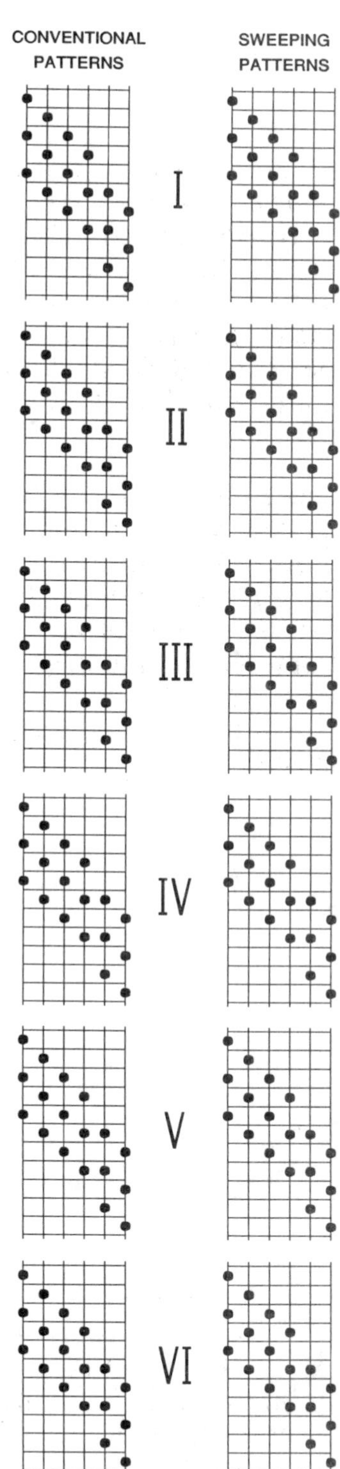

SCALE / MODE - CHORD CHART

I	WHOLE TONE	+
II	WHOLE TONE	+
III	WHOLE TONE	+
IV	WHOLE TONE	+
V	WHOLE TONE	+
VI	WHOLE TONE	+

DUE TO THE SYMMETRICAL NATURE OF THIS SCALE, IT HAS NO MODES.

NUMERIC SCALE / MODE CHART

		1		2		3	4		5		6		7	1		2		3	4		5		6		7
I	WHOLE TONE	1		2		3		#4		#5		#6													
II	WHOLE TONE			1		2		3		#4		#5		#6											
III	WHOLE TONE					1		2		3		#4		#5		#6									
IV	WHOLE TONE							1		2		3		#4		#5		#6							
V	WHOLE TONE									1		2		3		#4		#5		#6					
VI	WHOLE TONE											1		2		3		#4		#5		#6			

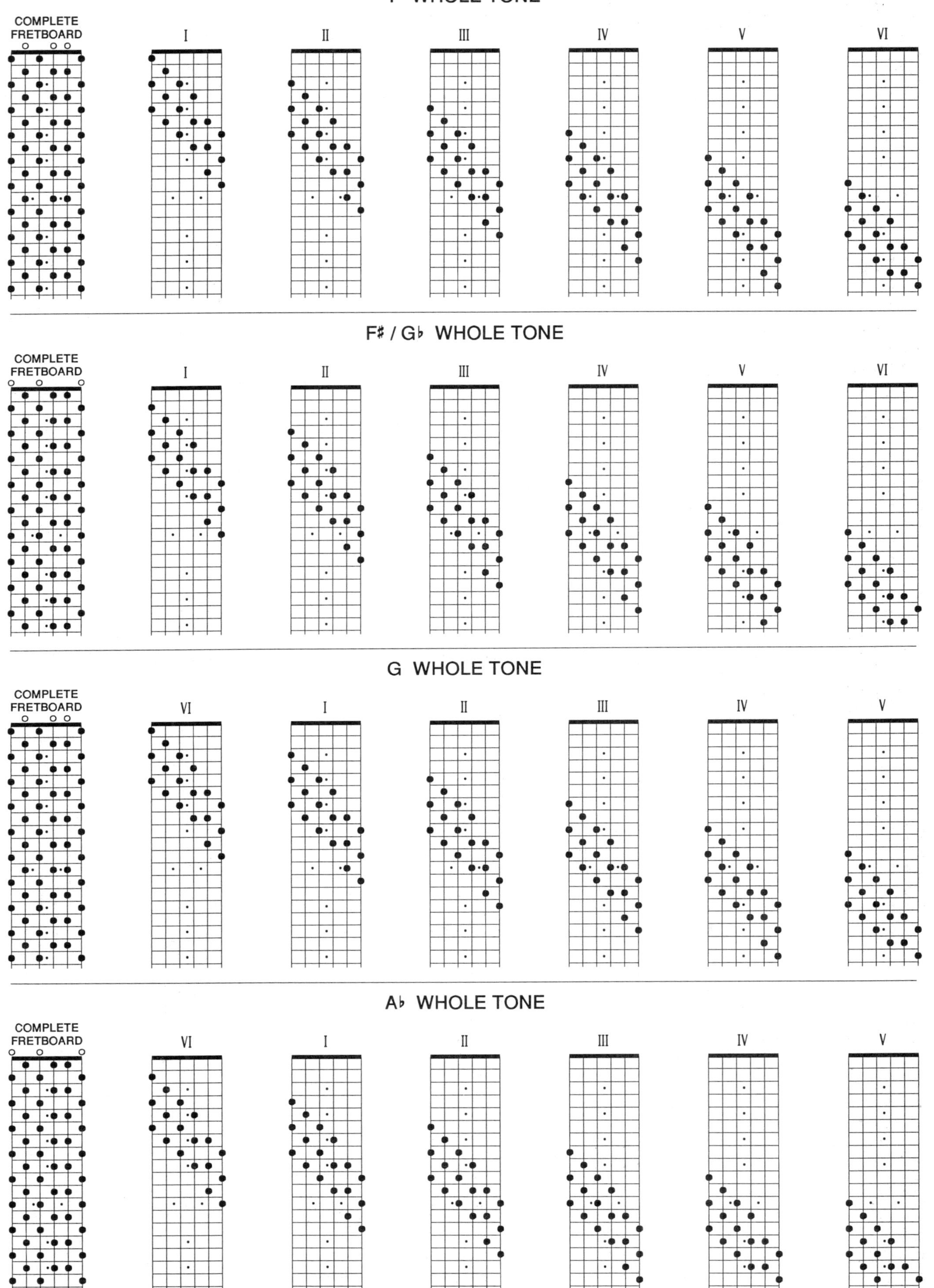
F WHOLE TONE
COMPLETE FRETBOARD
I
II
III
IV
V
VI
F♯ / G♭ WHOLE TONE
COMPLETE FRETBOARD
I
II
III
IV
V
VI
G WHOLE TONE
COMPLETE FRETBOARD
VI
I
II
III
IV
V
A♭ WHOLE TONE
COMPLETE FRETBOARD
VI
I
II
III
IV
V

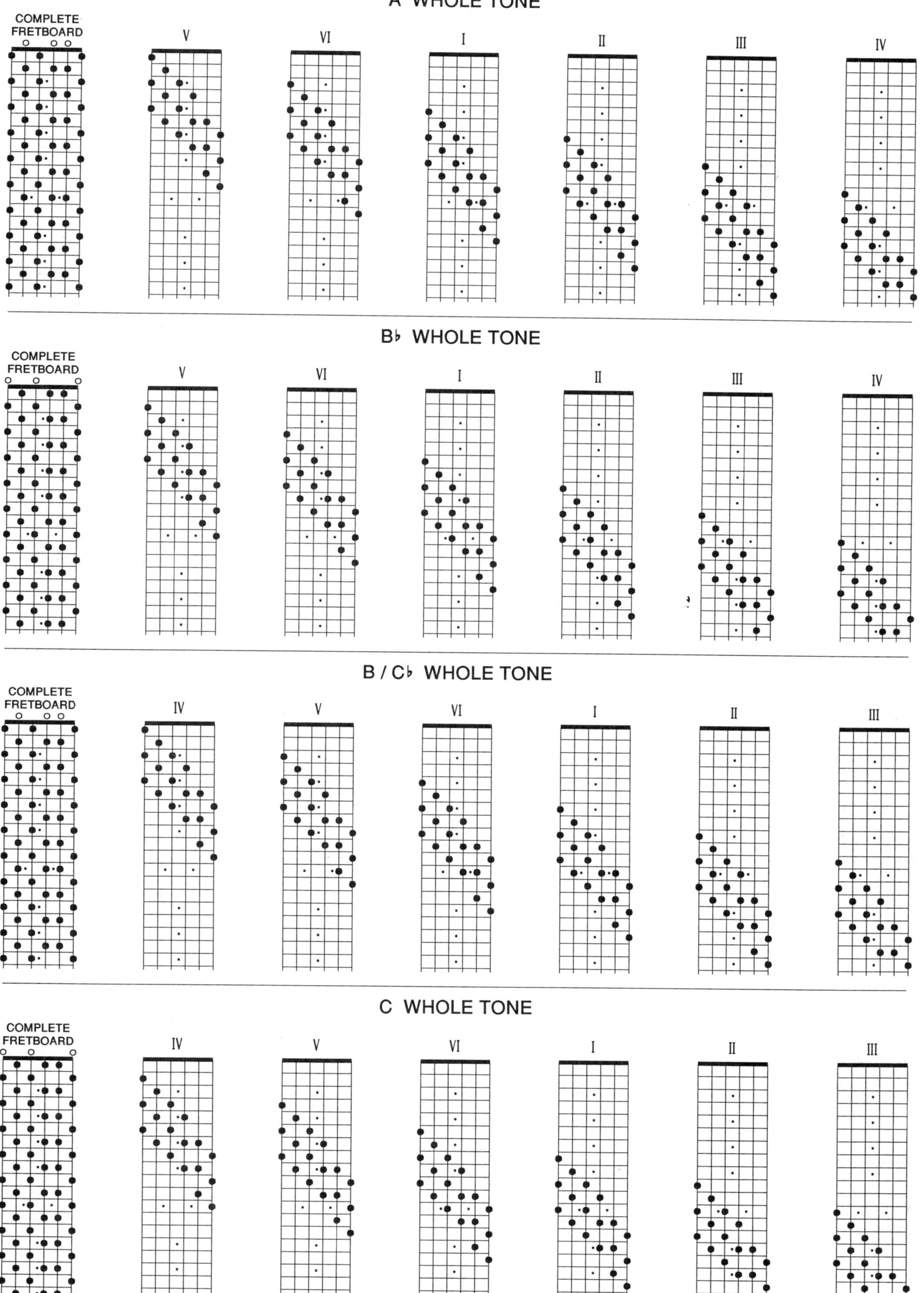
A WHOLE TONE
COMPLETE FRETBOARD
V
VI
I
II
III
IV
B♭ WHOLE TONE
COMPLETE FRETBOARD
V
VI
I
II
III
IV
B / C♭ WHOLE TONE
COMPLETE FRETBOARD
IV
V
VI
I
II
III
C WHOLE TONE
COMPLETE FRETBOARD
IV
V
VI
I
II
III

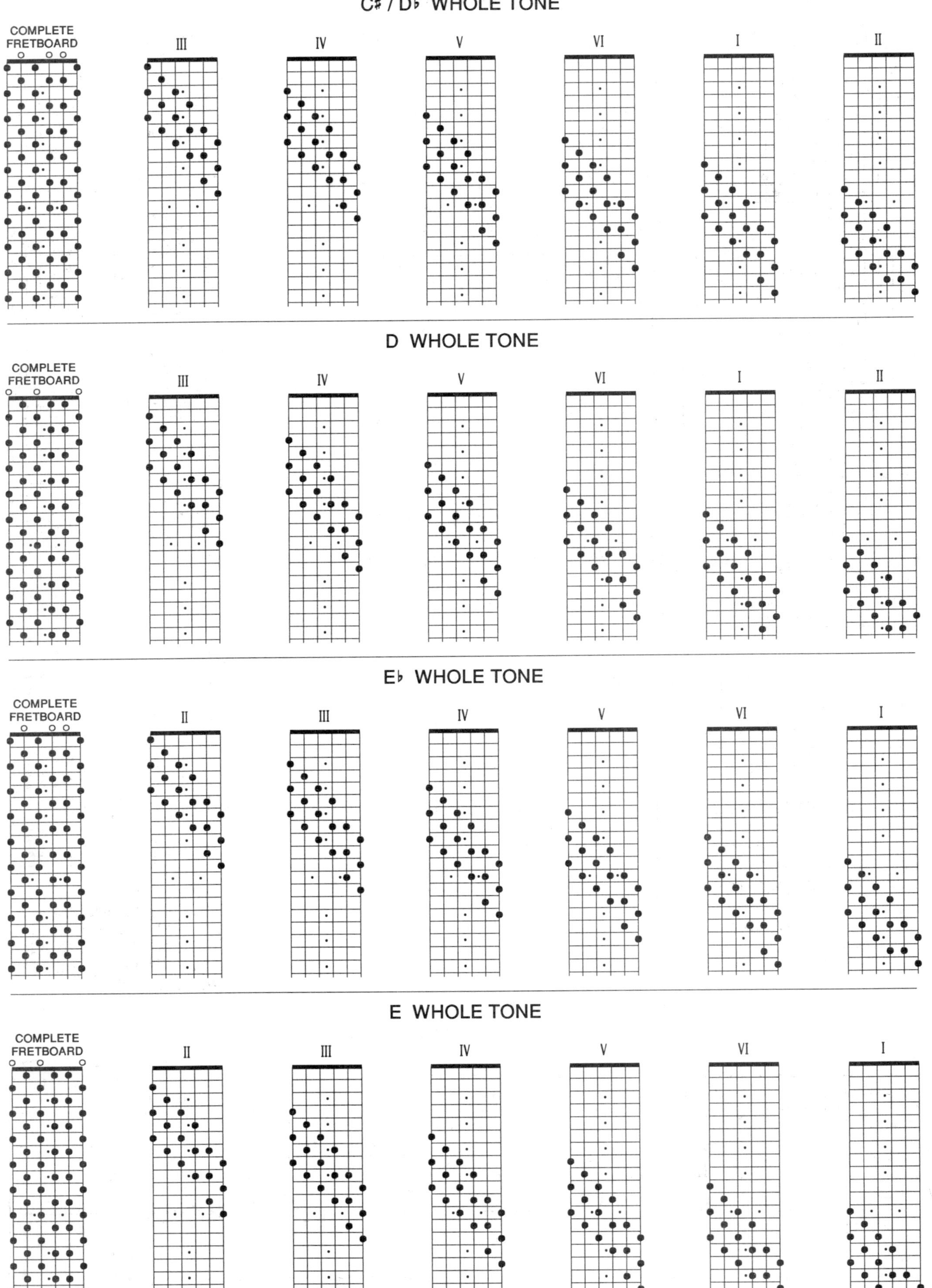
C♯ / D♭ WHOLE TONE
COMPLETE FRETBOARD
III
IV
V
VI
I
II
D WHOLE TONE
COMPLETE FRETBOARD
III
IV
V
VI
I
II
E♭ WHOLE TONE
COMPLETE FRETBOARD
II
III
IV
V
VI
I
E WHOLE TONE
COMPLETE FRETBOARD
II
III
IV
V
VI
I

KEYBOARD PATTERNS

AUGMENTED

QUICK MODE GENERATOR CHART

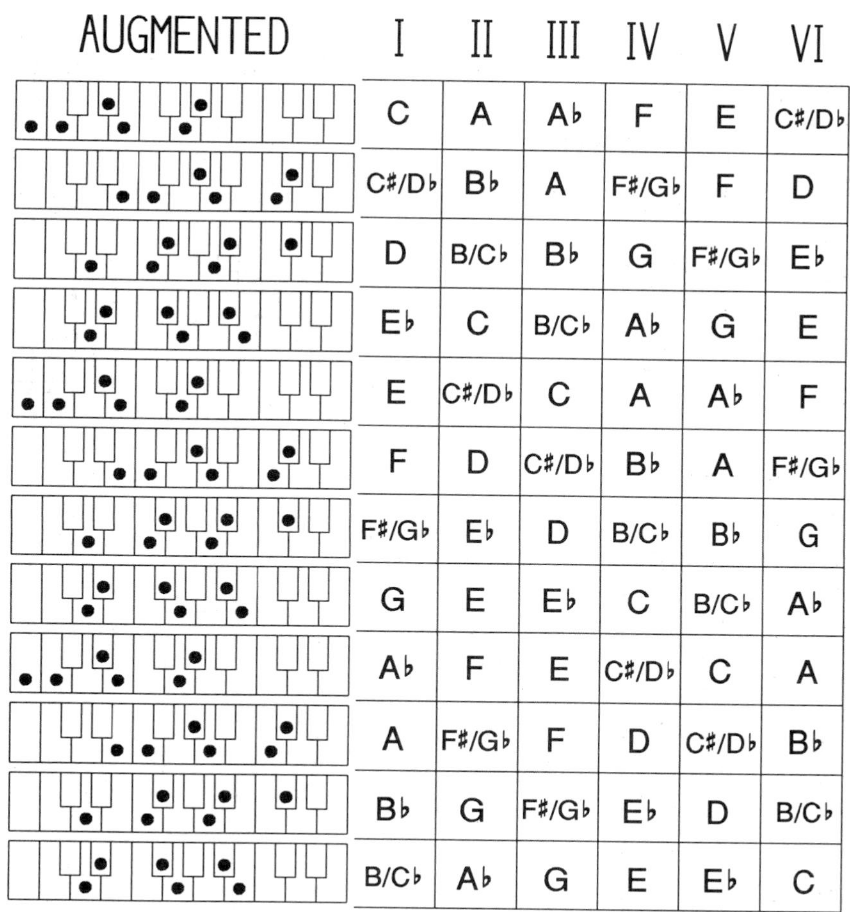

I	II	III	IV	V	VI
C	A	A♭	F	E	C♯/D♭
C♯/D♭	B♭	A	F♯/G♭	F	D
D	B/C♭	B♭	G	F♯/G♭	E♭
E♭	C	B/C♭	A♭	G	E
E	C♯/D♭	C	A	A♭	F
F	D	C♯/D♭	B♭	A	F♯/G♭
F♯/G♭	E♭	D	B/C♭	B♭	G
G	E	E♭	C	B/C♭	A♭
A♭	F	E	C♯/D♭	C	A
A	F♯/G♭	F	D	C♯/D♭	B♭
B♭	G	F♯/G♭	E♭	D	B/C♭
B/C♭	A♭	G	E	E♭	C

CONVENTIONAL PATTERNS / SWEEPING PATTERNS

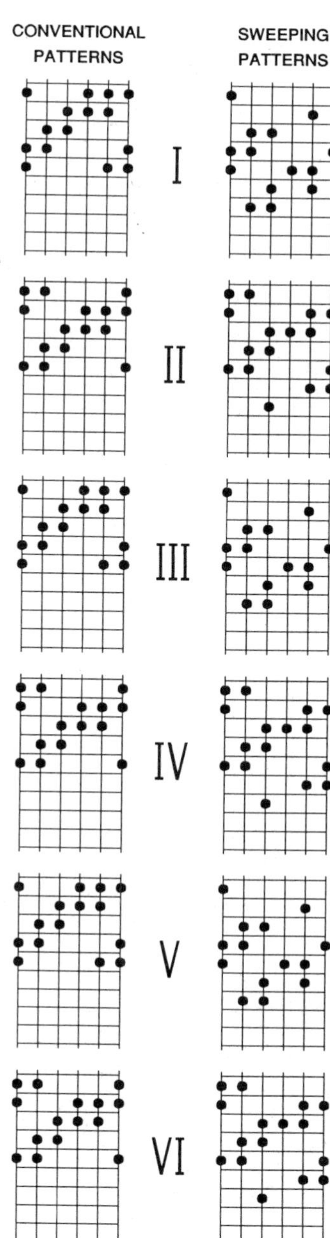

The Augmented scale is symmetrical, it has only 2 modes. Also, there are only 2 fingering patterns which repeat.

SCALE / MODE - CHORD CHART

I	AUGMENTED	$\triangle$, $\triangle^+$, $^-\triangle$, $^-\flat 6$
II	MODE 2	+ , 6^+
III	AUGMENTED	$\triangle$, $\triangle^+$, $^-\triangle$, $^-\flat 6$
IV	MODE 2	+ , 6^+
V	AUGMENTED	$\triangle$, $\triangle^+$, $^-\triangle$, $^-\flat 6$
VI	MODE 2	+ , 6^+

NUMERIC SCALE / MODE CHART

		1		2		3	4		5		6		7	1		2		3	4		5		6		7
I	AUG	1			♯2	3			5	♭6			7												
II	MODE 2				1	♭2			3	4			♯5	6											
III	AUG					1			♯2	3			5	♭6			7								
IV	MODE 2								1	♭2			3	4			♯5	6							
V	AUG									1			♯2	3			5	♭6			7				
VI	MODE 2												1	♭2			3	4			♯5	6			

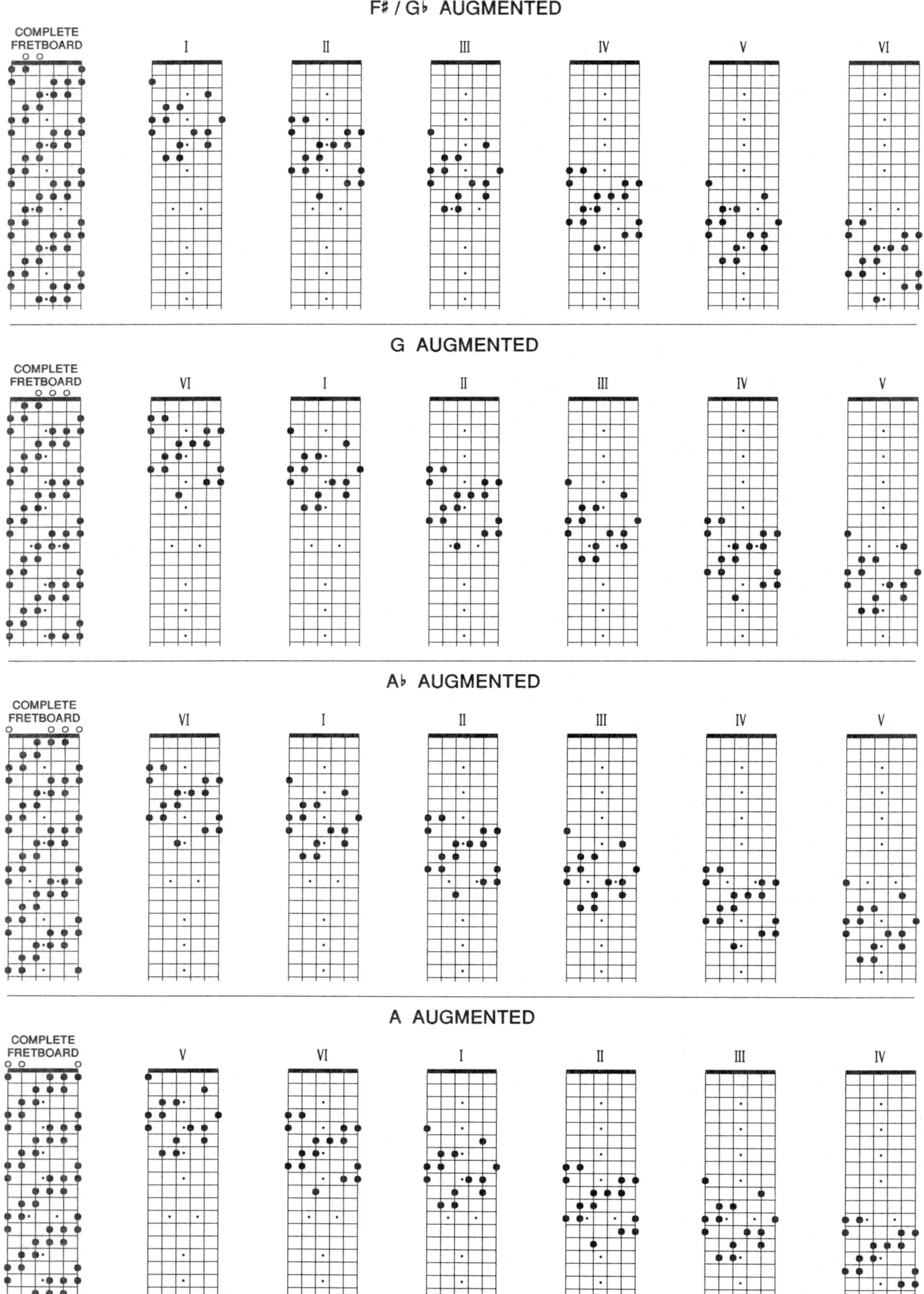
F♯ / G♭ AUGMENTED
COMPLETE FRETBOARD
I
II
III
IV
V
VI
G AUGMENTED
COMPLETE FRETBOARD
VI
I
II
III
IV
V
A♭ AUGMENTED
COMPLETE FRETBOARD
VI
I
II
III
IV
V
A AUGMENTED
COMPLETE FRETBOARD
V
VI
I
II
III
IV

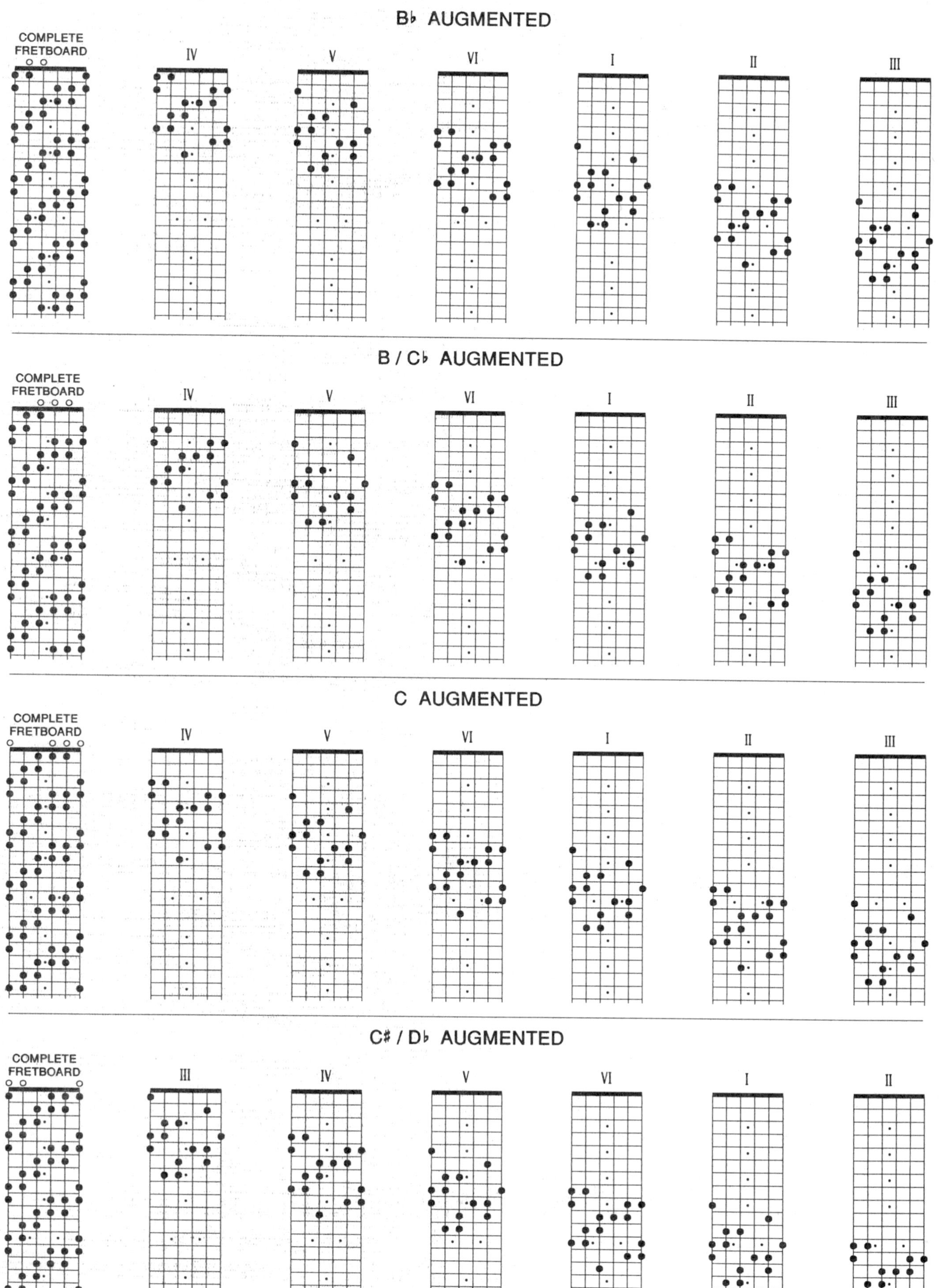
B♭ AUGMENTED
COMPLETE FRETBOARD
IV
V
VI
I
II
III
B / C♭ AUGMENTED
COMPLETE FRETBOARD
IV
V
VI
I
II
III
C AUGMENTED
COMPLETE FRETBOARD
IV
V
VI
I
II
III
C# / D♭ AUGMENTED
COMPLETE FRETBOARD
III
IV
V
VI
I
II

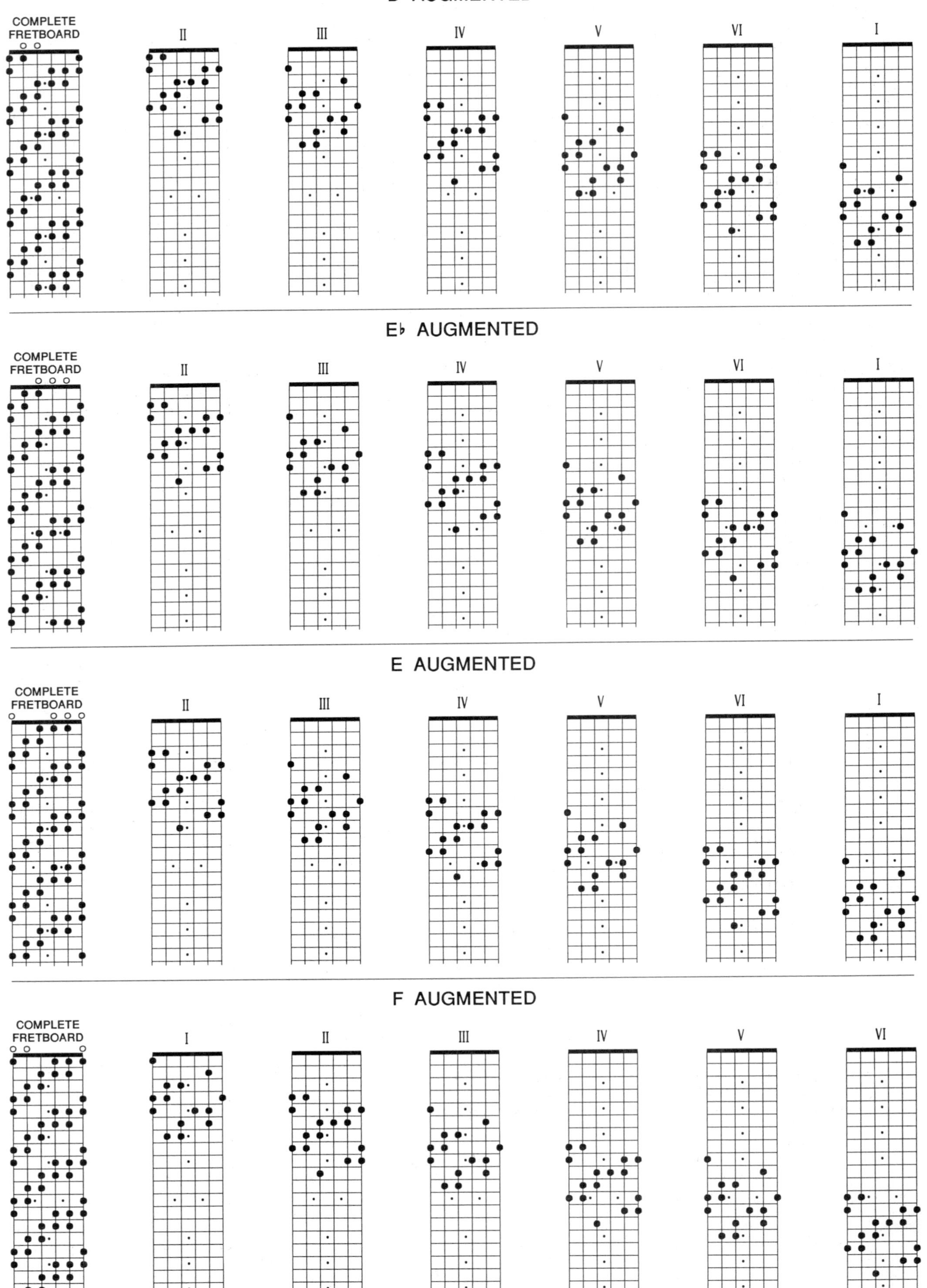
D AUGMENTED
COMPLETE FRETBOARD
II
III
IV
V
VI
I
E♭ AUGMENTED
COMPLETE FRETBOARD
II
III
IV
V
VI
I
E AUGMENTED
COMPLETE FRETBOARD
II
III
IV
V
VI
I
F AUGMENTED
COMPLETE FRETBOARD
I
II
III
IV
V
VI

KEYBOARD PATTERNS

PELOG

QUICK MODE GENERATOR CHART

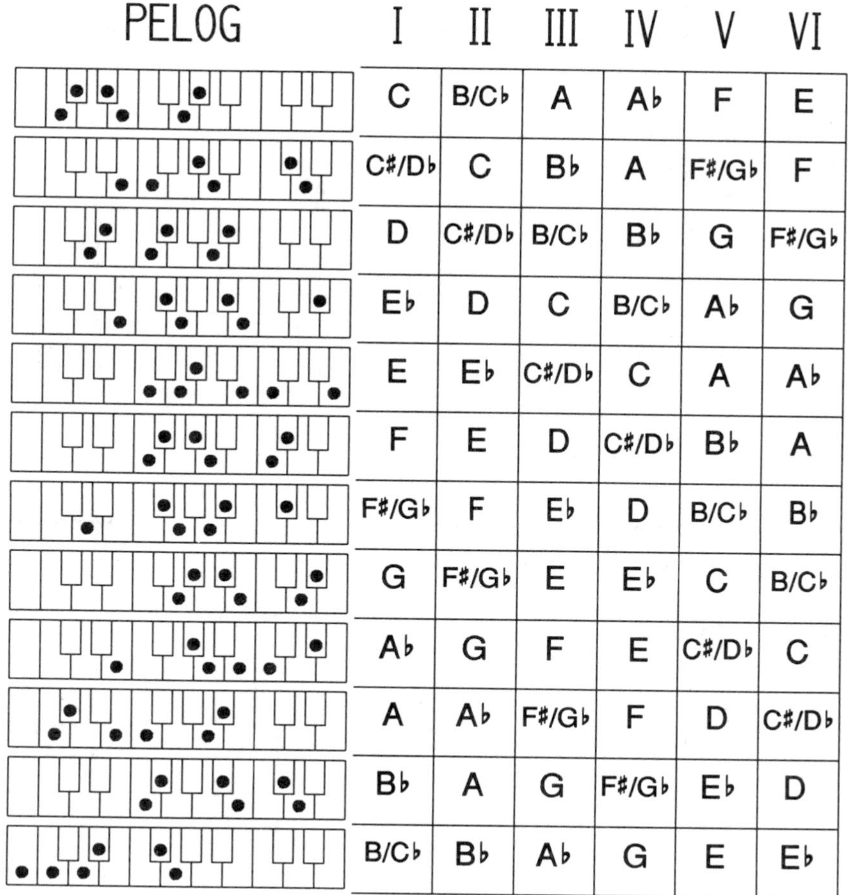

I	II	III	IV	V	VI
C	B/C♭	A	A♭	F	E
C#/D♭	C	B♭	A	F#/G♭	F
D	C#/D♭	B/C♭	B♭	G	F#/G♭
E♭	D	C	B/C♭	A♭	G
E	E♭	C#/D♭	C	A	A♭
F	E	D	C#/D♭	B♭	A
F#/G♭	F	E♭	D	B/C♭	B♭
G	F#/G♭	E	E♭	C	B/C♭
A♭	G	F	E	C#/D♭	C
A	A♭	F#/G♭	F	D	C#/D♭
B♭	A	G	F#/G♭	E♭	D
B/C♭	B♭	A♭	G	E	E♭

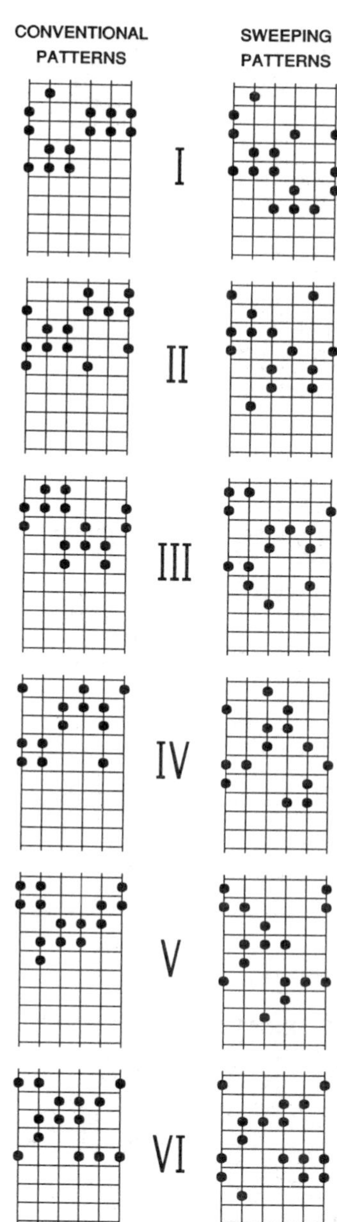

SCALE / MODE - CHORD CHART

I	PELOG	-♭6, ♭6, -
II	MODE 2	-△, -, sus2, △°
III	MODE 3	Q3
IV	MODE 4	△+
V	MODE 5	11
VI	MODE 6	△, ♭6, sus

NUMERIC SCALE / MODE CHART

		1		2		3	4		5		6		7	1		2		3	4		5		6		7
I	PELOG	1	♭2		♭3	♭4			5	♭6															
II	MODE 2		1		2	♭3			#4	5				7											
III	MODE 3				1	♭2			3	4				6	♭7										
IV	MODE 4					1			#2	3				#5	6		7								
V	MODE 5								1	♭2				4	♭5		♭6	𝄫7							
VI	MODE 6									1				3	4		5	♭6			7				

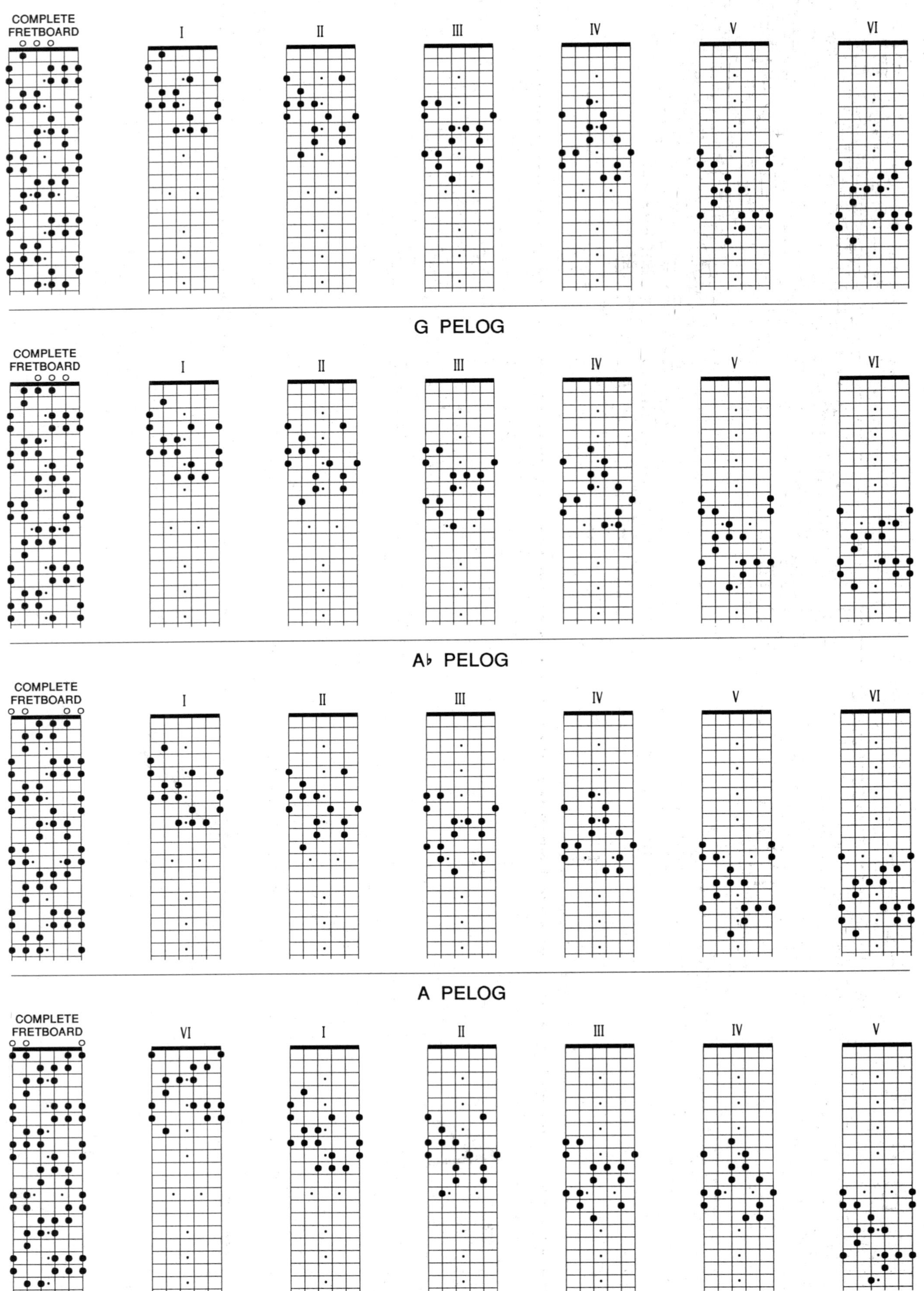
F♯ / G♭ PELOG
COMPLETE FRETBOARD
I
II
III
IV
V
VI
G PELOG
COMPLETE FRETBOARD
I
II
III
IV
V
VI
A♭ PELOG
COMPLETE FRETBOARD
I
II
III
IV
V
VI
A PELOG
COMPLETE FRETBOARD
VI
I
II
III
IV
V

B♭ PELOG

B / C♭ PELOG

C PELOG

C♯ / D♭ PELOG

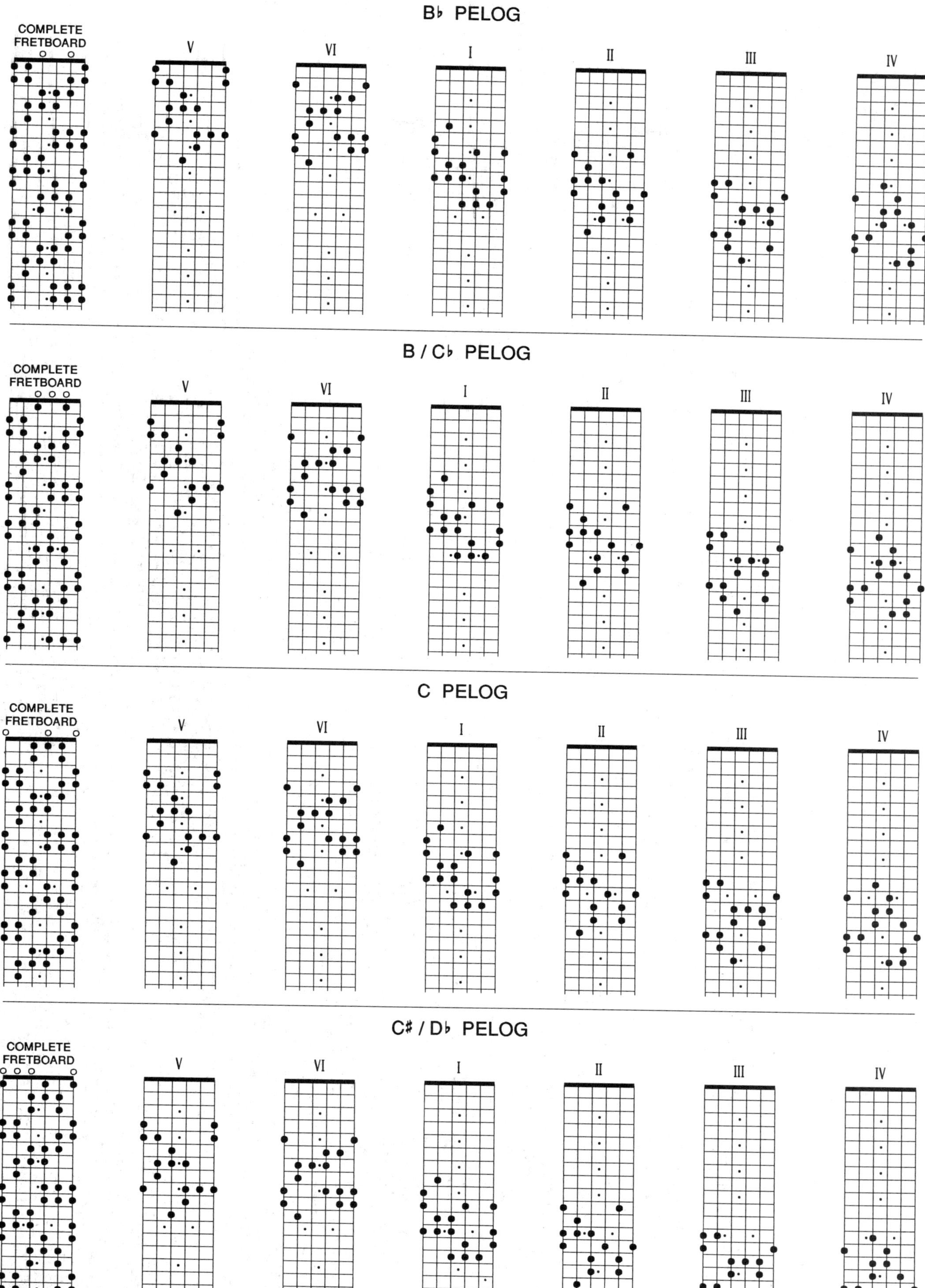

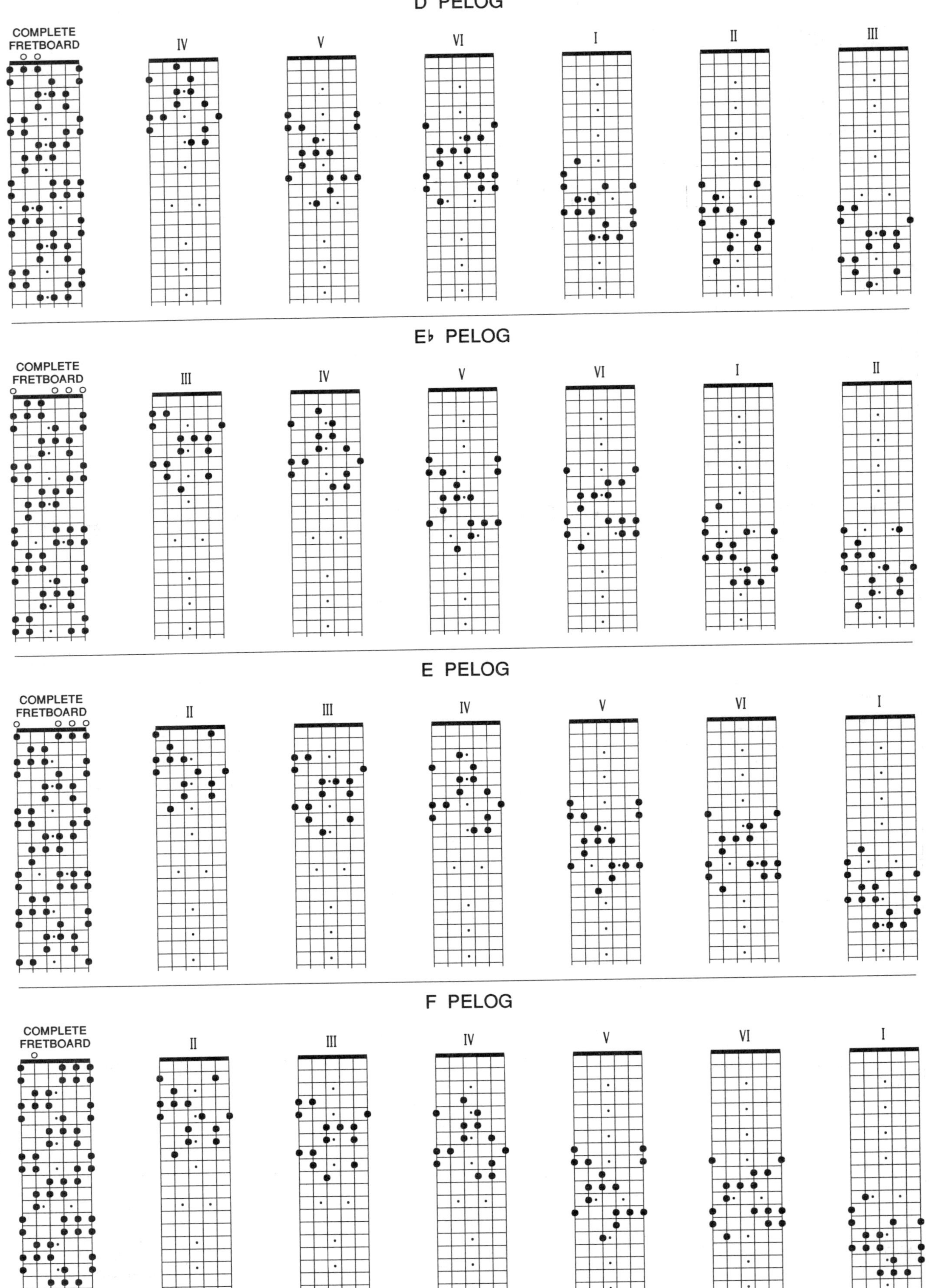
D PELOG
COMPLETE FRETBOARD
IV
V
VI
I
II
III
E♭ PELOG
COMPLETE FRETBOARD
III
IV
V
VI
I
II
E PELOG
COMPLETE FRETBOARD
II
III
IV
V
VI
I
F PELOG
COMPLETE FRETBOARD
II
III
IV
V
VI
I

KEYBOARD PATTERNS

QUICK MODE GENERATOR CHART

DOMINANT SUS

I	II	III	IV	V	VI
C	B♭	G	F	E♭	D
C♯/D♭	B/C♭	A♭	F♯/G♭	E	E♭
D	C	A	G	F	E
E♭	C♯/D♭	B♭	A♭	F♯/G♭	F
E	D	B/C♭	A	G	F♯/G♭
F	E♭	C	B♭	A♭	G
F♯/G♭	E	C♯/D♭	B/C♭	A	A♭
G	F	D	C	B♭	A
A♭	F♯/G♭	E♭	C♯/D♭	B/C♭	B♭
A	G	E	D	C	B/C♭
B♭	A♭	F	E♭	C♯/D♭	C
B/C♭	A	F♯/G♭	E	D	C♯/D♭

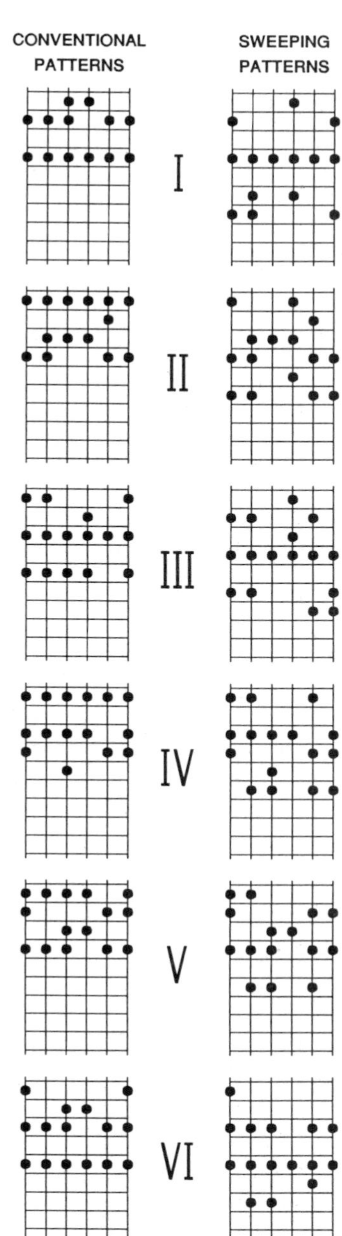

SCALE / MODE - CHORD CHART

I	DOMINANT SUS	sus2, sus, Q3, 9
II	MODE 2	⁻♭6, ⁻7, sus, Q3, 11
III	MODE 3	6, sus2 , sus, 9, 11, 13
IV	MODE 4	⁻7, sus2, sus, 9, ♯9, 11
V	MODE 5	Q3, ♭9, ♯9, 11, ♭13
VI	MODE 6	6, △, sus2, 9, 13

NUMERIC SCALE / MODE CHART

		1		2		3	4		5		6		7	1		2		3	4		5		6		7
I	DOMINANT SUS	1		2			4		5		6	♭7													
II	MODE 2			1			♭3		4		5	♭6		♭7											
III	MODE 3						1		2		3	4		5		6									
IV	MODE 4								1		2	♭3		4		5			♭7						
V	MODE 5										1	♭2		♭3		4			♭6		♭7				
VI	MODE 6											1		2		3			5		6		7		

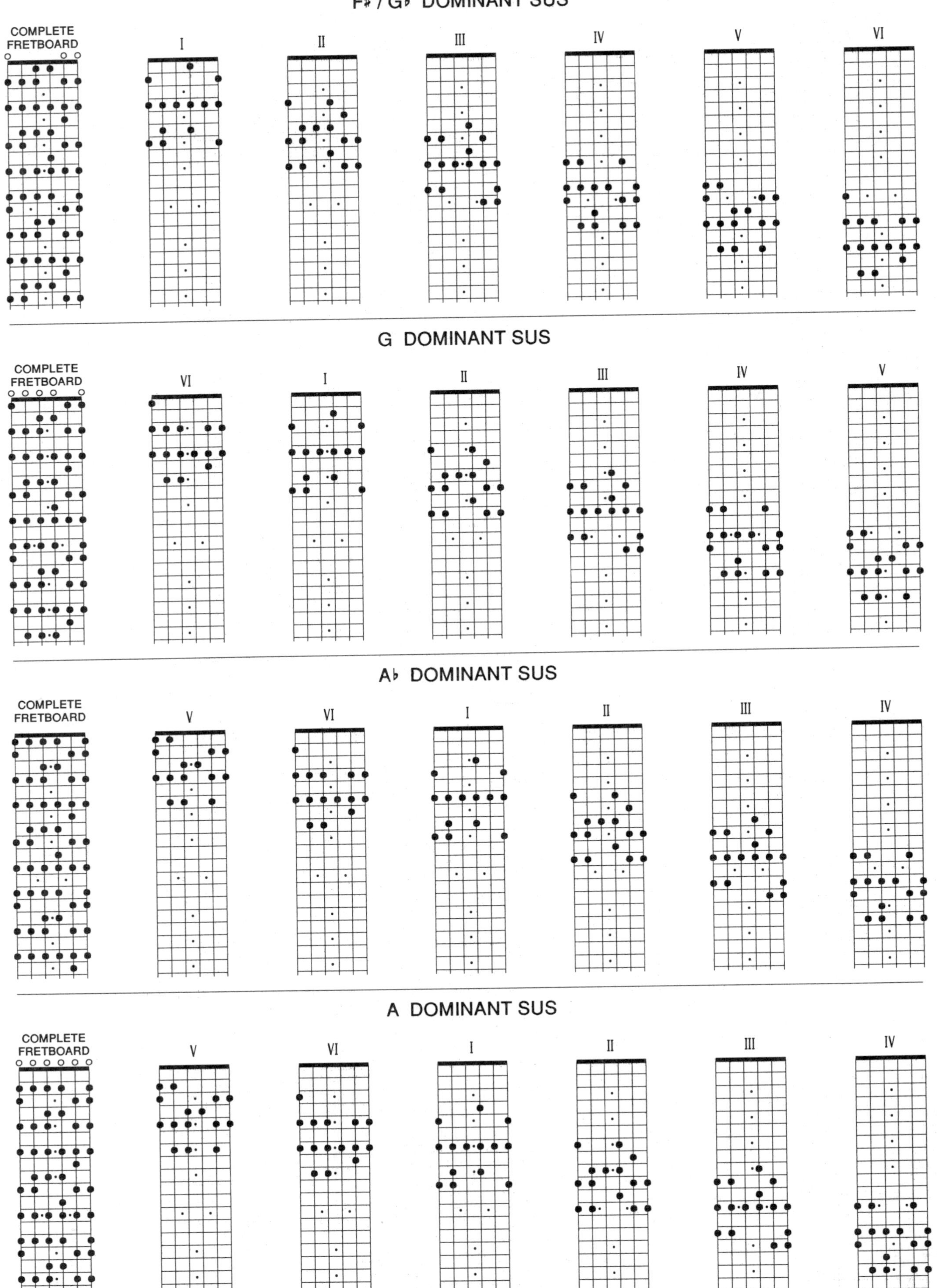
F♯ / G♭ DOMINANT SUS
COMPLETE FRETBOARD
I
II
III
IV
V
VI
G DOMINANT SUS
COMPLETE FRETBOARD
VI
I
II
III
IV
V
A♭ DOMINANT SUS
COMPLETE FRETBOARD
V
VI
I
II
III
IV
A DOMINANT SUS
COMPLETE FRETBOARD
V
VI
I
II
III
IV

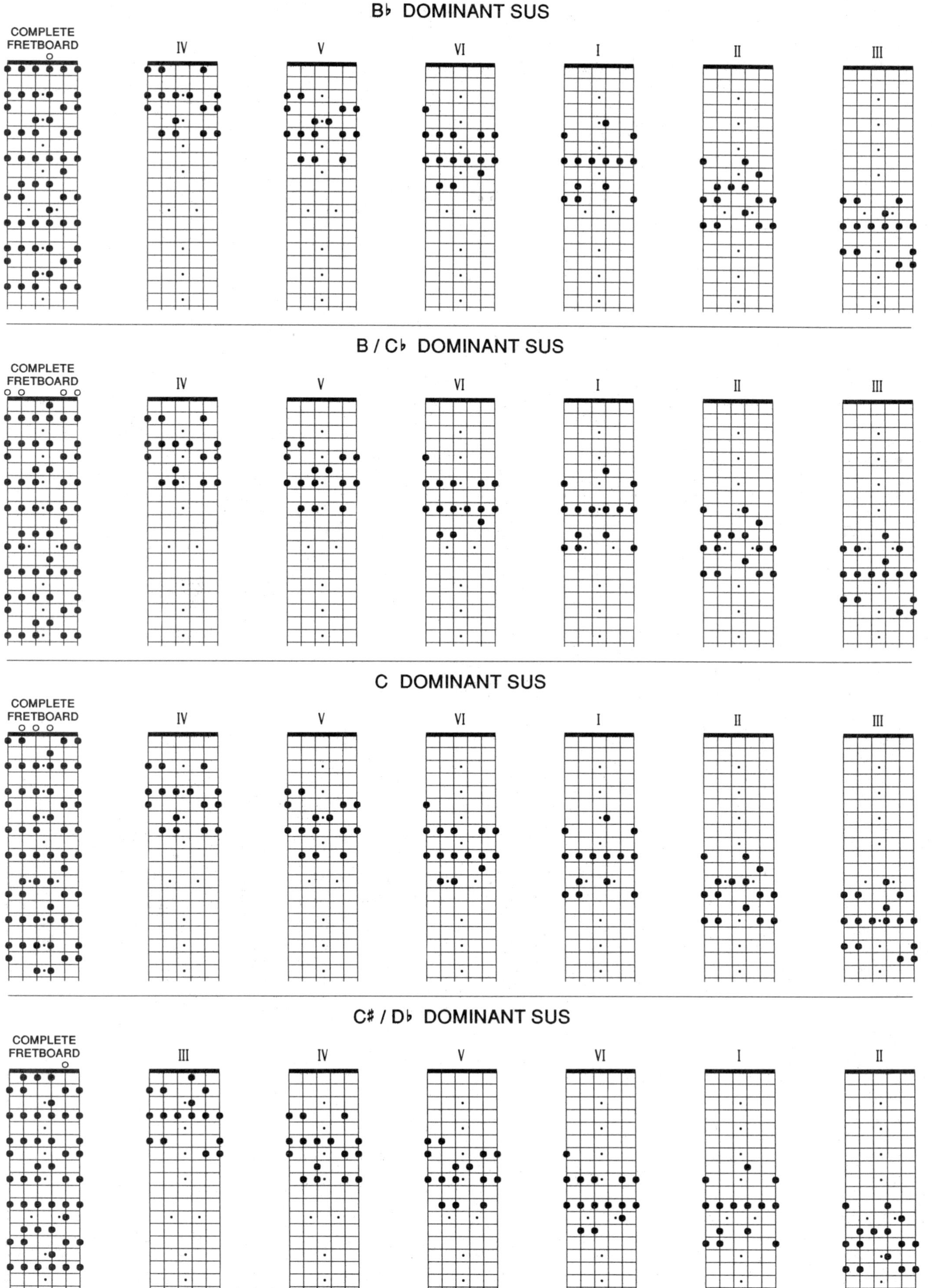

B♭ DOMINANT SUS
COMPLETE FRETBOARD
IV
V
VI
I
II
III
B / C♭ DOMINANT SUS
COMPLETE FRETBOARD
IV
V
VI
I
II
III
C DOMINANT SUS
COMPLETE FRETBOARD
IV
V
VI
I
II
III
C♯ / D♭ DOMINANT SUS
COMPLETE FRETBOARD
III
IV
V
VI
I
II

D DOMINANT SUS

E♭ DOMINANT SUS

E DOMINANT SUS

F DOMINANT SUS

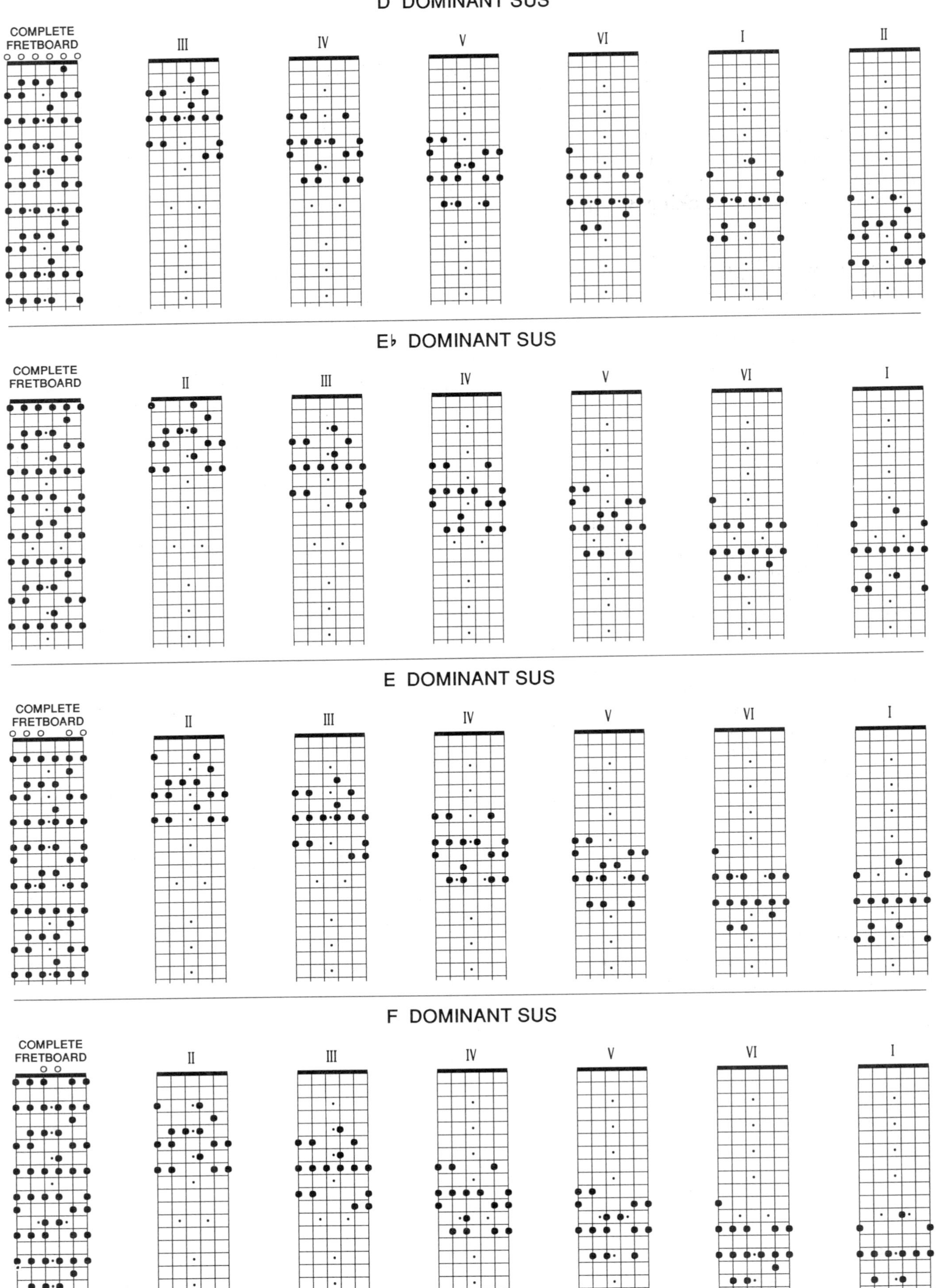

8 TONE SCALES

Just as scales can be created by deleting tones of a 7 tone scale, a scale can also be created by adding another tone, making 8 tones in all.

The chart on the right (fig. 47) is based on the diminished chord: 1 - ♭3 - ♭5 - 𝄫7. 4 other tones are then added to the original 4, making 8 tone scales.

→ → → → → → → → →

- The **X** in the boxes along with the numbers of *this* chart indicate the tones which are to be played•
- The scales: H / W *Half-Whole Diminished* and the W / H *Whole-Half Diminished* are the most common diminished•

DIMINISHED SCALE FORMULAS

	1		2		3	4		5		6		7
	1	X	X	**♭3**	X	X	**♭5**	X	X	**𝄫7**	X	X
H / W	1	X		♭3	X		♭5	X		𝄫7	X	
B	1	X		♭3	X		♭5	X		𝄫7		X
C	1	X		♭3	X		♭5		X	𝄫7	X	
D	1	X		♭3	X		♭5		X	𝄫7		X
E	1	X		♭3		X	♭5	X		𝄫7	X	
F	1	X		♭3		X	♭5	X		𝄫7		X
G	1	X		♭3		X	♭5		X	𝄫7	X	
H	1	X		♭3		X	♭5		X	𝄫7		X
I	1		X	♭3	X		♭5	X		𝄫7	X	
J	1		X	♭3	X		♭5	X		𝄫7		X
K	1		X	♭3	X		♭5		X	𝄫7	X	
L	1		X	♭3	X		♭5		X	𝄫7		X
M	1		X	♭3		X	♭5	X		𝄫7	X	
N	1		X	♭3		X	♭5	X		𝄫7		X
O	1		X	♭3		X	♭5		X	𝄫7	X	
W / H	1		X	♭3		X	♭5		X	𝄫7		X

fig. 47

During the bebop era, 8-tone scales were commonly used. It is at that time period that they were given the names bebop scales. With the exception of the Diminished and the 8-Tone Spanish, the 8- tone scales in this text will also be referred to as bebop scales.

KEYBOARD PATTERNS

DIMINISHED

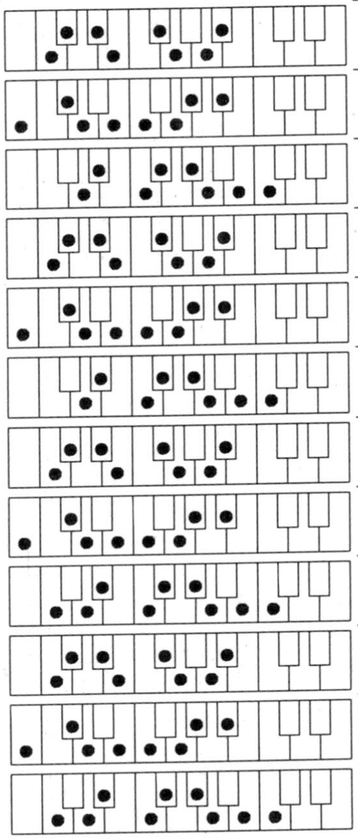

QUICK MODE GENERATOR CHART

I	II	III	IV	V	VI	VII	VIII
C	B♭	A	G	F♯/G♭	E	E♭	C♯/D♭
C♯/D♭	B/C♭	B♭	A♭	G	F	E	D
D	C	B/C♭	A	A♭	F♯/G♭	F	E♭
E♭	C♯/D♭	C	B♭	A	G	F♯/G♭	E
E	D	C♯/D♭	B/C♭	B♭	A♭	G	F
F	E♭	D	C	B/C♭	A	A♭	F♯/G♭
F♯/G♭	E	E♭	C♯/D♭	C	B♭	A	G
G	F	E	D	C♯/D♭	B/C♭	B♭	A♭
A♭	F♯/G♭	F	E♭	D	C	B/C♭	A
A	G	F♯/G♭	E	E♭	C♯/D♭	C	B♭
B♭	A♭	G	F	E	D	C♯/D♭	B/C♭
B/C♭	A	A♭	F♯/G♭	F	E♭	D	C

SWEEPING PATTERNS

I

II

III

IV

V

VI

VII

VIII

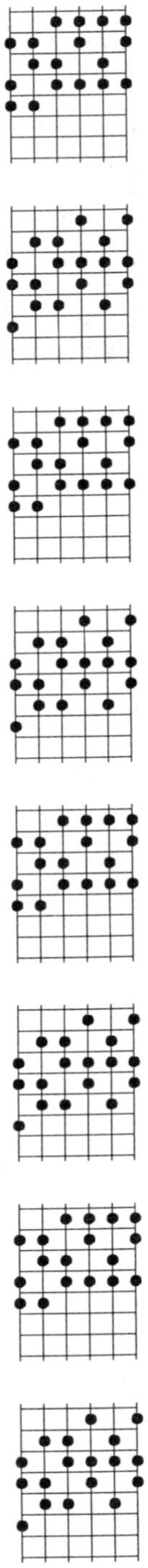

SCALE / MODE - CHORD CHART

I	WHOLE - HALF DIMINISHED	○, °7, △°
II	HALF - WHOLE DIMINISHED	∅, ○, -7, °7
III	WHOLE - HALF DIMINISHED	○, °7, △°
IV	HALF - WHOLE DIMINISHED	∅, ○, -7, °7
V	WHOLE - HALF DIMINISHED	○, °7, △°
VI	HALF - WHOLE DIMINISHED	∅, ○, -7, °7
VII	WHOLE - HALF DIMINISHED	○, °7, △°
VIII	HALF - WHOLE DIMINISHED	∅, ○, -7, °7

NUMERIC SCALE / MODE CHART

		1		2		3	4		5		6		7	1		2		3	4		5		6		7
I	W - H DIMINISHED	1		2	♭3		4	♭5		♭6	6		7												
II	H - W DIMINISHED			1	♭2		♭3	3		♯4	5		6	♭7											
III	W - H DIMINISHED				1		2	♭3		4	♭5		♭6	6		7									
IV	H - W DIMINISHED						1	♭2		♭3	3		♯4	5		6	♭7								
V	W - H DIMINISHED							1		2	♭3		4	♭5		♭6	6		7						
VI	H - W DIMINISHED									1	♭2		♭3	3		♯4	5		6	♭7					
VII	W - H DIMINISHED										1		2	♭3		4	♭5		♭6	6		7			
VIII	H - W DIMINISHED												1	♭2		♭3	3		♯4	5		6	♭7		

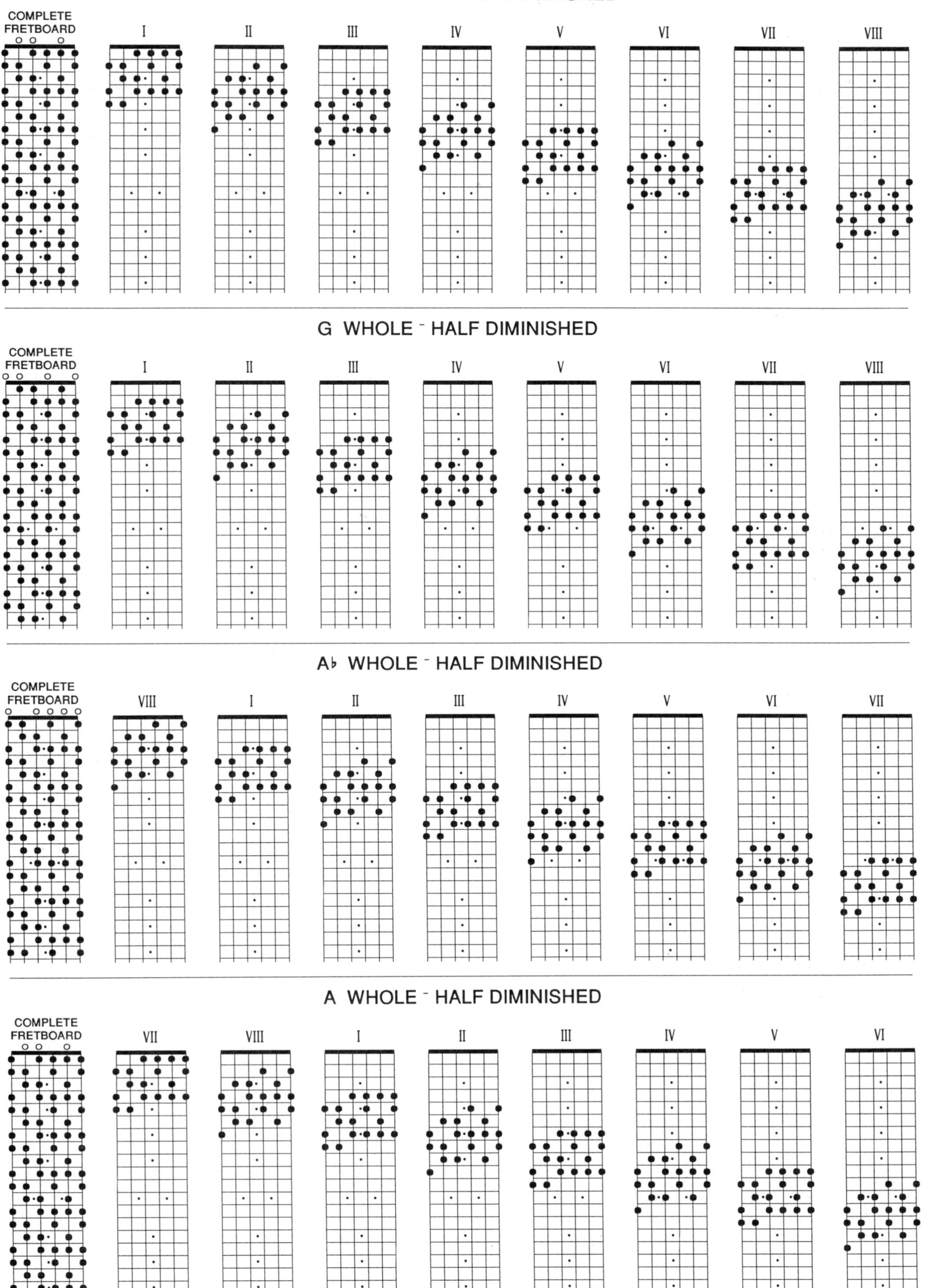
F♯ / G♭ WHOLE - HALF DIMINISHED
COMPLETE FRETBOARD
I
II
III
IV
V
VI
VII
VIII
G WHOLE - HALF DIMINISHED
COMPLETE FRETBOARD
I
II
III
IV
V
VI
VII
VIII
A♭ WHOLE - HALF DIMINISHED
COMPLETE FRETBOARD
VIII
I
II
III
IV
V
VI
VII
A WHOLE - HALF DIMINISHED
COMPLETE FRETBOARD
VII
VIII
I
II
III
IV
V
VI

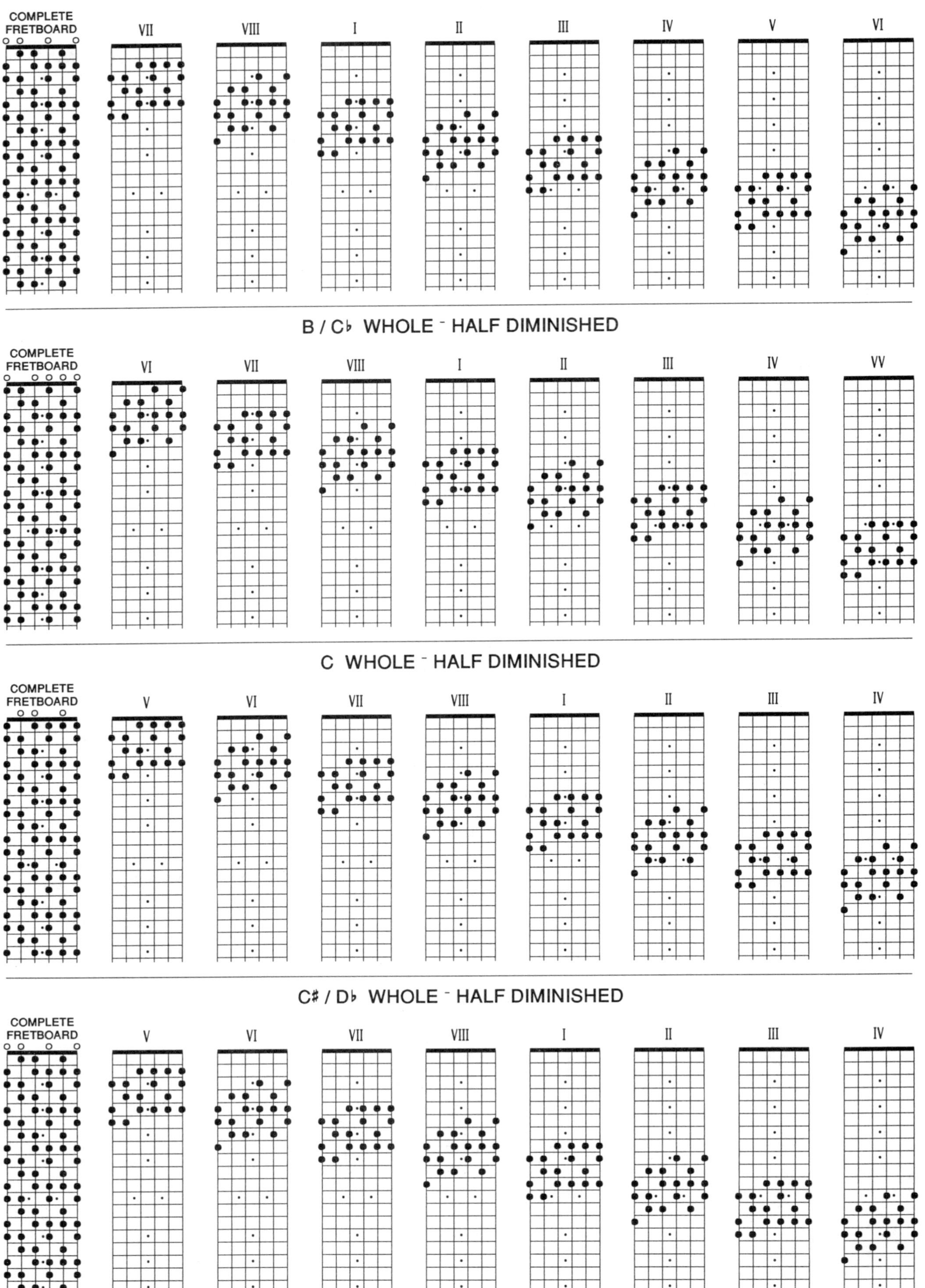
B♭ WHOLE - HALF DIMINISHED
COMPLETE FRETBOARD
VII
VIII
I
II
III
IV
V
VI
B / C♭ WHOLE - HALF DIMINISHED
COMPLETE FRETBOARD
VI
VII
VIII
I
II
III
IV
VV
C WHOLE - HALF DIMINISHED
COMPLETE FRETBOARD
V
VI
VII
VIII
I
II
III
IV
C♯ / D♭ WHOLE - HALF DIMINISHED
COMPLETE FRETBOARD
V
VI
VII
VIII
I
II
III
IV

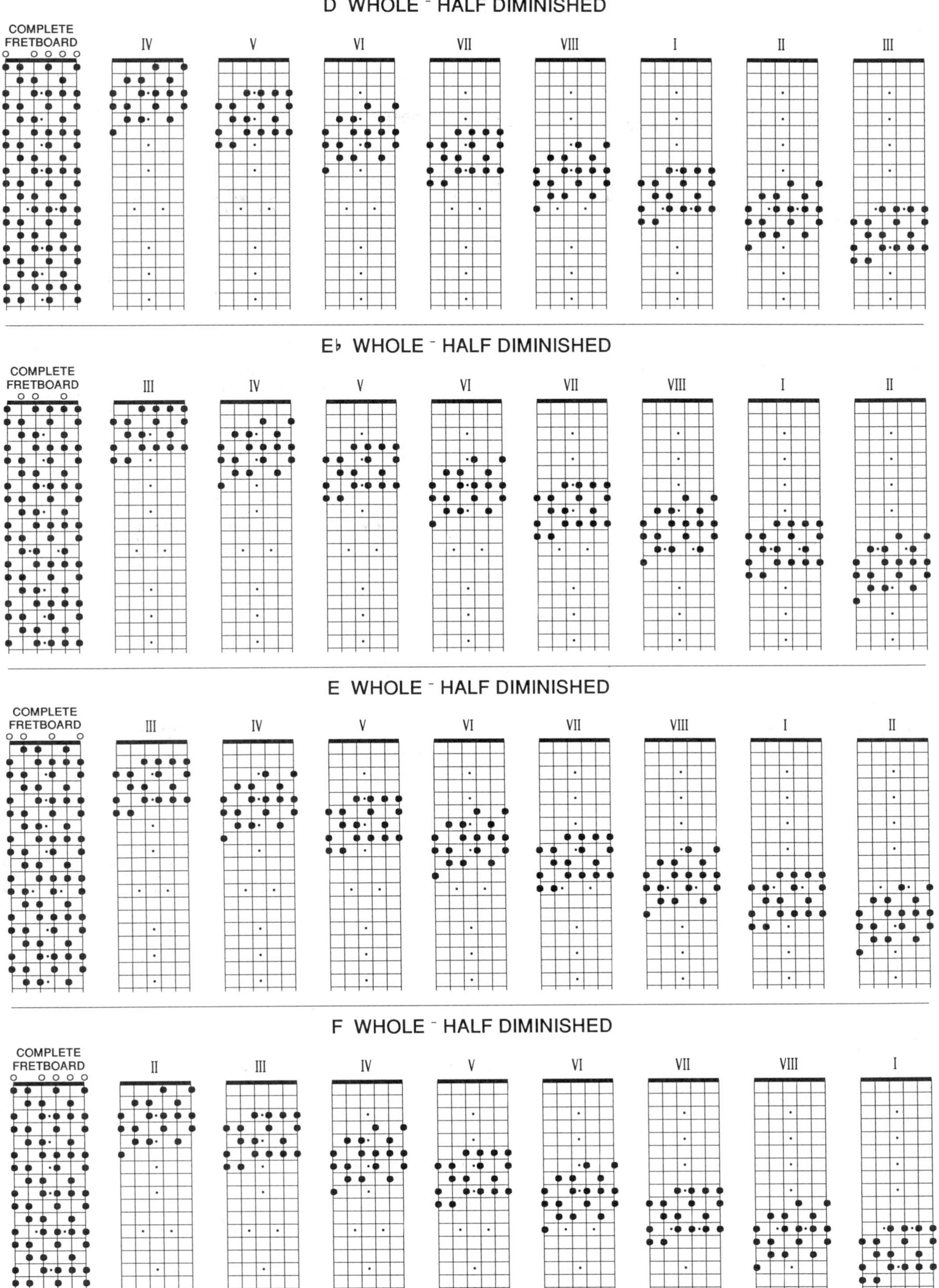
D WHOLE - HALF DIMINISHED
COMPLETE FRETBOARD
IV
V
VI
VII
VIII
I
II
III
E♭ WHOLE - HALF DIMINISHED
COMPLETE FRETBOARD
III
IV
V
VI
VII
VIII
I
II
E WHOLE - HALF DIMINISHED
COMPLETE FRETBOARD
III
IV
V
VI
VII
VIII
I
II
F WHOLE - HALF DIMINISHED
COMPLETE FRETBOARD
II
III
IV
V
VI
VII
VIII
I

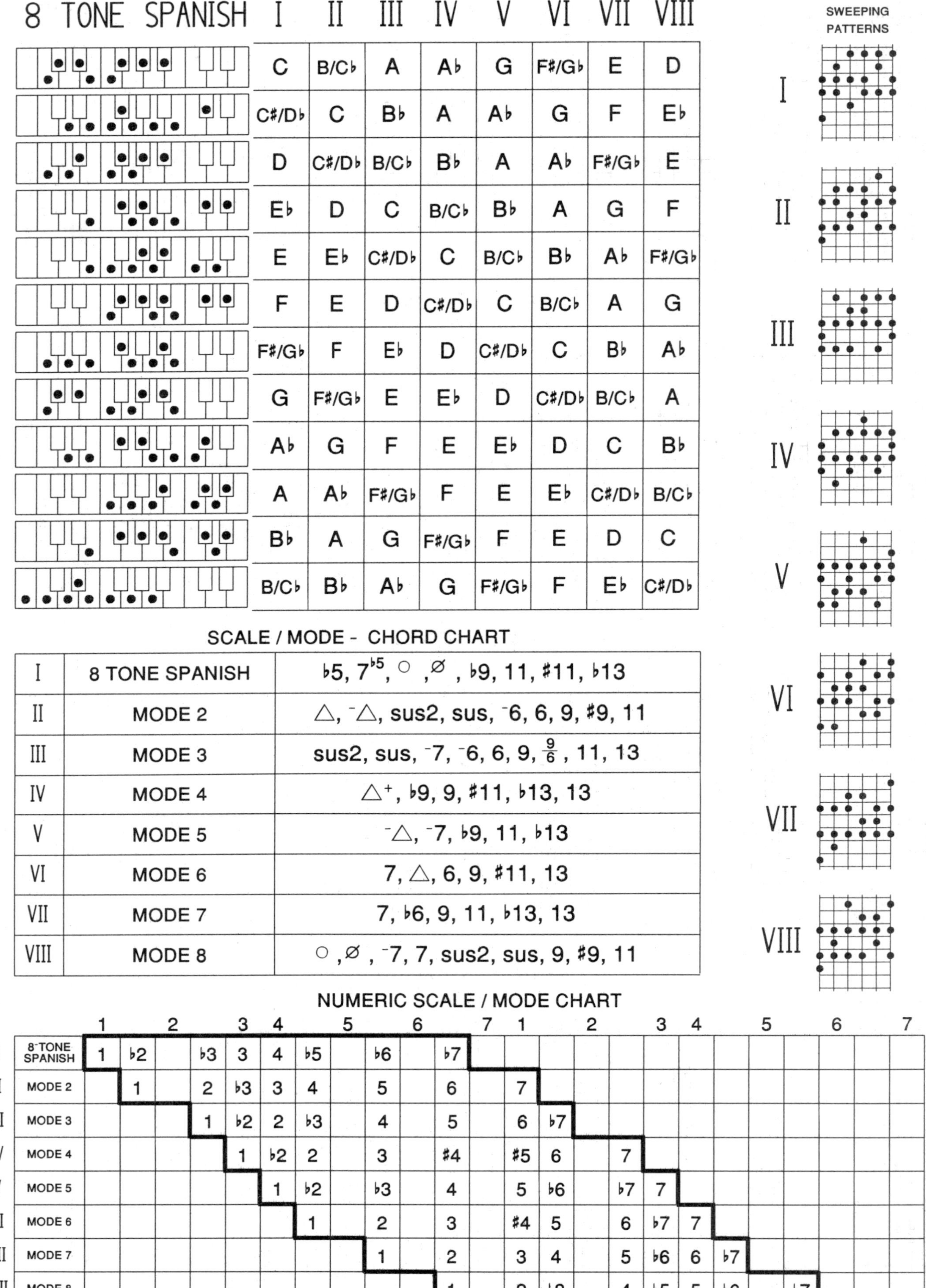

KEYBOARD PATTERNS

QUICK MODE GENERATOR CHART

SWEEPING PATTERNS

8 TONE SPANISH	I	II	III	IV	V	VI	VII	VIII
	C	B/C♭	A	A♭	G	F♯/G♭	E	D
	C♯/D♭	C	B♭	A	A♭	G	F	E♭
	D	C♯/D♭	B/C♭	B♭	A	A♭	F♯/G♭	E
	E♭	D	C	B/C♭	B♭	A	G	F
	E	E♭	C♯/D♭	C	B/C♭	B♭	A♭	F♯/G♭
	F	E	D	C♯/D♭	C	B/C♭	A	G
	F♯/G♭	F	E♭	D	C♯/D♭	C	B♭	A♭
	G	F♯/G♭	E	E♭	D	C♯/D♭	B/C♭	A
	A♭	G	F	E	E♭	D	C	B♭
	A	A♭	F♯/G♭	F	E	E♭	C♯/D♭	B/C♭
	B♭	A	G	F♯/G♭	F	E	D	C
	B/C♭	B♭	A♭	G	F♯/G♭	F	E♭	C♯/D♭

I II III IV V VI VII VIII

SCALE / MODE - CHORD CHART

I	8 TONE SPANISH	♭5, $7^{♭5}$, ○ , ∅ , ♭9, 11, ♯11, ♭13
II	MODE 2	△, ‑△, sus2, sus, ‑6, 6, 9, ♯9, 11
III	MODE 3	sus2, sus, ‑7, ‑6, 6, 9, $\frac{9}{6}$, 11, 13
IV	MODE 4	△+, ♭9, 9, ♯11, ♭13, 13
V	MODE 5	‑△, ‑7, ♭9, 11, ♭13
VI	MODE 6	7, △, 6, 9, ♯11, 13
VII	MODE 7	7, ♭6, 9, 11, ♭13, 13
VIII	MODE 8	○ , ∅ , ‑7, 7, sus2, sus, 9, ♯9, 11

NUMERIC SCALE / MODE CHART

		1		2		3	4		5		6		7	1		2		3	4		5		6		7
I	8 TONE SPANISH	1	♭2		♭3	3	4	♭5		♭6		♭7													
II	MODE 2		1		2	♭3	3	4		5		6		7											
III	MODE 3				1	♭2	2	♭3		4		5		6	♭7										
IV	MODE 4					1	♭2	2		3		♯4		♯5	6		7								
V	MODE 5						1	♭2		♭3		4		5	♭6		♭7	7							
VI	MODE 6							1		2		3		♯4	5		6	♭7	7						
VII	MODE 7									1		2		3	4		5	♭6	6	♭7					
VIII	MODE 8											1		2	♭3		4	♭5	5	♭6		♭7			

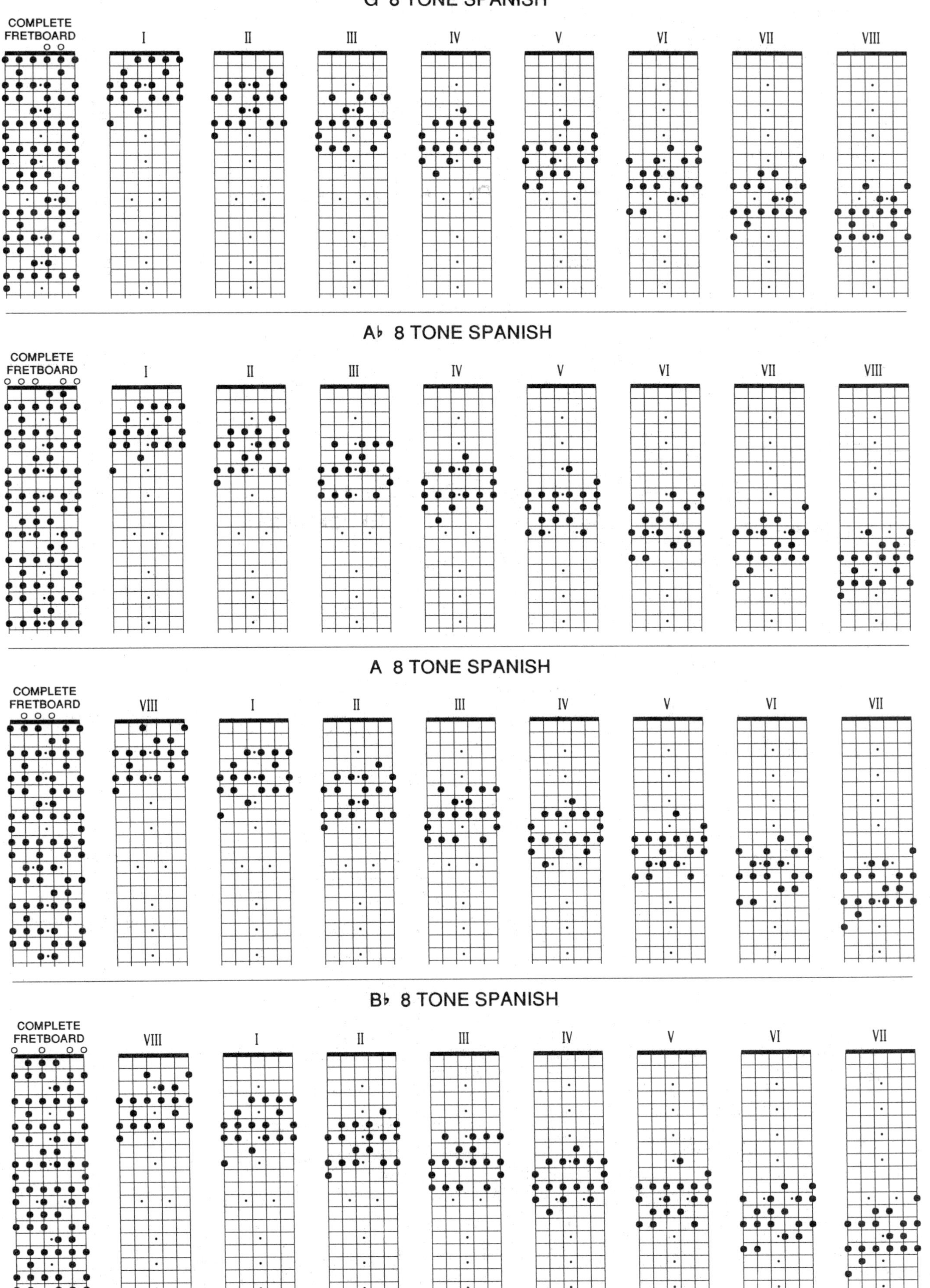
G 8 TONE SPANISH
COMPLETE FRETBOARD
I
II
III
IV
V
VI
VII
VIII
A♭ 8 TONE SPANISH
COMPLETE FRETBOARD
I
II
III
IV
V
VI
VII
VIII
A 8 TONE SPANISH
COMPLETE FRETBOARD
VIII
I
II
III
IV
V
VI
VII
B♭ 8 TONE SPANISH
COMPLETE FRETBOARD
VIII
I
II
III
IV
V
VI
VII

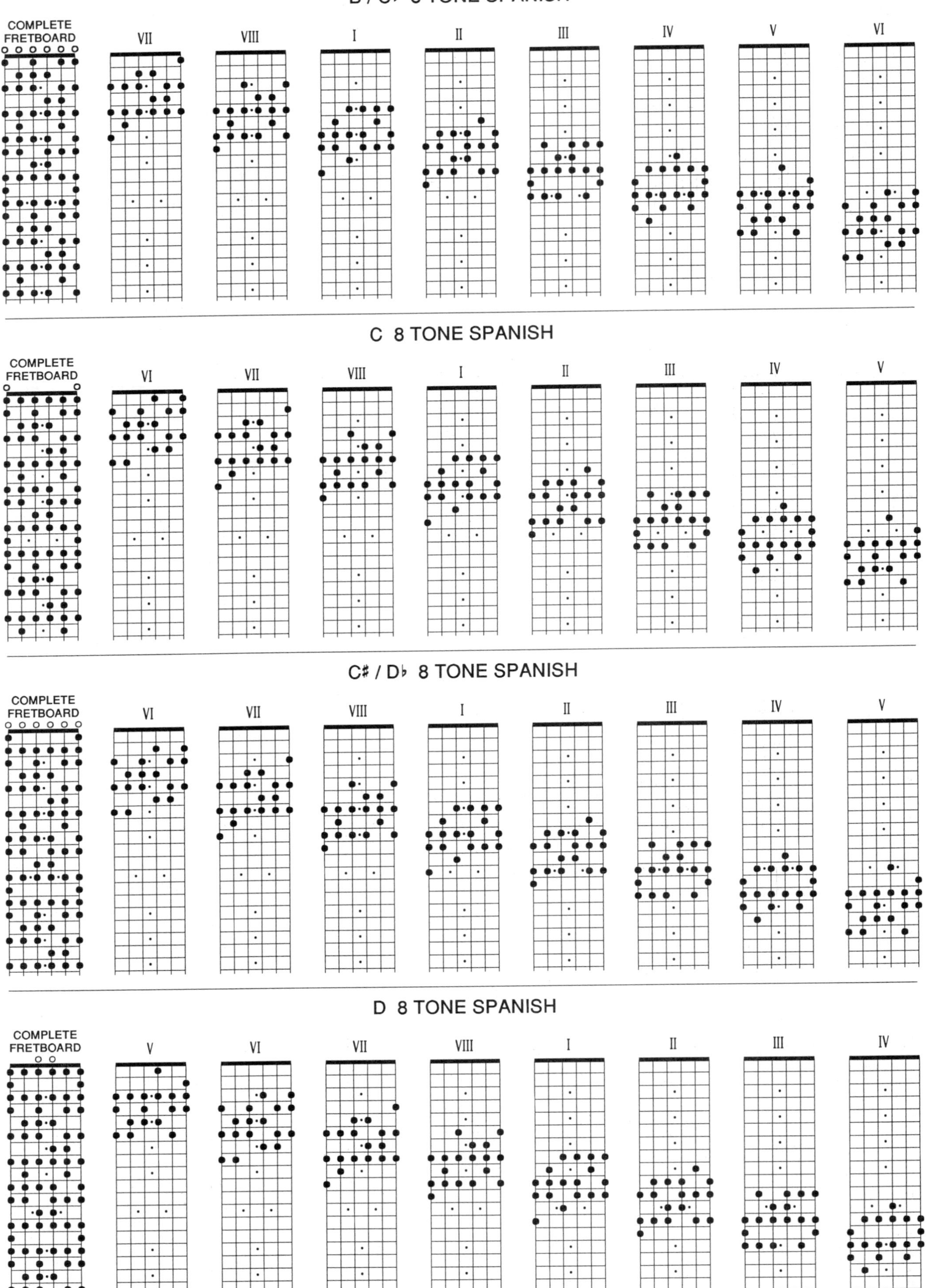
B / C♭ 8 TONE SPANISH
COMPLETE FRETBOARD
VII
VIII
I
II
III
IV
V
VI
C 8 TONE SPANISH
COMPLETE FRETBOARD
VI
VII
VIII
I
II
III
IV
V
C♯ / D♭ 8 TONE SPANISH
COMPLETE FRETBOARD
VI
VII
VIII
I
II
III
IV
V
D 8 TONE SPANISH
COMPLETE FRETBOARD
V
VI
VII
VIII
I
II
III
IV

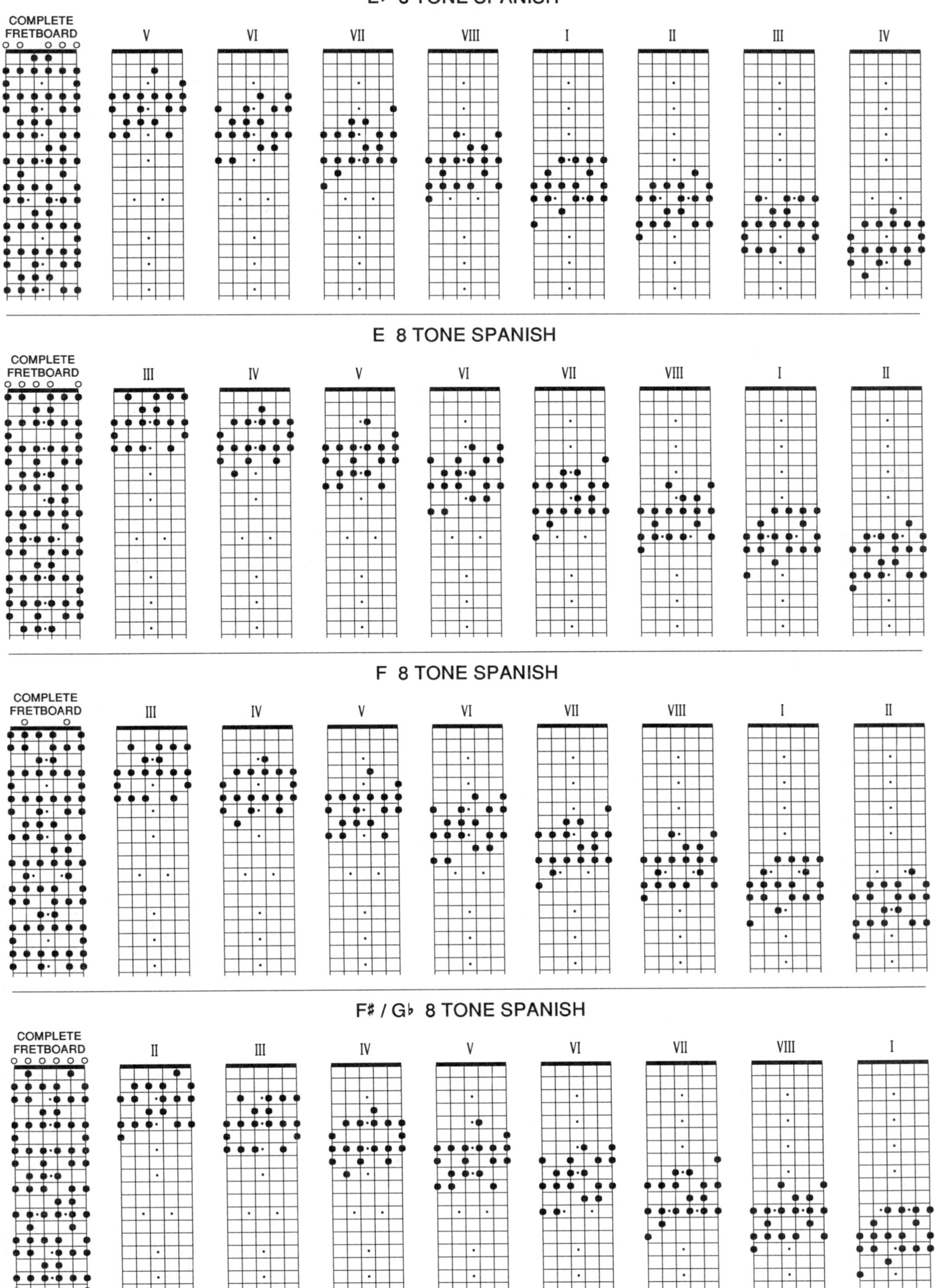
E♭ 8 TONE SPANISH
COMPLETE FRETBOARD
V
VI
VII
VIII
I
II
III
IV
E 8 TONE SPANISH
COMPLETE FRETBOARD
III
IV
V
VI
VII
VIII
I
II
F 8 TONE SPANISH
COMPLETE FRETBOARD
III
IV
V
VI
VII
VIII
I
II
F♯ / G♭ 8 TONE SPANISH
COMPLETE FRETBOARD
II
III
IV
V
VI
VII
VIII
I

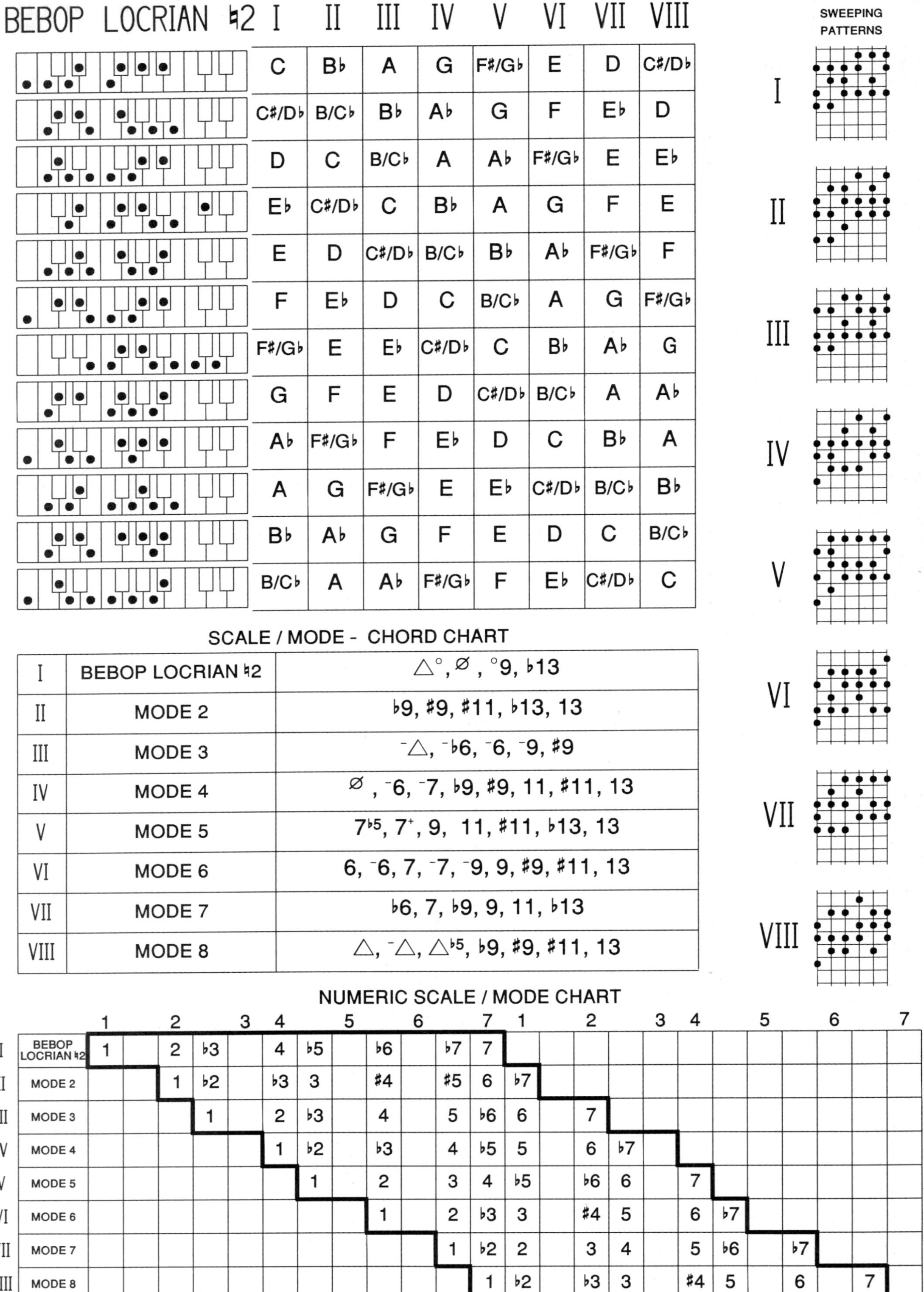

QUICK MODE GENERATOR CHART

BEBOP LOCRIAN ♮2

I	II	III	IV	V	VI	VII	VIII
C	B♭	A	G	F♯/G♭	E	D	C♯/D♭
C♯/D♭	B/C♭	B♭	A♭	G	F	E♭	D
D	C	B/C♭	A	A♭	F♯/G♭	E	E♭
E♭	C♯/D♭	C	B♭	A	G	F	E
E	D	C♯/D♭	B/C♭	B♭	A♭	F♯/G♭	F
F	E♭	D	C	B/C♭	A	G	F♯/G♭
F♯/G♭	E	E♭	C♯/D♭	C	B♭	A♭	G
G	F	E	D	C♯/D♭	B/C♭	A	A♭
A♭	F♯/G♭	F	E♭	D	C	B♭	A
A	G	F♯/G♭	E	E♭	C♯/D♭	B/C♭	B♭
B♭	A♭	G	F	E	D	C	B/C♭
B/C♭	A	A♭	F♯/G♭	F	E♭	C♯/D♭	C

SCALE / MODE - CHORD CHART

I	BEBOP LOCRIAN ♮2	△°, ∅, °9, ♭13
II	MODE 2	♭9, ♯9, ♯11, ♭13, 13
III	MODE 3	-△, -♭6, -6, -9, ♯9
IV	MODE 4	∅, -6, -7, ♭9, ♯9, 11, ♯11, 13
V	MODE 5	$7^{\flat 5}$, 7^{+}, 9, 11, ♯11, ♭13, 13
VI	MODE 6	6, -6, 7, -7, -9, 9, ♯9, ♯11, 13
VII	MODE 7	♭6, 7, ♭9, 9, 11, ♭13
VIII	MODE 8	△, -△, $△^{\flat 5}$, ♭9, ♯9, ♯11, 13

NUMERIC SCALE / MODE CHART

		1		2		3	4		5		6		7	1		2		3	4		5		6		7
I	BEBOP LOCRIAN ♮2	1		2	♭3		4	♭5		♭6		♭7	7												
II	MODE 2			1	♭2		♭3	3		♯4		♯5	6	♭7											
III	MODE 3				1		2	♭3		4		5	♭6	6		7									
IV	MODE 4						1	♭2		♭3		4	♭5	5		6	♭7								
V	MODE 5							1		2		3	4	♭5		♭6	6		7						
VI	MODE 6									1		2	♭3	3		♯4	5		6	♭7					
VII	MODE 7											1	♭2	2		3	4		5	♭6		♭7			
VIII	MODE 8												1	♭2		♭3	3		♯4	5		6		7	

F♯ / G♭ BEBOP LOCRIAN ♮2

G BEBOP LOCRIAN ♮2

A♭ BEBOP LOCRIAN ♮2

A BEBOP LOCRIAN ♮2

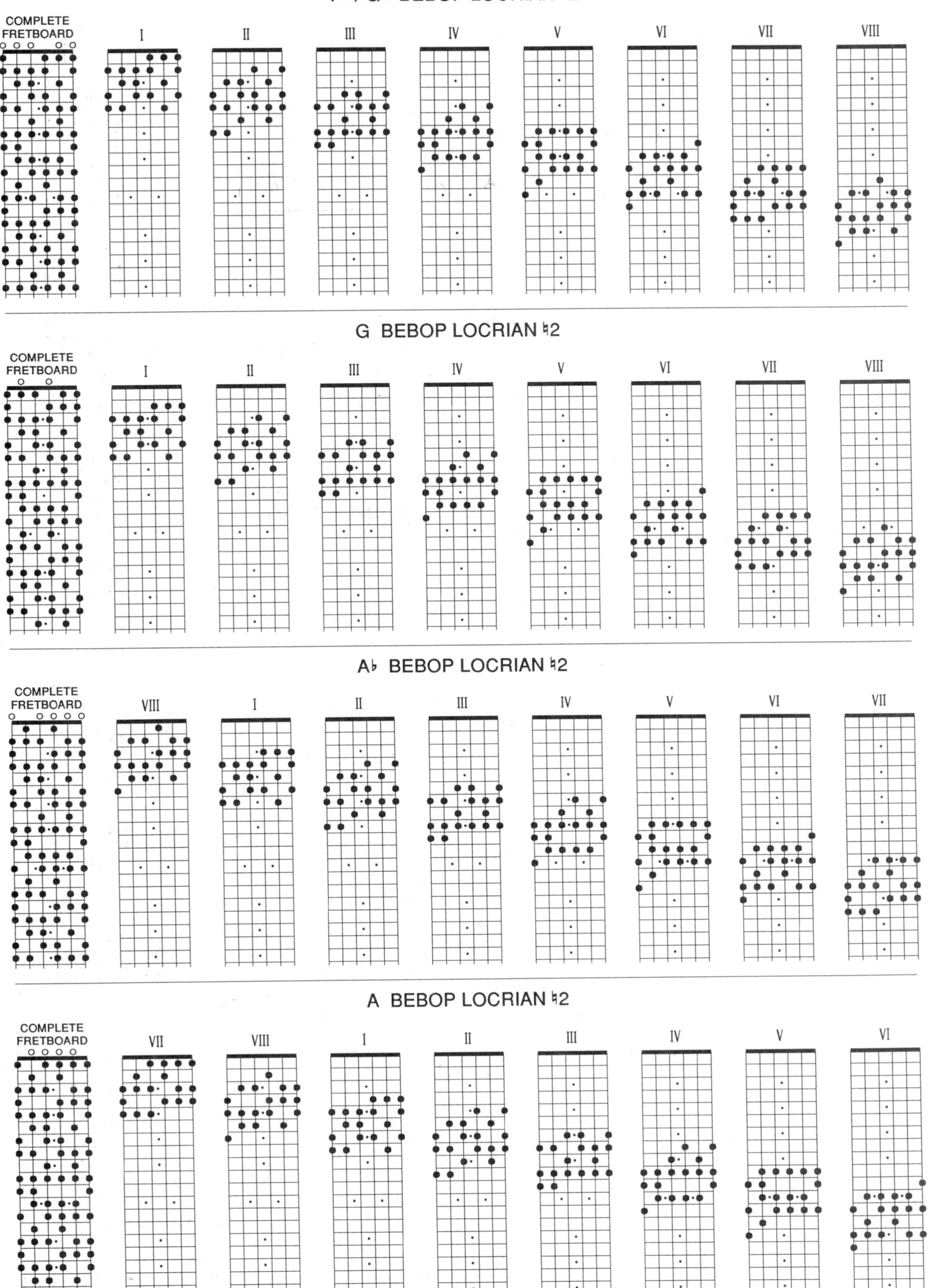

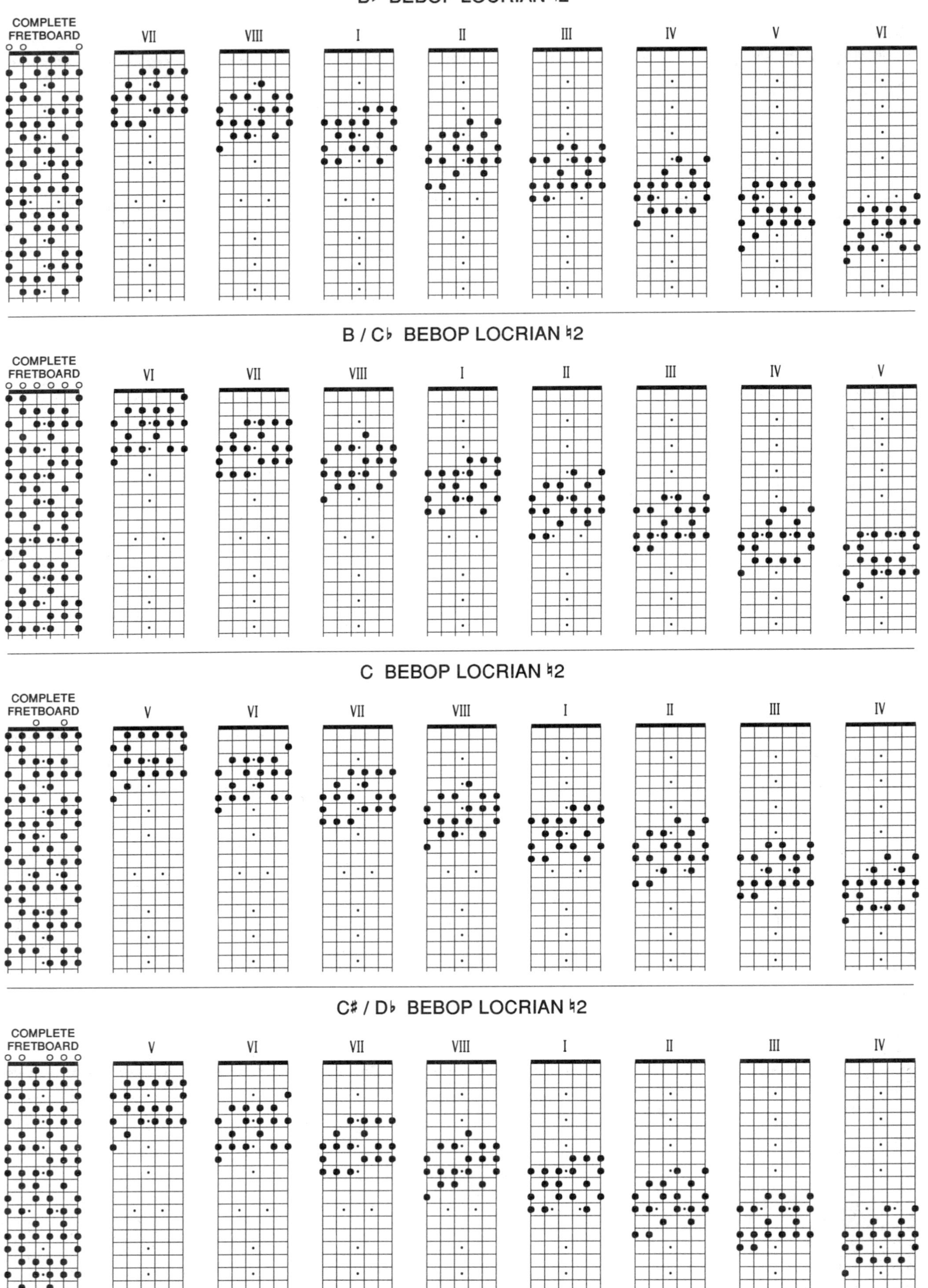
B♭ BEBOP LOCRIAN ♮2
COMPLETE FRETBOARD
VII
VIII
I
II
III
IV
V
VI
B / C♭ BEBOP LOCRIAN ♮2
COMPLETE FRETBOARD
VI
VII
VIII
I
II
III
IV
V
C BEBOP LOCRIAN ♮2
COMPLETE FRETBOARD
V
VI
VII
VIII
I
II
III
IV
C♯ / D♭ BEBOP LOCRIAN ♮2
COMPLETE FRETBOARD
V
VI
VII
VIII
I
II
III
IV

D BEBOP LOCRIAN ♮2

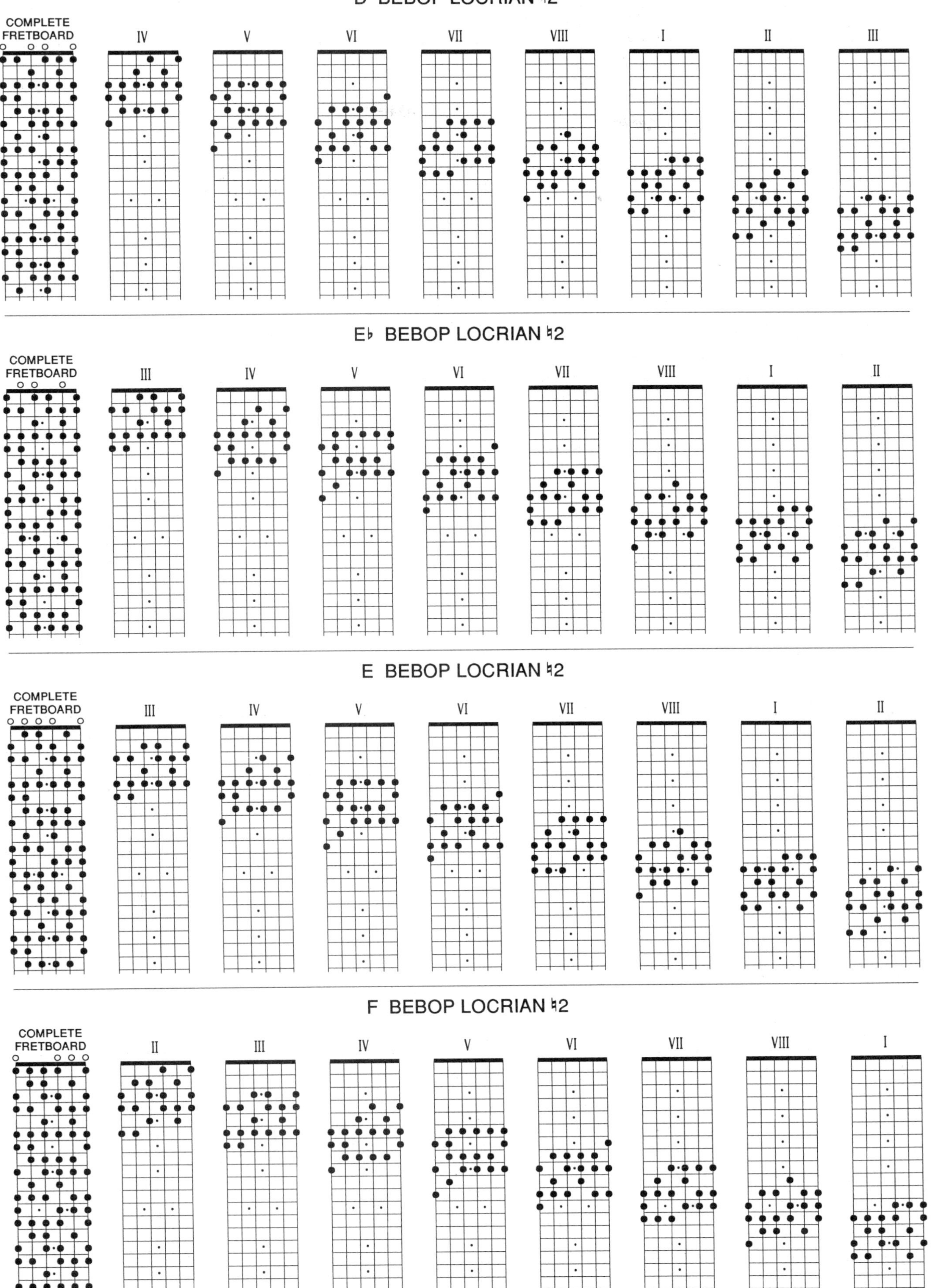

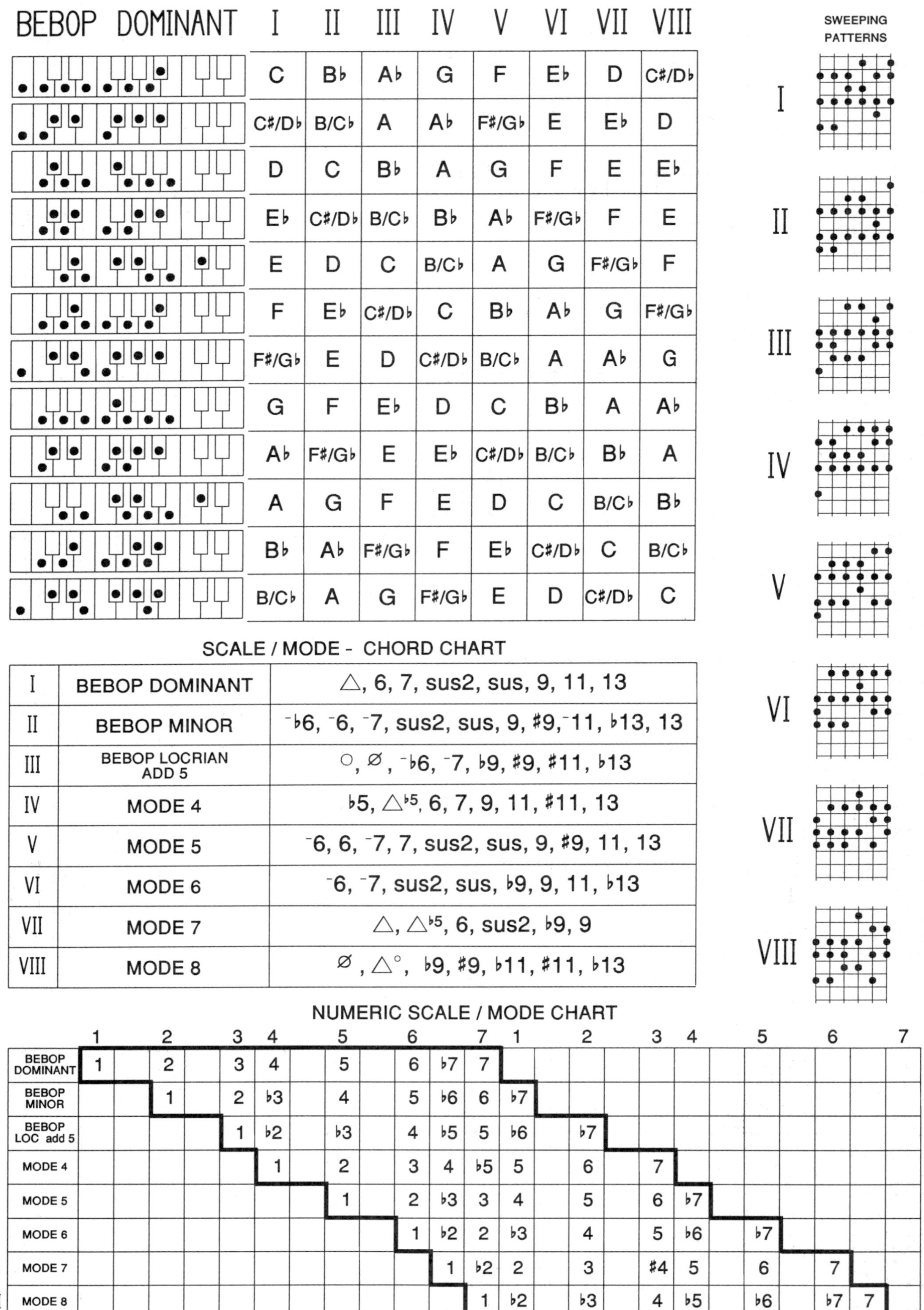

KEYBOARD PATTERNS

QUICK MODE GENERATOR CHART

SWEEPING PATTERNS

BEBOP DOMINANT	I	II	III	IV	V	VI	VII	VIII
	C	B♭	A♭	G	F	E♭	D	C#/D♭
	C#/D♭	B/C♭	A	A♭	F#/G♭	E	E♭	D
	D	C	B♭	A	G	F	E	E♭
	E♭	C#/D♭	B/C♭	B♭	A♭	F#/G♭	F	E
	E	D	C	B/C♭	A	G	F#/G♭	F
	F	E♭	C#/D♭	C	B♭	A♭	G	F#/G♭
	F#/G♭	E	D	C#/D♭	B/C♭	A	A♭	G
	G	F	E♭	D	C	B♭	A	A♭
	A♭	F#/G♭	E	E♭	C#/D♭	B/C♭	B♭	A
	A	G	F	E	D	C	B/C♭	B♭
	B♭	A♭	F#/G♭	F	E♭	C#/D♭	C	B/C♭
	B/C♭	A	G	F#/G♭	E	D	C#/D♭	C

SCALE / MODE - CHORD CHART

I	BEBOP DOMINANT	△, 6, 7, sus2, sus, 9, 11, 13
II	BEBOP MINOR	⁻♭6, ⁻6, ⁻7, sus2, sus, 9, #9, ⁻11, ♭13, 13
III	BEBOP LOCRIAN ADD 5	○, ∅, ⁻♭6, ⁻7, ♭9, #9, #11, ♭13
IV	MODE 4	♭5, △♭5, 6, 7, 9, 11, #11, 13
V	MODE 5	⁻6, 6, ⁻7, 7, sus2, sus, 9, #9, 11, 13
VI	MODE 6	⁻6, ⁻7, sus2, sus, ♭9, 9, 11, ♭13
VII	MODE 7	△, △♭5, 6, sus2, ♭9, 9
VIII	MODE 8	∅, △°, ♭9, #9, ♭11, #11, ♭13

NUMERIC SCALE / MODE CHART

		1		2		3	4		5		6		7	1		2		3	4		5		6		7
I	BEBOP DOMINANT	1		2		3	4		5		6	♭7	7												
II	BEBOP MINOR			1		2	♭3		4		5	♭6	6	♭7											
III	BEBOP LOC add 5					1	♭2		♭3		4	♭5	5	♭6		♭7									
IV	MODE 4						1		2		3	4	♭5	5		6		7							
V	MODE 5								1		2	♭3	3	4		5		6	♭7						
VI	MODE 6										1	♭2	2	♭3		4		5	♭6		♭7				
VII	MODE 7											1	♭2	2		3		#4	5		6		7		
VIII	MODE 8												1	♭2		♭3		4	♭5		♭6		♭7	7	

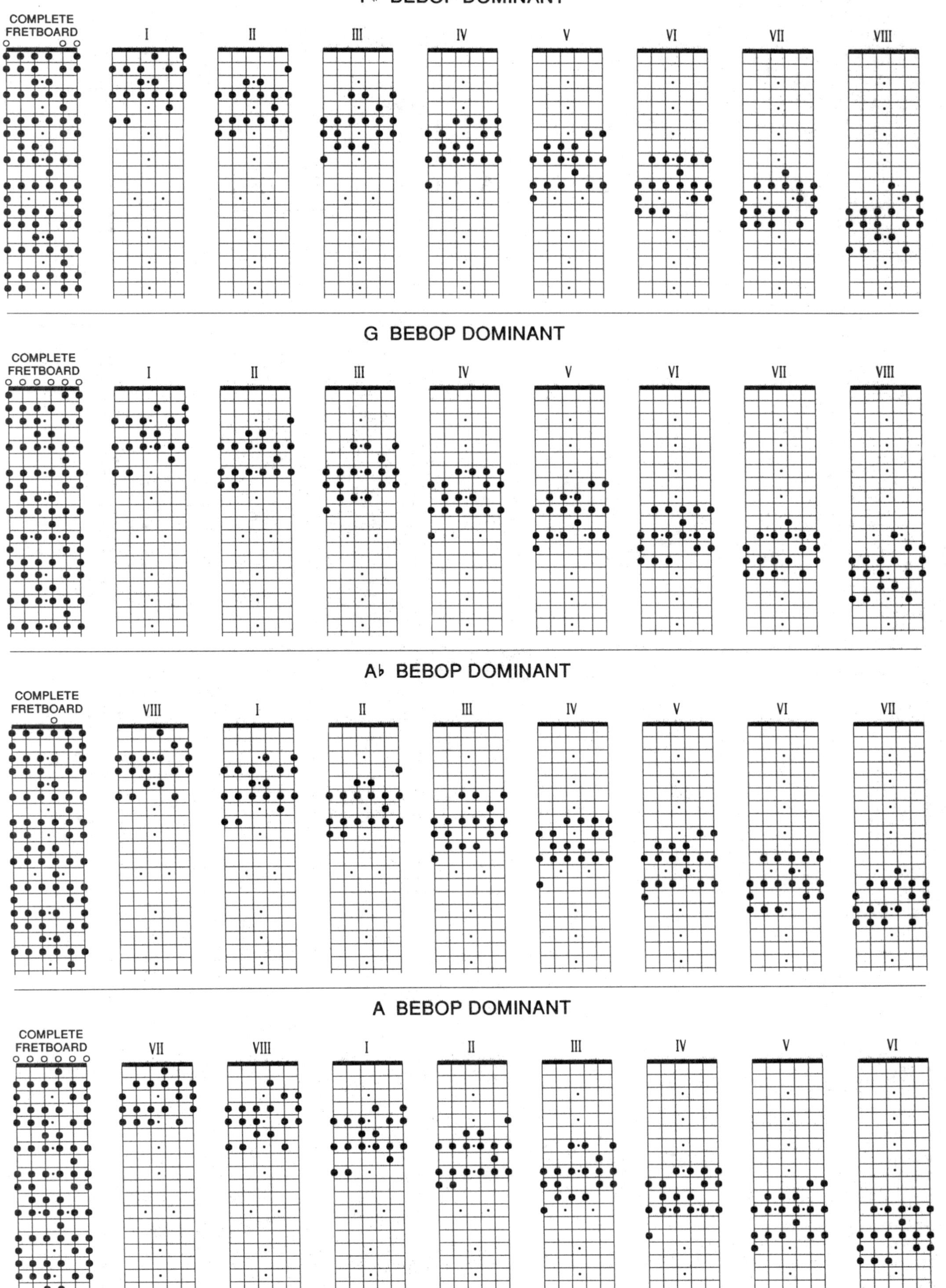
F♯ BEBOP DOMINANT
COMPLETE FRETBOARD
I
II
III
IV
V
VI
VII
VIII
G BEBOP DOMINANT
COMPLETE FRETBOARD
I
II
III
IV
V
VI
VII
VIII
A♭ BEBOP DOMINANT
COMPLETE FRETBOARD
VIII
I
II
III
IV
V
VI
VII
A BEBOP DOMINANT
COMPLETE FRETBOARD
VII
VIII
I
II
III
IV
V
VI

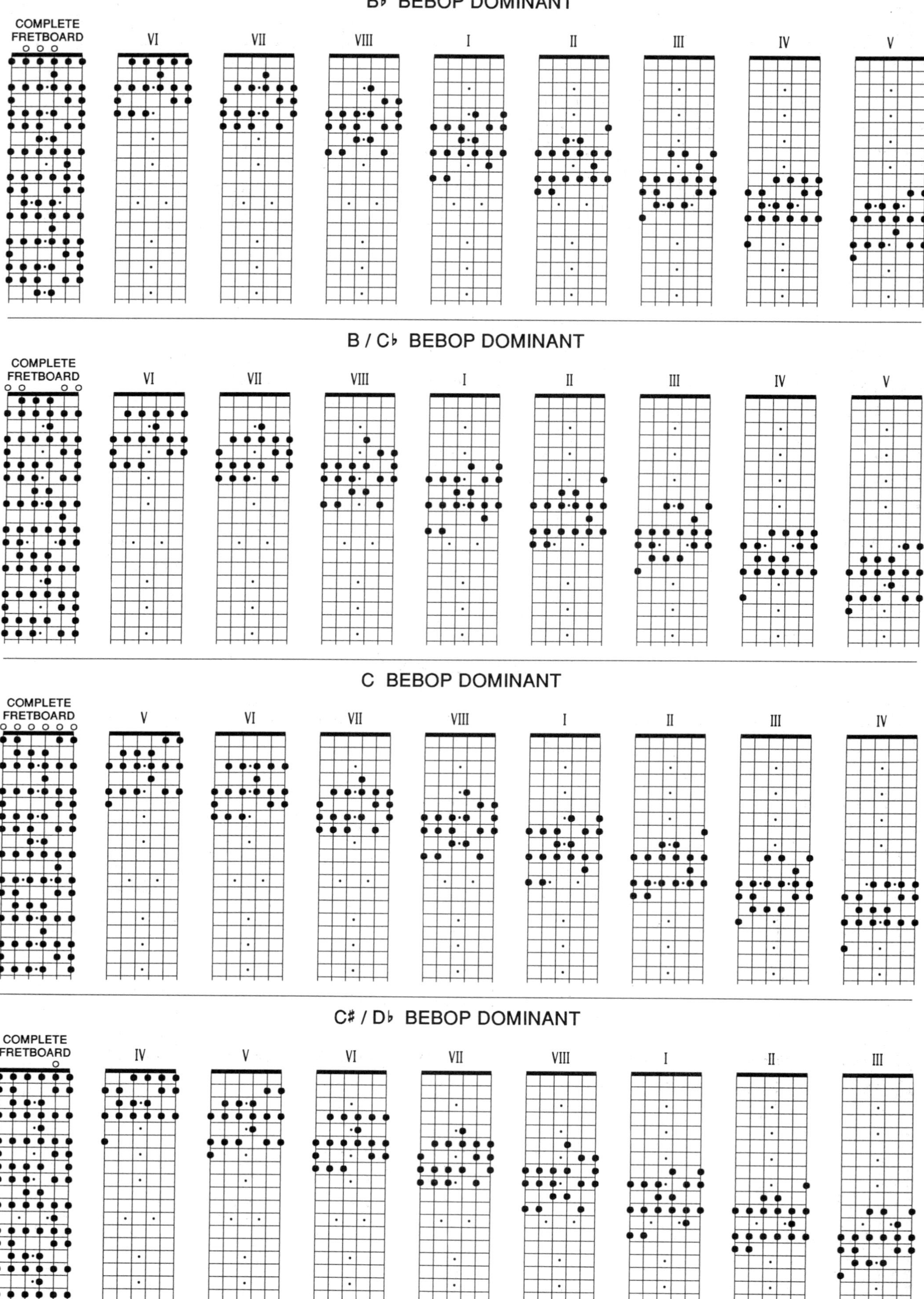
B♭ BEBOP DOMINANT
COMPLETE FRETBOARD
VI
VII
VIII
I
II
III
IV
V
B / C♭ BEBOP DOMINANT
COMPLETE FRETBOARD
VI
VII
VIII
I
II
III
IV
V
C BEBOP DOMINANT
COMPLETE FRETBOARD
V
VI
VII
VIII
I
II
III
IV
C♯ / D♭ BEBOP DOMINANT
COMPLETE FRETBOARD
IV
V
VI
VII
VIII
I
II
III

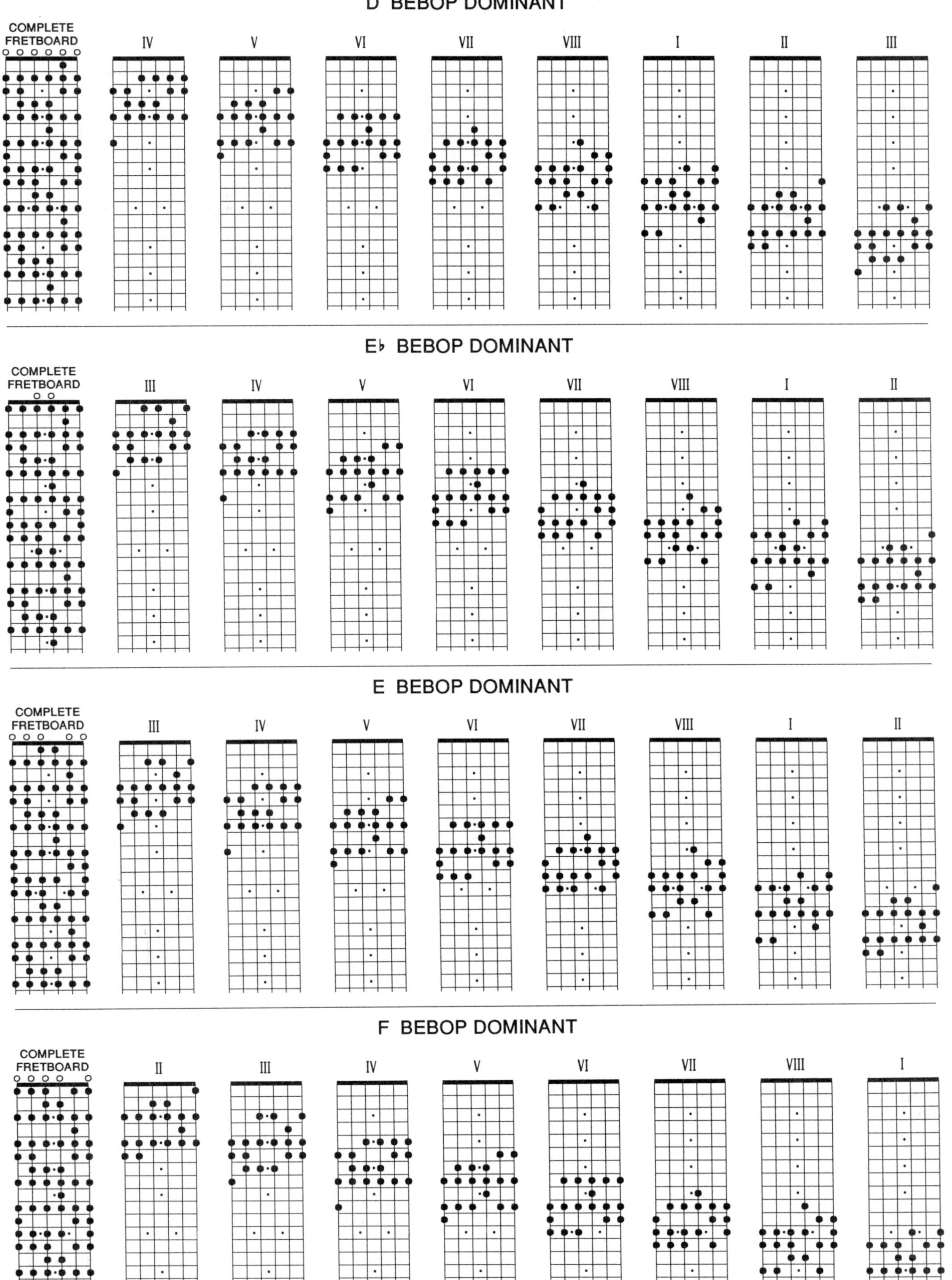
D BEBOP DOMINANT
COMPLETE FRETBOARD
IV V VI VII VIII I II III
E♭ BEBOP DOMINANT
COMPLETE FRETBOARD
III IV V VI VII VIII I II
E BEBOP DOMINANT
COMPLETE FRETBOARD
III IV V VI VII VIII I II
F BEBOP DOMINANT
COMPLETE FRETBOARD
II III IV V VI VII VIII I

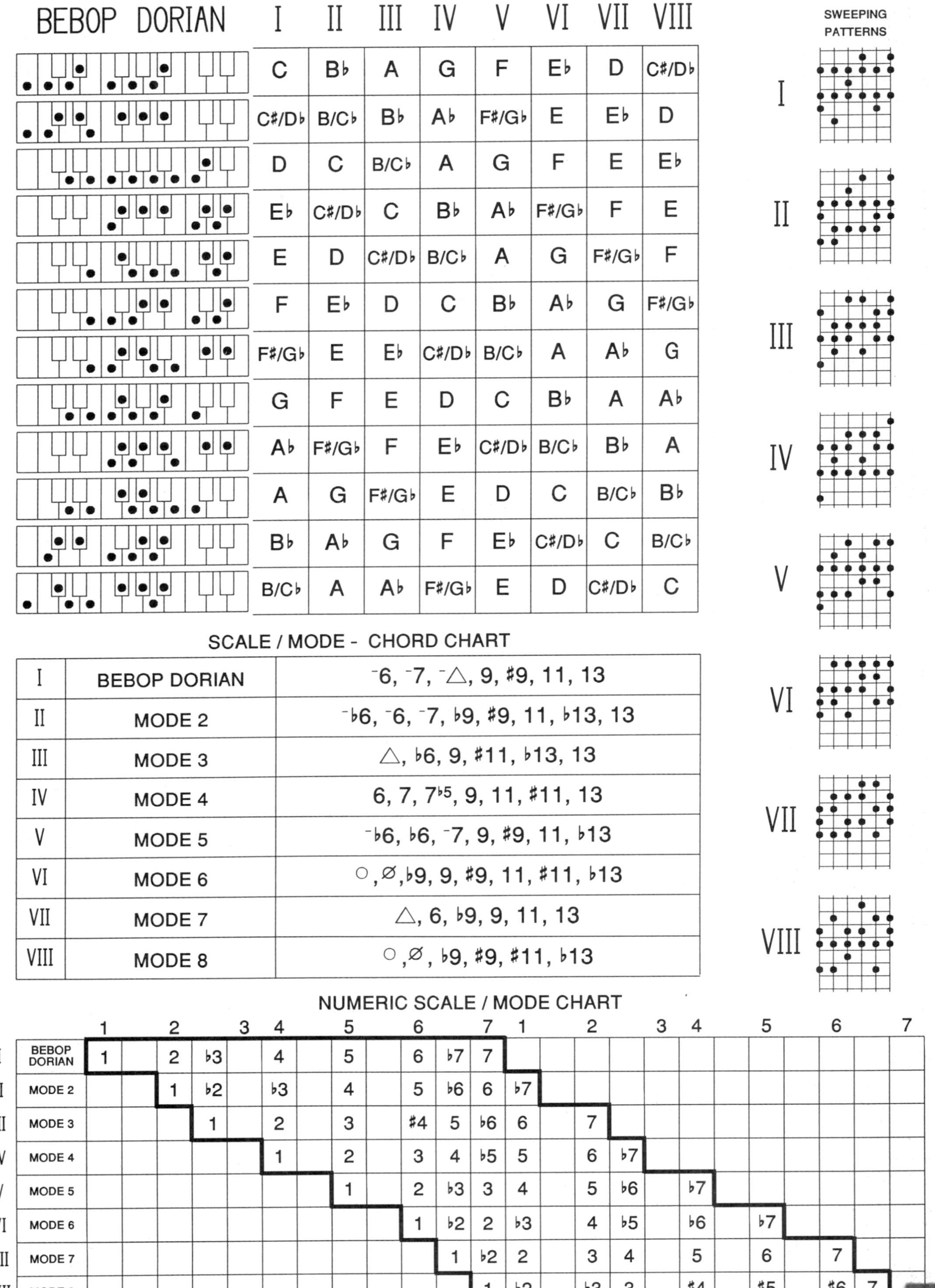

QUICK MODE GENERATOR CHART

BEBOP DORIAN

I	II	III	IV	V	VI	VII	VIII
C	B♭	A	G	F	E♭	D	C♯/D♭
C♯/D♭	B/C♭	B♭	A♭	F♯/G♭	E	E♭	D
D	C	B/C♭	A	G	F	E	E♭
E♭	C♯/D♭	C	B♭	A♭	F♯/G♭	F	E
E	D	C♯/D♭	B/C♭	A	G	F♯/G♭	F
F	E♭	D	C	B♭	A♭	G	F♯/G♭
F♯/G♭	E	E♭	C♯/D♭	B/C♭	A	A♭	G
G	F	E	D	C	B♭	A	A♭
A♭	F♯/G♭	F	E♭	C♯/D♭	B/C♭	B♭	A
A	G	F♯/G♭	E	D	C	B/C♭	B♭
B♭	A♭	G	F	E♭	C♯/D♭	C	B/C♭
B/C♭	A	A♭	F♯/G♭	E	D	C♯/D♭	C

SCALE / MODE - CHORD CHART

I	BEBOP DORIAN	-6, -7, -△, 9, ♯9, 11, 13
II	MODE 2	-♭6, -6, -7, ♭9, ♯9, 11, ♭13, 13
III	MODE 3	△, ♭6, 9, ♯11, ♭13, 13
IV	MODE 4	6, 7, $7^{\flat 5}$, 9, 11, ♯11, 13
V	MODE 5	-♭6, ♭6, -7, 9, ♯9, 11, ♭13
VI	MODE 6	○, ∅, ♭9, 9, ♯9, 11, ♯11, ♭13
VII	MODE 7	△, 6, ♭9, 9, 11, 13
VIII	MODE 8	○, ∅, ♭9, ♯9, ♯11, ♭13

NUMERIC SCALE / MODE CHART

		1		2		3	4		5		6		7	1		2		3	4		5		6		7
I	BEBOP DORIAN	1		2	♭3		4		5		6	♭7	7												
II	MODE 2			1	♭2		♭3		4		5	♭6	6	♭7											
III	MODE 3				1		2		3		♯4	5	♭6	6		7									
IV	MODE 4						1		2		3	4	♭5	5		6	♭7								
V	MODE 5								1		2	♭3	3	4		5	♭6		♭7						
VI	MODE 6										1	♭2	2	♭3		4	♭5		♭6		♭7				
VII	MODE 7											1	♭2	2		3	4		5		6		7		
VIII	MODE 8												1	♭2		♭3	3		♯4		♯5		♯6	7	

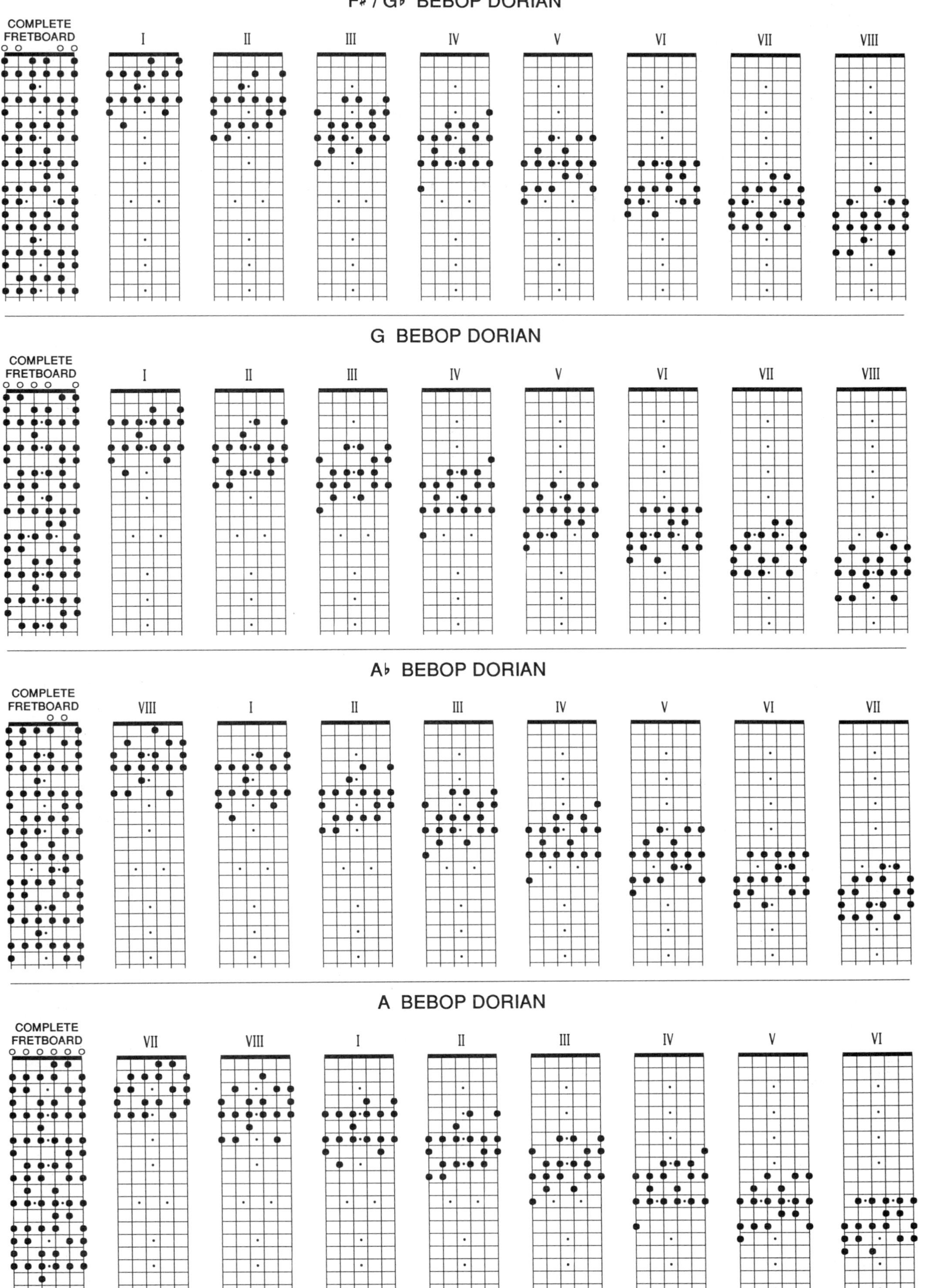
F♯ / G♭ BEBOP DORIAN
COMPLETE FRETBOARD
I
II
III
IV
V
VI
VII
VIII
G BEBOP DORIAN
COMPLETE FRETBOARD
I
II
III
IV
V
VI
VII
VIII
A♭ BEBOP DORIAN
COMPLETE FRETBOARD
VIII
I
II
III
IV
V
VI
VII
A BEBOP DORIAN
COMPLETE FRETBOARD
VII
VIII
I
II
III
IV
V
VI

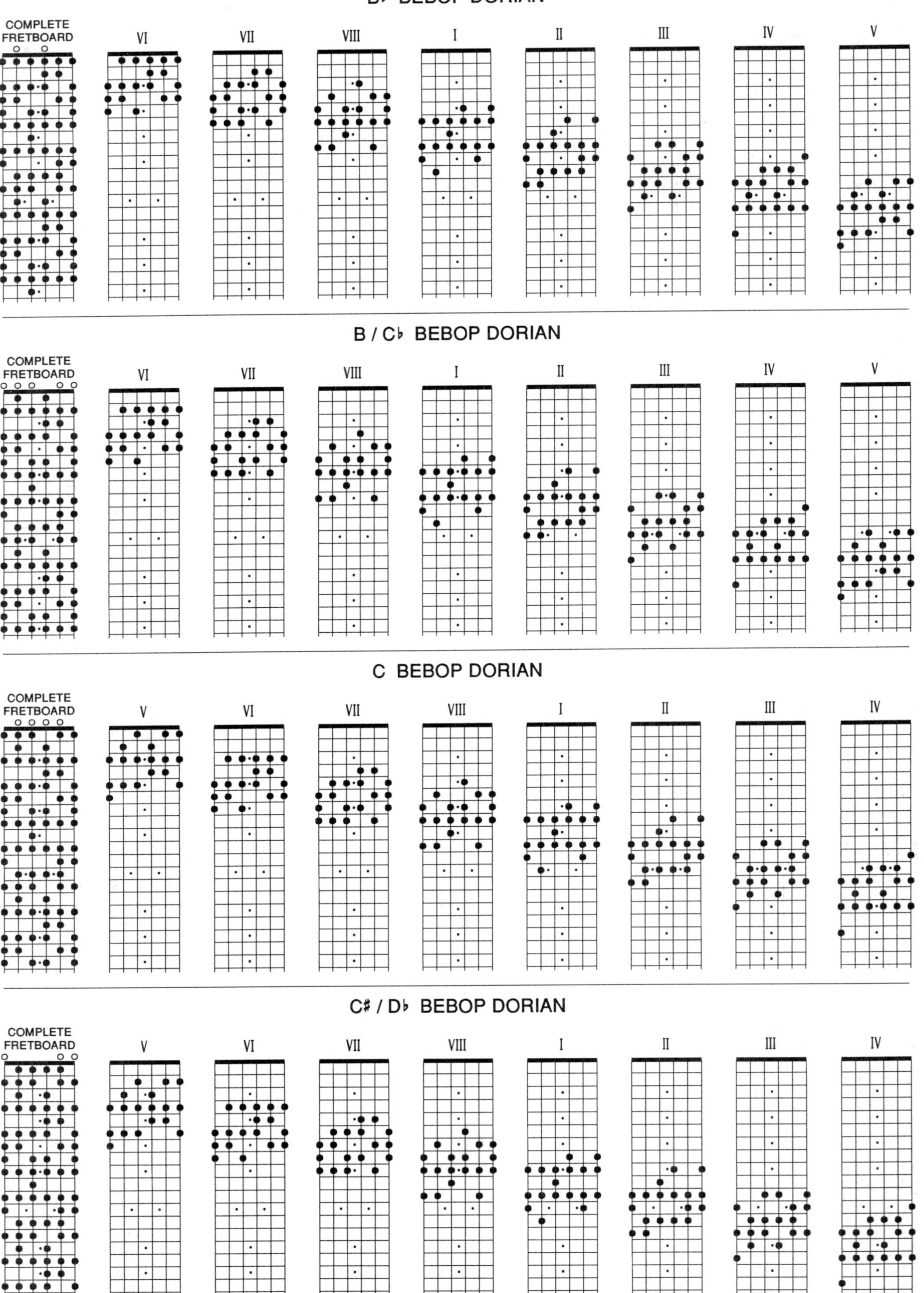
B♭ BEBOP DORIAN
COMPLETE FRETBOARD
VI
VII
VIII
I
II
III
IV
V
B / C♭ BEBOP DORIAN
COMPLETE FRETBOARD
VI
VII
VIII
I
II
III
IV
V
C BEBOP DORIAN
COMPLETE FRETBOARD
V
VI
VII
VIII
I
II
III
IV
C♯ / D♭ BEBOP DORIAN
COMPLETE FRETBOARD
V
VI
VII
VIII
I
II
III
IV

D BEBOP DORIAN

E♭ BEBOP DORIAN

E BEBOP DORIAN

F BEBOP DORIAN

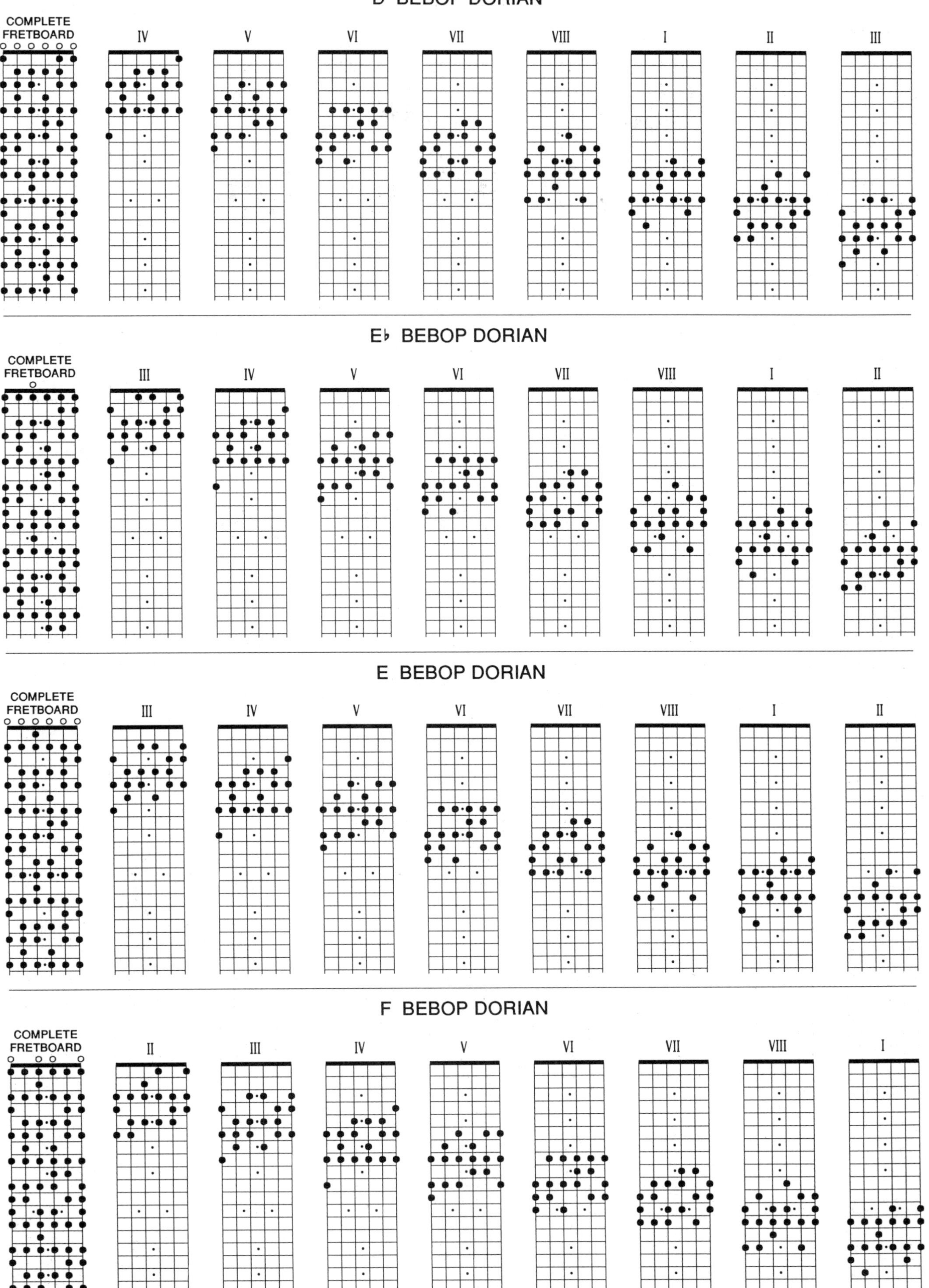

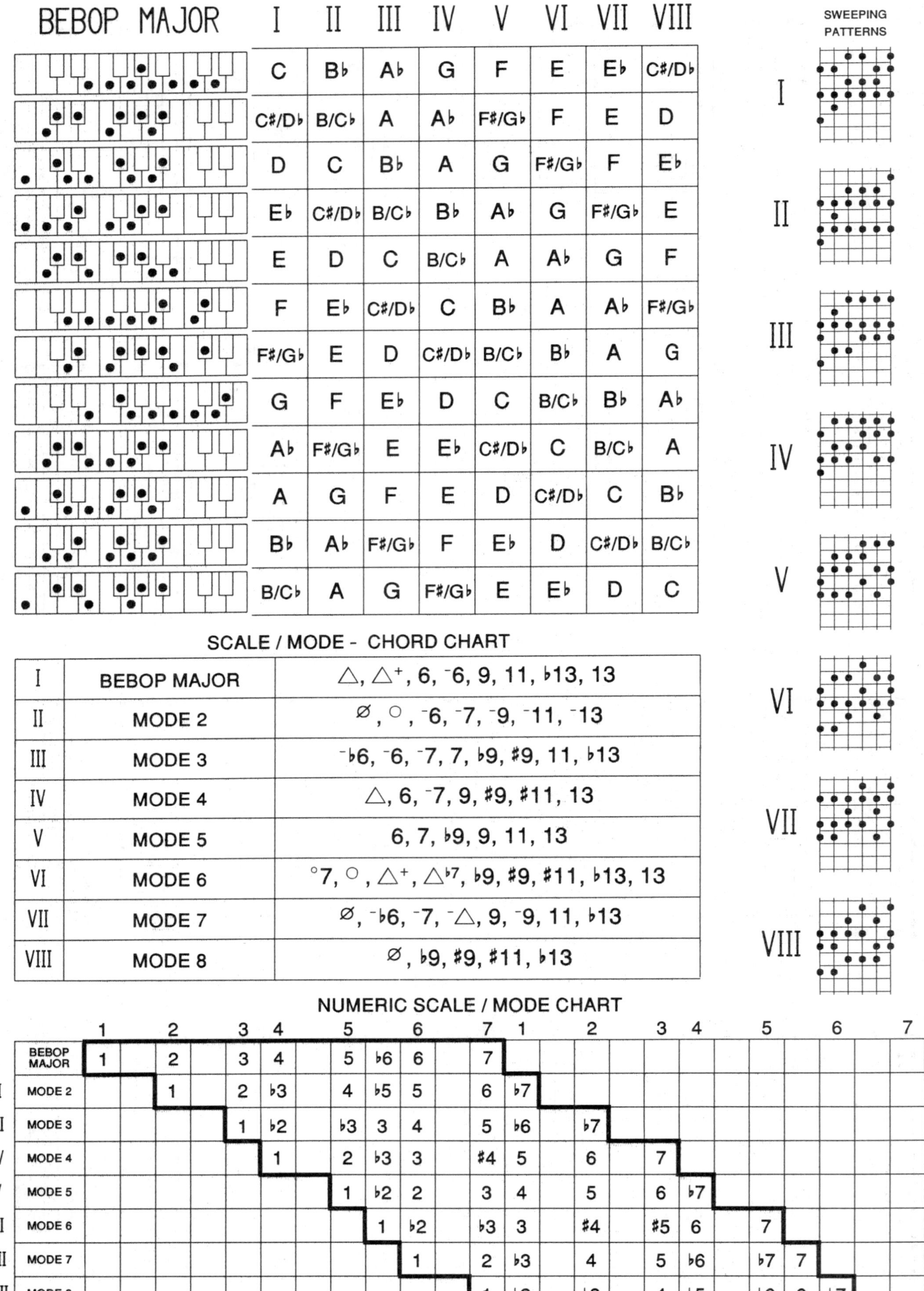

KEYBOARD PATTERNS

QUICK MODE GENERATOR CHART

BEBOP MAJOR	I	II	III	IV	V	VI	VII	VIII
	C	B♭	A♭	G	F	E	E♭	C♯/D♭
	C♯/D♭	B/C♭	A	A♭	F♯/G♭	F	E	D
	D	C	B♭	A	G	F♯/G♭	F	E♭
	E♭	C♯/D♭	B/C♭	B♭	A♭	G	F♯/G♭	E
	E	D	C	B/C♭	A	A♭	G	F
	F	E♭	C♯/D♭	C	B♭	A	A♭	F♯/G♭
	F♯/G♭	E	D	C♯/D♭	B/C♭	B♭	A	G
	G	F	E♭	D	C	B/C♭	B♭	A♭
	A♭	F♯/G♭	E	E♭	C♯/D♭	C	B/C♭	A
	A	G	F	E	D	C♯/D♭	C	B♭
	B♭	A♭	F♯/G♭	F	E♭	D	C♯/D♭	B/C♭
	B/C♭	A	G	F♯/G♭	E	E♭	D	C

SWEEPING PATTERNS

I

II

III

IV

V

VI

VII

VIII

SCALE / MODE - CHORD CHART

I	BEBOP MAJOR	△, △+, 6, -6, 9, 11, ♭13, 13
II	MODE 2	ø, ○, -6, -7, -9, -11, -13
III	MODE 3	-♭6, -6, -7, 7, ♭9, ♯9, 11, ♭13
IV	MODE 4	△, 6, -7, 9, ♯9, ♯11, 13
V	MODE 5	6, 7, ♭9, 9, 11, 13
VI	MODE 6	°7, ○, △+, △♭7, ♭9, ♯9, ♯11, ♭13, 13
VII	MODE 7	ø, -♭6, -7, -△, 9, -9, 11, ♭13
VIII	MODE 8	ø, ♭9, ♯9, ♯11, ♭13

NUMERIC SCALE / MODE CHART

		1		2		3	4		5		6		7	1		2		3	4		5		6		7
I	BEBOP MAJOR	1		2		3	4		5	♭6	6		7												
II	MODE 2			1		2	♭3		4	♭5	5		6	♭7											
III	MODE 3					1	♭2		♭3	3	4		5	♭6		♭7									
IV	MODE 4						1		2	♭3	3		♯4	5		6		7							
V	MODE 5								1	♭2	2		3	4		5		6	♭7						
VI	MODE 6									1	♭2		♭3	3		♯4		♯5	6		7				
VII	MODE 7										1		2	♭3		4		5	♭6		♭7	7			
VIII	MODE 8												1	♭2		♭3		4	♭5		♭6	6	♭7		

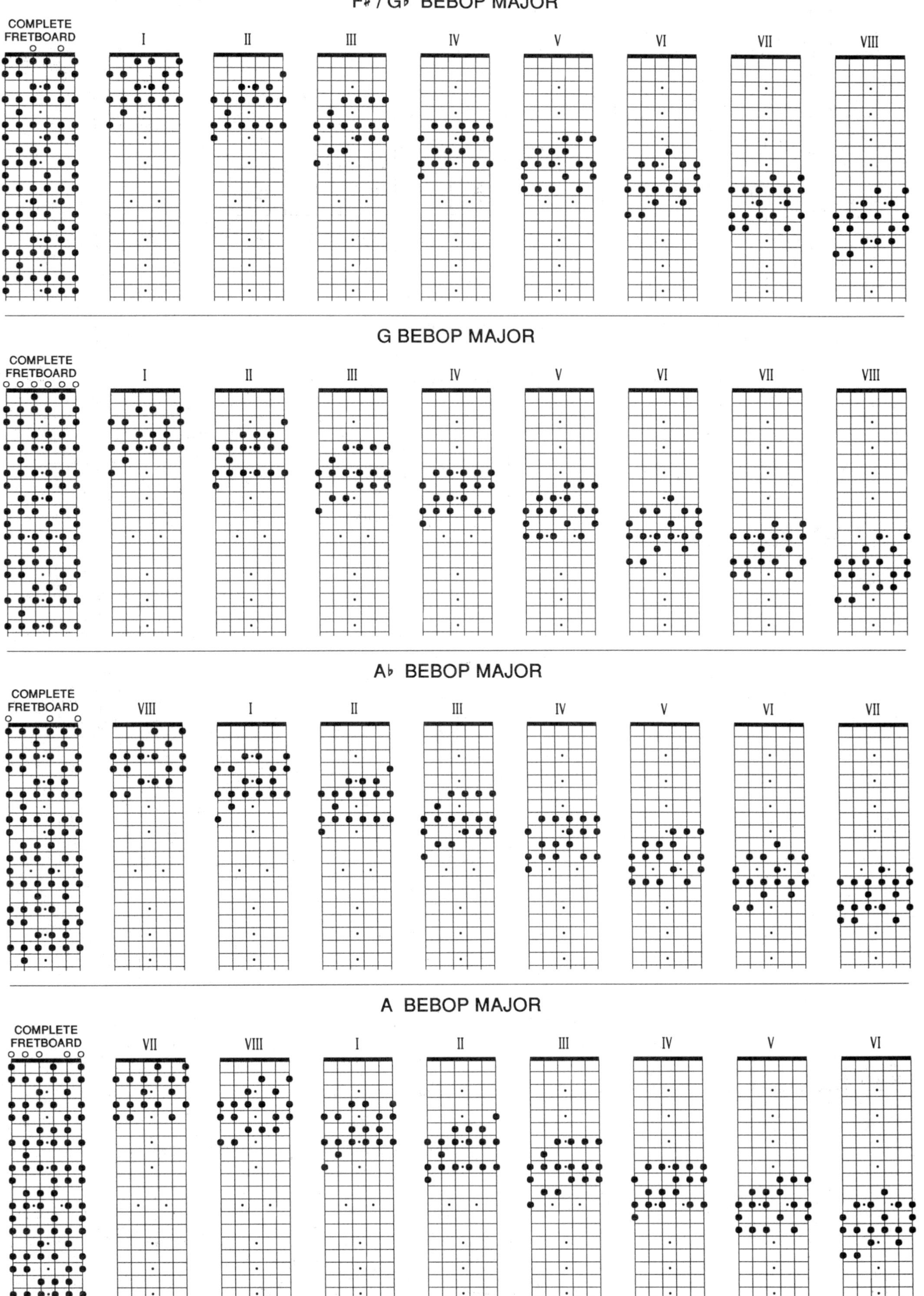
F♯ / G♭ BEBOP MAJOR
COMPLETE FRETBOARD
I
II
III
IV
V
VI
VII
VIII
G BEBOP MAJOR
COMPLETE FRETBOARD
I
II
III
IV
V
VI
VII
VIII
A♭ BEBOP MAJOR
COMPLETE FRETBOARD
VIII
I
II
III
IV
V
VI
VII
A BEBOP MAJOR
COMPLETE FRETBOARD
VII
VIII
I
II
III
IV
V
VI

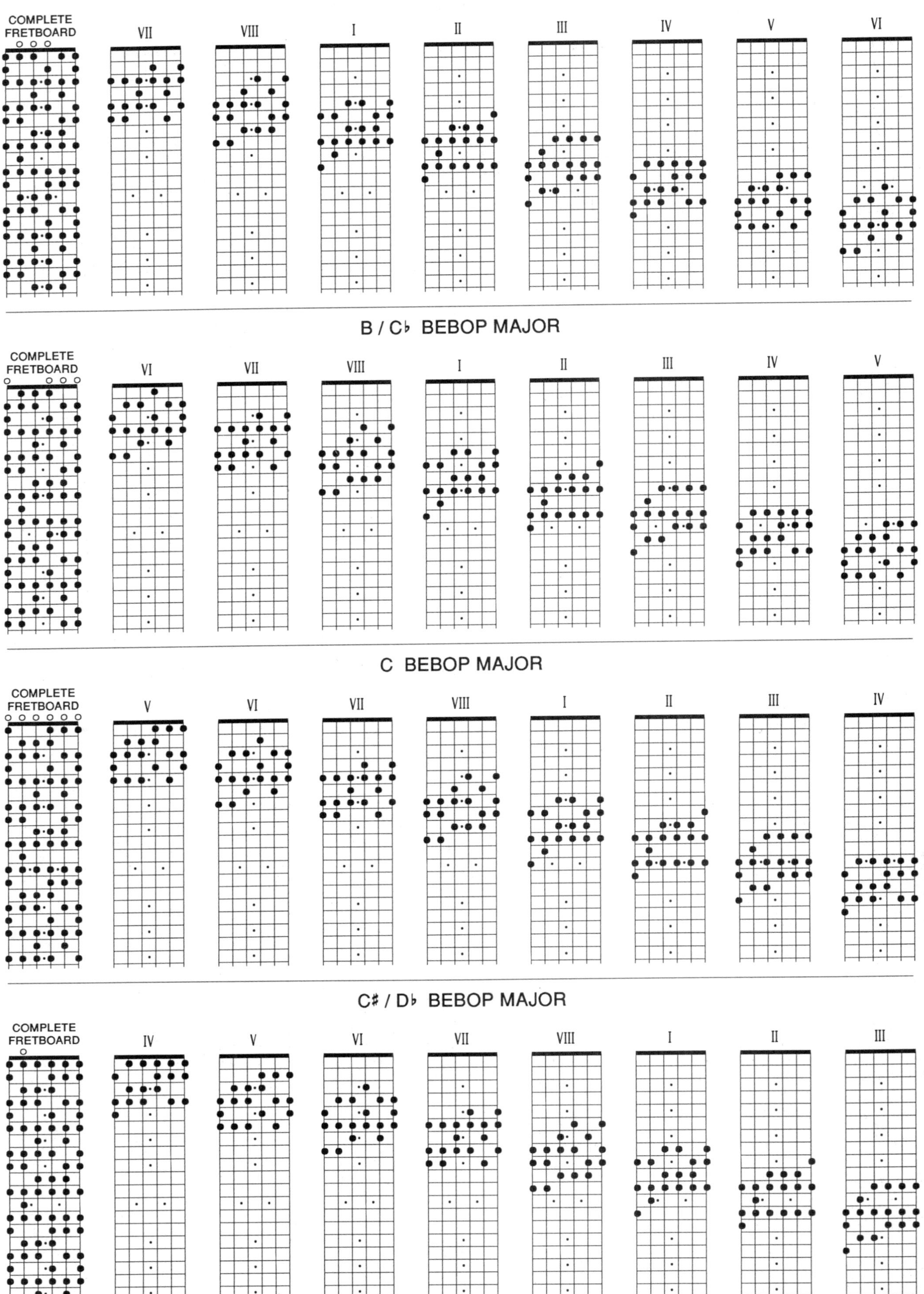
B♭ BEBOP MAJOR
COMPLETE FRETBOARD
VII
VIII
I
II
III
IV
V
VI
B / C♭ BEBOP MAJOR
COMPLETE FRETBOARD
VI
VII
VIII
I
II
III
IV
V
C BEBOP MAJOR
COMPLETE FRETBOARD
V
VI
VII
VIII
I
II
III
IV
C♯ / D♭ BEBOP MAJOR
COMPLETE FRETBOARD
IV
V
VI
VII
VIII
I
II
III

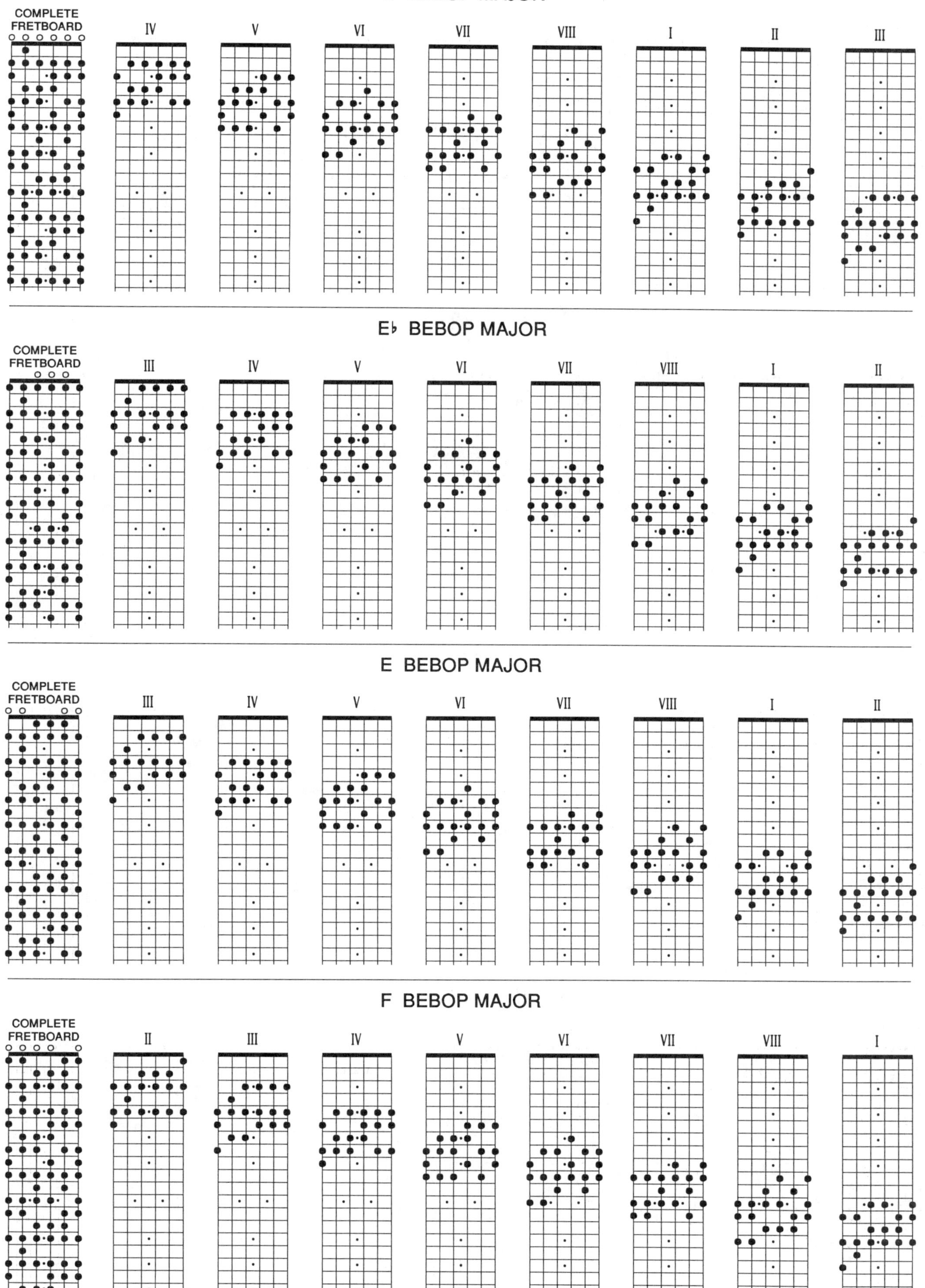
D BEBOP MAJOR
COMPLETE FRETBOARD
IV
V
VI
VII
VIII
I
II
III
E♭ BEBOP MAJOR
COMPLETE FRETBOARD
III
IV
V
VI
VII
VIII
I
II
E BEBOP MAJOR
COMPLETE FRETBOARD
III
IV
V
VI
VII
VIII
I
II
F BEBOP MAJOR
COMPLETE FRETBOARD
II
III
IV
V
VI
VII
VIII
I

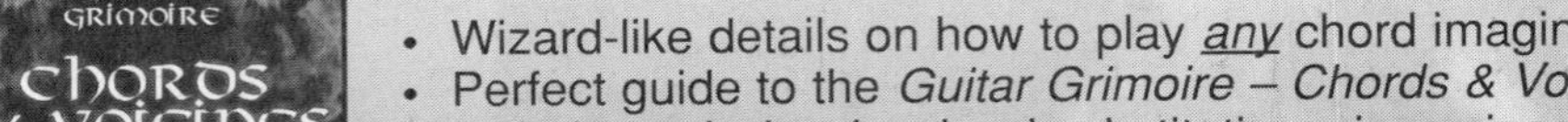